# Early Interracial Oneness Pentecostalism

# Early Interracial Oneness Pentecostalism

G. T. Haywood and the
Pentecostal Assemblies of the World
(1901–1931)

Talmadge L. French

PICKWICK *Publications* • Eugene, Oregon

EARLY INTERRACIAL ONENESS PENTECOSTALISM
G. T. Haywood, and the Pentecostal Assemblies of the World (1901–1931)



Pickwick Publications
An Imprint of Wipf and Stock Publishers
199 W. 8th Ave., Suite 3
Eugene, OR 97401

www.wipfandstock.com

ISBN 13: 978-1-4982-2685-1

*Cataloguing-in-Publication data:*

French, Talmadge L.

Early interracial oneness pentecostalism : G. T. Haywood and the pentecostal assemblies of the world (1901–1931) / Talmadge L. French, with a foreword by Allan H. Anderson.

xvi + 270 pp. ; 23 cm. Includes bibliographical references and indexes.

1. Haywood, G. T. (Garfield Thomas). 2. Oneness Pentecostal Churches. 3. African American Pentecostals—History. I. Anderson, Allan H. II. Title.

BR1644.3 F824 2014

Manufactured in the U.S.A.

# Contents

# Foreword

Several Pentecostal groups arose in the United States in the 1910s and 1920s with a doctrine called "Jesus' Name," "Apostolic Pentecostal," or "Oneness" by its proponents, and the "New Issue," or "Jesus Only" by its opponents. I had the privilege of supervising Talmadge French's PhD research on this subject over several years at the University of Birmingham. His research was meticulous and thorough, not leaving any stone unturned in his search for facts. Oneness Pentecostals, according to French, have some thirty million adherents worldwide, which makes them a significant minority within classical Pentecostalism. French is one of a handful of Oneness Pentecostal ministers with a PhD, and this historical study is unique, not least because he is an insider who manages to maintain critical distance from his subject, one that is also very close to his heart. Originally conceived as a study of the origins of Oneness Pentecostalism in one American city, Indianapolis, Indiana; it developed into a study of the most prominent African American leader in early "Finished Work" Pentecostalism, Garfield Thomas Haywood, also in Indianapolis; and then developed further to an analysis of the interracial nature of early American Oneness Pentecostalism spread across the United States, in which Haywood played a prominent role. Haywood was undoubtedly a most remarkable man whose achievements in attaining racial integration in an era of Jim Crow segregation laws that were de jure in the South and de facto in the North, were nothing short of amazing. This fascinating story with all its original sources is the result of these years of research.

Oneness Pentecostalism is an enigma to most scholars--of all forms of Pentecostalism globally today this form appears, at least to this observer, to have maintained most closely the countercultural and otherworldly character of early Pentecostalism. As French shows in this book, the "interracial fervor" of early American Pentecostalism remained in Oneness Pentecostalism longer than in other sections of the movement. There remains a deep divide between Oneness and other forms of Pentecostalism, largely on doctrinal grounds. It has been regarded by other Pentecostals variously as heretical or heterodox. The main issue is its Sabellian Modalistic approach to the Trinity, and the doctrine that baptism in the name of Jesus and Spirit baptism with speaking in tongues is necessary for salvation that is promulgated in many, but not all, Oneness circles. This is not a homogenous organization, for like Pentecostalism as a whole, Oneness Pentecostalism has split into many different groups independent of each other. The two largest in North America are the Pentecostal Assemblies of the World and the United Pentecostal Church International. There are even bigger Oneness Pentecostal groups in Ethiopia: the Apostolic Church of Ethiopia, and in China and the Chinese diaspora: the True Jesus Church. The latter has imbibed some of the features of Seventh-Day Adventism into its teachings and observes Saturday as the Sabbath. Most forms of Oneness Pentecostalism also practice foot-washing.

It might be helpful first to give a potted history and theology of early American Oneness Pentecostalism for the uninitiated, even though such a summary has to be arbitrary and selective. Racial, doctrinal and personal issues simultaneously caused the divisions that erupted in early American Pentecostalism. The first Pentecostals at Azusa Street under their African American leader William Seymour were in an integrated and socially inclusive movement of the Spirit. This was what French called an "interracial vision". Although Pentecostalism has its roots in the nineteenth century Holiness movement, some adherents had come from churches outside of this, and were more influenced by the Keswick view of progressive sanctification, which tended to deny a second instantaneous experience of holiness. William Durham in Chicago was undoubtedly one of the most influential Pentecostal preachers and the cause of the first major doctrinal schism in the movement. His Gospel Mission Church, also known as the North Avenue Mission, became a revival center that rivalled Azusa Street in influence and indirectly resulted in the creation of several European immigrant Pentecostal congregations in Chicago that spread worldwide.

In 1911 Durham, once so influenced by Azusa Street, went to the Azusa Street Mission to preach his "Finished Work of Calvary" doctrine in Seymour's absence, which resulted in schism and the departure of two-thirds of Seymour's workers. The Holiness teaching of "entire sanctification," which had been embraced by Seymour and most early Pentecostals, Durham declared to be unscriptural, teaching that sanctification was not a "second blessing" or a "crisis experience," but that Christ had provided for sanctification in his atonement and that this was received at conversion by identification with Christ in an act of faith. He therefore taught a "two-stage" work of grace (justification and Spirit baptism) instead of a "three-stage" one. His theology was thoroughly Christocentric, and it could be argued, deviated significantly from the Spirit-centered theology of both the Holiness movement and the first American Pentecostals. Durham's influence was enormous. Many of those who became major leaders of the Pentecostal movement embraced the "Finished Work" doctrine, including those who became leaders of Oneness Pentecostalism. After Durham's premature death from tuberculosis in 1912, his doctrine became the basis upon which the Assemblies of God, the Oneness denominations, the Foursquare Church, and several other smaller Pentecostal denominations were formed. Durham's assistant minister, Frank Ewart, who also became a Oneness leader, led the North Avenue Mission after Durham's death. There has been speculation that had he lived, Durham himself might have embraced Oneness, and that his Jesus-centered doctrine inevitably led to Oneness teaching. By 1914 some sixty percent of all American Pentecostals had embraced the "Finished Work" position. Durham's influence on the theology of the majority of Pentecostals was certainly immense and the division in US American Pentecostalism on this issue remains today.

The "Finished Work" controversy was the first of many subsequent divisions in American Pentecostalism. A more fundamental and acrimonious split erupted in 1916 over the doctrine of the Trinity. This was a schism chiefly in the ranks of the Assemblies of God that began as a teaching that the correct formula for baptism was "in the name of Jesus," and developed into a dispute about the doctrine of the Trinity. The "Finished Work" Pentecostals had an increasing expectation that God would continue to bring "further revelation" and do a "new thing". Remarkable revival meetings, especially those conducted by the woman evangelist Maria Woodworth-Etter in Dallas in 1912 and in Arroyo Seco, near Los Angeles in 1913, encouraged this heightened expectation but failed to unite Pentecostalism. In the Arroyo Seco camp meeting, Canadian evangelist Robert McAlister began to preach about baptism "in the name of Jesus Christ" from Acts 2:38, which he said was the common practice of the early church, rather than the triune formula of Matthew 28:19. Baptism was to be "in the name of Jesus" because Jesus was the "name" of God, whereas "Father, Son and Holy Spirit" were different titles for the singular name of Jesus Christ. This new teaching not only resulted in calls for rebaptism, but also developed into a theology of the name of God based on a combination of the Keswick emphasis on Jesus and the Old Testament names of God, and leading ultimately to what became known as the "Oneness" doctrine.

Early leaders in the Oneness movement included Frank Ewart, Seymour's former business manager Glenn Cook, the leader of a large interracial congregation in Indianapolis, Garfield T. Haywood, Iranian-born Assyrian Andrew D. Urshan (ordained by Durham), and Howard A. Goss, Pentecostal pioneer Charles F. Parham's former field superintendent. Ewart was credited with first formulating the distinctive Oneness theology on the nature and the name of God to accompany the new baptismal practice. This he first announced in a public sermon in 1914, when he and Cook rebaptized each other. The new doctrine spread through evangelistic meetings and in Indianapolis, Cook baptized Haywood together with 465 members of his large congregation. The "New Issue" created a schism in the Assemblies of God (AG) and Goss had been one of its organizing founders in 1914. In 1916, 156 ministers, including Goss, Ewart and Haywood, were barred from membership of the AG over the doctrine of the Trinity, which henceforth became a condition for membership. The AG emerged thereafter as a tightly structured, centralized denomination with a "Statement of Fundamental Truths" affirming the Trinity. The split also meant that the AG lost its black membership and became essentially an all-white denomination, especially with the departure of Haywood, the only prominent black leader associated with the AG, but never credentialed by them. The AG's stand for "orthodoxy" at this time was to ease their later acceptance by evangelicals. Oneness Pentecostalism in contrast was destined to remain isolated from the rest of Pentecostalism and Christianity in general, particularly through its practice of rebaptism and rejection of Trinitarian doctrine.

The details of this fascinating history and the subsequent events are presented in this book. Haywood's Pentecostal Assemblies of the World (PAW), the first American Oneness denomination, remained a racially integrated church until 1924, after which most of the whites withdrew and the PAW adopted episcopal government with Haywood as presiding bishop. After an abortive attempt to unite under the umbrella of the newly formed Pentecostal Church of Jesus Christ (PCJC) in 1931, the PAW has since been predominantly an African American church. The United Pentecostal Church (UPC) was originally a white denomination formed in 1945 from a union of the PCJC and the Pentecostal Church, Incorporated, but that tale belongs to a later historical period. Oneness Pentecostals have been excluded from fellowship with Trinitarian Pentecostals ever since the schism of 1916, except in the academic Society for Pentecostal Studies, where they have participated since 1973, and where I first met Talmadge French.

The central Oneness teaching as it has developed is a rejection of the traditional Christian concept of "separate but equal" Persons in the Trinity. Oneness Pentecostals hold that Jesus is the revelation of God the Father and that the Spirit proceeds from the Father, who is fully revealed in Jesus. Unlike the traditional idea that Jesus is the human name of Christ, in Oneness teaching Jesus is the New Testament name of God, and this name reveals His true nature. The one God of the Old Testament (Yahweh) reveals His immanence in the incarnation of Jesus, and His transcendence in the presence of the Spirit. God has now permanently taken up His abode in the human body of the Son. The Spirit indwells Jesus in fullness as God incarnate, and thus an attempt is made to resolve the intricacies of Trinitarian theology. Oneness Pentecostals think that Trinitarians have embraced tritheism because they believe in three separate and distinct "Persons" in the Godhead. Instead, Oneness teaching affirms that Jesus is fully God and not one divine being out of three. They prefer to refer to Father, Son and Spirit as "modes" or "manifestations" of God, all of which are present in the manifestation of each one. It follows that they also reject the traditional Christian teaching of the eternal Sonship of Christ, and that Oneness teaching on the dual nature of Christ tends towards a separation of the divine and the human. French explains carefully this theology of Oneness in the first chapter. Much of Oneness Pentecostalism teaches a threefold soteriology based on Acts 2:38: repentance, baptism in the name of Jesus Christ and the gift of the Spirit, all as essential parts of salvation. Oneness Pentecostalism therefore, with its several varieties and hundreds of denominations, emerged as an alternative to the Trinitarian doctrine and baptismal practice of early Pentecostalism, and was possibly the unavoidable outcome of the Christocentric "Finished Work" theology of William Durham.

By 1916, American Pentecostalism was doctrinally divided into three competing groups: "Second Work" (Holiness) Trinitarians, "Finished Work" Trinitarians and "Finished Work" Oneness Pentecostals, divisions that remain to this day. Other issues that divided Pentecostals were the authority of spoken prophecy (some held that there should be set apostles and prophets in the church), different eschatological interpretations, church polity, personality conflicts and racial differences. The process of schism and proliferation of new sects that had commenced in the nineteenth century Holiness movement was multiplied and perpetuated in the global expansion of Pentecostalism, and today might be considered a defining feature of the movement. In addition to doctrinal differences, within two decades the American Pentecostal movement had divided on racial lines. In the Oneness movement racial inclusion remained longer than in other forms of Pentecostalism, and this is recounted in the chapters of this book. The Oneness schism effectively meant that no black leaders remained in the AG. Racial divisions on the basis of African American, Hispanic American, and white American continued and proliferated throughout Pentecostalism for most of the twentieth century. By 1931 Oneness Pentecostals, the most integrated of all Pentecostal groups, were also split on racial lines. And yet, despite all these divisions, the Pentecostal movement continued to grow and as a whole probably retained as much friendly contact across racial divides as any other religious group in the United States.

What follows is a carefully-crafted, meticulously-researched history of early American Oneness Pentecostalism, based on original documents and hitherto-unknown sources. It has filled a large number of gaps in the historiography of American Pentecostalism and is essential reading for anyone who wishes to understand better and avoid a polemical attitude to these "without the camp" Pentecostals whom the author represents. This book will certainly clear up misunderstandings, foster better dialogue with Oneness Pentecostalism, and shed whole new light on American Pentecostal history and its struggle with racial prejudice. I want to warmly commend it to you.

Allan H. Anderson
Professor of Mission and Pentecostal Studies
University of Birmingham, UK

# Acknowledgments

The historical research and analysis published in this BOOK is adapted from my PhD Thesis from the University of Birmingham UK. I am especially beholden to the attentive and beneficial oversight of my supervisor Allan H. Anderson who not only proffers assistance in academic excellence but ultimately inspires in the progress. I want to thank my review committee which guided me to conclusion with insightful assistance, Mark Cartlege, Andrew Davies, and David Reed. I am eternally grateful for the unwavering support of my wife, Rebecca, and the constant encouragement of O. C. and Joan Marler. I am deeply indebted for the sponsorship for this research at its varied stages from Paul Mooney, Calvary Tabernacle, and Indiana Bible College in Indianapolis, Nate Wilson, the Rock Church, and Apostolic School of Theology in Sacramento, O'Neil and Jenean Smith, and Kenneth and Martha Pope. The embers of interest and the fire of possibilities for this work were first sparked in the halls of learning at Wheaton College and Graduate School, Wheaton, Illinois, especially in the excellent scholarship of Edith L. Blumhofer. I have been greatly assisted along the way by Darrin Rodgers at the Assemblies of God Flower Pentecostal Heritage Center, my secretary at Indiana Bible College, Jennifer Mast, TVA librarian research expert RaNae S. Vaughn, and Oneness studies scholar Alexander Steward. Two outstanding spiritual giants in the history of Pentecostalism have been enduring inspirations in my life, personally motivating my love for the pursuit of meticulously detailed, historically relevant research. The first, S. G. Norris, inspired a deep love of learning rooted in our Pentecostal heritage, and the other, Nathaniel A. Urshan, set an incomparable standard of integrity that has impacted generations.

# Abbreviations

| | |
|---|---|
| AAFCJ | Apostolic Assembly of the Faith in Christ Jesus |
| AAI | Apostolic Archives International |
| ACANJC | Apostolic Christian Assembly of the Name of Jesus Christ |
| AC | Apostolic Church |
| ACFCJ | Apostolic Church of the Faith in Christ Jesus [Mexico] |
| ACJ | Apostolic Church of Jesus |
| ACJC | Apostolic Church of Jesus Christ [originally—Apostolic Churches of Jesus Christ] |
| ACOP | Apostolic Church of Pentecost [Canada] |
| AFC | Apostolic Faith Churches [Hawaii] |
| AFMCG | Apostolic Faith Missionary Church of God |
| AG | Assemblies of God |
| AsCJC | Assemblies of the Church of Jesus Christ |
| ALJC | Assemblies of the Lord Jesus Christ |
| AMA | Apostolic Ministerial Association |
| AOHCG | Apostolic Overcoming Holy Church of God [originally—Ethiopian Overcoming Holy Church of God] |
| ABC | Associated Brotherhood of Christians [originally—Associated Ministers of Jesus Christ] |
| AMJC | Associated Ministers of Jesus Christ |
| BMA | Bethel Ministerial Association [originally—Evangelistic Ministerial Alliance] |
| BT | The Blessed Truth |
| BWC | Bible Way Church of Our Lord Jesus Christ Worldwide |

| | |
|---|---|
| CGA | Church of God (Apostolic) |
| CGCJA | Church of God in Christ Jesus (Apostolic) |
| CGSC | Christian Gospel Spiritual Church [Mexico] |
| COGIC | Church of God in Christ |
| CJC | Church of Jesus Christ |
| COOLJC | Church of Our Lord Jesus Christ of the Apostolic Faith |
| CLGPGT | Church of the Living God, the Pillar and Ground of the Truth |
| CLJC | Church of the Lord Jesus Christ |
| CPC | Christ Pentecostal Church [Yugoslavia] |
| CSOP | Center for the Study of Oneness Pentecostalism |
| CO | Christian Outlook |
| DPCM | Dictionary of Pentecostal and Charismatic Movements |
| ECSA | Evangelical Church in the Spirit of the Apostles [Russia] |
| EDN | Enumeration District Number—U.S. Census |
| ETBCAF | Emmanuel Tabernacle Baptist Church Apostolic Faith |
| ECJC | Emmanuel's Church in Jesus Christ |
| EMA | Evangelistic Ministerial Alliance |
| FCGCJN | Free Holiness Church of God in Jesus' Name |
| FPC | First Pentecostal Church of Jesus Christ, Little Rock, Arkansas |
| FUCJCA | First United Church of Jesus Christ Apostolic |
| GAAA | General Assembly of Apostolic Assemblies |
| GCGCA | Glorious Church of God in Christ Apostolic |
| GR | The Good Report |
| IPC | Indonesia Pentecostal Church |
| JOAC | Jesus Only Apostolic Church |
| KKK | Ku Klux Klan |
| LWC | Light of the World Church [La Luz del Mundo—Mexico] |
| MDS | Meat in Due Season |

| | |
|---|---|
| NBCGCP | New Bethel Church of God in Christ (Pentecostal) |
| NIDPCM | New International Dictionary of Pentecostal and Charismatic Movements |
| OSI | Oneness Studies Institute |
| PAJC | Pentecostal Assemblies of Jesus Christ |
| PAW | Pentecostal Assemblies of the World |
| PCCNA | Pentecostal and Charismatic Churches of North America [originally—Pentecostal Fellowship of North America] |
| PCAF | Pentecostal Churches of the Apostolic Faith |
| PCI | Pentecostal Church, Incorporated |
| PHCG | Pure Holiness Church of God |
| PMA | Pentecostal Ministerial Alliance [renamed (1932)—Pentecostal Church, Inc.] |
| PT | The Present Truth |
| SJC | Spirit of Jesus Church [Japan] |
| SPS | Society for Pentecostal Studies |
| TJC | True Jesus Church [China] |
| UPCI | United Pentecostal Church International [originally—United Pentecostal Church, Inc.] |
| VW | The Voice in the Wilderness |
| WG | The Witness of God |

# 1

# Introduction

## "Without the Camp"

HEBREWS 13:11

Perhaps the least known chapter in the history of American Pentecostalism is that of early Oneness Pentecostalism. The earliest era of this segment of the movement (1901–31) is especially relevant to Pentecostal history in general because of its unique and durative display of interracial fervor, an impulse which figured prominently into its formative development. This book is an in-depth look at the history and nature of this initial interracial vision as interpreted via the lens of one of the movement's primary architects, Garfield Thomas Haywood, and within the early development of Oneness Pentecostalism's central church and ministerial structures, the interracial Pentecostal Assemblies of the World.

It is also an attempt to rectify a one dimensional historical perspective currently pervasive in the overall historiography of Pentecostalism, and, therefore, decidedly inclusive of its Oneness dimensions, on the one hand, and a balance, on the other hand, to common interpretive models which have ignored the significance of race in the restorative framework of the early movement. As a starting point it is essential to trace this interracial fervor into the Azusa Street revival and to account for the Parham-influenced, power-struggle resistance to this impulse in the U.S. regionally. Several significant pieces of the historical puzzle have come to light in this research which give fresh and, in some cases, ground breaking insight into the events, such as the 1906 Azusa Street Mission founding of the interracial Pentecostal Assemblies of the World.

These and other sources have contributed to a much better understanding now of two of Oneness Pentecostalism's most obscure early leaders, J. J. Frazee and E. W. Doak, as well as of the movement's early major centers. African American Pentecostal leader G. T. Haywood, as it turns out, figures most prominently into this history, not only as one of its leading proponents, but as its central interracial voice, as well as its most renowned leader in its foremost early epicenter—Indianapolis, Indiana.

Therefore, an examination of its interracial authenticity necessitates an extensive look into the pre-Oneness context of the PAW, the related battle for the newly organized, intricately related, Assemblies of God, and the transition of the PAW itself from "Trinitarian" to "Oneness" Pentecostalism. In the final analysis this book makes an effort at investigation into the whole scope of the eventual racial schism which came to Oneness Pentecostalism and to the Pentecostal Assemblies of the World, in particular, in 1924, resulting in a majority withdrawal of the White segment of churches and ministers. The resulting rejection of the interracial impulse which followed within Oneness Pentecostalism as a whole produced a fractured movement with decades of resulting diffusion and the proliferation of separatism and independency. These events marked, indelibly, the movement's regional development in the U.S., as well as its critical global missionary and autochthonous segments, all of which were expanding rapidly by 1930.

## 1.1 Definitions and Parameters

The making of Oneness Pentecostalism, like that of the broader movement to which it is a prominent part, was largely dependent upon the motifs of restoration and revelation within its earliest development.[1] In turn, these elements greatly impacted its own theological receptivity to an early interracial impulse which largely shaped Oneness Pentecostal ideology for more than a generation. Yet it may very well have been equally impacted by the nature of the theological isolation and rejection experienced as a

1. Oneness origins are understood here to date to the popularly recognized initiating events which occurred in California at the Arroyo Seco Camp Meeting in April 1913. The initial epiphany-like events, the immediate scattered rebaptisms, and the planning, anticipation, and implementation of strategies resulted in a period of relative calm until April 1914.

result of its theological position, although it developed parallel to, if isolated from, broader forms of Pentecostalism.

The salient and emotive remarks of G. T. Haywood, for example, in the December 1916 issue of his influential periodical *The Voice in the Wilderness*, contain an excellent metaphor descriptive of the Oneness movement. They reveal his response to the events of October 1916—the resulting traumatic expulsion of the Oneness ministers from the young Pentecostal ministerial body in St. Louis known as the Assemblies of God:

> There were quite a number who withdrew from the Council at the close of the session, because there was a spirit of drifting into another denomination manifested, when they began to draw up a "creed," which they termed "fundamentals." It is no doubt the same thing under a different name. I have no complaints to make, but by the grace of God *I shall endeavor to press on with the Lord "without the camp, bearing His reproach, for here we have no continuing city, but we seek one to come."*[2]

Oneness Pentecostalism, the term which has become the most popular designation for the movement, and the term of preference in this book, is known also as the Apostolic Pentecostal and as the Jesus' Name movement, all being equally acceptable common self-designations. From its inception the movement has, indeed, remained "without the camp," as an enigma, and as a Pentecostal antagonist to the broader movement, experiencing both imposed and self-imposed isolation from the religious mainstream. This has been due largely to rigidity in its deviations from the classical doctrine of the Trinity and its soteriology.

Haywood's use, nonetheless, of such an Old Testament "without the camp" analogy encompassed more than the mere theological rejection of the Assemblies of God. It was, in fact, intricately linked as well to the AG racial rejection.[3] Some months prior to Haywood's remarks and the AG expulsion of its Oneness element in October 1916, well-known Pentecostal songwriter Thoro Harris also startled his AG Council compatriots by

2. Haywood, "St. Louis Council at St. Louis, Mo," 1; see Heb 13:11; cf. "They daily misjudge me and sneer, scoff and scorn; Reproach for Thy word and Thy name we have borne; Yet, Lord, we do love them, forgive them their wrong," Haywood, "O Lord, How Long," 15.

3. The terms "Unitarian" and "Jesus Only" are neither tenable nor common self-designations of the movement; cf. Yong, *Spirit Poured Out on All Flesh*, 205–6, who observed that Oneness affirmations distinguish it "from the Socinian and modern Unitarian denials of the Trinity" and served to reject "both Arian and modern theological liberal rejections of the deity of Christ."

converting to the Jesus' Name movement. As a rallying cry for the cause he immediately wrote "Baptized in Jesus' Name," and, in 1917, penned his most familiar of hymns, "All That Thrills My Soul Is Jesus." His baptismal hymn opens defiantly: "Today I gladly bear the bitter cross of scorn, reproach and shame; I count the worthless praise of men but loss, baptized in Jesus' Name."[4]

The Oneness proponents seemed to rather gladly identify such reproach with the suffering required for His Name, a theme which would loom large in Jesus' Name Pentecostalism. And, as Haywood vividly symbolized, their very identity was defined by a suffering "without the gate," a welcome plight, more or less, as the necessary spiritual badge of validation required in what they understood as the defense of restored truth.

### 1.1.1 Difficulties Inherent to Pentecostal Definition

In Pentecostal definition, Pentecostal-Evangelical assessments have typically stressed classical essentials, as in Menzies' 1971 research: "The 'baptism in the Holy Spirit,' is believed to be evidenced by the accompanying sign of 'speaking with other tongues as the Spirit gives utterance.'" Essentially, the dominant Evangelical, fundamentalist, and, ultimately, Assemblies of God definitions, as well as dominant history, were usually viewed as adequate and representative, as, more or less, "a microcosm of the Pentecostal movement as a whole," and even "the most representative of the Pentecostal organizations."[5]

Such a starting point is, obviously, a problematic definitional standard, not only for Oneness Pentecostalism, but for large segments of diverse Pentecostals, not the least of which are the burgeoning autochthonous Pentecostals worldwide. Also to the point, Assemblies of God and related denominational histories, until Edith Blumhofer's work, were typically critical and biased in their analyses of Oneness origins, and only a scant number of Oneness histories existed, none of which were broad, in-depth studies.

These earliest discussions of the movement refer to Oneness Pentecostalism as "The New Issue," setting the discussion in the "negative" terms of the AG perspective, as having come after another divisive issue, the sanctification issue which split Pentecostalism by 1910–1912.[6] The

4. Harris, "Baptized in Jesus' Name," 1.

5. Menzies, *Anointed to Serve*, 177–227.

6. Ibid., 114, for example, frames the events in terms of Oneness hysteria; cf.,

opponents, therefore, set the definitional parameters. For example, they inevitably over-emphasize the emergence of the movement in terms of mischaracterized new revelations to the exclusion of equally compelling alternative explanations.

Beyond this, the challenge of circumscribing Pentecostal category placement and definition in this manner is displaced, to some extent, in David Martin's sociological analysis of Pentecostal identity and trajectories. Martin suggests a definitional shift away from placing "the expansion of Pentecostalism under the rubric of American hegemony," noting, as well, the potential for an evangelical mimicking of the same "incline and decline" trajectory of "Liberal Christianity."

> Evangelical Christianity (of which Pentecostalism is a version) belongs to a phase in the process of modernity, with the corollary that the Pentecostalism now so expansive in the modernization of the developing world is likewise a phase . . . Insofar as Pentecostalism spreads it does so principally through a charismatic movement partly inside the older churches and partly "breaking bounds" in every sense.[7]

A more recent and far more "inclusive definition," however, is being suggested, for example, by David Barrett's new *World Christian Encyclopedia* and by such global studies as that of Allan Anderson in *An Introduction to Pentecostalism.* Beyond the earlier categories of "Pentecostal" and "Charismatic," the broad frame of reference for these emerging definitions make room for the inclusion of large segments of "Independents," including, notably the African Independent Churches and the Han Chinese Churches, which are Pentecostal-like, sharing the emphasis of empowerment and gifts, if not tongues.[8]

---

Brumback, *Suddenly from Heaven*, 191, ". . . a movement that brought forth a 'revelation' that almost tore the movement apart"; also, Brumback, *God in Three Persons*; Lindquist, *The Truth About the Trinity and Baptism in Jesus' Name Only*; and Rider, "The Theology of the 'Jesus Only' Movement."

7. Martin, *Pentecostalism*, 2–3; cf. also, the 250 million estimate for worldwide Pentecostalism (1), and the reference to "varied purposes of journalist rag-bags like 'fundamentalism'" in the explication regarding Pentecostal expansion (x).

8. Barrett, Johnson, and Crossing, "Christianity 2010," 36; Barrett's totals includes multiple non-tongues categories, such as "pre-," "post-," "quasi-,". See Barrett and Johnson, "Annual Statistical Table on Global Mission," 25, 13; Anderson, *Introduction to Pentecostalism*, 1, 10–11; cf. Anderson, "To All Points of the Compass"; also, Johnstone and Mandryk, *Operation World*, 755–65, with less optimistic totals which exclude "Independents."

These additional categories of "Pentecostal" groups, according to the *International Bulletin of Missionary Research,* boost the combined total to more than 614 million, and thus the basis for the oft-cited statistic of 600 million for the 2006 Azusa Centennial. Importantly, these totals include the diverse Oneness Pentecostal global constituencies, a characteristic feature of most assessments of general Pentecostalism's numerical strength. The number of Oneness Pentecostals, above and beyond the hard data of 27.4 million reported for specific groups by the Oneness Studies Institute in 2009, now exceeds an estimated thirty million.[9]

Somewhat enigmatically, Oneness Pentecostals fall within the range of "classical" Pentecostal definition with respect to the emphasis on tongues. Therefore, on the one hand, Oneness Pentecostals are accurately depicted as "classical" regarding evidentiary tongues. It must be observed that, on the other hand, by such a definition, perhaps as few as a third of Barrett's Pentecostal totals fit such a strong tongues categorization.[10]

Yet from almost every other perspective, the Oneness movement appears to be one of the most obvious examples of the difficulty of designating precise theological parameters to Pentecostal definitions. The observation that "Pentecostals have defined themselves by so many paradigms that diversity itself has become a primary defining characteristic" may, in fact, be nowhere better epitomized.[11]

### 1.1.2 A Consideration of Theological Parameters

This is representative of the fact that the Oneness movement's own definitive core is *theological,* deriving its distinctive identity from outside the mainstream, beyond the shared experiential Pentecostal elements of Spirit

9. Oneness Studies Institute, "Report of The Oneness Studies Institute," 1, 4–5, reporting 620 of a known 750 Oneness groups and Independents. The largest U.S. groups: (White) United Pentecostal Church International, Assemblies of the Lord Jesus Christ; (Black) Pentecostal Assemblies of the World, Church of Our Lord Jesus Christ of the Apostolic Faith, Bible Way Church of Our Lord Jesus Worldwide; (Hispanic) Apostolic Assembly of the Faith in Christ Jesus; The largest concentrations outside the U.S. are in China, Ethiopia, Colombia, Mexico, Indonesia, India, the Philippines, Nigeria, and Uganda.

10. Barrett, Kurian, and Johnson, *World Christian Encyclopedia,* "Table 1–5," 16–19. Oneness groups are not always identified in the WCE. Though dated, the WCE includes 18 million Oneness Pentecostals, see also, "Table 1–6a," 20–24, with newer stats for the TJC (1.83 million) and AWCF (6.63 million), Barrett, Johnson, and Crossing, "Missiometrics 2006," 27–30.

11. Anderson, *Introduction,* 10.

and gifts. The precursors for such a primacy of theological conviction were interwoven into the fabric of the Pentecostal experience long before the emergence of Oneness ideology in 1913. They became the pre-suppositional Oneness starting point which Jacobsen picks up on when he suggests that Haywood's Oneness theology leaves undefined precisely what the relationship is "between the human and the divine."[12] These precursors are seen in Pentecostal themes of "Back to the Bible," Jesus-centered worship, and the power of Jesus' Name. These latent elements were uniquely, and zealously, radicalized by Oneness reordering and redefinition.

With descriptions, rather than definitions, being the usual methodology within Pentecostalism, it is consistent that the chief self-descriptive identifier for Jesus' Name Pentecostals is that of "Apostolic." They are, first, experientially connected to the Spirit-life of the Apostles, but not without the essential life of the Word. In this way Oneness Pentecostalism should be understood as a prioritization of the Name of Jesus rooted in pre-Nicene Old Testament symbolism, intent upon capturing the essence of God's absolute "Oneness" in the person of Jesus Christ.

First of all, in order to grasp the framework of Oneness ideology it is essential to recognize its tenacious reordering of the varied and popular early themes of Pentecostalism itself. An important key to the Oneness theological position is the literal interpretive understanding of several critical scriptural referents, which observers often see as proof texts, regarding the nature of God and Christ, such as the biblical expression "God was manifest in the flesh." According to Oneness thought, Jesus is nothing less than the human manifestation of the One Mighty God, thus without allowance for differentiation within the divine nature. This starting point assures that the Old Testament El Shaddai Himself is the One Who is "God with us" in the Incarnation.[13]

The Oneness view conceives of Jesus as the Son, in that He is a man, but as the Father, in that He is the one God. Father and Son are seen as descriptive of composite human and divine natures in Christ in such a way that the man Jesus is understood as being indwelt of the Father, not of a *second* divine person. Similar reasoning is applied to the significance of Jesus' name. Being the God-Man, or God as a man, the result of a supernatural uniting of the divine and the human natures, the name Jesus

12. Jacobsen, *Thinking in the Spirit*, 212; cf., Haywood, "One True God," 2, and idem, "Dangers of Denying the Father," 3.

13. These aspects of the theology were most popularized in two of Haywood's most significant articles, "The One True God," appearing in *Meat in Due Season, The Present Truth*, and *The Voice in the Wilderness*, and "The Great Controversy."

is believed to be His exalted name, the Name above every name. "This then is substantially what baptism . . . really means," wrote early Oneness advocate Frank Ewart. "This is God's way to grant *remission* of sins. Every place in the New Testament that baptism is preached or commanded it is specifically stated that it is for the *remission* of sins, because we are thus *identified* with him in his death, which cancels or *remits* the entire debt, and sets us free."[14]

Observers of Oneness theology usually recognize that it emphasizes the preservation the Deity of Jesus within the context of a form of sequential modalism, with a theology of manifestations, offices, or roles, minus a theology of persons. Jesus is not to be limited to, or perceived as, merely a portion or person of, or in, the Godhead, but as *all* of God Himself, "*the* God of the whole earth," that is, the one "Mighty God."[15] This is what is usually thought of as the absolute or undivided Deity of Christ. Haywood stated boldly, "Jesus Christ is BOTH the Father and the Son," being both the one divine God and that same God in human manifestation. Jacobsen, therefore, regards his Christology as weak, calling it "more evocative than definitive," concluding that "Haywood's God was Jesus."[16]

As one might suspect, there is virtually zero allowance made in Oneness thought for creedal formulations, Nicene or otherwise, regarding a divine *ousia*, or essence, within the varied *hypostasis*, or persons, or any of the doctrinal formulations of church councils through the centuries. Father, Son, and Spirit are not viewed as separate persons, but, rather, as distinct manifestations. As with the Hebrew shema, the New Testament declaration "God is one" is taken as an absolute one, a profundity, in which Jesus, though genuinely man, is the *one* God, the *one* eternal "I Am," the *one* "Almighty."

Although most criticized for its scarcity of Christological solutions to questions regarding genuine interaction and relationship between the natures, versus persons, as well as between the manifestations, Oneness theology, nevertheless, conceives of only one divine person, manifested as Jesus, indwelt of the *totality* of God.[17] Deity, or divinity, in Oneness perspective, therefore, is a singular being, an unshared essence, demonstrating

14. Ewart, "Identification with Christ," 4; italics added.

15. 1 Tim 3:16; Matt 1:23; Phil 2:9; Isa 9:6 (AV); 54:5.

16. Haywood, "Jesus Is Both," 1; all-caps emphasis original; Jacobsen, *Thinking in the Spirit*, 211, 215.

17. Deut 6:4; Gal 3:20; 1 Tim 2:5; Exod 3:14; Rev 1:8; Col 2:9 (AV).

that Oneness theology does not so much ignore Nicaea, or Chalcedon, or any of the councils, for that matter, but rather disagrees with them.

Related theologically to the issues of theology proper and Christology are parallel restorative doctrinal beliefs within the Oneness movement, characteristic elements which are derived from the uniquely modal conclusions that the Father and Spirit are divine expressions of the person (singular) of God revealed in Jesus, the union of the Divine and the human in one person. These additional identifying doctrines to the "Oneness of God" are the importance of water baptism in the singular name of Jesus, rather than tripartite, speaking in tongues, and the experiential unfolding of these elements within the Acts 2:38, three-fold paradigm.

## 1.2 Definition in Context—Restorationism

"Dear Brother Haywood: . . . Praise God! Of a truth God is most graciously blessing his people who are willing to walk in the light."

—Lee Floyd, Kinder, LA[18]

Haywood's signature designation for the Oneness version of the miracle of incarnation is the popular Oneness expression "O Sweet Wonder," having become one of his own dramatic and theologically indelible imprints, from the poetic lines of his most famous hymn, "Jesus the Son of God."[19] From the mindset of early Pentecostalism rooted in an oft articulated vision of restoration, the wonder of new light via the Spirit's eschatological working was a guiding theological impulse, never more obvious than within Oneness Pentecostal circles.

It is not difficult, therefore, to see how the principle of "oneness" became a restorative theological foundation and a means of expressing both the divine reality, "I and the Father are one," as well as permeating the church experientially, "one, as we are."[20] Surely "Oneness" believers, they argued, would, of all people, insist upon the "oneness of believers" themselves—one God, one church. This perception became foundational to their impulse for interracial worship.

Nowhere is the movement's restoration tendencies more visible than in Haywood's own writings and hymnology, emphasizing, for example,

18. Reported in *Voice in the Wilderness,* No. 18, October 1916, 1.

19. Haywood, "Jesus, the Son of God," 5.

20. St. John 10:30 and 17:11 (AV).

the special nature of the name "Jesus," corresponding "in mystery" even to Father and Spirit, so as to be "the mystery revealed" and "the Name of Names."[21] Thus, for Haywood, His name is the paramount proof of His Oneness, linked from the outset to a Pentecostal "revelation" and "restoration" of truth. The highly popular early hymn by Hattie Pryor, published in Haywood's widely used hymnal, translated such ideology into vivid worship. "To get in the Church triumphant you must go the *water way*!" It illustrates the way in which the Oneness mindset held to this sense of restoration in the Oneness mindset, focusing, for example, on "evening time" events and a present fulfillment of prophetic latter rain. "*It shall be light in the evening time* . . . It is the *light* today, buried in His precious name."[22]

The new Pentecost was seen as jumping the intervening years back to "the way the apostles trod." Though shaped by identical motifs and impulses as the broader movement, it extracted its unique identity and self-understanding circumscribed by a distinct theological essence. Nowhere was this more pronounced than with respect to the Name of Jesus. Haywood's 1916 song, "The Name of God," is clearly characteristic of the way in which "the Name" was emphasized as a latter day revelation. The repeated final line emphasized this "truth" as a focus of worship: "Jesus is . . . the name of God!"

> Manna true came down from heaven, Bearing with it Jesus' name,
> Held in mystery through the ages, Now 'tis spoken clear and plain;
> Christ in you, the hope of glory, Lord of heaven, Lord of hosts;
> And in Jesus is the name of Father, Son and Holy Ghost.[23]

The restorative impulse and motifs were certainly not uncommon throughout the earliest Pentecostal period. B. F. Lawrence, one of the first to chronicle the Azusa Street revival, echoed shared sentiments of a dominant early Pentecostal restorationism in his 1916 history, *The Apostolic Faith Restored*:

> The Pentecostal Movement . . . leaps the intervening years crying, "Back to Pentecost." In the minds of these honest-hearted men and women, this work of God is immediately connected with the work of God in New Testament days . . . They do not recognize a doctrine or custom as authoritative unless it can be

21. Haywood, "Name of Names," 1–2.

22. Pryor, "Water Way," 20–21.

23. Haywood and Smith, "Name of God," 12, stanzas 1 and 5.

> traced to that primal source of church instruction, the Lord and His apostles.[24]

Blumhofer, who argues that a "strong restorationist component" was at the "heart of the definition of Pentecostalism," has also suggested that Oneness Pentecostals are best understood as simply "more zealously restorationist . . . than the mainstream."[25] Along with the "restoration" of "tongues," power, and healing to the church, they were including in the restoration priorities the additional theologies which they viewed as equally biblical—the power of Jesus' name, the Deity of Jesus, and the absolute Oneness of God.

## 1.3 Garfield Thomas Haywood

A major focus of this work has to do with the significant role of the Black Oneness pastor in Indianapolis, Garfield Thomas Haywood, as a preeminent leader within the early Oneness movement and as the chief architect of the post-Azusa Street revival interracial dream of the Pentecostal Assemblies of the World. Haywood was clearly the ultimate champion of the cause, defender and preacher par excellence, and foremost leader in the advancement and success of the movement's early interracial successes.

Gary B. McGee's popular history, *People of the Spirit: The Assemblies of God,* for example, although it does not reference the Oneness movement per se, does honor the solitary ministry of G. T. Haywood. As such, eighty eight years after Haywood's "without the camp" article concerning the Assemblies of God, McGee refers to T. K. Leonard's derision of Haywood in the 1916 General Council Assemblies of God debate. Leonard denounced the Oneness doctrine as "hay, wood, and stubble," raising the temperature of the debate a few degrees, but in doing so, demonstrating just how closely Haywood and Oneness theology were perceived.

McGee states observantly, though, that the "influence of Haywood on the Assemblies of God, however, could not be put down so easily." This is all the more amazing, considering Haywood was never a member of the AG. Haywood was so highly respected that he preached throughout the predominantly White AG circles, was a "featured speaker at early General

24. Lawrence, *The Apostolic Faith Restored,* 12; Lawrence associated with the movement for a time and was rebaptized.

25. Blumhofer, *The Assemblies of God,* 15, 237–38; cf., Ware, "Restorationism in Classical Pentecostalism," 1019–21; and Hall, "The Restoration Impulse."

Councils," and was even "granted the privilege of speaking from the floor" in AG Council meetings.[26]

Then, as now, Haywood's leadership, especially as the consummate representative of the Oneness position, was unparalleled. Although Blacks were unwelcome in the Assemblies of God, Haywood had long been a part of the lesser known, and largely western and northwestern regional group, the Pentecostal Assemblies of the World. A lesser known fact is that the PAW originated as an Azusa-based organization, interracial from inception, though largely White, readily credentialing Blacks and Hispanics. It served "under the radar," partly, perhaps, for this very reason, but certainly so as to avoid any taint of denominationalism and creed-making.

Nevertheless, historical and doctrinal details aside for the moment, Haywood fought long and hard to bring the Assemblies of God into the Oneness camp, in spite of the fact that, in 1914, it was a newly formed, intentionally lily white Pentecostal ministerial body, licensing only White ministers. He, evidently, had hopes for its interracial future, once secured for the Jesus' Name cause. After the Assemblies of God, though, was lost to Oneness effort, the eventuality of such interracial hopes and theological vision were tied to the success of winning over the Pentecostal Assemblies of the World.

### 1.3.1 Haywood, Indianapolis, and Interracial Pentecostalism

Growing very rapidly under Haywood's leadership, the Indianapolis church, by the time of his 1915 rebaptism, was one of the largest Pentecostal congregations in the country. His "Apostolic Faith Assembly" was also the most fully interracial Pentecostal congregation in the movement, "at one time . . . about sixty percent black and forty percent White."[27] In light of the cultural norms, the limitations placed upon Blacks of the period, and the alarming rising presence of the KKK in Indiana, Haywood's racial accomplishments were staggering.

26. McGee, *People of the Spirit*, 204–6 (a 665-page popular history). Haywood was emphatic that he was never credentialed, which is verified by the AG ministerial rosters, in Golder, *History of the Pentecostal Assemblies of the World*, 36.

27. Haywood, "The Convention," 1: "There were about 1,000 or more present, besides the throng outside looking in at the windows." Senate and Eleventh was enlarged by 1919 to seat 1,000, yet Apostolic Faith Assembly outgrew it, see Haywood, *Brief History of Christ Temple Church*, 37 and Golder, *Haywood*, 11.

Few ministers, regardless of race, were more beloved and admired for depth of ministry and leadership. In spite of its miscarried hopes, the Oneness movement's seven year "interracial era" and earlier interracial activities were entirely counter-cultural, inspired to success by a yearning for a return to a "new Pentecost," certainly, but also by the Pentecostal example of Haywood's life and ministry. Indianapolis became the focus of the fulfillment of the dream of interracial unity.

As Seymour's influence in the Azusa Street revival had caused the epicenter of Pentecostalism to shift to southern California, Haywood's international influence resulted in the Oneness movement's shift, from the west and northwest, to Indianapolis and the Midwest. In contrast, though, Seymour evidenced little organizational vision, except perhaps in the early efforts of the PAW, viewing Mason's Church of God in Christ as adequate, especially with its early White component.

With the 1910 division over Durham's sanctification views, Haywood, probably as early as 1911, represented a genuine schism within the Black Pentecostal leadership and thus a concern for both Seymour and Mason. As a radical convert to this new Finished Work theology Haywood was the chief visionary in the attraction and assimilation of large numbers of African Americans, a vision which also included the pre-Oneness PAW's original commitment to interracial unity. It was this very unity of purpose that would serve to later galvanize Haywood's influence as a major force for the Oneness movement early in 1915.[28]

Certainly, the interracial failures of the Azusa Street revival for Haywood hit close to home, producing a yearning for the aspirations of what many viewed as an essential element of the original Pentecost. Additionally, the sting of such failures were felt more acutely when demonstrated at Azusa in the very actions of Haywood's own doctrinal hero, William H. Durham. With the exclusionary race policies of the AG following closely on the heels of such controversies it is little wonder that so many hoped for the rejuvenating "winds of God" to prove both the authenticity of the Oneness aspirations and the vitality of an original, all-inclusive Pentecost. They trusted that their own Apostolic heirs to "Pentecost" would do better.

R. C. Lawson, one of Haywood's most notable converts, founder of the Church of Our Lord Jesus Christ of the Apostolic Faith, lamented their later, ultimate failure to do so. "We trusted that the apostolic people would rise to redeem man by example and precept. It is all right to sing and shout and pray and preach loud, but what this poor world is longing for is living

28. See, for example, Tyson, *Early Pentecostal Revival*, 196–97.

the real love of God. For, after all, the greatest badge of discipleship of the Master is love."[29] It was this belief in just such a "badge of discipleship" that successfully drew an ever increasing number of Black adherents to the movement.

More than perhaps any other figure, Haywood has remained a persistent legend, of sorts, for this racial heroism, as it were, and as a symbol almost larger than life. He has been described as a preacher's preacher, and a teacher par excellence, sought after the world over. He has been noted, too, as having an exceptional pastor's heart. Renowned Haywood convert, Morris E. Golder, said of him: "I can recall Bishop Haywood coming to our home, riding on a bicycle, to pray . . . . Holding us on his knee while praying . . . . He was a dynamic preacher, preaching always under the anointing of the Holy Spirit. His voice rang like an expensive cathedral bell when he spoke under God's unction."[30] He was also a truly exceptional musical talent, composer, and poet.

> Jesus, Thou art the good Shepherd, Our gateway to enter in
> Prophet Thou art, King and High-priest, Who sacrifice made for sin
> Altar Thou art, and the incense, Thou art the Lamb that was slain
> Jesus, Thou art the Temple, The Vail that was rent in twain.[31]

## 1.3.2 Haywood's Impact on Black Oneness Pentecostalism

Former AG Superintendent E. S. Williams, in an interview with James J. Tinney, unflatteringly and quite inaccurately, referred to Haywood as "a White man's Negro." The characterization is indicative, though, of the failure of many in early Pentecostalism, especially in the AG, to reconcile their racial attitudes with their theology. Tinney writes:

> The primary person responsible for the inter-racial character of Apostolicism was, of course, G. T. Haywood. In fact, it may be argued that Haywood, more than any other person, was responsible for the growth and development of the Oneness movement, especially in its formative years. No figure looms as large in all historical accounts of the movement . . . Haywood, as it turns out, becomes the central link between all the early leaders

29. Lawson, *The Anthropology of Jesus Christ*, 34.

30. Golder, *Life*, 70, 76.

31. Haywood, "Jesus Our All in All," *The Bridegroom Songs*, 34, the popular songbook released by Haywood in 1916.

of both the Trinitarian and Apostolic movements, and among both White and Black Pentecostals.[32]

In contrast, another commonly held perception is that Haywood seemed to transcend race, at least in as much as he overcame long held, previously unyielding resistances to integration, and initiated, along with an array of White, Black, and Hispanic leaders, a meaningful and viable interracial organism, genuinely unique to its day. Only after more than thirty years, from 1906 to the interracial failures of 1937, did adaptation to cultural racist "norms" and race division sever the interracial ties in irreversible finality.

Also attributable to Haywood's leadership, to a large extent, is the impressive growth of Black Oneness Pentecostalism, suggestive also of its broad appeal within the African-American and other Black culture populations. Black Oneness growth has, in fact, consistently outpaced that of Whites. A few small groups formed directly from the Azusa Street revival and from COGIC, but Haywood and the interracial vision of the PAW were the major influence attracting African American ministers. This tendency continues to the present, with the largest of the Oneness constituency groups being Blacks, with 40 percent worldwide, Asians thirty, Hispanics twenty, Whites only nine. The recent withdrawal of the Apostolic Church of Ethiopia from the UPCI made it the largest Black Oneness constituency globally, although the PAW remains the largest Black Oneness group in the U.S. In the U.S., of the estimated 4.5 million Oneness Pentecostals, 60 percent are African-American.[33]

## 1.4 Research Sources and Limitations

The paucity of prioritized preservation has resulted in minimal availability and accessibility of critical Oneness Pentecostal primary source archival material, reflecting a decidedly oral, non-reflective early history.

32. An early Azusa participant, Williams became AG Superintendent in 1929; see Tinney-Williams 1979 Interview, cited in Tinney, "The Significance of Race in the Rise and Development of the Apostolic Pentecostal Movement," 61, 66.

33. See Oneness Studies Institute "Report of The Oneness Studies Institute," May 2009, comparing a 1999 report constituency total of 15–20 million. Additionally, Blacks in the report totaled 11,230,000 in 215 U.S. groups and 208 groups outside the U.S. The PAW had 1.5 million worldwide (1998), approaching 2 million (2010), the UPCI, 3 million in 4,200 churches in the U.S. and Canada and 30,000 churches elsewhere.

The earliest historical account did not appear until 1947, when one of its key participants, Frank J. Ewart, published *The Phenomenon of Pentecost*.[34] Much later, in 1965 and 1970, respectively, two works by UPCI historians were published, Fred J. Foster's *Think It Not Strange* and Arthur C. Clanton's *United We Stand*.[35]

After this period African American historical works began to appear, the first being Morris E. Golder's 1973 *History of the Pentecostal Assemblies of the World*. The first Haywood biography, *Before I Sleep*, appeared in 1977 by James L. Tyson, along with Golder's second work, *The Life and Works of Bishop Garfield Thomas Haywood*.[36] In 1980 James C. Richardson published a broad study inclusive of the PAW, *With Water and Spirit: A History of Black Apostolic Denominations in the U.S.*, and Ross P. Paddock wrote a PAW history, *Apostolic Roots: A Godly Heritage*, in 1985 as a popular PAW history. Tyson later produced his two most significant studies, *Chalices of Gold* (1990) and *The Early Pentecostal Revival* (1992).[37]

A very brief work on Haywood appeared in 1968 by Paul Dugas, *Life and Writings of G. T. Haywood*. The other known Haywood biographies are more recent and thorough studies, the first being Victoria M. Peagler's *Garfield Thomas Haywood (1880–1931): From Migrant's Son to an Internationally Renowned Churchman* in 1993. The other, most recent biography, *A Man Ahead of His Times* by Gary W. Garrett (2002), is uniquely significant in its incorporation of author interviews with the last living key eye-witness participants in Haywood's life and times.[38]

The most comprehensive work on Oneness Pentecostalism has been *Our God Is One: The Story of the Oneness Pentecostals*, a work which has enjoyed a fairly wide circulation. *Our God Is One*, the author's Wheaton College MA thesis, published in 1999, is a detailed study of the movement's history, theology, and present expansion. A popular history of the

34. Ewart, *The Phenomenon of Pentecost*. A few, more limited autobiographical works also appeared.

35. Foster, *Think It Not Strange*, revised as *Their Story: 20th Century Pentecostals*; Clanton, *United We Stand*, revised, by Charles E. Clanton, *United We Stand: Jubilee Edition*.

36. Golder, *History of the Pentecostal Assemblies of the World* and idem, *The Life and Works of Bishop Garfield Thomas Haywood*; Tyson, *Before I Sleep*; cf., Sims, *From Grace to Glory*.

37. Richardson, *With Water and Spirit*; Paddock, *Apostolic Roots*; Tyson, *Chalices of Gold* and *Early Pentecostal Revival*.

38. Dugas, *The Life and Writings of Elder G. T. Haywood*; Peagler, *Garfield Thomas Haywood*; *Garrett, A Man Ahead of His Times*; Garrett is the Founder/Director of the Apostolic Archive International, Joplin, Missouri.

era was published in 2007 by J. L. Hall entitled *Restoring the Apostolic Faith.*[39] Remarkably few Oneness academic histories, though, have been produced, including biographical academic studies. The indication may be a limited interest in Oneness self-reflection, with emphasis remaining on the theological, although Robin Johnston's 2010 historical presentation, *Howard A. Goss: A Pentecostal Life*, is a clear exception.[40]

The early periodicals themselves, therefore, remain the highest priority resource, especially since, at least up to about 1918, these writings tended to virtually chronicle the emerging movement. The effort of amassing extant issues has served to open a crucial primary source window into the era and allow access to a fairly cohesive, if sketchy, recapturing of details of the movement's early history. The largest collection of available pre-1925 archived periodicals may be that of the Oneness Studies Institute, Atlanta, Georgia, used in this work. The UPCI's Center for the Study of Oneness Pentecostalism, though, houses the largest total collection of archival material. Another important archival source is that of the Apostolic Archives International, Joplin, Missouri.

With respect to the most critical data from the OSI periodical collection, Haywood's *The Voice in the Wilderness*, Ewart's *Meat in Due Season*, originally *The Good Report,* D. C. O. Opperman's *Blessed Truth*, and Andrew D. Urshan's *The Witness of God* have been the most significant. Though rarely biographical, these publications, like the books they spawned, chronicled the early events, people, places, and theology as it was actually happening. Haywood, for example, started his periodical in 1910, and by 1922 it had become the official organ of the PAW, changing its name to *The Christian Outlook.*[41]

39. French, *Our God Is One* and "Oneness Pentecostalism in Global Perspective"; Hall, *Restoring the Apostolic Faith.*

40. Johnston, *Howard Goss.* A section on Oneness history was also included in the third volume of Bernard's *History of the Christian Church*; cf., also, Bernard, *The Oneness of God*; Chalfant, *Ancient Champions of Oneness*; Norris, *"I Am"*; Segraves, "Oneness Theology," 344ff.; Boora, *Apostolic and Post Apostolic Baptism*; idem, *The Oneness of God and the Doctrine of the Trinity*, and idem, *Oneness and Monotheism.*

41. The OSI collection includes 5 issues of *The Voice in the Wilderness,* 1916, 1918, and 1921, 10 issues of *Meat in Due Season,* 1915–1919, 7 issues of *The Good Report,* 1911–1914, 8 issues of *The Blessed Truth,* 1918–1921, and 103 issues of *The Witness of God,* 1919–1933. *The Christian Outlook,* 1922–1931, has been made available via the Apostolic Archives, www.apostolicarchives.org.

## 1.5 Historiography of Oneness Pentecostalism

Historiography, considered "an established subfield within the discipline of history," has potential for offering its own interesting insights into Pentecostal self-definition and perspective. The scant historiographical interest within the Jesus' Name movement aside, the emergence of scholarly treatments and the altering of attitudes with respect to the movement toward a more broad-based inclusivity are important developments.[42]

An example of an inclusive scholarly treatment is Robert Mapes Anderson's ground-breaking 1979 study of Pentecostalism, *The Vision of the Disinherited.* Although from outside Pentecostalism itself, this scholarly history inclusively highlighted the substantial role of the Oneness movement as an integral part of the broader historical developments. "Interpretations for Fundamentalism which identify it as primarily theological in nature," he explains, "must take into account a Pentecostal doctrinal spectrum of such variety and complexity that even *unitarianism* may be found within it."[43]

Anderson, also, is one of the first to grasp the racial implications of the AG "Trinitarian Controversy" itself and was ground breaking from the standpoint of Oneness studies. The book's wide reception as a milestone in Pentecostal historiography influenced the initiation of an attitudinal shift toward Oneness Pentecostalism, from negligible, slanted, prejudicial treatment to more positive, scholarly, inclusive treatment.[44] As a balanced historical analysis of early Pentecostalism, it is probably unsurpassed, emphasizing the historical, socio-economic, and cultural paradigms, such as fundamentalism, dislocation and social deprivation, which shaped the movement.[45]

Another major breakthrough has been David Reed's 1978 Boston University dissertation which represented the first major scholarly, yet sympathetic treatment of the movement, entitled "Origins and Development of Oneness Pentecostalism in the United States." Though not published until 2008, this has been the landmark study of Oneness Pentecostalism, having been thoroughly revised under the title *"In Jesus' Name": The History and Beliefs of Oneness Pentecostals.*[46] The book was awarded

42. Cerillo, "The Beginnings of American Pentecostalism," 249.

43. Anderson, *Vision of the Disinherited*, 176–94; italics added.

44. Ibid., 177–78, 189, 330.

45. Ibid., 5, 136; cf. the critiques in Smith, "Disinheritance of the Saints," 15–28.

46. Reed, "Origin and Development"; *"In Jesus' Name"*; and "Oneness Pentecostalism," 936–44; cf., Howell, "The People of the Name."

the prestigious *Pneuma* Book Award of the Society for Pentecostal Studies in 2009.[47] A recognized scholar in Oneness studies, Reed's book and other scholarship are the most familiar available to academics and casual observers alike.

*"In Jesus' Name"* argues, essentially, for the identification of Oneness theology within the tradition and christologies of early Jewish Christianity, and, thus, for the movement's Christian legitimacy, drawn largely from interpretations of Danielou's *The Theology of Jewish Christianity* and Longenecker's *The Christology of Early Jewish Christianity*. These same Jewish tendencies, Reed suggests, later prevalent in aspects of early Evangelicalism, influenced Oneness ideology, including, for example, the strong Christological differentiation between natures. Oneness Pentecostalism is viewed as a plausible re-emergence of these Jewish categories of thought said to "recur in renewal movements" in church history.[48]

Reed also sees Oneness theology as a truncated, Jesus-centric view of God that results from a proclivity for christocentric reductionism which naturally obscures Christ's "identity within the Trinity."[49] "On the eve of the Oneness revelation most of the doctrinal elements were in place. Patterns and themes had already been developed and debated in Holiness, Evangelical and Pentecostal circles."[50] Ultimately, Reed argues that it is "a sectarian movement within the wider parameters of the Church rather than a cult, . . . heterodox rather than a heretical movement."[51]

Although pejorative treatments of the movement are usually theological, rather than historical,[52] Thomas Fudge's *Christianity Without a Cross* (2003) appears to be the exception. The study focuses on theorized differences regarding Oneness salvation theologies rather than primary sources.[53] Interestingly, though, Fudge's research highlights quite another

47. French, ""In Jesus Name,"" 267–73.

48. Reed, *"In Jesus' Name,"* 69, 233–44, suggests that the strong Oneness differentiation between natures hints of inevitable Nestorianism; cf., Danielou, *The Development of Christian Doctrine* 1:7–9, 148, 151, 407, 46, 154–56; also, Longenecker, *The Christology of Early Jewish Christianity*, 41–46, 128.

49. Reed, *"In Jesus' Name,"* 33–34.

50. Ibid., 50, 135.

51. Reed's analogies are based on Stark and Bainbridge, "Of Churches, Sects, and Cults," 117–31, and Hexham and Poewe, *New Religions as Global Cultures*, 27–40; see also, Reed, *"In Jesus' Name,"* 9.

52. Boyd, *Oneness Pentecostals and the Trinity*, 9, 10, 12; see also,, Dalcour, *A Definitive Look at Oneness Theology*; Reed, Review of *A Definitive Look*, 166–69; Ross, *The Trinity and the Eternal Sonship of Christ*; Beisner, *"Jesus Only" Churches*.

53. Fudge, *Christianity Without the Cross*, also from the perspective of a former

development initiated much earlier. Unwittingly, fresh interest in the movement was piqued by the 1980s due, at least partly, to the writings and scholarship produced in an exodus of former members eager, from their disparate perspectives, to reflect upon their familiar, if discarded, tradition.

A 1984 symposium convened at Harvard, called by a former Oneness participant, Jeffrey Gill, to explore "Aspects of the Oneness Pentecostal Movement." Although the symposium papers were unpublished, they were significant in demonstrating the direction of theological reflection and scholarly interest in Apostolic origins, theology, and expansion.[54] Some, who represented especially critical scholarship regarding the movement, including James Tinney, were represented, including, for example, those who were researching the movement's considerable expansion within autochthonous groups.

Roswith Gerloff was working on the Black Oneness trans-Atlantic and British movement. The first volume of her published work was subtitled *With Special Reference to the Pentecostal Oneness (Apostolic) and Sabbatarian Movements.* Presenters Ken Gill and the Oneness scholar Manuel Gaxiola were researching the Mexican Oneness movement.[55] It should be noted, too, that Iain MacRobert in 1988 published important research from his studies at the University of Birmingham, *The Black Roots and White Racism of Early Pentecostalism in the USA*,[56] broadly inclusive of Pentecostal racial issues in general. MacRobert, originally from the Oneness tradition himself, brings those insights into his analysis of the racial realities which have plagued Pentecostalism.

An example of the more sensible and inclusive treatment of the movement can be found in the popular Zondervan resource on Pentecostalism, *The New International Dictionary of Pentecostal Charismatic*

Oneness Pentecostal; Gill, "Book Review, Thomas A. Fudge, *Christianity Without a Cross*," 149–50, especially, "the hypothesis . . . he has failed . . . to substantiate."

54. See "First Occasional Symposium on Aspects of the Oneness Pentecostal Movement," Harvard Divinity School, Cambridge, MA, July 5–7, 1985. At least five of the Harvard presenters were formerly Oneness themselves: David Reed, Joseph Howell, Stephen Graham, Gregory Boyd, and Dan Lewis.

55. Gerloff and Gill completed their PhD research at the University of Birmingham, UK, and both were published by Peter Lang; see Gerloff, *A Plea for Black British Theologies*; and Gill, *Toward a Contextualized Theology for the Third World*. Gaxiola's PhD research was completed at Birmingham, unrelated to Pentecostal studies, but his MA research on Mexican Oneness history was completed at Fuller, see Gaxiola, "The Serpent and the Dove."

56. MacRobert, *The Black Roots and White Racism* and "The Spirit and the Wall."

*Movements*, containing more than seventy articles regarding aspects of Oneness Pentecostalism. Recent histories of the Assemblies of God, too, such as Blumhofer's, are far more inclusive than previous works. Also notable are the works of Douglas Jacobsen, *Thinking in the Spirit* and *A Reader in Pentecostal Theology: Voices from the First Generation*, which include sizeable sections on Haywood, Larson, and Urshan, as well as a chapter entitled "Oneness Option."[57]

Allan Anderson's *An Introduction to Pentecostalism* and Amos Yong's *The Spirit Poured Out on All Flesh* represent new ground in this regard.[58] Probably startling to many Oneness Pentecostals themselves, Yong, nevertheless, in "Oneness and Trinity: Identity, Plurality, and World Theology," posits the issues relative to Oneness Pentecostalism as primarily illustrative of both the possibility and the necessity of inclusivity within a newly envisioned trajectory for global theology. Yong's effort has been to allow for a Pentecostal acknowledgment of a working of the Spirit in the context of other religions. Yet what must not be missed here is the reversal of attitudes to such an extent that Oneness Pentecostalism is not merely included, but is now at the discussion's core.[59]

The SPS Trinity-Oneness Dialogue, though, seems to have been less significant than examples such as these.[60] In his most renowned writing to date on the Spirit, Frank Macchia, chair of the "Trinitarian side," reported a total ambivalence, in his words, of the meaning of "the Oneness protests."[61] Unfortunately, without the public release of the annual dialogue papers and discussion, the success or failure of the effort, including reports of frustration and ambivalence, cannot be analyzed.

57. Burgess and Van Der Maas, eds., *The New International Dictionary of Pentecostal and Charismatic Movements*; Blumhofer, *The Assemblies of God*; Jacobsen, *Thinking in the Spirit*; and idem, *A Reader in Pentecostal Theology*.

58. Cf., Anderson, *Introduction*, especially "Chinese Pentecostal Churches," 132ff., and Castleberry, "Pentecostal History from Below," 271–74.

59. Yong, *The Spirit Poured Out on All Flesh*, 203–34.

60. See "Oneness-Trinitarian Pentecostal Final Report, 2002–2007," 203–24; also, Catholic scholar, McDonnell, ed., *Presence, Power, Praise*, 526.

61. Macchia, *Baptized in the Spirit*, 115, 116, 110–25, 251. Macchia sees the problem as a Oneness failure to recognize their own Spirit baptism as a "Trinitarian act of God" and as a Trinitarian structured experience; cf., Macchia, "From Azusa to Memphis," 214–15.

## 1.6 Conclusion—Scope and Sequence

The ministry of G. T. Haywood, the history of the PAW, and the unfolding history the entire Oneness movement (1901–1931) cohere rather nicely as parallel events. Each of the following chapters attempts to retrace the sequence of these events, interpreted in light of the background and the context of the multiplicity of participants, yet without losing sight of Haywood's key role. First, the most significant pre-Oneness developments are the emergence of Parham's Pentecostal and Seymour's Azusa Street revival, especially in terms of their impact upon Oneness Pentecostalism (1901–1911).

By 1912 (Chapter Four) the structures taking shape which will be pivotal to the development of Jesus' Name Pentecostalism include both the AG and PAW, but most importantly the leadership of J. J. Frazee and the "pre-merger," pre-Oneness PAW (1912–1918). This Pentecostal force, which had been aggressively moving forward since 1913, moved into a new era by late 1918, the fully interracial, integrated era of the leadership of the E. W. Doak and G. T. Haywood (1918–1924). Unfortunately, the unraveling of this vision occurred in 1924, and the era of diffusion and independency ensued from 1925–1931 and beyond.

Of course, beyond the sequence of events lies the focus and scope of emphasis and impact on developments. The Azusa Street revival can be seen as central in its ideological influence, its shaping of leadership, and its structural influence, via the PAW. Considerably less obvious is the Frazee era obscurity historically which demands special attention. These previously obscure events must be traced through Frazee's inter-connectedness to Los Angeles, the relocation to Portland, Oregon, the nature of the PAW, and Frazee's own personal theological journey, all of which can be evaluated, for the first time, in light of relevant new documentation. The swirl of historical events must be included in this analysis as thousands were swept into the so-called "new issue" from the AG, the PAW, and the length and breadth of Pentecostalism.

Elucidation is also necessary regarding the Indianapolis context, with the roots of the early AG in its borders, shaping Haywood's ministry and hopes of real unity and an interracial Pentecost eradicating race divisions. Even more important is a meaningful comprehension of that interracial golden era in which the unique counter-cultural ideology of the Spirit of Pentecost actually informed and shaped the human structures and relationships of both church and ministry. On the other hand, several issues are critical in the overall analysis, none more significant than the query regarding the Black "roots" of Pentecostalism or Haywood's particular forms of response to the racism that would shatter the dream of interracial harmony in the PAW. And regardless of varied attempts one might make at contextual, historical distancing, ultimately, the questions regarding present application resurface, not the least of which is whether or not historical hindsight can result in an ability to learn from past mistakes.

In the busy days immediately prior to the 1916 AG convention and the finality of their own ouster from their own ministerial body, many, like Haywood, were pressing hard for a new vision of fellowship. Rushing just such a message to the presses, Haywood wrote the following prayer for widespread distribution.

> God help us not to be afraid to break our alabaster boxes . . . Today many of God's People have some nice little alabaster boxes, which they prize very highly . . . Break your denominational boxes and let the odor fill the house! Break your second work of grace boxes . . . Break your manmade views concerning water baptism and let the name of Jesus have preeminence . . . Break your trinity boxes and let the glory of God be revealed in the face of Jesus Christ.[62]

Oneness Pentecostalism, perhaps, then, was the story of a tenacious breaking of the boxes of tradition within just the right context and such that these creative minds were able, surprisingly, to succeed in actually capturing the imaginations of a generation of hopeful proponents bent upon a dream of restoration of a meaningful, living new Pentecost. That vision carried with it a Spirit-centered commitment to an "all flesh" acceptance of all races, though, admittedly, in radically new theological "boxes."

62. Haywood, "The Alabaster Box," 1.

# 2

# G. T. Haywood and The Black Roots of Pentecostalism

A considerable consensus of scholarship has come to view the emergence of Pentecostalism in the U.S. as rooted in the American revivalism and Black spirituality prevalent in the early twentieth century. Charles Fox Parham's association of tongues speaking with Spirit baptism radically shaped the movement via his Apostolic Faith Bands, but his lack of racial integration and international impetus assured him a limited legacy. By 1906 more than thirteen thousand were associated with Parham's ministry and the rumblings of a movement were increasingly evident. Having spread to Los Angeles, William J. Seymour, the Azusa Street mission African American leader, called Parham "God's leader" of the new movement.[1]

## 2.1 Racial Implications of Parham's Views

That assessment would be radically redacted within a matter of weeks, as an overt racism from Parham became increasingly apparent. According to Anderson this was traceable to a much earlier period, but by 1902 was evident in the embrace of a full-blown racist British Israelism.[2] As demonstrated in his treatment of Seymour, it was certainly antithetical to the Black roots of the emerging international movement. But, whereas

1. See "The Old-Time Pentecost," 1. Parham's Pentecostal revival dates to January 1, 1901, Topeka, Kansas.

2. Anderson, "The Dubious Legacy of Charles Parham," 51–64; cf. Goss, *Fields White unto Harvest*, 132.

Parham's ministry had been largely confined to Kansas, Missouri and Texas, its success was now dwarfed by the magnitude of the unprecedented Seymour revival. California suddenly became the epicenter of a full-scale influx into the Pentecostal movement in the Nazareth of Los Angeles, with many African Americans, including such prominent names as G. T. Haywood and Charles H. Mason,[3] being impacted by the spreading fires.

### 2.1.1 Spirit Baptism and the Parham Tongues Movement

Parham's most important contribution was not tongues speaking per se, but his formulation linking tongues to the "biblical evidence," or what was viewed as the initial evidence of Spirit baptism. His most notable biographer, James Goff, considers Parham's most significant impact on the movement to be that of the theological connecting of "the basic tenets that later defined the movement" and "gave Pentecostalism a definable theological corpus."[4] Tongues as a *necessary* sign of the baptism became the defining characteristic of Pentecostalism and, perhaps more strongly, of Oneness Pentecostalism.

Clearly, the Azusa Street revival served as a catalyst in the widespread dissemination of tongues theology. To one degree or another, the emphasis on tongues in Spirit baptism influenced all other definitional parameters, setting up the ultimate tension in Pentecostal definition between the theological and experiential. Oneness Pentecostalism was in near unanimous agreement.[5] Some, like Haywood, believed in the essentiality of Spirit baptism long before their espousal of Oneness beliefs. "We conclude that the new birth and the baptism of the Holy Ghost are synonymous."[6]

As to the classical view of Pentecostalism, historian Vinson Synan argues that, with only slight exceptions, and even "despite these exceptions,"

3. Mason journeyed to Los Angeles where he was Spirit filled in February 1907, becoming head of the Church of God in Christ, now the largest Pentecostal group in the U.S., and, according to DuPree, the "fifth-largest U.S. denomination." See DuPree, "Explosive Growth of the African American Pentecostal Church," 7–10.

4. Cf., Anderson, *Disinherited*, 52–57; Goff, "Parham, Charles Fox (1873–1920)," 955; see also McGee, *Initial Evidence.*

5. Haywood, *The Birth of the Spirit in the Days of the Apostles,* in Dugas, *Haywood,* 88, 67–90; cf., Kinzie, *Handbook on Receiving the Holy Ghost*, 81ff., and Reeves, *Holy Ghost With Tongues,* 31–36.

6. Haywood, "Baptized Into One Body," 3. Haywood's position on Spirit baptism as an essential element of the new birth and on speaking in tongues was probably his most significant doctrinal contribution to the emerging Oneness movement.

initial evidence theology "carried the day throughout most of the Pentecostal world." "In the end tongues as initial evidence became the distinctive doctrine of the Pentecostal churches."[7] This is the belief in the essentiality of tongues, but only in the sense that they are the necessary sign that one is Spirit filled. Oneness Pentecostalism commonly holds this view, but usually goes further, holding to a distinct view of the essentiality of Spirit baptism itself.

Although not true of Oneness Pentecostalism, it is true that a considerable segment of the broader tongues movement no longer holds to the initial evidence. The trend is toward preference of less restrictive, less theologically-oriented, and, therefore, broader classifications of Pentecostal Spirit baptism.[8] This allows, of course, for the inclusion of non-tongues groups under the Pentecostal classification, although no standard classification prevails, as noted earlier in the research preferences of Johnstone and Mandryk. Nevertheless, even with the broader parameters, most observers minimally define Pentecostalism as "usually including a post-conversion experience" baptism, with the additional emphasis of a "renewing experience of the Holy Ghost" and the "gifts."[9]

## 2.1.2 Parham's Impact on the Southwest States Region

Certainly, merely having Parham influences, or even southern cultural influences, are in no way implication of racial impact, but in either instance any negative potential requires historical scrutiny. Influence can be subtle, yet profound; quite difficult to analyze, yet easily misinterpreted. Something that has become crystal clear in the course of this research is that Charles Fox Parham did, in fact, draw into the Pentecostal movement through his ministry a relatively large number of associates who later became a part of the Oneness forces. It is also true that these very ministers later participated in the profound interracial ministry of the flagship organization the Pentecostal Assemblies of the World.

7. Synan, "The Role of Tongues as Initial Evidence," 10; cf., Palma, *Baptism in the Holy* Spirit, 57.

8. Hunter, "Baptism in the Spirit," 108–109; Macchia, *Spirit Baptism*, 72–74; McDonnell and Montague, *Christian Initiation and Baptism in the Holy Spirit*, 24–30, 39–40; see also, Fee, *Gospel and Spirit*, 83–85, 105–11.

9. Johnstone and Mandryk, *Operation World*, 3, 21; Anderson, *Introduction*, 11; see also, Synan, "Role of Tongues," 15–16.

The most significant Oneness association to that of Parham is Howard A. Goss, whose wife Ethel E. Goss compiled the book *The Winds of God* in 1959 as his biography of the period and up to the AG formation. He never, though, wrote about his pivotal participation in the emergence of Oneness Pentecostalism.[10] Of course, Parham's greatest impact was in the southwest, but the nature of influence upon associates is less easily determined.[11] He had begun a Holiness healing ministry in Topeka by 1898, where, by 1900, he had also opened a Bible school in an old mansion known as Stone's Folly. He and some of his students spoke in tongues in January 1901, but for three years very few converts were made. The breakthrough came late in 1903 with a healing revival in Galena, Kansas.[12]

Parham's ministry became quite successful for the next three years, mostly throughout Oklahoma, Missouri, Arkansas, and Texas.[13] As Parham's center of operation shifted to Houston, where Seymour was introduced to the tongues movement, the region was clearly taking shape which would, certainly before 1930, become a Oneness epicenter rivaling Indianapolis and Los Angeles.

The highly publicized struggles between Seymour and Parham were known throughout the southwest, as well the entire movement, and the more than a dozen key leaders in Parham's ministry who would later embrace Oneness Pentecostalism were equally aware of the nature of their differences. Howard Goss (1883–1964), the most notable of these leaders, first Superintendent of the UPC when it formed in 1945, came from Clinton, Missouri, though his family moved to near Galena, Kansas in 1898.[14]

During Parham's successful 1903 Galena revival the twenty year old Goss received his call and joined the Apostolic Faith movement. He did not receive Spirit baptism with tongues until April 1906, on a train in Alvin, Texas, during an evangelistic tour with an Apostolic Faith band.[15]

10. Goss, *The Winds of God*, revised by Ruth Goss Norgje.

11. The foremost Parham authority is James R. Goff, Jr., see *Fields White unto Harvest.* The first-hand account of the Parham era was compiled in 1930 by Parham's wife, Sarah E. Parham, see *The Life of Charles F. Parham.*

12. Parham, *Life of Charles F. Parham*, 90–91; Goss, *Winds of God*, 34.

13. Goff, "Parham," 955.

14. Goss' original ancestry is traced to Granville and Wilkesboro, North Carolina. They would later settle just north of Galena in Empire City, Kansas. *Biography Index,* Sept 1955-Aug 1958, vol. 4 (New York: H. W. Wilson Co., 1960; *Who's Who In America,* vol. 7, 1977–1981 (Chicago: Marquis Who's Who, 1981); "March 6, 1883," WWI Registration Card, September 7, 1918; *1900 U.S. Census,* Empire City, Cherokee Co., Kansas, 5.

15. Goss, *Winds of God*, 27–28, 80–81. Goss' own early description of the event

Later, Howard Goss and E. N. Bell, to whom he turned over his successful Malvern, Arkansas church in 1910, were the key AG founders. Bell became its first AG Chairman.

Originally, Daniel C. O. Opperman was an educator with John Alexander Dowie's healing movement in Zion, Illinois. He was healed of tuberculosis while working with the Parham ministry in Texas at the time Seymour was departing for Los Angeles. He joined the Apostolic Faith evangelism teams in 1907, although he did not receive Pentecostal baptism until January 1908 in San Antonio, Texas.[16] A leading organizer of early short-term Bible schools, Opperman later, in 1917, became the first Chairman of the newly formed Oneness organization the General Assembly of Apostolic Assemblies after their AG expulsion.

When Parham separated from the Apostolic Faith organization, several ministers were brought into Pentecostalism under Goss, to whom the leadership mantle had fallen, such as David Lee Floyd. Originally from Red River County, Texas, in 1910 Floyd received Spirit baptism in Wilburton, Oklahoma. He was a 1914 AG charter member, but is best known for establishing one of the earliest Oneness periodicals *The Blessed Truth.* He turned his influential paper over to Opperman after joining his ministry in Eureka Springs, Arkansas.[17] Samuel C. McClain, G. C. McDaniel, and Clarence T. Craine, who joined Opperman's nearby Bible school in Joplin in 1910, converted in Goss's 1909–1910 sixteen week Malvern revival in which sixty-five preachers received their call.[18]

Walter H. Lyons, in 1906, and Lemuel C. Hall, in 1907, converted under Parham, but shifted allegiance to Goss as Parham's moral problems surfaced. The San Antonio mission where Parham had been speaking when arrested, July 1907, was under L. C. Hall's direction. This West Point graduate and former Dowie disciple was the grandson of Alabama

---

is also preserved in Lawrence, *The Apostolic Faith Restored*, 60–61; see also, Gurley, "Howard Goss and the Revival in Alvin," 9–10.

16. Goss, *Winds of God*, 100–105, 205; Blumhofer, "D. C. O. Opperman," 946–47; cf., Gohr, "D. C. O. Opperman and Early Ministerial Training"; see also, Hall, "Contending for the Faith," 13–17; see also, Cook, *Zion, Illinois*.

17. "Transcript of the David Lee Floyd Interview with Larry Booker–1979–1980," Miami, Oklahoma, 6; Martin, *The First Pentecostal Church of Garden City/First Pentecostal Church of Tulsa Story*, 3–4; Wacker, *Heaven Below*, 28; *1900 U.S. Census*, Red River County, Texas, 22. Floyd first began publication of *the Blessed Truth* in about 1916 in Louisiana.

18. Martin, *Tulsa*, 38; McClain, *Seek First the Kingdom*, 17–19, 22; Goss, "The Blessed Revival at Malvern, Arkansas," 2; Hansford, "Grover C. McDaniel," 136–40, 142; Reed, "T. Richard Reed," 199.

governor and U.S. Senator Arthur P. Bagley. He married the young widowed Mabel Smith, who was converted in Parham's Galveston meetings. Later joining the Azusa Street ministry, she became known for her gift of xenolalia and for convincing William Durham to visit Azusa. Hall and Opperman received Spirit baptism in the same San Antonio revival, where Hall was pastor of a CMA congregation.[19]

Much later, Hall became the first head of the Pentecostal Ministerial Alliance after its racial split from the PAW in 1924. At the same time, Lyons, an important Dallas area leader, became head of a separate withdrawing group, the Emanuel's Church in Jesus Christ.[20] Lyons converted at Millicent McClendon's Arlington, Texas revival, although he had actually only attended in order to stop the meetings. McClendon, a featured Parham preacher, married Goss in February 1907, but died in childbirth in 1910.[21] R. L. Blankenship, another influential Texas Oneness leader, was connected to Goss' early ministry, converting at least as early as 1910.[22] In Welch, Oklahoma Frank Yadon received Spirit baptism under Edward M. Pearson, one of the ministers who worked directly with Parham in Baxter Springs, Kansas.[23]

Jerry E. Osborn (1879–1964) received "Pentecostal" baptism prior to Parham's claim to having restored it, and a full ten years before the Azusa revival—in 1896 in Glenn Rose, Texas near Dallas. Ministering between Texas and Oklahoma between 1900 and 1906, Osborn worked with Pentecostal minister Frank Talmedge Alexander in Erick, Oklahoma, and identified early on with Parham's ministry in Texas. He was in "Beulah," Oklahoma by 1906 working with Emanuel Bible College, famed

19. Anderson, *Disinherited*, 137; see also Ewart, *Phenomenon*, 107; Alexander, *Women of Azusa Street*, 135, 138; Goss, *Winds of God*, 105–7; Blumhofer, *Aimee Semple McPherson*, 106.

20. The PMA later became the Pentecostal Church, Inc. The ECJC later merged to become the Pentecostal Assemblies of Jesus Christ. In 1945 the PCI and PAJC merged to become the UPC.

21. Clanton, *United We Stand*, 54; Goss, *Winds of God*, 145, describing Millicent as "freckled-faced," 146; Wallace, *Old-Time*, 272–73; Treece, *Come to Beulah Land*, 248–59.

22. See *The Pentecostal Outlook*, November 1937, 13; Howell, "People of the Name," 180–81; Synan, *Holiness-Pentecostal Movement in the United States*, 160. Blankenship, head of the 1945 Texas District PAJC, opposed the merger with the PCI and formed his own organization, the Apostolic Church.

23. Yadon, by 1912, was among the earliest participants in Idaho Pentecostalism. The Yadons figured prominently in Oneness Pentecostalism, see Martin, *Tulsa*, 9–10; Yadon, *Historical Record of the Oneness Movement in the Northwest*, 3–4; Wiens, *Unto You and Your Children*, 36.

songwriter R. E. Winsett, and evangelist Daniel Awrey, who, for example, conducted the Bible school in Eureka Springs in 1910.[24]

Oliver F. Fauss (1898–1980) became involved with Parham's Houston meetings as a young boy. Moving from Waynoka, Oklahoma to Texas, sometime after 1900, he received Spirit baptism in 1911, and was involved with the early ministries of A. P. Collins and Robert LaFleur. Fauss' ministry spanned several decades, serving as the UPC Assistant General Superintendent from 1947–1972, and briefly, in 1967, as General Superintendent.[25]

## 2.2 Early Pentecostal Origins and Oneness Motifs

Many precursors to Oneness theology, such as a strong emphasis on restoration, were found in the theology of Charles Parham, but the most important was his practice, as early as 1902, of baptism in Jesus' name.[26] Goff has noted, "though Parham never acknowledged the position himself," that is, the Oneness of God, "the Oneness organizers no doubt found a receptive audience among Pentecostals previously baptized by the Parhamite model."[27] Restoration motifs of the Holiness and Keswick movements were shared in common with Pentecostalism, for, as Wacker has pointed out, "nineteenth-century Protestantism brimmed with restorationist impulses."[28]

> Pentecostalism gradually emerged as a discrete religious movement among people who were certain that they lived in the days of prophecied restoration, revival, and consummation. Molded by a view of history that anticipated that an intense, brief recurrence of pristine New Testament faith and practice would immediately precede Christ's physical return to earth, early Pentecostalism is best understood as an expression of restorationist yearning that was shaped in significant ways by

24. Treece, *Beulah*, 68, 98–120, 84–94; Goss, *Winds of God*, 250.

25. Fauss, *What God Hath Wrought*, 18–19; *1900 U.S. Census*, Waynoka, Woods County, Oklahoma, 2; see also, Hall, "Oliver F. Fauss," 304–5; Tenney, *The Flame Still Burns*, 14.

26. Parham, *A Voice Crying in the Wilderness*, 22–24; Blumhofer, *Restoring the Faith*, 47 n. 23; Anderson, *Disinherited*, 176.

27. Goff, *Fields White unto Harvest*, 153 n. 24.

28. Wacker, *Heaven Below*, 3.

> the hopes and dreams of disparate groups of late nineteenth-century restorationists.[29]

It did not take long for Parham to fade to the background once moral allegations surfaced in 1907, for the leadership spotlight had already shifted to Seymour and the dramatic Azusa Street outpouring. It is understandable that historians have often favored Seymour in the protracted debate over which of them, if either, is the movement's founder. The debate, though, highlights an ambiguity within Pentecostalism regarding both origins and race, as variously discussed, for example, by Cecil Robeck, one of the foremost Azusa Street scholars, and James Goff, the foremost Parham, scholar.[30] Tinney points out that the conflicts over origins readily "illustrate the tensions between the two segments of the movement."[31]

In the expanded debate, a seminal question as to whether or not the origins are U.S. based at all, but rather traced to multiple points of global origin, is answered in the affirmative by such scholars as Allan Anderson in his detailed account of the spread of early Pentecostalism, *Spreading Fires: The Missionary Nature of Early Pentecostalism*. From such a perspective, earlier revivals, such as that of the Welsh revival (1904–5), the Pandita Ramabai led revival in India (1905–7), and the "Korean Pentecost" (1907–8), rival that of Parham and Azusa Street.[32]

Robeck, on the other hand, has concluded that all evidence for origins does, in his opinion, point to North America, as opposed to multiple, independent, and spontaneous points of origin, and, evidently, to an American founding. Additionally, Goff dismisses the a-historical notions of "the fabled 'no founder' school, of those content to acknowledge only divine intervention."[33] The legitimacy of suggesting, therefore, an apparent founder seems appropriate, as does favoring Seymour, although Parham's limited impact preceded the events of the Azusa Street revival. A strong case can be made for Seymour as the twentieth century founder and father of the American movement, at the very least, if not the global movement,

29. Blumhofer, *Restoring the Faith*, 11–12; cf., Dayton, *Theological Roots of Pentecostalism*, 40–54, 18; cf., Wacker, *Heaven Below*, 3; see Faupel, *The Everlasting Gospel*; Reed, *"In Jesus' Name,"* 78; Hall, "Restoration Impulse," 2.

30. Cf. Robeck, "Pentecostal Origins from a Global Perspective," 166–80, and Goff, "Problem of History," 186–91.

31. Tinney, "Significance of Race," 58 n. 11.

32. Anderson, *Spreading Fires*, 27–28, 29, 31.

33. Robeck, "Pentecostal Origins," 170; Goff, "Problem of History," 188.

based upon the necessity of international and interracial appeal before the fires of Pentecost could rightly be categorized as a movement.

To simply precede Seymour, obviously, does not imply a prior position as founder, for many examples, other than Parham, can be sighted regarding localized belief in and practice of tongues speaking throughout the previous decades leading up to Azusa Street. These were predecessors and perhaps even represented rumblings of a movement, but are not appropriately viewed as the initiators or the founder of the movement itself.

Goff, though, concludes conversely, that the movement originated with Parham, with arguments crucially dependent, again, upon Parham's historical definition of evidential tongues. Nelson, on the other hand, concludes, on the basis of weight of contribution to the movement, that Seymour is the modern founder, but a fact obscured, according to Nelson, due to racial prejudice.[34]

## 2.3 The Black Roots of Early Pentecostalism

Without question, Tinney's corollary observation is, indeed, pointed, that "without the important role of blacks there might be no Pentecostal movement of any magnitude today in the United States or the world."[35] Clearly, the discussion of origins must include the critically important consideration of the roots, or primary influences, within the early movement, especially apropos to an understanding of interracial Oneness Pentecostalism. The mounting evidence demonstrates the primacy of the Black roots of Pentecostalism in the analysis of the movement, including an appreciation of the implications of the Black experience in the context of the influences within Pentecostalism.

Therefore, preparatory of an examination of the interracial roots of Oneness Pentecostalism, first within the context of the Azusa Street influences, and then that of the Black influences original with Haywood's participation in the emerging movement, these root elements can be discussed from varied perspectives. Especially helpful is the related perspective of Cheryl Sanders' *Saints in Exile: The Holiness-Pentecostal Experience in African American Religion and Culture*. It allows insight into the topic from the prospect of "exile" by first evaluating the views of Black

34. Goff, "Problem of History," 189 n. 2; Nelson, "For Such a Time as This," 4, 13, 18, 49.

35. Cited in Clemmons, *Bishop C. H. Mason and the Roots of the Church of God in Christ*, 38

intellectuals, such as Chancellor Williams' view of African uniqueness, E. Franklin Frazier's social pathology, James Baldwin's cultural and religious impoverishment, as well as Howard Thurman's interpretation of the spirituals.[36]

Sanders' work highlights the fact that the Black Pentecostal experience of "exile" represents a dimension "on the extreme margins of an American society stratified by race, class, and denominational status."[37] She highlights the study of Black Pentecostal origins, especially the arguments of James S. Tinney[38] and Leonard K. Lovett,[39] similar to those of Gerloff and MacRobert. Walter Hollenweger, as a leading expert on worldwide Pentecostalism, noted that MacRobert's scholarship "goes a long way to explain the root cause for the division between black and White churches."[40]

In terms of the Black roots, or origins, of Pentecostalism, Sanders' ideological premise suggests convincingly that the Black Church, as well as Pentecostalism in particular, incorporates elements which are rooted in both slave religion ethos and experience. Turner sees this in the Black Baptist, Methodist, Holiness-Pentecostal traditions, in that they "flow in a common course." "They each make a vigorous effort," Turner then adds, "to preserve a spirituality that is not intellectualized to an extent that would diminish direct and immediate witness of the Spirit."[41]

The Black elements, therefore, are part and parcel of a myriad of racial realities, and, thus, the insight, forged during 400 years of slavery and oppression, components which reunited the faith of Pentecost and championed an unparalleled interracial fervor. Of course, even in pre-Pentecostal worship, as Baer and Singer have observed, such as in the Great Western Revival of Methodism in the early 1800s, the interracial joining together in the Holiness services, Blacks "eagerly participated in the tumultuous exercises which became characteristic of frontier revivalism."[42]

36. Sanders, *Saints in Exile*, 106–17.

37. Ibid., 118–20.

38. See Tinney, "Theoretical and Historical Comparison of Black Political and Religious Movements," "Exclusivist Tendencies in Pentecostal Self-Definition," "The Blackness of Pentecostalism," and "Black Origins of the Pentecostal Movement." In 1977 he established *Spirit: A Journal of Issues Incident to Black Pentecostalism.*

39. See Lovett, "Black Holiness-Pentecostalism" and "Black Origins of the Pentecostal Movement."

40. Hollenweger, "Towards an Intercultural History of Christianity," 526.

41. See Turner, "Black Evangelicalism," 40–56, 41.

42. Baer and Singer, *African American Religion in the Twentieth Century*, 5.

Tinney, Lovett and MacRobert, when observing these elements in the Pentecostal setting, consider them to be characteristically Black. In addition, Mason's biographer, Ithiel Clemmons, suggests that White Pentecostals have, to one degree or another, failed to appreciate, or even recognize, these essential contributions.[43] Sanders suggests that Tinney essentially "argued that Pentecostalism is *inherently* black." The inherently spiritual, "every kindred" Pentecostal component must never, though, be rendered merely cultural or ethnic.[44] More to the point is Lovett's emphasis: "It may be categorically stated that black Pentecostalism emerged out of the context of the brokenness of black existence." "One cannot meaningfully discuss the origins of contemporary Pentecostalism," he adds, "unless the role of blacks is clearly defined and acknowledged."[45]

The Black roots and influences, which Tinney calls Africanisms, with respect to worship practices, for example, were inculcated into the music and dance which characterized not only early Pentecostalism, but aspects of frontier religion as well. "The jerking, rolling and shouting associated with the American Revivals," MacRobert points out, "was, in part at least, due to the influence of the Black camp meetings of the 18th and 19th centuries."[46] Interestingly, Goss recalled that demonstrative practices common at Azusa, such as "dancing," simply "had had no place" in Parham's group.[47] Obvious difficulty accompanies an attempt to assign specifically racial connotations to psychological or deeply emotive worship responses. Nevertheless, the emotional parallel between deliverance from slave repression and that of spiritual deliverance, can hardly be missed in a Pentecostalism resiliently adaptive to the human condition.

Additionally, writers such as MacRobert see in Pentecostalism's undeniable Black influences and antecedent slave experience, as in Hollenweger's words, "not only the reason for their survival in a hostile environment," but also the very things "responsible for the success of early Pentecostalism."[48] The Black component is thus seen as an essential element, not only in meaningful Pentecostal historiography, but experience. Therefore, the fundamental premise which builds on MacRobert's

43. Clemmons, *Mason*, 57, 36–37.

44. Sanders, *Saints in Exile*, 120.

45. Lovett, "Black Origins of the Pentecostal Movement," 138.

46. Cited from Herskovits, *The Myth of the Negro Past*, 63; see MacRobert, "Spirit and the Wall," 46; Clemmons, *Mason*, 57; Kay and Cary, *Slavery in North Carolina (1748–1775)*, 180–83; see Gerloff, "Blackness and Oneness (Apostolic) Theology," 83.

47. Goss, *Winds of God*, 192; cf., also, Grant Wacker, *Heaven Below*, 3.

48. Hollenweger, "Priorities in Pentecostal Research," 9.

conclusion is that the very "reason for its growth lies in its black roots."[49] The penultimate Pentecostal element is from this perspective considered to be the Black component.

J. Nico Horn concludes, therefore, that "MacRobert makes an understanding of the African origins and the conditions of slavery prerequisites for the understanding of black Pentecostalism."[50] Hollenweger, in accord with MacRobert's work, offers the following summation regarding the significance of Pentecostalism's Black origins:

> The black churches developed an oral liturgy, a narrative theology, a maximum participation at the levels of reflection and decision-making. They used dreams and visions as a form of iconography in their communities and expressed their understanding of the body/mind relationship in praying for the sick. All this was, and still is, considered to be inferior to White Christianity. Yet it is not inferior. And it could become vital for White churches to recover some of the oral culture of our common past.[51]

This pragmatic approach is similar to Gerloff's attempt to outline the significance of the cross-cultural "Blackness," or Black spirituality, of Oneness Pentecostalism. Gerloff conceptualizes the Black Oneness movement as being "owned by the dispossessed and poor" and "filtered through the spectrum of the experience of the Black diaspora, i.e., through the history of pain and suffering."[52] For Gerloff the Oneness plight is to be conceived of as a sort of African "collective unconscious," in which the struggle for Trinitarian re-interpretation is "part and parcel of the much greater conscious and unconscious struggle of the oppressed and dispossessed against the 'ruling classes' and their White/Western impositions."[53]

She also makes a clear separation between the Black Oneness reality of Pentecost and that of "its all-White" counterpart, both theologically and experientially. Similar to Hollenweger's five roots of Pentecostal origins, Gerloff sees three aspect of the superiority of Pentecostalism's "Blackness," first, in its oral or narrative worship which, secondly, emphasizes the brokenness of human existence, and, thirdly, in its emotional empowerment

49. Hollenweger, "Intercultural History," 529; italics added.

50. Horn, "The Experience of the Spirit in Apartheid," 122.

51. Hollenweger, "Intercultural History," 529, 531; cf., Clemmons, *Mason*, 41.

52. Gerloff, "Blackness and Oneness," 72.

53. Ibid., 76–77.

and healing, not by means of the ocular, but rather a non-abstract religious reality.[54]

Neither the issues regarding the movement's Black origins, nor the emerging issues within Pentecostalism regarding race, which eventually split Oneness Pentecostalism in the 1920s, are known to have been addressed directly by Haywood, except for brief comments in a handful of articles. Haywood's stance, though, is probably best understood within the context of his primary, overriding commitment to two parallel visions, the interracial and the theological, which, even in the face of White abandonment, dominated his actions, even more so than the culture, mediating his restraint in critique and censorship.

Tinney, on the other hand, offers a balanced comprehension of any such perceived motives, in the recognition of the interracial predominance in Haywood:

> The survival of Black culturalisms over White ones can be largely attributed to those things he [Haywood] countenanced; and the curious mixture of these with White culturalisms was also his doing, intentionally and unintentionally. If some of the things he borrowed from Whites were later rejected by other of his Black brothers and sisters, this can only be viewed as a witness to the resilience of Black religious culture, not as a denigration of his influence.[55]

In Tyson's analysis of the 1924 PAW racial schism, while not speculating as to Haywood's approach and motives in dealing with the devastating events, he has stated: "There was a concerted effort by the P.A.W. to rise above the racist attitudes of the times."[56] By comparison, if Haywood's methodology can be characterized as patiently silent, R. C. Lawson, Haywood's protégé, followed an opposite course, not only speaking out, but refusing participation in events that, in the end, would leave them so vulnerable.

54. Ibid., 82–83; see Hollenweger, "The Black Roots of Pentecostalism," 32–44.

55. Tinney, "Significance of Race," 62.

56. Tyson, *Early Pentecostal Revival*, 272.

## 2.4. Profile of the Black Experience—Haywood Slave Origins

Even a summary account of the historical Haywood participation in the realities of the twentieth century Black experience of slavery provides profound depictions of the themes of emancipation and freedom which were later key aspects of Pentecostal spirituality. Haywood family oral tradition, preserved by biographers Tyson and Peagler,[57] as well as in recorded interviews collected by biographer Gary Garrett, confirms the scant details of these slave origins. The parents of G. T. Haywood, Ben and Ann Haywood, and their parents before them, were born into slavery in Raleigh, North Carolina.

Unfortunately, the available slave records are notoriously illusive, leaving the task of finding more precise family slave information a daunting task.[58] As detailed in *A Genealogist's Guide to Discovering Your African-American Ancestors*, a viable option for locating slave family members also exists in the careful comparison of the pertinent *U.S. Slave Schedules* with the oral accounts regarding Raleigh.[59] Also, federal census records, unfortunately, from 1790 to 1860 listed the total number of slaves by slave owner, and the age, sex, and color of each slave, but not their names.[60]

Hubert Benbury Haywood, Sr.'s superb genealogical study, *Sketches of the Haywood Family in North Carolina*, and the corresponding censuses and slave schedules, indicate that there are only four Haywood generations in North Carolina up to the birth of G. T. Haywood's father. The first, John Haywood (1685–1758), migrated to Halifax County, North Carolina, as a surveyor in 1730 from Christ Church Parish, Saint Michaels Island, Barbados. But John's ancestry traces back to 1337 in England with the spelling "Heywood."

Members of the William Haywood family were the immediate descendants of the family of John and Mary (Lovett) Haywood.[61] John

57. Tyson, *Before I Sleep*, 2; Peagler, *Haywood*, 6.

58. See "Finding Slave Records," http://statelibrary.dcr.state.nc.us/iss/g/slaveprep3.htm; *Guide to Research Materials in the North Carolina State Archives: County Records*; and Cain, McGrew, and Morris, *Guide to Private Manuscript Collections in the North Carolina State Archives*.

59. Smith and Croom, *Genealogist's Guide*, especially 129–38.

60. "Slave Schedules" were produced by the U.S. Census as separate lists from the census.

61. Haywood, *Sketch of the Haywood Family in North Carolina*, 2, 3b, 16a; Armstrong, *Notable Southern Families*, 2:151–60; Inscoe, *Mountain Masters, Slavery, and the Sectional Crisis in Western North Carolina*, 61–65.

Haywood (1755–1827), son of William I and Charity, was the most renowned North Carolina Haywood, becoming the state Treasurer in 1787.[62] He moved to Raleigh in 1792, where he built his estate bounded by New Bern Avenue and Blount, Edenton, and Person Streets. The estate, built in 1800–1801, is now a museum, Haywood Hall.[63] John Haywood's move to Raleigh resulted in the relocation of all of his brothers as well, and William Henry Haywood II (1770–1857), Sherwood Haywood (1762–1820), and Stephen Haywood (1772–1850), moved at the same time and built homes on adjacent city squares. The White Haywood families in Raleigh were Episcopalian and charter members in the formation of Christ Church.[64]

Both of Haywood's parents were born in Raleigh, North Carolina—Ben Haywood into a slave family in 1855 and Ann Uzzle in 1859.[65] Ben Haywood's slave owner was one of the five grandsons of William Haywood I: Dr. Fabius Julius Haywood, Dr. Edmund Burke Haywood, Dr. Richard Bennehan Haywood, Gen. Robert W. Haywood, or William Haywood III (via his widow, Jane F. Haywood).[66]

Such an accounting, though, doesn't represent mere fact, but rather indelible realities which etch themselves into the ongoing psyche of experience and meaning—an African slave reality. Eaton has concluded that "the Southern colonies received their slaves largely from the West Indies instead of directly from Africa," perhaps as many as ninety-five percent of their slaves.[67] Almost all of these were exported from West Africa, nearly half from the west central areas of the Congo and Angola, and half from

62. Boyd, *Federal Period*, 113.

63. See http://ced.ncsu.edu/2/adventure/haywood /history.html.

64. Haywood, *Sketch*, 21b, 23, 27–28; see also, Pyatt, *African-Americans in North Carolina*, 131–34.

65. Slave names are not listed in the schedules. Nevertheless, oral family history confirms Raleigh as the city of Ben and Anne's birth and slave ownership. For confirmation of Ben's birth date, "March" 1855, see *1900 U.S. Census*, Wayne Township, Marion County, Indiana, A12, (but lists "1860" in error); "N. Carolina" and the age "25" are confirmed (b. 1855), see *1880 U.S. Census*, Monroe Township, Putnam County, Indiana, 5.

66. See *1860 Slave Schedules*, Raleigh, NC, for (Ben Haywood, b. 1855), five year old male, lists only five slave owners–all the grandsons of William Haywood I; see "Appendix A: The Slave Owner Family of Ben Haywood," in French, "Early Oneness Pentecostalism," 322ff.; *1860 Slave Inhabitants*, Raleigh, NC, 3, 5, 14, 17, 18. The number of slaves owned by these five families include Fabius J. Haywood, in two locales, (22 and 25), Edward B. Haywood (18), Robert W. Haywood (48), Richard B. Haywood (31), and Jane F. Haywood (widow of William I) (32).

67. Eaton, *A History of the Old South*, 33.

the areas of Togo, Benin, and Nigeria.[68] Although such trade was banned by Britain in 1833, largely due to William Wilberforce's heroic campaign to end slavery, slave ships smuggled slaves into the Southern colonies at least until the year 1859.[69]

Undeniably, in light of the complexities and severity of these many centuries of forced servitude, the overwhelming challenge is to comprehend the reality of slavery's human toll as it is intertwined with, as well as central to, their societal and psychological making. The crucial task is to recognize the imprint of slavery upon the Black experience. Bassett's insensible suggestion, for example, that "to have come to America as a slave was not without an advantage to the negro," represents a consummate failure to grasp the shattering experience and meaning of slavery.[70]

Perhaps some of the best windows to such a comprehension, as James Rucker demonstrates regarding the "taproots" of African-American folk culture, are the old slave songs or spirituals produced within the very crucible of slavery: "The story of the roots of *African-American Folk Culture* would, of course, start with slavery and the 'middle passage,' which is what the slaves called the sea voyage from West Africa to the shores of the American Continent and its accompanying islands."[71]

Unmistakably, the echo of a similar ethos of hope and of longing is later spiritualized by slave descendents, such as G. T. Haywood, in their songs of the soul. In what may be one of his earliest songs, for example, Haywood, who began composing in 1914, writes with this voice of crying, interspersed with the refrain, "some day, some happy day!"[72]

This variety of Haywood song is reminiscent of the African survival spiritual, such as "Lord God Almighty, I'm Free At Last." Howard Thurman, a recognized interpreter of Black religion and culture, sees in such familiar slave spirituals the resonance of the spiritual desolation of Africans in survival, a desolation of anguish reaching for hope. The response of progenitors in Thurman's contemplative verse is a poetic, rather than didactic, address:

68. Kay and Cary, *Slavery in North Carolina*, 144–45; also, http://en.wikipedia.org/wiki/Transatlantic_slave_trade. Less than a fifth came from Senegal, Gambia, Sierra Leone, Liberia, Mozambique, and Madagascar.

69. See, for example, Metaxas, *Amazing Grace*.

70. Bassett, *Slavery and Servitude in the Colony of North Carolina*, 11.

71. Rucker, "Heroes and Hard Times," 1.

72. Haywood, "Some Day," 6. The notation "Not Copyrighted. Let no one do so" suggests the likelihood that this hymn was one of Haywood's earliest.

> O my Fathers, what was it like to be stripped of all supports of life save the beating of the heart and the ebb and flow of fetid air in the lungs? In a strange moment, when you suddenly caught your breath, did some intimation from the future give to your spirits a hint of promise? In the darkness did you hear the silent feet of your children beating a melody of freedom to words which you would never know, in a land in which your bones would be warmed again in the depths of the cold earth in which you will sleep unknown, unrealized and alone?[73]

### 2.4.1 The Southern Black Experience—Raleigh, North Carolina

The first North Carolina slaves, like the vast majority of other states, were brought in from Barbados in 1627, with the first imported slaves arriving in 1636. North Carolina's very first Haywood likewise came from Barbados, John Haywood who was an ancestor to the slave owners of G. T. Haywood's father Ben. This John Haywood emigrated from Barbados to Raleigh in 1730.[74]

In 1899 John Bassett estimated in his Johns Hopkins University research that the number of Blacks in North Carolina increased from about 36,000 in 1776 to 331,059 slaves and 30,463 free Blacks by 1860. Such statistics indicate, then, that the number of pre-emancipation slaves in North Carolina was rather substantial, thirty three percent of the state's total population.[75]

Religious fervor, though, in the south was making its impact, as well, amidst the Methodism of John Wesley, who once called the slave trade the "sum of all villainies." By 1839 the Black to White ratio of North Carolina Methodists had grown to thirty five percent, a "rapid proportional gain," 26,404 Whites, 9,302 Blacks. The 1787 Methodist Black to White ratio was 10%. And, by 1853, Raleigh's main Methodist Episcopal Church (Edenton Street) had divided into separate Black and White charges.[76]

73. Thurman, "On Viewing the Coast of Africa," cited in Sanders, *Saints in Exile,* 117.

74. Haywood, *Sketch of the Haywood Family*, 2.

75. Bassett, *Slavery in the State of North Carolina*, 77.

76. Ibid., 53, 56; http://wesley.nnu.edu/wesleyctr/books/0801–0900/HDM0828.PDF; www.docsouth.unc.edu/nc/bassett99/bassett99.html.

By the time of the birth of Haywood's parents in the 1850s, Raleigh was an area which Clement Eaton referred to in his book, *The Old South,* as the "Black Belt" of North Carolina. This was a reference to the concentration of the majority of slaves in North Carolina by the year 1860 into the counties mostly around Raleigh and north into Virginia. Slavery existed throughout North Carolina, but "The Black Belt" highlighted the largest concentrations, that is, only areas in which the slave population was 50 percent and over.[77]

The slavery question remained most acute throughout the 1840s and 1850s, with the 1850 Fugitive Slave Bill making it more dangerous for runaways to remain in the urban North. The context, therefore, of the Black experience in the United States cried out, "Emancipation." James Buchanan was elected president in 1856, one year after Ben Haywood's birth. Buchanan's bid for the presidency has been characterized as one of the bitterest campaigns in American history. This was due to the slavery issue. The South even called Buchanan's party the "Black Republicans" due to their anti-slavery platform.

The issues of slavery and emancipation were the most volatile at the time throughout the south. The die was cast shortly after Buchanan was sworn in, due especially to northern resentment of the Southern victory in the Dread Scott Supreme Court decision. The Scott case was viewed as lending support to the ideology of a "non-rights" slave status for any slave returning to his or her original slave state, and as basically rejecting federal citizenship of slaves.[78]

Raleigh, too, was the birthplace of Andrew Johnson (1808), 17th U.S. president, following Lincoln, who was sworn in as the 16th President March 4, 1861. One month prior, February 4, 1861, Jefferson Davis was elected President of the Confederacy.[79] By 1860 the population of Raleigh, the North Carolina capital, barely exceeded 5,000.

### 2.4.2 Emancipation—Reality and Symbol

Ben Haywood was only six years of age when Johnson took office. He knew the meaning of slavery in this Raleigh context, but before reaching his teen years he had also experienced the fulfilled hope of emancipation. Unfortunately, much of the nation was ill-prepared for the societal and

77. Eaton, *Old South*, 234.

78. Ibid., 480–82; Murley, "Unionists to Secessionists."

79. Ashe, *History of North Carolina*, 505, 536, 554, 561; Eaton, *Old South*, 478.

economic difficulties which ensued. Having grown up in servitude, and as a young adult at the dawn of the post-war reconstruction era, he lived at the end of the epoch of transatlantic trade in human cargo.

Ben, listed variously in sources as "Bennett," and sometimes "Benjamin," lived in Raleigh until he moved his family to Indiana in 1879.[80] He was only nine at the time of Sherman's North Carolina campaign, and the Raleigh occupation was still ongoing at the time that President Lincoln was assassinated.[81] The North Carolina surrender in April of 1865 at "Bennett Place" farm in Durham was the largest surrender of confederate troops in the Civil War. Haywood's mother, variously listed as "Ann," "PenAnn" or "Penann," and commonly known in the Haywood biographies as "Penny Ann," was six when the historic, and life-changing, southern surrender took place in Durham, just a short distance from Raleigh.[82]

Their names, "Ben," "Penny," and "Ann," are listed among the most common African names in Kay and Cary's chapter on "Slave Names and Languages" in the book *Slavery in North Carolina*. Kay and Cary note that it is likely that slaves normally "continued to use their correct African names among themselves." The many common names, such as Ben and Ann, were actually "Anglo-American" versions "derived from like-sounding African names." Such "naming practices" are believed to have occurred "usually from debarkation onward."

> Africa profoundly affected the names of slaves and the languages they used to communicate with one another and with Whites . . . Slaveowners as a rule acquiesced to demands by slaves that they be allowed to control their own names and those of their children . . . It is not difficult to envision how Africans named Adeben, Bem, Bena, Benda, Beni, Benin, Beng, or Kwabena could all become Ben or Benn . . . Panyin, Pendu, Pene, or Pinde would be called Penny.[83]

80. "Ben," *1880 U.S. Census*, 5; "Bennett," *1900 U.S. Census*, 12; *1910 U.S. Census*, 7; Tyson, *Before I Sleep*, 2; Garrett, *Haywood*, 29; "Benjamin," *Indianapolis Star*, 1910 Fall Creek Renovation Notification; Golder, *Life and Works*, 1.

81. Haywood, *Sketch*, 73.

82. The earliest census, "Ann," *1880 U.S. Census*, Indianapolis, IN, 5, and *Indianapolis Star*, Fall Creek Renovation Notification, May 27, 1910; cf. *1900 U.S. Census*, 12, *1910 U.S. Census*, 7, which also indicates that both Ben and Ann's parents were from North Carolina; "Penny Ann," see Garrett, *Haywood*, 29, and Golder, *Life and Works*, 1; Tyson, *Before I Sleep*, 2, "Penn Ann"; Haywood's death certificate lists his mother as "Pennan Uzzle," see *Certificate of Death*. Although "Uzzle" slave owners do not appear in the *1860 Raleigh Slave Schedules*, "Uzzle" families were listed as Raleigh residents.

83. "Ben" may have meant "a child born on Tuesday," 146; see, for example, Kay and Cary, *Slavery in NC*, 137–38, 141–42.

In the reconstruction years Raleigh held hopes for many Blacks, establishing, for example, the country's first African-American college, Shaw University, in 1865. The Episcopal Church of which the White Haywood families were prominent also established St. Augustine's College for freedmen in 1867. On the other hand, the reconstruction south was a most challenging place for a young, aspiring Black couple after the 1865 Union victory.

By 1869, for example, after the Ku Klux Klan had been introduced in North Carolina for only a period of three years, the extreme racist KKK had reportedly reached a membership of 70,000. The difficult circumstances which contributed to such a state of affairs in the former confederate states encouraged thousands of freedmen across the South to migrate to the northern cities in search of a better life and in hopes of greater racial equality.[84]

Ben Haywood and Ann Uzzle married in late 1876, when Ann had just turned seventeen. Tyson's oral sources from his early interviews for the first Haywood biography definitively placed them in Raleigh and there is no indication that they ever lived outside Raleigh. Raleigh is the city to which they "bade farewell forever" when they migrated to Indiana in the late 1870s. Simon, their first son, was born in Raleigh in the first half of 1877.[85] Their second child, Carolina, was born in early 1879, after which the young couple, with two year old son and infant daughter, left Raleigh behind them forever.

## 2.5 Haywood in the Late 19th Century U.S. Midwestern Context

Although Haywood was reared as a child and lived his entire youth and adult life in Indianapolis, he was born in Greencastle, Indiana, approximately forty miles east of Indianapolis, a farm region into which Ben and Ann Haywood migrated west from Raleigh, North Carolina. Greencastle is at the very center of Putnam County, one county east of Vermillion County, Indiana. The *1880 U.S. Census* lists Ben and his small family along

84. Ashe, *History of North Carolina*, 1060–61; also, the Dr. Manassa T. Pope story, "The Pope House Museum Foundation, Family History," http://www.popehousemuseum.org/family3.html.

85. Tyson, *Before I Sleep*, 5; In the *1900 U.S. Census*, 12, they had been married twenty three years; the marriage license does not appear in the Wake County records; The June *1880 U.S. Census*, 5, lists their son "Simon" as three years old.

with one boarder working "on a farm," amidst mostly White neighbors, in rural Monroe Township of Putnam County. Monroe is a farming community township directly north of Greencastle, Indiana, and Ben and Ann Haywood lived there from 1879 to 1883. Within a year of settling in this area, Garfield Thomas Haywood was born on July 15, 1880 in Greencastle. In February 1882, a fourth child was born, a daughter Jesse.[86]

The given and surname "Garfield" during this period was not uncommon. The likely inspiration for Haywood's name, though, was President James A. Garfield (1831–1881), originally an Ohio U.S. Congressman, who, as a Lincoln Republican, won his 1879–1880 campaign for the presidency. In June of 1880 the popular candidate, James Garfield, spoke at the Republican National Convention. He was a graduate of an abolitionist college, a Civil War Brigadier, and then a Major General. The greatest impact of Garfield on the common voter may have been a reputation of being perhaps the poorest candidate to ever campaign for the highest office of the land.

President James Garfield possessed several characteristics which ingratiated him to the disinherited, the poor and the downtrodden, not the least of which was his emphatic position regarding the advancement of African Americans. Even in his inaugural address Garfield made the needs of Blacks a central issue:

> There is no middle ground for the negro race between slavery and equal citizenship . . . Freedom can never yield its fullness of blessings so long as the law or its administration places the smallest obstacle in the pathway of any virtuous citizen . . . The elevation of the Negro race from slavery to the full rights of citizenship is by far the most important political change we have known since the adoption of the constitution in 1787.[87]

In the Black struggle for freedom, Garfield also remarked that African Americans had "followed the light as God gave them to see the light."

86. *1900 U.S. Census*, 12; *1880 U.S. Census*, 5, Alfred Nubens, boarder; 1875 Map, Putnam County, Indiana, Higgins Belden & Co., http://home.att.net/~Local_History/Putnam-Co-IN.htm; even the name "Garfield Thomas Haywood" is found in Greencastle, a Haywood family in 1856.

87. http://www.loc.gov/exhibits/treasures/inaugural-exhibit.html#garfield, 7–9, with the handwritten inaugural speech of President James A. Garfield; Rutkow, *James A. Garfield*, 1–4, 115–22; http://biographypresgarfield.homestead.com/biography.html.

Unfortunately, sworn in March 4, 1881, he served only two hundred days before he died from an assassin's bullet on September 19, 1881.[88]

### 2.5.1 Indianapolis and the Black Experience

Leaving the farm in Greencastle, Indiana in 1883, Ben and Penny Ann Haywood moved their family of six to the Haughville area of west Indianapolis in order to improve themselves. Ben Haywood began work at an east side foundry, to and from which he had to walk. With the arrival of five more Haywood children in Indianapolis between 1887 and 1902, all nine were raised in Haughville. They certainly knew the nuanced changes in the plight of African Americans in the post-reconstruction era in the U.S. Midwest.[89]

Uncertainty regarding exact starting dates for Haywood's schooling is probably best solved by assuming the age sixteen, as Tyson suggests, as the accurate age at which he was forced to drop out in order to work to help support the family, a scenario not uncommon in the 1890s.[90] Therefore, at the age of six, Haywood would have started school in 1886 at the Elementary School #52, which he attended through the 1893–94 term.

In 1894 he entered the integrated Indianapolis Shortridge High School for a period of two years. Shortridge, named after Indiana educator Abram C. Shortridge, championed education for all, and admitted its first Black student in 1872.

> The school act of 1877 clarified the matter of high school attendance by providing that when a child attending a Negro school showed that he was prepared to be placed in a higher grade than that afforded by the school, he was to be admitted to a White school. There was no high school for Negroes, and a sizable number of black students attended Indianapolis, later Shortridge, High School with almost no problems until the 1920s.[91]

By 1878 the students were almost exclusively White children of laborers. But, by 1894, Shortridge, then located at Michigan and Pennsylvania Streets, provided the young Garfield with an excellent breadth in

88. http://www.loc.gov/exhibits/treasures/inaugural-exhibit.html#garfield, 7–9. Garfield lived eighty days after he was shot by Charles Guiteau on July 2, 1881.

89. Peagler, *Haywood*, 7; Tyson, *Before I Sleep*, 3.

90. Tyson, *Before I Sleep*, 3–4.

91. Gaus, *Shortridge High School 1864–1981 in Retrospect*, 15.

secondary education. During his time at Shortridge High School, due to overcrowding, the interracial Shortridge was also using the Virginia Street annex, referred to as "High School #2."[92] Haywood, though, would not see racist educational segregation in Indianapolis for thirty years, or until 1927, the exact historical time frame in which he also saw the interracial hopes of the Indianapolis-based PAW dashed within the context of the organization's ministerial racial upheaval.

As the 1800s drew to a close, Simon and Carrie had left home and transferred their family responsibilities to the oldest remaining son, Garfield. In 1896 it was necessary, therefore, for Haywood to leave school in order to assist with the financial support of a family with six younger siblings.[93] Nevertheless, by the time Haywood left Shortridge, at the age of sixteen, he had demonstrated exceptional academic skills and a profound artistic ability, which later landed him a job, as a sketch artist, with more than one of Indianapolis' professional newspapers.

By the time the Topeka revival broke out in Kansas, January 1901, Haywood was a young twenty year old, working at various jobs about Indianapolis, but who had been seeking opportunity to get on at a newspaper that could use his talent at drawing. Also, he had met Ida Howard sometime in the late 1890s, a young lady four years his junior, who had moved to Indianapolis from Owensboro, Kentucky. Owensboro is thirty two miles from the Indiana southern border, near Evansville, Indiana.

During this time, prior to the events of the Azusa-inspired Indianapolis revival, the Haywood family was attending the Haughville St. Paul Baptist Church. According to the 1900 census report, the young 19 year old Haywood was working as a "day laborer" in Indianapolis and living with his family at 948 Bismarck Avenue, in the Wayne Township community of Haughville.

Garfield Thomas Haywood and the eighteen year old Ida Howard were married on February 11, 1902. It would be six years later almost to the day that they would both receive Pentecostal baptism at a downtown Indianapolis mission. The Haywood's only child, Fannie Ann, was born the year after their marriage, in 1903. Information regarding Haywood's parents during this period is sketchy, but after 1910, as Haywood's ministry

92. Shortridge High School Collection, 1870–1981, 1995, http://www.indianahistory.org/library/manuscripts/collection_guides/m0482.html; Gaus, *Shortridge*, 28.

93. *1900 U.S. Census*, Indianapolis, Indiana, 12.

was on the ascendency, Ben and Ann Haywood no longer appear in U.S. Census records together.[94]

## 2.5.2 Reflections of the Black Experience in Black Publishing

The rare opportunity to view the African American experience through the lens of the inner-workings of Black newspaper publishing was provided Haywood at a young age, broadening his perspective of the issues relative to the Midwest, African Americans, culture, religion, and a variety of vital concerns. The young Haywood became a newspaper illustrator, writer, and artist.

G. T. Haywood possessed an exceptional talent, as well as a strong determination, to be a successful professional illustrator, gaining him a position with the prominent Black newspaper, *The Freeman,* in Indianapolis. He also did some work for the *Recorder,* which became a weekly in 1896.[95] *The Recorder* dealt with local Black issues, whereas *The Freeman* was "the first and only illustrated journal of the African-American race," nationwide in scope, with columnists from across the country. *The Recorder,* established by George P. Stewart and William H. Porter, and inherited by Fannie Caldwell Stewart in 1924, used few sketches, cartoons, or illustrations before 1906.[96]

The experience at *The Freeman,* undoubtedly, provided Haywood with exceptional opportunity for the broadening of his horizons early on. *The Freeman* was owned by an ex-slave from Tennessee George L. Knox, who purchased the paper from the founder, Edward E. Cooper, in 1892. Knox had made his earlier fortune as an owner of a large barbershop in Indianapolis, becoming "the city's most conspicuously successful black businessman" by 1884.[97] When Haywood joined the *Freeman* in 1902,

94. Tyson, *Before I Sleep*, 4–5; *1900 U.S. Census*, Indianapolis, 12; *Index to Marriage Record 1901–1905*, Indiana, 555.

95. *The Freeman,* which became a weekly by 1888, circulated from 1884 to 1927, whereas the *Recorder* continues to the present; cf. also Tyson, *Before I Sleep*, 10; Important Indiana Black newspapers of the period included *The Argus* (1886–1887), *The Courier* (1893–late 1890s), *The Leader* (1879–1890), *The Ledger* (1913–1925), and *The (Colored) World* (1883–1932). See Miller, *Indiana Newspaper Bibliography*.

96. Bigham, "Black Press in Indiana," 55; see also Madison, *Indiana Way*, 169–73, 241–44, 318–20; http://www.indianahistory.org/library/manuscripts/collection_guides/P0303.html.

97. Knox, *Slaves and Freemen*, 4, 18–20.

the paper was Republican, and circulation, from 1903–1913, went from 16,000–20,000.[98]

Before his 1884 move to Indianapolis, Knox was working for the cause of Black justice in Greenfield, Indiana, twenty five miles due east of Indianapolis, by assisting to transport Blacks north. Knox writes that the *Hancock Democrat* "castigated local Republicans for encouraging the 'pauperized exodusters' from the South to settle in Indiana, claiming that it was merely a political scheme to strengthen the Republican party."[99]

Even the Haywood family itself could very likely have been assisted by Knox in their trek to Indiana. The Knox autobiography, in fact, describes a train with twenty five Black immigrants coming to Greenfield, Indiana, which the *Hancock Democrat* reported as the arrival, on January 8, 1880, of "another lot of North Carolina Negroes."[100] It is also possible that Knox and Haywood attended the same Methodist Episcopal Church, at least for a while, known as the Simpson Chapel.[101]

Knox's life also intersected Haywood's at another interesting juncture. A White, female healing evangelist, Marie B. Woodworth-Etter, began revivals in Greenfield in the early 1880s. Her camp meeting near Los Angeles in 1913, which Haywood attended, played a pivotal role in the emergence of Oneness Pentecostalism, though Woodworth-Etter did not embrace it herself. Knox reported that, by 1884, he was "in charge" of the "racially integrated" meetings (1884–1886) which had reached six thousand in attendance, and in which "Whites and colored" were "all kneeling at the same bench."[102]

Warner similarly notes that her meetings had "racial equality from start to finish," and that "black participation began as early as her 1885 Hartford City, Indiana meeting, where she used a black barber, Ananias Frazier, as her soloist." Woodworth-Etter, according to Warner, was "one of the most popular evangelists and miracle workers of the late nineteenth century." Knox described her camp meeting in Lawrence, Indiana, in 1886, recalling that "On Wednesday she had several in a trance, men fell, White

98. Ibid., 30–32.

99. Ibid., 213 n. 72, 110.

100. Ibid., 214 n. 74. By the June *1880 U.S. Census* the Haywoods were already living in Greencastle, Indiana, although Garfield was not born until July 15, 1880 and, therefore, not included in the census.

101. Knox, *Slave and Freeman*, 20, and Melton, "Garfield Thomas Haywood," 106.

102. Knox, *Slave and Freeman*, 123, 125, 126 n. 114.

and black, mainly White, as though they had been shocked." These worshipers, he noted, were rendered "unconscious" for three or four hours.[103]

Attestation to the extraordinary talents of G. T. Haywood extended, of course, beyond the phenomenal work that he produced for *The Freeman* and *Recorder*. His level of artistic sophistication was exceptional, reflected in his association with some of the era's finest talent and in their recognition of his abilities, including artist W. E. Scott and poet A. B. Thompson, both African Americans. Haywood maintained, for example, a "very close" friendship with the Indianapolis-born, worldwide renowned professional African American artist, William Edouard Scott (1884–1964). Scott, who studied in Paris beginning in 1904, was known for his refusal to paint Blacks as slaves in order to help reverse old stereotypical perceptions. In fact, many of Scott's paintings had nothing to do with race.[104]

The aspiring Indianapolis African American poet Aaron Belford Thompson (1883–1929) published a third book of poetry in 1907 known as *Harvest of Thoughts* and the illustrator for the project was none other than Garfield Thomas Haywood. The well-known Indiana poet James Whitcomb Riley (1849–1916), who was designated the "Hoosier poet," wrote the introduction to Thompson's new work in which Haywood had sketched seven illustrations to accompany his poetic themes. As such they therefore highlighted Thompson's overall autumn themes which included love, race, frivolity, as well as slavery and religion.[105]

## 2.6 Haywood's Racial Voice as a Black Newspaper Illustrator

Haywood's *Freeman* sketch work extended over a longer period of time than previously assumed, from at least as early as December 1902 and extending well into the period after which he had begun his Indianapolis pastorate, at least into the year 1909. This employ continued, therefore, well over a year after Haywood's initial Pentecostal experience, yet he apparently began his pastoral ministry very shortly after his conversion at a downtown Indianapolis mission.[106]

103. Ibid., 127; Warner, "Maria B. Woodworth-Etter," 212, 205.

104. Tyson, *Before I Sleep*, 4; see Taylor, *A Shared Heritage*.

105. Thompson, *Harvest of Thoughts*, 21, 39, 50b, 58b, 72b, 84b, 104b.

106. See Tyson, *Before I Sleep*, 10; Peagler, *Haywood*, 9; Garrett, *Haywood*, 32, regarding Haywood's "factory" or "iron foundry" employment. Certainly, in 1909, long after he became pastor, Haywood's *Freeman* work continued, indicating that he held both positions.

Throughout his lifetime Haywood continued to do produce notable artistic sketches, charts, and paintings, for both family and church, which are now far more widely known than any of his earlier professional material. He drew the masthead which first appeared on Frank Ewart's earlier periodical *The Good Report* in November 1913.[107] But, obviously, his sketches for the Indianapolis newspapers are of special interest due to their representation of Haywood's earliest known mindset regarding the racial issues of the period.

During the years that he was the regular Saturday cartoonist for *The Freeman*, for example, his political/racial themes were actually quite common, even dominant, comprising well over half of the total Haywood sketches annually. The sketches accompanied articles, most of which were unsigned, but which may have been authored by Haywood. His work at *The Freeman* spanned the period of the Republican presidential victories of Roosevelt (1901–1909) and Taft (1909–1913). In 1903–1904, twenty two of thirty three sketches were racial cartoons, depicting the government, for example, as a "Dr. Jekyll" in its treatment of a 1903 Black postal worker in Tennessee.

During this early period, 1902–1903, voter "disfranchisement" was the most addressed issue, but other themes were advanced, such as unions and industry, citizenship, work prejudice, the lack of protection from mobs, and even "Uncle Sam's" putting foreign relations above negro relations. One of the most intriguing depictions is that of "prejudice" as a three-headed monster, and one of the earliest Haywood cartoons shows a Black man being beaten with a whip. Also, Benjamin T. Tillman, the South Carolina Governor (1890–1894) who became a U.S. Senator (1895–1918), is often depicted or noted, whose blatant racist policies were used to fight against the interracial Republican coalition.[108]

Early in 1904, Haywood was very effectively satirizing the prejudice, for example, that disallowed Blacks in certain train sleeper cars. Yet another sketch shows a man, labeled "negro," about to fall, being attacked by large mosquitoes labeled "race hatred," "union," "poverty," "injustice,"

107. Ewart, "Editorial," 1, 2: "The plate of the beautiful and expressive heading of this paper is taken from a drawing sent to us by Elder G. T. Haywood of Indianapolis, Indiana. It is a real work of art, and in keeping with the name and pretentions of our paper, it incriminates no one . . . We rejoice to believe also that God inspired our Beloved Brother Haywood to draw this new heading and present it to us."

108. See the three-headed monster sketch, Haywood, "A Formidable Foe"; Knox, *Slave and Freeman*, 30, and Haywood, "What Credit Is It For An Elephant To Crush An Infant."

and "violence." One arm is chained by "labor opposition" and the other by "prejudice," as southern states pierce his legs with sharp thorns and the blood drips to the ground.[109] Clearly, these political and racial depictions were anything but haphazard, but rather, extremely pointed, most effective, often quite moving, and a means of addressing some of the most important societal issues of the day facing Blacks.

By 1907 Haywood introduced an interesting identifying mascot, a tiny "coon," which he used as a humorous, yet, evidently, clever satirical reversal on racist attitudes, as an artistic means of clarifying issues in each of his later cartoons, to the end of, but not after, 1908.[110] By this period, it was becoming more evident that Haywood found less and less hope in the political process for displacing societal injustice. After 1907, and following his Pentecostal experience, religious-moral themes became more prominent, depicting, for example, Jesus and moral concepts from the Proverbs.[111]

One of the later sketches, in the summer of 1909, depicts a large hog, labeled "evil society," pulling a lamb to which it is yoked, labeled "the innocent," into the "degradation mire." Another moralistic portrayal in October 1909 shows a scene from a man's life, now in prison, being disobedient to his mother as a child, with the caption: "Bend the sapling, lest it grow up crooked and trouble you."[112] In 1907 and 1909, just over 40 percent of the sketches were racial, but for 1908 there was an increase to 70 percent of the illustrations depicting racial concerns. In fact, one of the most pointed illustrations showed a lynching, with the seriously satirical caption reading: "Protection in America by Uncle Sam."[113]

109. Haywood, "It Looks Like A Case of Dr. Jekyll & Mr. Hyde," "The Negro Looks Quite as Well as Any in That Bunch," and "Can He Make It?"

110. Compare the negative use of "coon" relative to race, *Historical Dictionary of American Slang*, 1:477, stating that "coon" was used contemptuously "of a black person," perhaps as early as 1829.

111. Haywood, "The First Easter Morn," "To the Graduate," "Fools and Their Money Soon Part," "What Have I Done?," and "Home Life."

112. Haywood, "The Inevitable Consequences," and "Bend the Sapling."

113. Haywood, "Liberia–Shall It Be Like This?" A 1907 sketch uses the biblical Goliath as the "political enemy" of the "the negro" (shown as David) holding a sling labeled "conservative action," see Haywood, "A Modern Goliath."

## 2.7 Conclusion

"No other figure looms as large," Tinney wrote of Haywood, "in all historical accounts of the movement."[114] Even in his early life and career, through the talent and insight displayed in journalism, this is evident, in his reflection upon the race issues within the nineteenth century American context. Like his later ministry, too, they reflect a unique racial balance as well. These were indications of a thoughtful perspective which would serve as driving metaphors for his religious and ministerial attitudes regarding society and race sufficient to motivate and inspire.

Though counter-cultural within their common societal norm, White, Hispanic, and Black Pentecostals would seek the basis of genuine interracial, harmonious fellowship, forcing them individually to search deep for the root and source of their shared Spirit experience. What they discovered was the "all flesh" divine reality, a potent epiphany that resists the negation of the elemental components which made it all possible. Leaders, such as Urshan, Ewart, Haywood, and Lawson, may have been multi-talented and capable, but they would find that what they were attempting racially would take far more than mere human qualities to succeed against the odds.

Digging deep into their experiential roots, though, they would find themselves best served by the context of emancipation and deliverance, creatively expressed in their common song. "And in these days of *darkness*, when faith has fled away, we hear the voice of Jesus to His faithful servants say, '*These signs* shall follow them that believe on my name'!"[115] Inclusive identification of the signs with Joel's prophetic Spirit poured out on *all flesh* as the working metaphor of racial equity, they found themselves inspired and willing to take the risk of its fulfillment in spite of the disintegration of that hope all about them.

114. Tinney, "Significance of Race," 61.

115. Haywood, "These Signs Shall Follow Them," 33, stanza 4; italics added.

# 3

# The Azusa Street Revival and Early Oneness Pentecostalism

The Azusa Street revival, for most Pentecostals, is viewed as "the formative and definitive event of early Pentecostalism." Robeck suggests that Azusa was the multicultural and interracial experiment of the Azusa Street revival which contributed most to the globalization of the movement, "the paramount center from which the Pentecostal movement spread prior to 1915."[1] Considering the impact it had on Haywood's conversion, he may have visited Azusa, having been in service with Ewart in Los Angeles and at Arroyo Seco. Interestingly, during Haywood's teen years Seymour lived and worked in Indianapolis from 1895 to 1899. While living in Indiana he left his Catholic upbringing to join Simpson Chapel, a Methodist church, which Haywood is also known to have attended, as did the owner of *The Recorder*, George Knox.[2]

1. Robins, "Azusa Street Mission," 98; Robeck, *Azusa Street Mission and Revival*, 16.

2. See Borlase, *Seymour*, 48, 44–47; Nelson, "For Such a Time," 48 n. 18, 33; Robeck, *Azusa Street Mission*, 28, "we do not know which congregation," suggests that he may have attended one of the other Methodist churches; Sanders, *Seymour*, 50, cites Nelson's contention that Simpson Chapel was the "only legitimate possibility." Several of Haywood's members are known to have converted to Pentecostalism from Bethel AME and Allen Chapel AME, Golder, *Haywood*, 4.

## 3.1 Interracial Impact of the Azusa Street Revival

By 1903 Seymour was living in Houston working with the African American led Holiness church of Lucy Farrow.[3] By 1905 Farrow had introduced Seymour to Parham's Apostolic Faith meetings at which African Americans had to sit or stand in the back. Seymour was not allowed to seek Spirit baptism at the altar with Whites.[4] After arriving in Los Angeles in February 1906, the famed revival erupted on April 9th when Edward and Mattie Lee, who later embraced the Oneness position, were the first to receive Spirit baptism, but at the Bonnie Brae location.[5] Frank Bartleman, another of the prominent Azusa Street revival participants to later joined the Oneness movement, wrote: "It seemed that everyone had to go to 'Azusa.' Missionaries were gathered there from Africa, India, and islands of the sea. Preachers and workers had crossed the continent, and come from distant islands, with an irresistible drawing to Los Angeles."[6]

Robeck says of participant Frank Bartleman that his "significance as a social and religious critic" regarding his important eyewitness account of the Azusa Street revival "cannot be overestimated."[7] The Azusa Street mission racial attitudes were summed up in his often quoted personal observation: "The 'color line' was washed away in the blood." "All classes began to flock to the meetings," according to Bartleman's account for "God was working mightily." And, he added, "There were far more White people than colored people coming."[8]

The interracial and international essence of the revival was a critical component, as well, which was linked to the "all points of the compass"

3. Martin, *Seymour*, 73–75, places Seymour first in Chicago before moving on to Cincinnati, and, then, after leaving Cincinnati in 1902, possibly living in Columbus, Ohio before Houston.

4. Regarding Parham's distinctly racist views, see Anderson, "Dubious Legacy," 51–64, Robeck, *Azusa Street Mission*, 43–50, Anderson, *Disinherited*, 60–61, and Nelson, "For Such A Time," 167.

5. Seymour arrived in February to assume duties at Julia Hutchins' Los Angeles Black holiness church, but by March he had been locked out due to his message regarding tongues, forcing him to meet in the home of members Richard and Ruth Asberry on Bonnie Brae, while staying with Edward and Mattie Lee on South Union Avenue, see Borlase, *Seymour*, 102–3.

6. Bartleman, *How Pentecost Came to Los Angeles*, 54

7. Robeck, *Witness to Pentecost*, xxiii.

8. Bartleman, *Los Angeles*, 49, 54, 58–59; cf., also, "Whites and Black Mix in a Religious Frenzy," *Los Angeles Daily Times*, September 3, 1906, 11.

missionary expansion, an unmistakable hallmark of Azusa Street, another feature which clearly distinguished Seymour's revival from that of Parham's. Jacobson has suggested that Azusa Street played the role of "Grand Central Station" for Pentecostalism.[9] Yet the most significant impact upon the Jesus' Name movement was, in fact, the *aftermath* of the eight year interracial Azusa experiment, especially its resulting failure and resulting division of Pentecostalism along racial lines.

Parham condemned Seymour for "unseemly" race mixing, finding "conditions even worse than I had anticipated." Yet Wacker calculates that, in a total of 17,000 published words, Seymour "mentioned race only once."[10] To this weight of racial failure would soon be added Durham's attempted takeover of Azusa and the White rejection of Mason's COGIC.[11]

Recounting events before this fallout Goss briefly mentions Azusa in *The Winds of God*, referring to Lucy Farrow at Parham's in Houston. She "preached and told about the great outpouring at Azusa Street." "Although a Negro," he writes, "she was received as a messenger of the Lord to us, even in the deep South of Texas." Goss, though, clearly takes Parham's side in the accounting of the later Seymour skirmish, even if he took exception to his racial references: "But, as is often the case, *they felt that they had received a greater power in Los Angeles* than had been known before, so Brother Parham's saving advice and council went unheeded and was rejected."[12] Referring to the historical perspective of Goss and Ewart, Goff has concluded that "Oneness Pentecostals have been much more sympathetic to Parham" than other earlier historical accounts and "recognized Parham's role long before other denominational treatments."[13]

Soon, though, Parham's reputation was irreversibly tarnished as the rumors of the unfolding moral issues, even as early as late 1906, began to worry the faithful. These allegations of moral misconduct, as Wacker points out, effectively destroyed his career.[14] Yet the racial unraveling al-

9. Jacobsen, *Thinking in the Spirit*, 10; Anderson, *Introduction*, 171, idem, "To All Points of the Compass," 164–72, and idem, *Spreading Fires*, 46–65, 109–11, 149–51; Robeck, *Azusa Street Mission*, 235–80; Clemmons, *Mason*, 31

10. October 1906; Parham, *Parham*, 163; Wacker, *Heaven Below*, 234.

11. 1911/1913, respectively; see Blumhofer, *Restoring the Faith*, 47; Cox, *Fire from Heaven*, 61.

12. Goss, *Winds of God*, 74, 98, italics added.

13. Goff, *Fields White Unto Harvest*, 232 n. 25.

14. Wacker, "Travail of a Broken Family," 31; Goss, *Winds of God*, 100–101, 145, and 105–6; Goff, "Problem of History," 190, citing the *San Antonio Light*, July 19, 1907, 1, the *San Antonio Daily Express*, July 20, 1907, 12, and the *Houston Chronicle* July 21,

ready set motion sparked an opposite, resisting reaction within the latent, emerging Oneness segment—north, south, east, west. No evidence suggests that even the most Parham-influenced southwest was ready to follow a call to abandon their restorationist racial instincts. "The rise of Oneness, or Apostolic, Pentecostalism" Howell writes, "must also be seen as a *reaction against racism* in the early movement."[15]

Seymour's efforts as an African-American to hold an interracial movement together, in MacRobert's words, "were left in tatters" by the ensuing divisions.[16] But, in the end, Oneness Pentecostals faced precisely the same race issues that had plagued Seymour. Many White Pentecostals, as Nelson notes, reasoned that racial separation was necessary to an "effective proclamation and expansion of the gospel," a mere excuse which was actually the "very essence of sin, a form of self-deception." "The simple truth of Seymour's theology," he concludes, "means that separated Christianity is not Christian at all but rather its denial."[17]

> As the movement turned away from Seymour it began to separate along racial lines sometimes camouflaged by administrative or doctrinal disagreements . . . The wonder is not that Seymour could not permanently maintain leadership of such a counter cultural movement, but that such a surprising historical breakthrough could happen at all and continue under him for so long.[18]

## 3.2 Precursors to Oneness Theological Ideology

Howell sees Oneness Pentecostalism as a restorationist fervor to "recapture the vitality of the Azusa revival" and to reverse negative trends in Pentecostalism which had led to extinguished, waning fires by 1910 at Azusa. It is a "counter-reformation of the Azusa revival" itself.[19] If so, it assumed, nonetheless, the vision for the continuation of the Azusa Street revival

1907, 14; Goff, *Fields White Unto Harvest*, 136–41.

15. Howell, "People of the Name," 25, italics added.

16. MacRobert, *Black Roots*, 64.

17. Nelson, *Seymour*, 300; cf., also, Clemmons, *Mason*, 42. In Clemmons' estimation Nelson's contribution, "a White Methodist scholar, has been an exception in his recognition of the spiritual legacy of pentecostalism."

18. Nelson, "Black Face of Church Renewal," 180–84.

19. Howell, "People of the Name," 14, 16, 25, 27; cf., Reed, *"In Jesus' Name,"* 82–83.

ideal, its imagination and its hope, vividly displayed in its international and interracial impact. Perhaps no group was more impacted by the fires of Azusa than the Oneness movement itself, and, not the least of all, via its direct and indirect influence upon an array of leaders.

### 3.2.1 Use of the Jesus' Name Formula by Parham and Seymour

It is also true that much of the early mindset which permeated the Pacific Apostolic Faith movement was anticipatory of the Oneness issue. The self-identifying name, "Apostolic Faith," became a designation for Oneness adherents and organizing bodies more than any other segment of the movement, a marker which remains true to the present. Even the restoration impulse linked to baptism is reflected in the Apostolic Faith movement, including Seymour, as demonstrated in the ministry of Joshua W. Sykes who, early in 1907, established a separate, but related mission in East Los Angeles, the Apostolic Church.

By mid-1908 Sykes teamed with H. A. Garrison and Mary Taylor, an African-American, to open a work on West Tenth Street. Like Parham before him, Sykes baptized in Jesus' name, a practice for which he was remembered in 1913, when the Oneness debate began in earnest in Los Angeles. Sykes, though, is not known to have either participated in or influenced the Oneness movement.[20] Joshua W. Sykes, apparently, is the "Dr. Sykes" referenced amidst McAlister's Jesus' Name baptism sermon at Arroyo Seco in 1913:

> There was an inaudible shudder that swept the preachers on the platform and the people in the vast arena. The preacher noticed it, and stood in awesome silence. Brother Denny, a missionary from China . . . told him not to preach that doctrine, or it would associate the camp with a Dr. Sykes, who so baptized.[21]

Parham's use, referenced earlier, of an altered Jesus' Name baptismal formula "in Jesus' Name, into the name of the Father, Son and Holy Ghost," was a similar precursor. He later explained that "unscriptural" teachings were being "wiped from my mind."[22] Goss was baptized in Jesus' Name

20. Robeck, *Azusa Street Mission*, 189, 282–83.

21. Ewart, *Phenomenon*, 76–77; cf. Reed, *"In Jesus' Name,"* 138–39, citing "The Outpouring of the Spirit in Los Angeles," *Pentecostal Testimony*, 2/3 (1912) 15.

22. Parham, *A Voice Crying in the Wilderness*, 5; Blumhofer, *Restoring the Faith*, 47, 64 n. 21, 23; Parham, *Parham*, 27.

twice. "E. N. Bell was called upon to do the baptizing. Howard A. Goss . . . could no longer stand against truth. Although he had been baptized in Jesus' name by Parham twelve years before this time, he had not realized the significance, but would now accept it fully for himself. He was one of the first baptized by Bell in this camp, and many lay members."[23] The significance here, though, may have more to do with Bell's mindset than Goss' baptism.

Perhaps Parham used the formula only "occasionally," in spite of the fact that his implementation of the teaching was said to be by divine revelation,[24] though he did repudiate the Oneness position much later. Some have assumed, nevertheless, that Parham baptized consistently in the formula prior to 1914, and that Seymour also, at least at times, followed Parham's example at the Azusa Street mission. Amidst the 1915 controversy of Jesus' Name baptism, Seymour endorsed Trinitarian baptism only. Yet at least two separate eye witness Azusa accounts indicate that Seymour baptized in Jesus' Name in the earliest years on occasion. These are Luis Lopez, a Hispanic convert, later with the Apostolic Assembly of the Faith in Christ Jesus, baptized by Seymour in Jesus' Name in 1909,[25] and William and Maggie Bowdan, similarly, before 1909.[26]

David Lee Floyd, a Parham convert and AG charter member, joined the Oneness cause early on, serving originally as Secretary of the Oneness GAAA. In his recorded interviews, he notes that even J. Roswell Flower discussed *with him* that he had used the Jesus' name formula himself for some years, but, then, abandoned it when the controversy arose over its use.[27]

23. Foster, *Think It Not Strange*, 71, 56; Bell, "Sad New Issue," 3.

24. Anderson, *Disinherited*, 140.

25. Cf., *Doctrines and Disciplines of the Azusa Street Apostolic Faith Mission of Los Angeles*; Anderson, *Disinherited*, 176; see, for example, Booker, "Azusa Street," 24–25, and "Jesus' Name Baptism and the Azusa Revival," 30–33; Historical Committee of the Apostolic Assemblies of the Faith in Christ Jesus, *Historia la Assemblea Apostolica de la Fe Cristo Jesus (1916–1966)*, 6; Espinosa, "Apostolic Assembly of the Faith in Jesus Christ," 321; cf. Walsh, *Latino Pentecostal Identity*, 19 n. 65.

26. LeBlanc, *Like A Rose*, 5, and the "Apostolic Encyclopedia," http://grou.ps/jcami/wiki/11538.

27. Clanton, *United We Stand*, 23–24; Floyd, Interview with Larry Booker, 54–55; Booker, "Jesus' Name," 32–33.

### 3.2.2 Key Oneness Leadership Impacted by Azusa Street

The impact of Azusa upon the movement cannot be ignored. Canadian minister, Robert E. McAlister, for example, whose sermon on baptism sparked the Oneness controversy at the Arroyo Seco camp meeting in 1913, one of the movement's most prominent early advocates, received Spirit baptism at Azusa December 11, 1906.[28] The Wisconsin-Minnesota Oneness movement, for example, traces its beginnings to Mrs. Malmberg, and her daughter, Ragna in Superior, Wisconsin who received Spirit baptism July 1907 after receiving tracts from the Azusa Mission. They embraced Jesus' name baptism after a camp meeting in St. Paul at which Haywood was the speaker in 1915.[29]

The most significant, though, was Haywood himself, in 1908, with the outbreak of the "Indianapolis Azusa." The revival, aided by a visit from Seymour, was spearheaded by Glenn A. Cook, who later became one of the most successful itinerant Oneness evangelists, working closely with Ewart. It was Henry Prentiss, an African-American, who came from Azusa to pastor the Indianapolis African American mission.

Cook, though, like McAlister, received Spirit baptism at Azusa in 1906 and then served in Los Angeles on the Azusa Street mission Board of Elders and as the mission's secretary. Cook likely played a key role in bringing Pentecostalism to other key leaders, as well, such as L. V. Roberts in Indianapolis, his brother-in-law James A. Frush in Newark, Ohio, B. F. Lawrence, Mother Lenore Barnes, and Mother Mary Gill Moise, all from St. Louis.[30]

Like Haywood, though, other important leaders of the period also experienced this type of strong, but indirect, Azusa Street revival influence, including Andrew D. Urshan in Chicago who, like E. N. Bell, received Spirit baptism at William Durham's Chicago mission. According to his later accounts Urshan had actually already begun to baptize in Jesus' Name in 1910.

> This truth became so clear to me that I was influenced by God To . . . publish a little leaflet on the New Birth and also to print Acts 2:38 on the cover of our baptistery tank and began to baptize the

28. Miller, *Canadian Pentecostalism*, 25, 62, 65–66, 111, 117.

29. Johnson, "First Jesus' Name Pentecostal Church in Wisconsin," 2; Vernon and Ragna (Malmberg) Johnson were later missionaries to Sweden.

30. Bartleman, *Pentecost*, 110; Hall, "Early Pentecostalism in St. Louis, Missouri," 10.

> new converts into the Name of the Lord Jesus Christ, *which is the one name* of the Father, Son and Holy Ghost.[31]

Likewise, Frank J. Ewart received Spirit baptism in Florence Crawford's camp meeting in Portland, Oregon in 1908, meetings sponsored by Azusa Street. The tongues phenomenon experience of Ewart and Haywood, then, were only months apart. Later Ewart would refer to the Azusa Street revival as the "burning bush" and the "blazing shekinah" of the early movement. The Crawford camp meeting, which Ewart fails to specifically mention by name, was held in June-August 1908 in the Mt. Tabor area, evidently just as Crawford split with Seymour.

By 1911 Ewart was assisting Durham in Los Angeles. He took charge of his mission after Durham's untimely death in 1912, bringing him in close proximity to Seymour and the Azusa Street mission.[32] Although he recognized the important early contribution of Parham, Ewart consciously associated Pentecostal origins with the Los Azusa Street revival: "As at the beginning in Los Angeles, God sent his signal stamp on baptism in the Name of Jesus by healing and baptizing believers in the water."[33] Elmer G. Lowe, another Los Angeles pastor, connected with Ewart's ministry, was an early Azusa participant as well.[34]

After the initial revival erupted in Toronto in late 1906, Franklin Small, organizer of the Oneness movement in Canada from 1913, received Spirit baptism in 1907 in Winnipeg in A. H. Argue's meetings. Argue had received Spirit baptism at Durham's Chicago mission. In eastern Canada, Lottie McLean brought the Pentecostal message from Azusa Street in 1911, with Hubert S. Perkins and Leslie Estabrooks being the first to receive Spirit baptism in New Brunswick. All were later participants in the Oneness revival in that province.[35]

31. Ewart, *Phenomenon*, 72; Urshan was Spirit filled in 1908, see Urshan, *Pentecost as It Was*, 77; Hunter, "Urshan, Andrew (Bar-) David," 1208.

32. "When I came into this great movement by the baptism of the Holy Spirit . . . I found a burning bush in the midst of the people. The bush is burning yet, but its radiant glory has noticeably diminished. It is only a faint spark compared to the blazing shekinah of Azusa Street Mission" (Ewart, *Phenomenon*, 9, 6, 20, 49; see http://www.azusabooks.com/what.shtml#3). Note, also, Bartleman preaching in Portland, Oregon in March 1908, Bartleman, *Pentecost*, 113.

33. Ewart, *Phenomenon*, 102.

34. E. G. and A. B. Lowe, *1917 & 1919 PAW Minute Book*; Paddock, *Apostolic Roots*, 91.

35. Gohr, "Franklin Small," 1075; Larden, *Our Apostolic Heritage*, 27–28; Morehouse, *Pioneers of Pentecost*, 198–99, 302.

William Booth-Clibborn, one of the earliest of the Oneness advocates, received Spirit baptism in London in 1908 at age fifteen, after the "European Azusa" ignited in the wake of the revival initiated by T. B. Barratt in Norway and A. A. Boddy in England after their contact with the Azusa Street revival. William, the son of Arthur S. Booth-Clibborn and grandson of the founder of the Salvation Army, William Booth, attended Harry and Margaret Cantel's mission in Plumstead, London which had been initiated into the revival via Boddy's Sunderland meetings.[36]

For many others the Azusa Street influence was much more direct, with several ministers, later to assume significant positions of leadership within the Oneness movement, finding their Pentecost in the actual Los Angeles mission. Several of these were African-American, including Edward S. and Mattie Lee, noted as the first to receive the Spirit at Azusa. Lee, eleven years Seymour's senior, married Seymour and Jennie Moore in May 1908.[37] Ministers William and Maggie Bowdan, parents of PAW leader Frank R. Bowdan, were also early Azusa Street participants.[38]

Frank W. Williams received Spirit baptism at Bonnie Brae in 1906. He returned to Mobile, Alabama and established several strong African-American works. Although he embraced the Oneness position in 1915, he rejected Finished Work theology, in spite of Haywood's influence. Williams retained, instead, a Wesleyan view of sanctification, which prompted him to found his own Oneness organization, the Apostolic Faith Mission Church of God, separate from those African-Americans joining with Haywood. Williams, in turn, converted W. T. Phillips in 1917, also in Alabama, founder of the Apostolic Overcoming Holy Church of God, which also organized as a separate African-American Oneness group. Williams and Seymour had been close, but his Oneness defection, like that of Haywood, was yet another strain on the unity of the faith of Azusa Street.[39]

Evidently, with Haywood's Finished Work views prevailing, more and more, in the Pentecostal Assemblies of the World, African American

36. Booth-Clibborn, "The Baptism in the Holy Spirit," 22–24; Ewart, *Phenomenon*, 107; see also, Bundy, "Barratt, Thomas Ball," 366, and "Boddy, Alexander Alfred," 436–37.

37. *PAW Minute Book and Ministerial Record 1930–1931*, 19; Lee was twenty four years older than Mattie, whom he married in 1904; *1900 US Census*, Fresno, California, 5; *1920 US Census*, Los Angeles, 3B; Robeck, *Azusa Street Mission*, 307.

38. LeBlanc, *Like A Rose*, 1–3; William Sylvester Bowdan married Maggie America Pryor, September 12, 1899, Austin, Texas, but moved to Los Angeles in 1900, http://trees.ancestry.com; Martin, *Seymour*, 205.

39. Sanders, *Seymour*, 13; Martin, *Seymour*, 326.

leaders like Williams and Phillips, could find little to attract them. The outcome of the AG turmoil was of little consequence, for even if the Oneness position had prevailed, it was overrun with non-Wesleyan theology. Thomas J. Cox, head of the Church of God (Apostolic), founded in 1897, found himself in a similar circumstance when he was converted by Lawson to the Oneness position sometime before 1919.

Frank Bartleman (1871–1936), the foremost "chronicler of Pentecostal origins in Los Angeles," due to his Azusa Street history, *How Pentecost Came to Los Angeles,* and with 550 articles, 100 tracts, and 6 books to his credit, was, perhaps the most well-known figures of the revival who was later to become Oneness. Cerillo refers to Bartleman as "arguably ranked as one of the most significant early American Pentecostal leaders." Bartleman's small tract, "The Earthquake," concerning the April 18, 1906 devastating San Francisco quake, drew considerable attention because the catastrophe occurred the very day that the *Los Angelis Daily Times* published its first article attacking the Azusa Street meetings.[40] In 1908 he established his own "nameless" mission at Eighth and Maple, which he turned over to William Pendleton, a charter member and first Chairman of the pre-Oneness PAW, and later Oneness PAW minister.[41]

Harry Morse, prominent Oneness leader in the west, established significant works located in Stockton and Oakland and an important Bible college and mission school. Morse, who was leading the San Pedro Peniel Mission south of Azusa Street, was informed by Bartleman of the revival, which prompted his first visit in 1906. Though he sought hard, it was six months before Morse received Spirit baptism.[42] Morse was one of the earliest of the Oneness participants, working early on with Ewart and Cook to spread the Oneness message throughout California.

George B. Studd, brother of British missionary to China and Africa C. T. Studd, left the Peniel Mission in 1907 to attend Azusa, which he did

40. Cerillo, "Frank Bartleman," 107, 113–14. Cerillo is doubtful of Bartleman's Oneness position and assumes it only an "*apparent* acceptance during the war years," italics added; see also, Robeck, "Frank Bartleman," *NIDPCM,* 366; Reid, "Frank Bartleman," 119. Bartleman, *Los Angeles,* 43–44; Bartleman's steps previous to Azusa are traced in his earlier book *From Plow to Pulpit: From Maine to California*; cf., Bartleman, "Why I Was Re-Baptized in the Name of Jesus Christ," 1.

41. Robeck, "Frank Bartleman," *DPCM*, 304–5; Robeck, *Azusa Street Mission*, 76–79; The mission at Eighth and Maple was later led by Ewart, see Bartleman, *The Deity of Christ*; Robeck, *Witness to Pentecost*, x; Bartleman, *Pentecost*, 92, in which Bartleman notes that "we never gave it a name."

42. Wallace, "Harry Morse," 2:284; Olive Haney, *The Man of the Hills*, 32; Bartleman, *Pentecost*, 93.

for more than a year, until joining Elmer Fisher's Upper Room Mission to co-edit *The Upper Room* paper.[43] He became Ewart's assistant and worked closely with the coordination and funding of Oneness missions.

John Schaepe, who received Spirit baptism at Azusa, February 23, 1907, received a "revelation" six years later of Jesus' Name baptism at Arroyo Seco. Many, including Harry Morse, heard him shouting the news throughout the camp in the early morning hours, persuading many of the new doctrine, and impacting Ewart himself, with whom Schaepe's Los Angeles ministry was associated.[44] Others associated with Ewart's ministry were Spirit filled at Azusa, also, including Elmer K. Fisher in Los Angeles, Robert G. Hammond, and Frederick E. Poole and Sarah E. Poole.

May Heath was a missionary to Japan who later married Frank Gray in 1910 and returned to Japan in 1914.[45] C. P. Nelson was a young Swede who stumbled upon the Azusa Street mission 1906, later basing his ministry in St. Paul, Minnesota.[46] George Carlisle, ordained by L. V. Roberts, based out of Indiana[47] and H. G. Rodgers, out of Tennessee organizing the historic July 1915 camp meeting in which AG Chairman E. N. Bell was baptized in Jesus' Name.[48]

## 3.3 The Los Angeles-based Pentecostal Assemblies of the World

The founding of the Pentecostal Assemblies of the World has long been disputed, especially as to its date and location, due mostly to contradictory

43. Ewart, *Phenomenon*, 56, 80, 106; Robeck, *Azusa Street Mission*, 299; George Studd was 52 before he married Mabel in 1911 (Oct 20, 1859–Feb 13, 1945), *1930 U.S. Census*, Los Angeles, 8A; Wilson, "George B. Studd," 1108; see also, a reprint article by Studd, "One Baptism," 1.

44. See Robeck, "John G. Schaepe," 1042; *1930 U.S. Census*, Christy, Arizona, 8B; Brumback, *Suddenly from Heaven*, 191; Clanton, *United We Stand*, 16; Reed, *"In Jesus' Name,"* 140; Schaepe, "The One Name," 6.

45. Ewart, *Phenomenon*, 54; Interview with Tracey O. Hammond, Freemont, Indiana, November 2006; Fred & Sarah Poole, *1910 U.S. Census*, Los Angeles, 3B; *1920 U.S. Census*, Visalia, CA, 1A, *1930 U.S. Census*, Chico, CA, 7B; Haney, *Clyde J. Haney*, 87–90, 160; Haney, "Azusa Street Revival," 7–8.

46. Nelson, "Charles Peter Nelson," 2:295–304; Reinking, "Charles Nelson," 18–20.

47. Paddock, *Apostolic Roots*, 91; Neal, *Keepers of the Flame*, 13; Carlisle, "The World's Saturday Night," 4, 3.

48. Jackson, *Tennessee District Heritage*, 16–20; Rodgers, "Henry Green Rodgers"; Rodgers was Spirit baptized May 8, 1906; cf., Lawrence, *Restored*, 94.

interpretations of the limited data. Nevertheless, the exciting discovery during the course of this research of earlier PAW documents than previously available allows for a more plausible and conclusive determination. These documents, to be detailed in the clearer context of events in the following chapter, assist in a correct interpretation of the PAW Minutes' "Brief Record" relative to these issues.

First of all, therefore, a composite of evidence appears to support the traditional view of the Azusa Street mission founding of the PAW in 1906 for the purpose of evangelism and keeping pace with its expanding, increasingly visible ministry. Secondly, this conclusion, admittedly, assigns special weight to the Haywood source, quoted and defended by historian Morris Golder: "It was started in 1906 in Los Angeles."[49]

## 3.3.1 Evaluating the "Brief Record" of the PAW Minute Book

The above mentioned exciting discovery was that of a large FBI archival file[50] containing the entire record of a previously unknown investigation of the Pentecostal Assemblies of the World. That, by itself, is a shocking discovery. Just imagine discovering that FBI Report #55234 had contained, for nearly a hundred years, a copy of the earliest known *PAW Minute Book*—a ministerial directory for *1917*. Previously, the earliest known Minute Book was from 1918. The *1917 PAW Minute Book* represents, then, the oldest extant records of the PAW, records, as will be seen, that may be its first published records as well.[51] Concerns regarding a government investigation in war time would have been adequate motivation for producing the first printed PAW minutes and rosters as an updated, reviewable record.

In terms of it importance to an understanding of an early founding, first of all, the ministerial listing represents the pre-1917, pre-Oneness list so vital for comparative analysis with the years 1918 and 1919, and,

49. Golder, *History*, 31, 36; Peagler, *Haywood*, 76; MacRobert, *Black Roots*, 71–72.

50. See FBI Report #55234, Publ. M1085, "Investigative Case Files of the Bureau of Investigation 1908–1922."

51. *Minute Book and Ministerial Record of Pentecostal Assemblies of the World*, Portland, Oregon, U.S.A., Year 1917–1918, in FBI Report #55234, Publ. M1085; cf., Tyson, *Early Pentecostal Revival*, 188, "earliest records available of the embryonic PAW are found in the minute book and ministerial record dated 1918 and 1919," records unavailable for this study.

secondly, it offers fresh evidence by which to assess the "Brief Record." Had earlier records been published? Had a need for the "Brief Record of Minutes 1907–1917" suddenly arisen? Not surprisingly, the *1917 PAW Minute Book* appears to have been compiled precisely *for* the government's investigation of its anti-war pacifism. Complete records, including the inclusion of summary minutes for the previous decade, not only served to demonstrate the PAW's longevity, but may indicate that no previous minutes had ever been published, per se.

These summaries contain very short PAW business reports from five earlier PAW meetings, the earliest being from 1907, recording the earliest activities of the PAW. It was, apparently, a considerably loose-knit ministerial organization, rather than tightly knit, to avoid being mischaracterized as denominationalism. Minutes indicate it was a ministerial cooperative "in the Azusa Mission" itself, obviously, by design very loosely organized. It operated for the "different Pentecostal Assemblies," yet with little or no fanfare. After initially forming in 1906, without a formally called meeting of the varied ministers who would be involved in the scope of its operation, the "first ministerial meeting" took place in 1907 at which they chose "the BIBLE as their Charter, Constitution and By-Laws" with "willing and unanimous consent."[52]

## 3.3.2 The 1906 Azusa Founding of the PAW

The 1906 date is not reflected in the PAW's early minutes, but rather in its oral history, as indicted in Haywood's precise confirmation. The 1907 first elections, reflected in the minutes, were not held, therefore, simultaneously with the PAW founding.[53] Little commends a challenge to the early date of 1906 prior to elections, at which the eldest of Azusa's board members were present, Hiram W. Smith and B. H. Irwin.[54] Later dates

52. FBI Report #55234, *Minutes,* 33; cf. Robeck, *Azusa Street Mission*, 96–98; also, the Azusa "incorporation" and purchase of the building were soundly criticized, ibid., 290.

53. Haywood's matter-of-fact declaration of the date and place can hardly be misconstrued as a mere cursory identification of the PAW *with* Azusa, and thus its 1906 beginning.

54. Cf. Jacobsen, *Thinking in the Spirit*, 196; Reed, *"In Jesus' Name,"* 96; *1917 PAW Minutes*, 8. Irwin was founder of the Fire-Baptized Holiness Church who was Spirit baptized at Azusa, later becoming a leader of the International Pentecostal Holiness Church, Borlase, *Seymour*, 191; see also, Paddock, *Apostolic Heritage*, 35; Lovett, "Black Holiness-Pentecostalism," 80; www.economicexpert.com/a/Pentecostal:Asse

simply reflect other historical markers, such as an assumed 1913 or 1914 Portland charter.[55]

Under Seymour's watchful eye, it may very well be that the PAW was set in order first, toward the latter part of 1906, as the itinerant schedules, such as those of Glenn Cook and Florence Crawford, resulted in long absences from the mission. Certainly, the 1907 meeting would have been a-typical, at best, for a first session organizational meeting, which requires the establishment of a name, mission, purpose, etc. Those items had clearly *already* been determined less formally before October 27, 1907. Although the election of officers took place on this date, the establishment of the by-laws governing the election did not. It is likely that the PAW had been operating without elected leadership for some time, but a duly called election became essential.

### 3.3.3 Early Pre-Oneness Leadership of the PAW

William Pendleton was the first "elected chairman, pro tem" of the PAW. Pendleton had been the pastor of the Los Angeles Holiness Church, Hawthorne Street, before his 1906 Spirit baptism at Azusa caused his ouster. He was PAW Chairman less than nine months, until July 1908.[56] A "Bro. Clark" served briefly as secretary with Pendleton, but he was "called by the Holy Ghost" as a missionary to India. Most likely this refers to J. E. and Margaret Clark in Bombay, who became Oneness in 1916. After her husband's death in 1917 Margaret Clark remained as a PAW missionary for some years.[57]

---

mblies:of:the:World.html; www.dunamai.com/Azusa/azusa_pages/Introduction.htm; and Braddy, *PAW History*, www.mca postolic.org/PAW_History/ PAW_History01.doc.

55. Anderson, *Disinherited*, 177, 278 n. 7 and n. 9; Bell, "Bible Order," 2–3; cf. Foster, *Think It Not Strange*, 73; Reid, *Dictionary of Christianity in America*, 884. Tyson seems to accept the 1907 reference in the minutes as the founding date; see Tyson, *Chalices*, 208, and idem, *Early Pentecostal Revival*, 188; cf., Reed, *"In Jesus' Name,"* 96, 110.

56. FBI Report #55234, 34; No available evidence links Seymour to an *official* PAW capacity.

57. See *Voice in the Wilderness*, "Missionary Report," October 1916, no. 18, 2, December 1916, no. 19, 3; *The Blessed Truth*, December 1, 1919, vol. 4, no. 22, 3; Anderson, *Spreading Fires*, 94. "Mrs. J. E. Clark" is listed in the *1917 PAW Minute Book* as a one of seven "Foreign" "Field Missionary Superintendents," though not listed in the ministerial roster, FBI Record #55324, 31.

Soon after he and most of his congregation were Spirit filled, including Ivey Campbell,[58] he became pastor of Bartleman's mission which opened August 1906. He remained close to Seymour, later working with Ewart. Already in his late sixties, he became one of the very first to embrace the Oneness position after the Arroyo Seco camp meeting in 1913.[59]

A "Sis. Hopkins" was elected to serve as the "temporary chairman," or chairwoman, in 1908, but her leadership has proven to be the most obscure of the early period, about which even less is known than that of J. J. Frazee, who served as secretary for the four years of her tenure. Hopkins' temporary tenure, evidently, was fulfilled as if it were permanent in that she appears to have served as head of the PAW for the four years 1908–1912.

Unfortunately, little else about her, including her first name, is known. Hopkins, like Emma Cotton, Rachel Sizelove, and Florence Crawford, was an early Azusa revival participant. Cotton referred to themselves as "pioneers," remaining in touch with these ministers, including Hopkins, in later years.[60] The timing of Hopkins' leadership, on the heels of Crawford's early 1908 severing of ties with Seymour, may have served to silence suggestions that sentiment against women preachers had been involved in their rift.[61]

Most importantly, these earliest summaries of PAW activity contribute to an understanding of the obscure era of J. J. Frazee, giving the date of his ordination, PAW, March 22, 1908. Frazee's ordination, therefore, occurred just months before the July 1908 replacement of Pendleton and Clark. He became Secretary for four years, serving with Hopkins, then, Chairman, March 1912, a position he served for six more years.[62]

58. Robeck, *Azusa Street Mission*, 187, 189, 191–92, 318; Bartleman, *Pentecost*, 67, 82–83, 92; Owens, *Azusa*, 59; Martin, *Seymour*, 257–58.

59. See *1900 US Census*, Los Angeles, 22. Ewart became Pendleton's co-pastor, and, after Pendleton's death in January 1917, assumed the pastorate of the mission, which had relocated to Kohler Street about five blocks south of Azusa Street.

60. She is not listed in the *1917 PAW Minute Book*. See Cotton, "Letter to Rachel Sizemore," http://www.azusastreet.org/participantHopkinsSister.htm; Butler, *Women in the Church of God in Christ*, 62–64; Alexander, *Women of Azusa*, 177.

61. Clemmons, *Mason*, 49–50; Robeck, *Azusa Street Mission*, 285, 301–7; Nelson, "Seymour," 240.

62. FBI Report #55234, 7, according to an August 2, 1917 FBI interview with Frazee; cf. Ross, *Apostolic Heritage*, 35.

## 3.4 THE REVIVAL WITHIN THE RACIAL COMPLEXITY OF INDIANAPOLIS

The Pentecostal revival that swept Indianapolis in 1907–1908 was both initiated and led by Azusa Street, and G. T. Haywood entered the movement at this height of Azusa fervor and success. In many ways Indianapolis represented an exceptional sort of parallel to Seymour's Los Angeles success, especially in the sense that both were bastions of interracial conviction led by two of the most prominent leaders Pentecostalism has produced, and both African American.

Just as the initial Indianapolis revival became the hub from which several early Pentecostal leaders, such as John G. Lake, Thomas Hezmalhalch, and J. R. Flower, were propelled into key involvement, so it would ultimately develop into a major early success story for Oneness Pentecostalism. Flower played a major role in resisting the Oneness movement within the Assemblies of God. During this period, in 1911, Haywood made the pivotal decision to join the ministerial ranks of the Los Angeles based PAW, and then, in 1915, to join ranks with the Jesus' Name camp. Indianapolis, which would quickly emerge as an early Oneness epicenter, also had a rapidly growing Black population, and become a U.S. bastion of prejudice and racism.

Consider, for example, the sharp contrast in the growth of the Black population in Indianapolis, compared to that of such cities as Los Angeles. Rapid growth in Los Angeles by 1906 resulted in a population of 238,000, but, even by 1910, it had only 7,599 Blacks out of a population of 319,000.[63] In Indianapolis, though, by 1900, the Black population had begun to explode, jumping from 16,000 to nearly 35,000 in 1920. This was an enormous increase from nearly 10% of the Indianapolis population to 43 percent.

> So in 1910 Indianapolis had the highest percentage of black population of any Northern city in America with over 100,000 residents; the black percentage for Boston was 2 percent, for Chicago 2 percent, and for New York 1.0 percent but for Indianapolis 9.3 percent. When Indiana had 80,810 blacks in 1920, 43 percent of them (34,678) lived in Indianapolis.[64]

63. Robeck, *Azusa Street Mission*, 53; Fogelson, *The Fragmented Metropolis*, 76, 78.

64. Rudolph, *Hoosier Faiths*, 545.

This "great migration" of African-Americans into Northern cities, during the first two decades of the twentieth century, had an obvious impact upon Indianapolis in terms of the uniquely high percentage of migrants. The "increase of the black population between 1910 and 1920 (50 percent)," as documented by Brady, "was significantly greater than that of the city population as a whole (35 percent)."[65] During this period, with its declining agricultural economy, Baer and Singer have argued that "Blacks became an easy target for White hostility."[66]

Accordingly, the availability of jobs in northern industries created by World War I, as well as the economic prosperity of the 1920s, "propelled massive numbers of Blacks to leave the rural areas of the south."[67] Also, during this period, cultural perceptions and racial prejudice reached such a fever pitch amidst the societal racial adjustments and tensions throughout the country that thousands of African-American lives were taken in the act of tragic, barbaric lynching.[68]

The majority of Indianapolis Blacks in 1910 were in the Fifth Ward, bounded by the White River, Tenth, West and Washington streets. The Fifth Ward was 48 percent Black. Anti-interracial sentiment in the city often prevailed, requiring court action, for example, to rule unconstitutional an ordinance, in 1926, which made it illegal to move into a White neighborhood, without the residents' approval.[69] By the 1920s Indiana was experiencing a resurgence of the Ku Klux Klan which quickly made the Klan "the largest social organization in Indianapolis and dominant force . . . from 1921 to 1928."[70]

The impact upon early racial relations in the city has been enormous. According to Moore, 25 percent "of native-born White men" in Indianapolis' Marion County had become members of the KKK by 1925. Rudolph argues that the Indiana Klan became the largest in the nation. In 1923, for example, it published 50,000 copies of the *Fiery Cross* weekly, signed up 117, 969 new members, and had, as members of the Klan, forty

65. Brady, "Indianapolis at the Time of the Great Migration, 1900–1920," 1, http://www.carolynbrady. com/indymigration.html.

66. Baer and Singer, *African-American Religion*, 38.

67. Brady, "Indianapolis at the Time of the Great Migration, 1900–1920," 1.

68. Franklin, *Illustrated History of Black Americans*, 103–11; cf. Nelson, "Seymour," 254–59.

69. Brady, "Great Migration," 4–5; Bodenhamer and Barrows, *Encyclopedia of Indianapolis*, 7.

70. Schneider, "Changing Face of Indianapolis"; Bodenhamer and Barrows, *Encyclopedia of Indianapolis*, vii.

nine Indianapolis pastors.[71] In 1921, when an African-American dentist moved into a White Indianapolis neighborhood, it required a Superior Court order to remove the twelve foot high fences the neighbors built on either side of his property.[72]

Haywood's own high school, Shortridge, had been integrated from the time that Abram Shortridge, White superintendent of the then "Indianapolis High School," escorted Black "test student" Mary Ann Rann to class in 1872. Yet, in 1927, Haywood witnessed the progression of increased prejudice in the city, with the first ever segregated Indianapolis high school, the separate, all Black Crispus Attucks High School. Crispus, the Black sailor killed in the Boston Massacre in 1770, had long been a symbol of abolition. Black schools in Indianapolis from 1927 to 1942 were barred from the state basketball tournament and Indiana High School Athletic Association leagues.[73]

Richard Pierce suggests in his discerning study of the race complexities in the city of Indianapolis, *Polite Politics,* that African Americans there "created a style of race relations" which may be, more or less, unique to Indianapolis. He argues that they maintained, amidst determined segregation by Whites, a gentle diplomacy.[74] This, indeed, sounds a great deal like Haywood himself, an African American who not only survived, but thrived in the racial matrix of Indianapolis, repeatedly excelling in spite of mounting race challenges.

Haywood's personal aspirations of racial unity were, obviously, not born out of a cultural naiveté. Yet these early societal racial issues in Indiana coincide with the crucial years in the racial unification of the Pentecostal Assemblies of the World, especially those immediately prior to the 1924 racial schism. Both the societal prejudice and a ministerial apathy were working to nullify the efforts of Haywood, and the many other early Apostolics, White and Black, who believed "Pentecost" worthy of a truly interracial vision.

71. Moore, *Citizen Klansmen*, 49; Rudolph, *Hoosier Faiths,* 547, 549.

72. Brady, "Great Migration," 5.

73. Gaus, *Shortridge,* 15, 116–18; see Jackson, "The Endless Journey."

74. Pierce, *Polite Politics*, 3–4.

## 3.5 Indianapolis, Indiana—"The Midwest Azusa"

These Apostolics were, of course, in their interracial idealism, championing the original Azusa Street vision of Pentecost, an idealism into which the young convert to the movement, G. T. Haywood, had been spiritually born, only ten months into the Azusa outbreak. The racial complexities of the Indianapolis revival, which began in early 1907, paralleled that of Los Angeles.

The city's press labored hard to segregate the congregations of the earliest Apostolic Faith converts. The negative, sardonic antagonism of the press, including the unique nomenclature, "gliggy bluk" churches, was maintained for many years, at least until as late as 1915.[75] David Bundy, an Indianapolis church expert and historian of Pentecostal history in the city, has noted:

> The excitement caused by the development of Pentecostalism was unprecedented in Indianapolis religious history, with scrutiny from the city establishment paralleled only by the experience of the tradition in Los Angeles. It is against this backdrop that one must understand the early ministry of Haywood.[76]

### 3.5.1 Glenn A. Cook and the Interracial Indianapolis Revival

The events transpiring in Los Angeles had begun, by the end of 1906, to impact the city of Indianapolis, and like-minded folks, such as George N. Eldridge's CMA congregation in Indianapolis' northeast downtown area, began seeking Spirit baptism. Eldridge rejected the movement at the time, but later, after becoming a CMA district superintendent in the Los Angeles area, he visited Azusa Street and was Spirit baptized in 1910.[77]

75. See "Judge Discharges Man Who Laughed in Church," 11: "He attended what he said was a 'Gliggy Bluk' service on Roosevelt avenue, near Cooper street."

76. Bundy, "G. T. Haywood," 239.

77. He established Bethel Temple in Los Angeles and, by 1919, was an AG minister and "General Presbyter." See Robeck, "Azusa Street Revival," 347; Martin, *Seymour,* 285; Borlase, *Seymour,* 207–8; *Minutes of the General Council of the Assemblies of God 1919,* 30; *1850 US Census,* Orrington, Penobscot County, Maine; Eldridge was born in Maine in 1847, *1880 US Census,* Calais, Washington County, Maine, 18; *1910 US Census,* Pasadena, CA, 7A.

Glenn A. Cook (1869–1947), born in Ohio, yet raised in Brownsburg, Indiana since 1870, but his family moved in 1870 to Ohio. By the early 1890s he was married, "wayward," and, at least as late as 1900, working in Chicago as a printer. In late 1900 or early 1901, Glenn and Sophic Cook moved back to Indianapolis and converted in the holiness movement, which, before their move to California, brought them into contact with Eldridge and the N. East Street CMA.[78]

Gospel Tabernacle, near downtown, was one mile east of Senate & Eleventh, soon to be the locale of Haywood's church. Cook was staying just off East Street, at 612 Terrace Avenue, near his sister, Eveline Surver, at 726 Terrace Avenue, and his mother. Although Cook's father, Nathan Cook, a Civil War veteran, died in 1899, his mother, and four of his (married) sisters, remained in the Indianapolis area.[79]

Cook, as Robeck points out, joined a holiness group in Los Angeles known as the Metropolitan Church Association, which had formed in 1894, and, by 1902, he was the printer of the MCA's paper, *The Burning Bush*. "At one time," before 1907, in Indianapolis, according to *The Indianapolis Star,* Cook had been a barber. He worked as a printer, though, most of his life in the Los Angeles area, operating a print shop from his home, working closely with Ewart's *Meat in Due Season*. Cook published his own paper, *Messiah's Coming Kingdom,* as well, in the late 1920s.[80]

Hearing of the revival while preaching a tent meeting one mile southwest of Azusa Street at W. 7th Street and S. Spring Street, Cook attended to "straighten the people out in their doctrine."

> I dropped into the meetings on Azusa Street some time in April, having heard that some people were speaking in tongues, as they did on the day of Pentecost. Although I had been trying to preach Pentecost for five years, the speaking in tongues was as strange to me as though it had never been mentioned in God's word . . . As I was indoctrinated in the second blessing being the baptism of the Holy Ghost, I branded the teaching as heretical.

78. Flower, "When Pentecost Came to Indianapolis," 5–7.

79. Cook, "Pentecost in Lamont, Okla.," 1; *1870 US Census,* Lincoln Township, Hendricks County, Indiana, 30, *1880 US Census,* Brownsburg, Indiana, 11, and *1990 US Census,* Chicago, Cook County, Illinois, 3. At the time of her death, Cook's mother, Mary Jane Cook, was living with her daughter Eveline Surver, September 1909, see "Son Conducts Funeral," 7.

80. Robeck, *Azusa Street Mission*, 101, 107, originally Metropolitan Holiness Association; "Seek New Religious Speech," 6.

> [Later in July 1906] I was laid out under the power five times before Pentecost really came . . . I had been seeking about five weeks, and on a Saturday morning I awoke and stretched my arms toward heaven and asked God to fill me with the Holy Ghost. My arms began to tremble, and soon I was shaken violently by a great power . . . About thirty hours afterwards, while sitting in the meeting on Azusa Street, I felt my throat and tongue begin to move, without any effort on my part. Soon I began to stutter and then out came a distinct language which I could hardly restrain. I talked and laughed with joy far into the night.[81]

In October 1906, Cook signed his letters to T. B. Barratt in Oslo, Norway, regarding Spirit baptism, as *The Apostolic Faith* managing editor. He could not, though, have continued as editor for long with the travel itinerary he kept in 1907. Even earlier, for example, he had carried the message of the Azusa Street revival in July to Monrovia and to the Los Angeles People's Church in September. Then, when his testimony appeared in *The Apostolic Faith* in November, the thirty-seven year old Cook became an even more sought after evangelist. Five months after his experience of Spirit baptism, he left Los Angeles, December 4th, for Oklahoma, Missouri, Indiana, and Tennessee. Sarah Cripes wrote requesting he come to Indianapolis. He arrived January 18th: "Arrived here Friday morning after spending two days in Chicago. Quite a number are seeking the baptism."[82]

Cook began preaching at the East St. church, though Eldridge was away, and folks immediately began receiving Spirit baptism, including, on February 7, 1907, Richard and Maude Cordell. But Eldridge, upon his return, soon banned these "tarrying" meetings. They were, in fact, forced out of several places, Cook noted. They met briefly at Senate Avenue and St. Clair Street, then for several weeks at 1111 ½ Shelby Street, just north of E. Morris Street. [83]

The press hype subsided somewhat in February and March. Tom Hezmalhalch arrived with a band of White Azusa workers, Celia Smock, Elnora Hall, and Fred Dexheimer, although he was away for most of May.

81. Cook, "Receiving the Holy Ghost," 2, and "The Azusa Street Mission," published some years later while pastor at 133 ½ S. Alma St., Belvedere, California.

82. Bundy, "Spiritual Advice to a Quaker," 163–66; Cook, "Pentecost in Lamont, Okla.," 1; Robeck, "Azusa Street Revival Timeline," 104.

83. Gene Cordell Interview, Calvary Tabernacle, Indianapolis, Indiana, January 10, 2006, son of Richard and Maude Cordell; Cook, "Pentecostal Power in Indianapolis," 3.

He then departed Indianapolis for South Africa by April 1908. But Cook had returned to Indianapolis late in April through the first week of May, returning from Oklahoma at the end of the month in preparation for Seymour's June arrival. Among the early converts of the period were Alice Reynolds (Flower), her parents, the Flower family, Louie Scheiderman and the Jacob Lehman missionary family.[84]

The meetings were then moved to an upper room at Fountain Square, where they continued until the end of March. Describing his last service before his temporary return to Azusa Street in mid-March, Cook reported: "Many received the baptism . . . The meeting seemed to have wings, and the whole room had to be used for the altar service." His anticipatory remarks in the March issue of *The Apostolic Faith* portended accurately the scope of the events: "This will be a *center* of power, being an inter-urban railway center like Los Angeles."[85] Tom Hezmalhalch arrived from Azusa Street to assist in the work in Cook's absence.

### 3.5.2 Indianapolis Pentecostalism Dubbed the Gliggy Bluk Revival

The crowds, by April, necessitated the move to Murphy Hall, a mile and a quarter North, at E. New York and N. Alabama Streets, just four blocks from the Black mission which would soon open on W. Michigan Street. April, May, and June erupted into a Midwest revival in many respects rivaling that of Azusa Street, due in part to the free publicity, the daily, incendiary press coverage of the *Indianapolis Star* and *Indianapolis News,* which employed overt racism in protesting the interracial services which the Indianapolis Pentecostals were enjoying.

> This is stirring up the ministers and people, and the newspapers are lying and trying to put the people against us, but God is overruling . . . Yesterday afternoon God took a young colored brother and a young sister, and in a most marvelous manner the Holy Ghost spoke through them in tongues, giving the

84. Lehman became one of the first Pentecostal missionaries to South Africa; "Seek New Religious Speech," 5; Bundy, "Haywood," 239; see also, Smock, "Reminiscences of God's Faithfulness," 4; see "Trance Followed Sermon by Cook," 3, and *Enrichment,* Spring 2006, 105.

85. Cook, "Pentecostal Power in Indianapolis," 3; italics added.

> interpretation, and with such power and force that the whole audience was stricken with awe.[86]

The city's Black papers, though, including the two for which Haywood worked, *The Freeman and the Recorder*, reported on neither the religious phenomenon itself, nor the race issues involved. The twenty-five-year old Haywood, who lived only a short distance west of the ongoing events, could not have avoided the torrent of vitriol on display in the White press. Cook, unplanned, quickly returned, as crowds came from "all over the state" and adjoining states. Alice Flower noted that "out-of-towners could take one of the 26 interurban lines which made getting in and out of the city very easy." J. Roswell Flower soon joined his parents in attendance once meetings moved over to Murphy Hall.[87]

Seymour himself joined the meetings by June 2, 1907 for two weeks, in the face of incessant press coverage. Hezmalhalch's *Apostolic Faith* report in mid-April mentions the interracial services, which were apparently the norm early on, although the public outcry against it came in early May. Also, by mid-April, the press had already dubbed the movement with the demeaning term "Gliggy Bluks," meant as a "humorous" attempt at mimicking speaking in tongues.

One Indianapolis newspaper report created the following farcical lines: "Oogie google wago mo, Fasto maro Cook de bo, Lalu galu sando fando here's for *luck*; Ingle wingo fer so kink, Sando fago wastel dink, If I only was a *Gliggy Bluk*." The first such article appeared in the *Indianapolis Morning Star*, April 17, 1907, 1, with attempts made at making other terms stick, such as the "Glug" meetings. But "Gliggy Bluk" quickly won the day.[88]

May 4, 1907 Ernest Buel Lloyd, twenty-six, African-American, and single, was propelled to prominence in the revival due to his nearly inciting a race riot during the Saturday service. Lloyd, who was to later join Haywood's church and license with the PAW, once again made the revival front page news in the *Indianapolis Star*: "Ernest Lloyd . . . narrowly escaped violence at the hands of a mob when at the altar he seized 12-year-old Naomi Groves by the head and shook her until her screams stirred the

86. Hezmalhalch, "In Indianapolis, Ind.," 1. His report is dated April 20, from his residence at 2341 Fletcher Avenue.

87. Seymour refers only to the extended trip to Zion, Illinois, and not to either Indianapolis or the race conflict disrupting the city, see "'Latter Rain' in Zion City, Ill.," 1; Flower, "When Pentecost Came," 6.

88. Robeck, "Azusa Street Revival Timeline," 9; "Gliggy Bluks Meet," 1; see also, "Stutterer Speaks at 'Glug' Service," 15.

large audience in the hall. The police were called and took a hand before quiet was restored."[89]

The *Star* also suggested that "members of the Apostolic faith believe that he has great power," and that, in an attempt to beat a demon out of the girl, "seized her with both hands by the hair." The assistance of six to eight policemen was needed to settle the opposition crowd positioned in the rear of the hall. "Religion is religion, but it is another thing," the paper stated, "for a burly n----- to grab a little girl and frighten her to death."[90]

Lloyd, who was born February 12, 1881 in Topeka, Kansas, and also lived in Oklahoma before moving to Indiana with his family, remained in Indianapolis most of his life and ministry. A month after the initial June 5th story, the *Star* repeated portions of the account with photos of Cook and Lloyd together. The caption read: "'Bluk' Apostle and One of the Bluks." The press coverage for an article entitled "Negro Bluk Beats Demon From Girl," which ran in the *Indianapolis Sunday Star,* May 5, 1907, seems to indicate that the meetings were, indeed, interracial from the start. It states that Lloyd "has been meeting with the band since it invaded the city."[91]

Over the next weeks police were in attendance at the services periodically, but, ultimately, for the purpose of protecting the church from the increasingly tense crowds of angry protesters. Cook, for example, in mid-June, was attacked and hit "about the head." The announcement, the actual June 2nd arrival, and the visit of African-American leader William Seymour served to fan the editorial rancor even more, with the Indianapolis papers more than doubling their coverage of varied details of the revival.[92] The coverage of Seymour's first service was reported as "Negro Bluk Kissed," emphasizing Cook's form of greeting.

89. "Negro Bluk Beats Demon From Girl," 1.

90. Ibid., 1

91. *1890 U.S. Census,* Hennessey, OK, 28; *1895 Kansas Census,* 8; *1910 US Census,* Indianapolis, IN, 2A; Lloyd does not appear in the pre-Oneness roster of the *1917 PAW Minutes,* but only later in the *1919–1920 PAW Minutes;* "Negro Bluk Beats Demon From Girl," 1; "'Bluk' Apostle and One of the Bluks," and "Negro Bluk 'Blows,'" 20.

92. "Police Visit Bluks," 12; "Police Are Spectators at Bluks' Meeting," 4; "Hit Brother Cook"; "Young Mob Assails Bluks' Temple"; and "Bluks Appeal to Police," 3, 7. Also, the neighboring community attempted to have the services closed at Murphy Hall, see "Desire the Bluks to Go," 1; "Mayor Will Protect 'Gliggy Bluks,'" 1; "Police Have No Power to Stop Bluks' Meetings," 8. Also, June 14th Captain Asch of the Indianapolis Police interviewed Cook as to possible criminal charges, Robeck, "Azusa Street Revival Timeline," 105. Outgoing African-American missionary, William H. Cummings, with his large family, accompanied Seymour, with his elder son, Frank, assisting with the June 15th baptism.

By June 19th the Indianapolis Republican Mayor, Charles A. Bookwalter issued statements in defense of the rights of the group to meet under the protection of the law. The press, though, continued to spotlight their use of offerings, the threats of husbands to divorce their "Bluk" wives, the baptism of thirteen in Fall Creek, and even the foot washing service which followed.[93] Therefore, within a week of Seymour's arrival, the crowds were so large that people were being turned away. The paper was especially quick to point out, not only the increase in African-American attendance, but the inappropriate "familiarity with which the colored members of the flock were greeted" by White members.

On June 9th Seymour and Cook decided to segregate the races, more out of safety concerns than the size of the crowds, and held separate services upstairs and down in Murphy Hall. The antagonism of the press over the next weeks regarding the interracial baptism and foot washing may be, in itself, an indication that all other services had remained segregated, and thus, a partial victory for the White press.[94]

By the year's end a separate African-American mission was established at W. Michigan Street, just west of N. Blake Street. Azusa minister, Henry Prentiss, evidently at Cook's invitation, became pastor of the African American group, probably, in the fall of 1907. Cook appears to have overseen the White congregation, while continuing itinerant evangelistic work, until late 1909 or early 1910.[95]

Twenty year old J. Roswell Flower edited the important paper *The Pentecost* from 1908 to 1910, resulting in his leaving Indiana for almost two years in April 1909. Although, for many months, *The Pentecost* included a featured U.S. and missions "Apostolic Faith Directory" of *all* churches, Flower never listed Prentiss, Haywood, their African-American

93. "Negro Bluk Kissed," 3; "Bluk Divides Home," 1; "Oddy Asks Divorce Because of Bluks," 3; "Gliggy Bluks Bathed at Fall Creek Waters," 7; "Bluk Feet, Little and Big, Scrubbed," 10.

94. "Bluk Crowd Runs Over," 12. See also Bundy, "Haywood," 243, and Martin, *Seymour*, 308.

95. The January 1908 *Apostolic Faith* opens: "Indianapolis, Ind.—Many souls have been baptized in Indianapolis, saved and sanctified," see "Indiana Missionary Convention," *The Apostolic Faith*, 2; Cook returned to Chicago, his wife's home, and ran a "printing shop," by April 1910, *1910 U.S. Census*, Cook County, Chicago, IL, 12B; "Son," *Star*, 7, refers to Cook as "pastor of the church" at "New York and Alabama streets." The segregated congregations were less than a mile apart, see Martin, *Seymour*, 311. L. V. Roberts assumed leadership of this Apostolic Faith Assembly, then on New Jersey Street, in January 1913. Later named Oak Hill Tabernacle, Roberts led the entire church into Jesus' Name baptism in 1915, see Roberts, "More Blessed Revival Fires: Fresh Blaze in Indianapolis," 3; cf. Blumhofer, "Thomas F. Zimmerman," 4.

church (originally part of his own church), or *any* African American mission or individual.[96]

Seymour and Cook conducted the June 15th baptism near the Fall Creek Indiana Street bridge, in which Mabel, Cook's own daughter, Sarah Cripe, Ida May Oddy, Ernest B. Lloyd, Joseph Ingland, Naomi Groves, and seventeen year old B. F. Lawrence were among the baptized.[97] The baptism took place slightly over a mile east of Haywood's home, at a time when, no doubt, Blacks across the city were keenly aware of the racial upheaval impacting Indianapolis and the interracial band of Bluks.

## 3.6 HENRY PRENTISS AND THE DOWNTOWN INDIANAPOLIS MISSION

Haywood was converted in the Black mission downtown which Henry Prentiss, a truly unique Azusa Street minister, had come to pastor. The historical detail of Prentiss' role in the Indianapolis revival has been one of the most elusive of all the early participants. His ancestry, like so many African-American descendants, due to slavery, has been difficult to decipher. It is now clear that he was born Christmas Day 1873 on a "Beverly Manor" farming estate near Staunton, Virginia in the Shenandoah Valley.[98]

*The Apostolic Faith* carried the phenomenal story of Henry Prentiss, his conversion, ministry, and repeated arrests, in the December issue 1906. It was simply signed "A Worker." Prentiss wrote: "I came from Frisco to Los Angeles five days after the earthquake." Admittedly, Spirit baptism did not come easy, or quickly, for him. After "having the devils cast out of me," Prentiss reveals, and after "much study of the word," he finally "spoke with new tongues" in late September. Thirty-two when he received Spirit baptized at Azusa, Prentiss was, positively, one of the mission's most colorful figures.[99]

96. Flower moved to Kansas City, Missouri, April 1909, to work with A. S. Copley, who later took over as editor of *The Pentecost*. Flower left in November, returning to Indianapolis by February 1910; Flower, "God Honors Faith," 1; see also, Bundy, "Haywood," 244.

97. This baptism was mocked in cartoon-fashion in the *Indianapolis Star*, in stark racist caricature of Seymour and the entire Pentecostal group, "The Gliggy Bluks' Water Carnival," see "Baptismal," *Enrichment*, Spring 2006, 34; Martin, *Seymour*, 309, plus, photos courtesy of the Indiana Historical Society, 318–19; Lawrence, *Apostolic Faith Restored*.

98. *1880 U.S. Census*, Beverly Manor District, Augusta County, Virginia, 20.

99. "Arrested For Jesus' Sake," 3, contra Peagler, *Haywood*, 11; Robeck, "Azusa

In June 1906 he was nearly lynched for disturbing the peace at a tent meeting in progress less than two miles from Azusa, when he pointed his finger at a White Church of God minister's daughter and declared her a sinner. Found guilty of the charges, he served thirty days on a chain gang. Police arrested Prentiss again in October at a downtown street service, fearing his tongues speaking a sign of insanity.[100] The next month, in Whittier, along with three other Azusa comrades, Prentiss was arrested, but the case was declared a mistrial and later dismissed. In December, on his thirty-third birthday, he was nearly lynched in Anaheim, California. Three days later he was arrested, again, in Whittier, and, again, the trial ended in a mistrial and was later dismissed.[101]

After Prentiss' court appearance in January 1907, he began a series of itinerant evangelistic trips up the West coast, preaching for Adolph Rosa in San Francisco, for example, in February and March. *The Apostolic Faith* published his itinerary as he traveled in April and May with Florence Crawford and "Sister Rees" from Santa Rosa, to San Jose, then on to meetings in Portland, Oregon. John Glassco's mission on 2nd Avenue, shortly after he received Spirit baptism in early May, was turned over to Crawford, who later left Azusa to pastor this work.[102]

After the summer of 1907 and Seymour's Indianapolis visit, house meetings became the norm for the African-American members, although they were partially integrated initially. After the arrival of Prentiss as pastor in the fall, having worshipped in house meetings and a rented hall for a short while, a tiny tin shop building on W. Michigan St., just west of Blake St., was secured, in close proximity to most of the members. The early flock included among the faithful charter members Ernest Lloyd, Charles and Elizabeth Smith and family, Simon and Mary Barber and family, notably their son, Oddous Barber, later the Smith's son-in-law, and the Allen Woodring family, whose daughter Prentiss married in June 1908.[103]

---

Street Revival Timeline," 70, with each of the article's details being that of Prentiss' timeline, notably, the singular Oct. 4, 1906 "board of insanity" incident, and his fall attendance of the "Bible school up at Azusa St.," cf. Robeck, *Azusa Street Mission*, 95; also, "Unusual Noise," 1.

100. Martin, *Seymour*, 252–54; "Negro Preacher on Trial in Police Court"; Robeck, "Azusa Street Revival Timeline," 68; Borlase, *Seymour*, 188; Nickel, *Azusa Street Outpouring*, 15–18; "Pentecost Among the Young People," 1. Mistaken assumptions of Prentiss' young age at the time have likely been derived from this article.

101. Robeck, "Azusa Street Revival Timeline," 103–4.

102. Adolph Rosa, "In San Francisco," 3; "Pentecost In San Jose and Portland," 4; Amos Morgan, "Mother Crawford," www.azusabooks.com/profile.shtml, 8.

103. They used the homes of the Smiths (732 Adelaide St.) and Maggie Clark

In February 1908 Prentiss put the Apostolic Faith Assembly back on the front page with the press coverage of another Prentiss arrest and trial. Just days prior to this incident, which took place at Allen Chapel on February 23rd, Garfield and Ida Haywood, and his sister Gertrude, had trudged through ice and snow to attend Prentiss' mission for the first time. Prentiss may have been known for his many aggressive antics and scrapes, but recollections of Indianapolis' faithful have rather made reference to his famous praying, which was, reportedly, "like listening to an angel."[104]

## 3.7 G. T. Haywood's Conversion and Early Ministry

Ben and Ann Haywood raised their family in the 900 block of N. Bismarck Avenue (renamed Pershing during WWI) just to the west, over the White River, in the Haughville community, bounded by 16th on the north and W. Michigan on the south. Garfield and his young family were living next door to his parents. His mother and sister, Celia, had already received Spirit baptism.

Reflecting on the plight of "the Negro" in his 1908 weekly sketches for *The Freeman,* February 8th, Garfield depicted a young Black man standing on a bluff looking out, with the caption: "It is the West that the Negro's hope of the future lies." The tiny mascot, with his suitcase, says, "I wonder what's he waiting on?" Haywood was contemplating the means of success for the African-American, amidst all the obstacles.[105] His personal decisions, in terms of his own future, were also being cast.

After weeks of Barber's attempts to convert him, Haywood was finally convinced by Prentiss, and determined to visit the mission. After Haywood slipped into the crowded service, eyewitness oral accounts of his Spirit baptism that night state that "he was sprawled prostrate on the floor." Then, suddenly, "the power of the Lord fell on him like a lightning

(White), Golder, *Haywood*, 3, whose account relies heavily on Barber. The Barbers were originally on Rhode Island St., and moved to Colton, just off Walnut St., where the Woodrings lived; *1900 U.S. Census,* Marion County, Indianapolis, IN, A12, B12; *1910 US Census,* Marion County, Indianapolis, IN, 3A, 9A. See details of the group in "Gliggy Bluk Preacher Fined For Contempt," 16, cited also in Garrett, *The Chronicles of Pentecostalism and the Apostolic Movement*, 165.

104. Golder, *Haywood*, 3.

105. "The Land of Promise," 1; see also, his sketch depicting "The Negro Path to Success," 1.

bolt."[106] In a rare semi-biographical, historical sketch, Haywood himself said, concerning the mission at that time: "Night after night scores of anxious souls would make their way to that little dusty, bay window building and tax it to its capacity. Long before one could reach the door, songs of praise could be heard floating in the air for several blocks away."[107]

Within days of Haywood's conversion visit, Prentiss, with some of his saints, attended the Allen Chapel AME, on February 23rd, a couple of miles east of the mission, and interrupted the service by bursting into speaking in tongues during the sermon. After Prentiss was arrested, the press immediately connected him to Cook's Gliggy Bluk interracial revival of the previous year. They, therefore, followed the March 4th trial with great interest, and in April, Prentiss was found guilty. The Allen Chapel trial coverage evidenced considerable growth in Prentiss' church, numbering his trial supporters at about a hundred. Several had joined him from Bethel AME on W. Vermont Street, just blocks from the W. Michigan Street mission.[108] They had to relocate to larger quarters half a block down Michigan at Minerva, a street which is now eliminated by the Indiana University campus.

Furthermore, two important inter-related issues regarding the historical record have remained unclear. First, how and when did Haywood assume leadership? But, also, why and when did Prentiss leave? Answers to these questions have been exacerbated by conflicting interpretations of both the oral accounts and of Haywood's own written statements.

An important piece of the historical data has been mostly overlooked, as well, that of a news clip of Haywood and an article containing

106. *1900 U.S. Census*, Marion County, Indianapolis, IN, 12, confirms the address given twice in 1908 for Haywood in *The Apostolic Faith*. Tyson, *Before I Sleep*, 9. Golder, per the timing in February, sequences the events with Haywood's baptism preceding the arrest of Prentiss, and Barber's own brothers, who were with Prentiss at Allen Chapel and also arrested (Golder, *Haywood*, 4). Ben Haywood evidently died in the mid-1910s, not being listed in the 1917–18 WWI Registration records. "Anna" is widowed by the *1920 US Census*, Marion County, Indianapolis, IN, 13A. They were in Haywood's church "in their later years," Tyson, *Before I Sleep*, 9.

107. Haywood wrote the account in 1924, and it is reproduced, in slightly altered form, in both Golder, *Haywood*, 31–37 and Tyson, *Before I Sleep*, 16–18, 24; see also, Tyson, *Chalices*, 331.

108. "Bluks Invade Allen Chapel and Stop Sermon," 1; "Gliggy Bluks Are Fined"; Robeck, "Azusa Street Revival Timeline," 106; Martin, *Seymour*, 254. Other *Indianapolis Star* articles included "Gliggy Bluk Pleads Own Case and Pays 3 Fines," March 5, 1908, and "Invade the Bluks' Temple," April 25, 1908, 1. The *Indianapolis News* also carried the story: "For Disturbing Service," March 4, 1908, 7; "Tongues at Allen Chapel," April 24, 1908, 7.

his testimony, printed in the final two 1908 issues of *The Apostolic Faith*, during or after the split between Seymour and Crawford. The second, "Pentecost in Indianapolis," quotes an original written testimony sent by Haywood:

> A light shined about me and I fell to the floor, and when I tried to get up found that I was helpless. I could see no one . . . I tried to say, "What is it?" but could not, for the flow of Latin words which were readily recognized. It was no longer I that spoke, but the Spirit of God that was in me. Suddenly my speech was changed and German words flowed from my lips. I was wonderfully blest.[109]

The July issue reports: "At least 200 have received the baptism of the Holy Ghost in Indianapolis in the past year." The June news clip states that "several hundred have been baptized with the Holy Ghost, *now under the leadership of Brother Haywood*."[110] The conventional interpretation of the various Haywood statements has been that he worked for a year under Prentiss, who turned the church over to Haywood in February, then departed back east. Haywood's statements and the related data do not appear to support these assumptions. *The Apostolic Faith* announcement clarifies that Prentiss no longer led the mission in June 1908, but that Haywood had become pastor within four months of his Spirit infilling.

The record is also clear that Prentiss did not mentor in any way the ongoing developments of the congregation, or follow Haywood's rise to prominence, or emulate his entrance into either the PAW or the Oneness movement. If he left Indianapolis at this time, it was temporary. Thirteen years her senior, Prentiss married Josephine Woodring in Indianapolis June 2, 1908, a union which may have even precipitated the change in leadership at the mission. Nonetheless, Henry and Josie remained, or later returned, as Indianapolis residents in mid-1910.[111] Prentiss was still indi-

109. "Pentecost in Indianapolis," 4. See also Robeck, *Azusa Street Mission*, 284–87, for a discussion regarding the debate of the "authenticity" of these two issues. The debate is related to the authority and location of publication, not content.

110. "Indianapolis, Ind.," 1; italics added; cf., also, Robeck, "Haywood, Garfield Thomas," 693: "By the *end* of 1908 Henry Prentiss had turned the Indianapolis work over to Haywood," italics added.

111. Marion County, Indiana, *Index to Marriage Record 1906–1910*, County Clerks Office, Book 49, 261, at www.ancestry.com, "Indiana Marriage Collection, 1800–1941." *1910 U.S. Census*, Marion County, Indianapolis, IN, 3A. "Days Statistics: Births," *Indianapolis Star*, June 29, 1910, 12, "*Rev.* Henry and Josephine Prentiss," italics added. Whether they may have left on a missionary term has not been determined.

cating, at this point, that he was a "minister" and "missionary," living with her family on Douglas Street, just off Minerva. Their son Francis was born in Indianapolis, as well, in June 1910. Haywood, by this time, was already becoming prominent throughout Pentecostalism.

The scenario that best accounts for Prentiss' remaining in the city, yet having no involvement with Haywood's ministry, as well as for the conventional assumption of an eastern departure, is a separation. No hints as to a cause are mentioned, and Haywood, for that matter, never mentions Prentiss in his account. Yet Haywood's few comments and his actions are consistent with a separation characterization: "In February, 1909, with about thirteen Saints, we opened up *another* little Assembly in a vacant storeroom on the corner of Twelfth and Lafayette Streets."[112] Apparently, therefore, Prentiss intended to relinquish leadership of the mission to Haywood in June, as indicated in *The Apostolic Faith*, but, due either to his remaining in Indianapolis, or to a later return, Haywood willingly and quietly surrendered leadership of the W. Michigan and Minerva mission.

Haywood's 12th Street mission, then, was an additional mission, which Haywood had located a respectable distance away, a mile and a quarter North to Lafayette Street. This interpretation explains why he started over with thirteen, rather than the hundreds reported just nine months prior. When the church relocated again, in the fall of 1910, or, as Haywood points out, "a little more than a year" before the first convention in November 1911, it was only a few blocks west down 12th to Missouri St.

After the convention in 1911, they moved permanently into the Peniel Mission which they first rented at Senate Avenue and Eleventh Street. They later purchased the building and, in 1919, by adding a second level, enlarged the seating capacity to over a thousand, allowing the rapidly growing Apostolic Faith Assembly to remain at this location until the current "Christ Temple" was completed in 1924.[113]

Few early Pentecostal leaders experienced the level of ministerial success and influence that accompanied Haywood's rise to prominence, and, soon, his church became the dominant influence in Pentecostalism in Indianapolis. The rapid expansion of Haywood's church began late in 1911, with the popularity of his annual convention, the widening circulation of

112. Tyson, *Before I Sleep*, 16, italics added.

113. Ibid., 17, 24, with Haywood stating: "In November 1911, we moved from the little storefront on 12th and Missouri Streets with a little band of about 50 saints." "'Gliggy Bluk' Meeting Set," 7. Also, by 1910, Haywood had moved his family to Fayette St. and West St., not far from the church location, see *1920 U.S. Census*, Marion County, Indianapolis, IN, 4A.

*The Voice in the Wilderness,* his writings and music, his interracial and revival zeal, his acclaim as a Bible scholar and preacher, and the recognition of his extraordinary leadership abilities.

Eventually, too, there was an assimilation of saints from Prentiss' original work into the Eleventh Street work, but precisely what became of Prentiss' ministry is not known. By 1917 he was in Chicago, evidently not in ministry, and his wife was not listed as the "nearest relative." By 1920 the Prentisses disappeared from the records, and their nine year old son was living with her parents and family, who had relocated to Detroit.[114] Haywood's influence, though, continued unabated. As Wacker has noted in *Heaven Below*:

> Adherents undoubtedly received baptism and healing under Haywood's ministry, but those were not the gifts for which he was (and remains) most widely and proudly remembered. Instead, contemporaries and biographers emphasized his astonishing mastery of the King James text of the Bible, including his ability to fire biblical passages like bullets from a Gatling gun . . . Individuals who possessed or were perceived to possess exceptional learning, and who demonstrated an ability to integrate that learning with daily life, found honor among their fellow believers.[115]

## 3.8 Conclusion

The Haywood conversion was a most opportune event indeed for developing early Oneness Pentecostalism, love for memorizing the King James Bible, exceptional giftedness, and all, participating as he did in guiding the essential coalescing of theological and ecclesiological elements in the forging of a solidly viable movement. Although a mixture of Azusa Street influences, it dared to soar upon its own wings, chance the complete loss of the support of the broader movement, and nest itself in the heights of a new, radical vision of Pentecostalism.

114. *1918 WWI Registration Card,* "Henry Prentiss," "Local Board for Division #3," Chicago, 1645, listing the nearest relative as "Mrs. Shelton, 1720 South St., Philadelphia, Penn," suggesting a separation, or that Josie had passed away; *1920 U.S. Census,* Wayne County, Detroit, MI, 16B; see also, *1930 U.S. Census,* Wayne County, Detroit, MI, 2A.

115. Wacker, *Heaven Below*, 153.

In doing so the Oneness movement swept the flagship organizational body of Azusa Street, the PAW, into the vital flow of its theological and structural development, so that it served the needs of assimilating the diverse, but newly re-aligned elements of the tongues movement into an orderly unit. At the center of that order were the emphases of the theological, of experiential faith, of God's power, and of the reality of a tenacious racial equality. For the Oneness proponents their dream of Pentecost was viewed as the re-fulfillment of opportunities lost in translation and blurred in the failures of Azusa Street's experiences, but of which they were confident.

The Oneness element, therefore, was birthed within the developing Pentecostal dynamism, not in the least peripheral to the core of the broader movement's ethos and vitality. The early success of Jesus' Name, Apostolic Pentecostalism *is* the story of early Pentecostalism itself. Though determined to make their way, separating as a matter of inclination, whether for better or worse, they were, nonetheless, heirs to Azusa. From their perspective, nothing the Spirit was compelling them to do was incongruent with their shared envisioned restoration. Like Faupel says of the early AG, these were yearnings derived and inculcated from the broader context of restoration fervor, a faith steeped in the early Evangelical and Holiness milieu of countercultural religious life.[116]

116. Faupel, "Restoration Vision in Pentecostalism," 938–41, http://www.religion-online.org/showarticle.asp?title=818. The original article is a review of Edith Blumhofer's two-volume *The Assemblies of God: A Chapter in the Story of American Pentecostalism*, in which Faupel states, "Had Blumhofer used the restorationist framework to interpret the history of the denomination as she did its prehistory, the work would have been even more illuminating. For example, that the early leaders could denounce the church fathers as apostate one minute and then turn to embrace them the next in order to declare the 'oneness' view of the Godhead to be heresy, was quite remarkable indeed."

# 4

# The Frazee Era Emergence of Oneness Pentecostalism and The Transitional Pentecostal Assemblies of the World

The PAW historical trail, even the period of its early transitioning into Oneness Pentecostalism, has been extremely scant, with relatively little, if anything, known of either Hopkins or Frazee. Now, with the uncovering of the FBI records in this research, the near total obscurity of the Frazee era begins to yield to new light.[1] These documents have been the key to unlocking several important previously unknown aspects of the PAW story. Paddock's PAW history expresses this typical earlier obscurity: "Elder Frazee . . . served until he disappeared from the scene in 1918. We have no knowledge of what happened to him. We believe he died in the influenza epidemic of that time."[2]

J. J. Frazee did not disappear due to death in the 1918 pandemic. Frazee, though, disappeared totally from Oneness history amidst the tumultuous changes and political uncertainties which so thoroughly shook Pentecostalism during the movement's emergence. Even after the AG expulsion in late 1916, Oneness difficulties were far from resolved. With the controversy in the AG lost to the Oneness cause, the battle necessarily shifted to another front, a uniquely challenging battle within the PAW.

1. FBI Report #55234, Publ. M1085, "Investigative Case Files of the Bureau of Investigation 1908–1922." Records research expert R. S. Vaughn retrieved the FBI for the author March 2008. The Bureau of Investigation became the FBI in 1935.

2. Paddock, *Apostolic Heritage*, 47–48. Paddock (1907–1990), a white minister from Kalamazoo, Michigan, served as PAW Assistant Presiding Bishop (1953–1967) and Presiding Bishop (1967–1974).

## 4.1 The FBI Records—Shedding Light on the Frazee Era

The significance of the FBI documents to the understanding of J. J. Frazee and the pre-Oneness PAW can hardly be overstated. The agency, known at that time as the Bureau of Investigation, sealed more than one hundred pages of material regarding the PAW into the FBI Report #55234, the most important of which was the earlier discussed *1917 PAW Minute Book.*[3] An amazing wealth of data is also revealed within the context of the numerous draft exemption documents, letters to and from the war department, church infiltration and interview agent reports, and documents regarding the ministers in question.

The implications of this material, interpreted mostly in this chapter, require a thorough rethinking of the Frazee era, especially as it impacts four areas of major significance. The first, already discussed, is a contextual understanding of the PAW summary minutes, but the second is the light shed on J. J. Frazee himself. The intriguing unfolding of the events of the actual FBI probe, examined later in this chapter, highlights Frazee's role, as it does that of Haywood. The third, though, the invaluable evidence regarding the pre-Oneness, pre-1917 PAW ministry rosters, represents the most important and startling of them all. Finally, comparison of 1917 and 1919 data reveals the withdrawal of the PAW Trinitarian majority.

### 4.1.1 Initial Glimpses of Frazee in Light of the FBI Data

J. J. Frazee led the PAW during what must be recognized as the most dramatic time of transition imaginable for the fledgling organization, first, its transition to the Finished Work theology of Durham, then, the transition to Oneness Pentecostalism, away from its Trinitarian, yet diversely Pentecostal ministerial recent past. Neither of these, it is obvious, could have transpired at all without unique leadership from the top. Although the enigmatic whirl of 1918 events would serve to nearly erase Frazee's role, his decade of official PAW leadership (1908–1918) was crucial.

3. *Minute Book and Ministerial Record of Pentecostal Assemblies of the World*, Portland, Oregon, U.S.A., Year 1917–1918 (19 pp) in FBI Report #55234, Publ. M1085 (missing the 18th page or "S" section); The entire report has 108 pages with documents dating from June 1917 to August 1918. Pagination was assigned by the author to the FBI Publication #M1085 PDF file *as retrieved* for purposes of sequence, retrieval and citation.

The events of the period, as ascertained from primary source Oneness records available, had left behind a seemingly blank record of the emerging movement's first Oneness PAW leader—no liturgies, no periodical articles, no rebaptism accounts, no doctrinal insights, and certainly no explanation of his disappearance. Although Frank J. Ewart and J. J. Frazee were both working in close proximity, Los Angeles and Portland, Ewart's *Phenomenon of Pentecost,* the earliest historical account, does not even mention Frazee. W. E. Kidson served as Frazee's PAW/GAAA merger Secretary in 1918, yet he surprisingly recalled later that the head the PAW at the time was a "Frazier."[4] Fortunately, several of the documents of the FBI Report #55234 relate directly to Frazee, including an agent's interview report in Portland with Frazee and letters to and from Frazee regarding the PAW position on the war.

The 1917 ministerial rosters are the first glimpse back to the Frazee Era PAW, revealing a most enlightening portrait of the transitioning PAW. Slightly more than a decade after its founding, a majority of the PAW ministers continued to be from the west coast, a number of which were those most closely associated with Azusa. Ultimately, though, the vast majority of these pre-Oneness ministers would withdraw from the PAW, as did Frazee himself slightly later. What surfaces is a continuing enigmatic story in microcosm, a fracturing of Pentecostalism, a tenuous array of Oneness defenders and defectors, even at the height of the controversy, and a period best understood as that of the *transitional* Pentecostal Assemblies of the World.

### 4.1.2 Initial Gleanings from the FBI Report's 1917 PAW Minute Book

Even after nearly four years of resilient adaptation, neither Frazee nor the majority of ministers in the PAW were able, in 1918, to continue to successfully absorb tumult, and opted instead to simply withdraw amidst the transitional foment. The 1917 PAW, before the GAAA Oneness influx, had grown to 548 ministers under Frazee leadership, although, less than

4. W. E. Kidson was PCI Secretary, 1928–1943, see Kidson, *History of Pentecostal Organizations*, cited in *The Encyclopedia of American Religions*, 1:266–67; *MDS*, "Minutes," February 1918, 3, PAW/ GAAA merger minutes; Tyson, *Early Pentecostal Revival*, 289ff.; Paddock, *History*, 47; McClain, *Seek First the Kingdom*, 49; Anderson, *Disinherited*, 177.

one quarter of them were Oneness, appearing on no post-merger Oneness rosters.[5]

Several factors influence this interpretation of the rosters, especially the conclusion that the 1917 published information was probably the very first, prepared specifically in response to the FBI probe impacting PAW pacifist exemption.[6] The corroboration of this possibility may be the internal evidence of the minutes themselves. First of all, contrary to expectation, Frazee included no evidence of earlier minute books or an incorporation charter, only the summaries, with the *Minute Book*. Afterward, the FBI found the PAW to be "very loose" in its system of "organization."[7]

Also, the *Minute Book*, while listing current names, refers to page numbers which evidently coincide with a comprehensive list kept elsewhere. The *1919 PAW Minute Book*, for example, refers to this separate, single ledger, or handwritten roster as "the" Minute Book, but this is not an indication of earlier annual published minutes.[8] The PAW was so attentive to the publishing of an *updated* 1917 roster that the *1917 PAW Minute Book* had accurately removed the name of Pendleton, whose death had occurred in January, from the roster released to the FBI in June 1917.[9]

Internal evidence also demonstrates that the "Brief Record of Minutes," which Frazee attached to the 1917 minutes sent to the FBI, had not been published earlier in annual ministerial rosters. Indications that these summarizations were actually written in 1917 include the anachronism referencing Frazee himself, as being "of Portland," though speaking about 1908. This would have been an anachronism, indeed, since all the evidence, including the federal census, places him in Los Angeles, if he were not speaking retrospectively. This is even clearer in Frazee's use of the past

5. FBI File#55234, *1917 PAW Minute Book*, 34–44; The ordeal of FBI investigation of the PAW, therefore, paralleled the time of the merger efforts of the PAW/GAAA.

6. FBI File#55234, 14, 8, Haywood Letter to Frazee, January 22, 1917, lack of official records, via no "official letter heads" and an FBI request for "your minute books," 13.

7. FBI File #55324, 92.

8. FBI File #55324, 21; The evidence the PAW offered to validate its minister in question, by the name of Sherman, was that his name was "on Page 98" of "the Minute Book" in 1915, *not* the 1915–1916 Minute Book. For example, in the later *1919 PAW Minute Book*, at each letter of the alphabetical listings of ministers, the page is noted on which those minister's names appear in a separate "Minute Book," which uses a 10-page section for names for each letter of the alphabet; see Tyson, *Early Pentecostal Revival*, 301ff.

9. See *1900 U.S. Census*, Los Angeles, 22.

tense: "The purpose and desires *were and are still* that the Pentecostal Assemblies might be governed by the Word of God."[10]

On the one hand, the roster shows evidence of having been rushed in production, with, for example, a substantial number of names having no address and/or no designated city (69%), misspelled names, and a complete lack of alphabetized sequence, quite unlike later issues. The fact of no official PAW business having taken place 1912 may have contributed to a sense of urgency in the production of 1917 minutes, suggested as well by the obviously hasty January 1917 Portland meeting, at which not even the secretary, John Mautz, was present, and Portland-only "elders" were in attendance. The urgent need to respond to the FBI prevailed, and the January business was included, rather than that of the far more representative meeting held in St. Louis in March.[11]

## 4.2 Frazee Historical Sketch

Other than an initialized form of his name and his PAW titles, almost nothing else about his out-of-the-ordinary Oneness contribution remained in the dust of history, except that he had disappeared. In spite of the mergers and victories, changes and challenges taking place in the PAW at the time, Frazee's exit after a decade of leadership was an unexpected loss which necessitated yet another meeting and election in the fall of 1918.

But it is now evident that Frazee, 67 years of age when he left the PAW leadership, had been plagued with poor health much of his life. He died at age 79 in the Oregon State Hospital in 1930 where he been institutionalized for some years. His given name was actually Stephen Jacob Jackson Frazee, born January 29, 1851 in Leando, Iowa. His family farmed in this southeastern Iowa farming community along the Des Moines River's south bank.[12] Because he shared his name, Stephen J., in common with his father, Frazee soon came to use his middle initials, J. J., instead.

Tragically, at the young age of nine, as the result of a serious knee injury, caused from a bad fall from the hayloft, he became crippled for

10. FBI File#55234, 34–35, 33.

11. FBI File#55234, "Brief Minutes," 34; "To the Jew First," *MDS*, March 1917, 1. An early 1917 date and St. Louis location may have intentionally fostered contact with leadership of the recently organized GAAA.

12. *1860 U.S. Census*, Van Buren Township, Iowa, 287, "White," father and son both listed, "Stephen J."; elsewhere listed "Jacob J."; also, www.ancestry.com, "5 Generation Pedigree Chart, Jacob Jackson Frazee."

the rest of his life and was generally confined to a wheelchair. This fatiguing and limiting disability, no doubt, impacted his leadership in unique ways, both frustrating and challenging his best efforts, and, eventually, taking its toll emotionally and mentally.[13] Yet he exemplified enormous determination and fortitude at an early age, attending college, like his two sisters before him, and becoming not only a music school teacher, but an accomplished vocalist and a musician proficient with several instruments. He reported competing in the vocal competition at the 1876 Philadelphia World's Fair at the age of twenty five.[14]

Not marrying until the age of fifty, Frazee remained at home in Iowa, except for moving for a short while to La Junta, Colorado at the turn of the century.[15] Returning to the farm, due to his mother's failing health, in 1901, Frazee met Anna, daughter of neighbors William "Clarence" and Mary Brizendine, the young 18 year old who had been helping his mother during her illness. Despite the disparity between Louvisa Anna's age, who was born in 1883, and Frazee's, they were married in 1901. He was 32 years Anna's senior and older than both of her own parents. Three years later, by 1904, after the death of their first son in childbirth in 1902, followed by the death of his mother in late 1903, they relocated to Mesa, Arizona. By either late 1906 or early 1907, at the height of the Azusa revival, they had settled in the Los Angeles area.[16]

Their earliest association with the Azusa Street mission in Los Angeles is not known, but later they were certainly connected with Azusa Street by 1910 via a mission in or near Rialto. Frazee relocated his family to what is now the old downtown area of Rialto, probably as the new pastor.[17] In

13. "Tracking Down Rumors," 17 Mar 2009, by "truitti" family post, www.ancestry.com; *1880 U.S. Census*, Van Buren Co., Iowa, 22; An OSI archival photo from 1914 has him in a wheelchair at age 63; Census records list him "Maimed, Crippled, Bedridden, or Otherwise Disabled."

14. "Rumors," family post by "truitti," www.ancestry.com; Local city directories list Frazee as a music teacher, including Mount Zion, *Iowa State Gazetteer*, "Mount Zion Directory," 1884–1885, 1266, and the 1900, 1910, and 1920 U.S. Censuses.

15. *1900 U.S. Census*, Otero County, LaJunta, Colorado, 18, a "music teacher & real estate dealer." His father died in 1882.

16. Cf., Louvica "Anna" Brizendine, *1900 U.S. Census*, Burlington, Iowa, with the Tombstone, "Anna Smead," Woodland, CA, born "February 29, 1883"; see also, "Mama's Family" and "Our Family" by "truitti," www.ancestry.com; *1910 U.S. Census*, Rialto, California, 12.

17. Frazee himself gives the date of his ordination, March 22, 1908, in the FBI Hudson's Report, 2, also, FBI Record #55324, 7; *1910 U.S. Census*, Rialto, CA, 12; *1917 PAW Minute Book*, 19, 10.

any case he was not ordained until nearly sixty years of age. Nevertheless, he was probably commended to PAW Secretary on the basis of his exceptional education as a school teacher and because of his seasoned age of fifty seven.

Also, he, like Haywood, appears to have been an advocate of women preachers, serving as he did with Hopkins in her PAW leadership role for four years.[18] John and Elizabeth Rosa Mautz were Hungarian-born Germans who immigrated to Ohio in 1906, but moved to San Antonio, Los Angeles County shortly thereafter.[19] Mautz became PAW Secretary in 1912, and Frazee the Superintendent, although the Mautzes remained behind in California later in the year when the headquarters relocated to Portland, Oregon.[20]

## 4.3 The PAW Transition to Finished Work Theology

The first of the major transitional issues to rage within Pentecostal circles, especially impacting the PAW and the AG, was the doctrinal controversy raised by William Durham over sanctification which was known as the Finished Work debate. As the issue began to emerge in 1910, the PAW had expanded well beyond its Azusa Street origins, and the peaking of the controversy in 1912 coincided with Frazee's rise to key leadership.

18. Frazee's wife, Louvisa, was also an ordained minister. Haywood joined the PAW in 1911 during the Hopkins era of leadership. Also, 32 percent of the 1917 PAW ministers were women, twice that of the 1917 AG, see *1917 PAW Minute Book*, FBI Report #55234, 34; cf., *1917 General Council of the AG—Combined Minutes*, 27, with 15 percent; cf., Morse, "Woman's Place in the Body," 2.

19. *1920 U.S. Census*, San Antonio, CA, 3B, born c. 1876, German-speaking; Jacob and Jenny Mautz, also, both PAW ministers, and a younger brother, immigrated in 1903 and 1900, respectively; Unlike John, they remained with the PAW after the GAAA merger.

20. Frazee and Mautz remained in leadership from 1912 to 1918, the period of the emergence of the Oneness movement and the resulting transition of the PAW. Elsworth Davidson served briefly as "pro tem" secretary, merely for the January 1917 Portland meeting; *1920 U.S. Census*, "Asa E. Davidson," Portland, OR, 2B. Mautz may have simply been unable to attend, but he remained, nonetheless, on all official PAW correspondence letterhead sent to the government as late as 1918, see FBI File#55234, 34.

### 4.3.1 The PAW's 1912 Relocation to Portland, Oregon

A comprehension of a critical puzzle piece in the Frazee history depends upon an accurate interpretation of the timing of both Frazee's own Finished Work conversion and his Portland relocation. Prior to Frazee's leadership, but as late as 1911, and the time Haywood himself joined, Haywood says that the PAW "was still based in Los Angeles." His 1911 PAW affiliation is confirmed by his own statements in 1921 in *The Voice in the Wilderness.*[21] The headquarters was also still in Los Angeles at the time that Frazee assumed the leadership of the PAW in March of 1912.

In all probability, Frazee, then, continued in the Los Angeles area into the year 1912, since the PAW meetings and the election of Frazee were held there during this time as well. The minutes, though, for this period record no attempt to incorporate the PAW in Los Angeles. Clearly, too, the 1910 Census that confirms Frazee was still in Los Angeles, not Portland. Noted earlier, Frazee's own reference about his 1908 election, which says he was "of Portland," has been routinely misinterpreted to suggest he moved at this earlier date.[22]

It is true, though, that the Finished Work debate was a raging controversy in California by the time of the 1912 PAW elections. Evidence suggests that Frazee was clearly with Haywood on this issue, and that it may have influenced, or even motivated, his decision to relocate the PAW to Portland. It isn't known where Hopkins stood on these issues, but she did step down at the height of the controversy. In early 1912, Los Angeles and the diminishing Azusa Street revival were no longer the dominant center of the burgeoning tongues movement. As the divisive controversy widened across the country, Frazee relocated the Pentecostal Assemblies of the World to property at 773 Third Street, Portland, Oregon which served both as a residence and as the PAW headquarters.

Although it boasted a "big sign on the building," the 1917 investigative government report reveals that FBI Special Agent Hudson could not even imagine that this property was a valid headquarters for a church organization, describing it in August 1917 as "little more than a shack" in the "remote southern part of the city."[23] With the prospects of severed

21. See quote in Golder, *Haywood*, 53; Golder, *History*, 35.

22. "Brief Record of Minutes 1907–1917," *1917 PAW Minute Book*, 8. Peagler's suggestion that the PAW met in 1912 to "officially incorporate," Peagler, *Haywood*, 77–79, remains uncorroborated; *1917 PAW Minute Book*, 34; *1910 U.S. Census*, Rialto, CA, 12.

23. FBI File #55324, 81, Letter, Special Agent Byron, March 11, 1918; Special Agent Hudson, Report, August 8, 1917, 7–8.

ties with Azusa and the Finished Work ministry opportunities in Portland, Frazee decided to base the newly infiltrated PAW out of the more favorable Portland Pentecostal climate. It would remain, nevertheless, a mutual haven for both Azusa-like Holiness ministers and Finished Work advocates like Frazee, Ewart, and Haywood, all later Oneness partisans.

### 4.3.2 Initial Links between the Finished Work and Oneness Movements

The Pentecostal movement was ripped apart by Durham's Finished Work controversy which represented a rejection of the original Pentecostal Wesleyan- Holiness belief in sanctification.[24] In terms of its divisive success, though, it was a model for Oneness emulation in the introduction of the "new issue," except in its racially disappointing elements exemplified by both Durham and his theological heir, the AG. Durham, for example, after preaching at Azusa from February to May 1911, attempted to take over Seymour's Azusa Street mission while he was away. As Robeck has point out, the racial effrontery of this coup was thwarted only by the official board literally padlocking Durham out of the building on May 2, 1911.[25]

Durham's failure to take over Azusa forced him instead to start his own mission, which he promptly opened on Seventh Street. Frank Ewart, entirely committed to his new doctrine, immediately relocated to Los Angeles and subsequently served as Durham's assistant.[26] The Finished Work theology quickly emerged as the dominant view in Pentecostal circles, although Durham himself, at the height of the controversy, died suddenly of pneumonia on July 12, 1912.[27] The Pentecostal landscape had been altered completely, including a new alignment of ministers theologically in need of a separate organizational structure, the answer to which was the 1914 formation of the Assemblies of God.

The Finished Work and Oneness theological issues arose within the same context, just as Jesus-centered affection central to Oneness ideology derived from its unmistakable prevalence throughout early Pentecostalism. Early Oneness proponent R. E. McAlister, for example, before the emergence of an articulated Oneness theology, was thoroughly

24. Riss, "Finished Work Controversy," 638.

25. Robeck, *Azusa Street Mission*, 316–17; Martin, *Seymour*, 287–88.

26. Ewart, *Phenomenon*, 7, 74–75, 105.

27. Riss, "Finished Work Controversy," 638.

Christocentric even as he was transitioning into Finished Work theology. The 1911 theme for his periodical *The Good Report* was, "Everything in Jesus, and Jesus everything," which became the masthead motto in 1913. The transitional time span for such advocates, from Holiness, to Finished Work, to Oneness theology, was extremely short.

McAlister had left a ministry in Portland, on good terms with Florence Crawford, to deputize in the fall of 1910 for missionary funds for Egypt. Delayed indefinitely in Ottawa, Canada, he started *The Good Report,* with a 70,000 annual circulation.[28] Late in 1911 he and its editors had joined with Durham and aggressively promoting his Finished Work view.[29] McAlister published a strong defense of the doctrine in a "supplement" issue which he entitled "The Finished Work of Calvary."[30]

Ewart wrote in 1912: "The Apostolic Faith platform has been in the process of construction. The creeds have been slaughtered, doctrines have been rejected, and others have been added to the platform through much suffering and sacrifice."[31] In 1913 *The Good Report* was moved to Los Angeles, with McAlister and Ewart as editors. It spoke of Spirit baptism and Finished Work doctrine in common restorationist terms such as "greater light" and "the true Gospel," as they would do later in their Oneness advocacy. Argue, for example, wrote: "As these truths have been revealed one by one . . . Does it not appear that Luther, Wesley, Edwards, Cookman, Fox, Finney, and other good men did not have the full Gospel as we have it today?"[32]

Maria Woodworth-Etter had moved into the Finished Work camp by the time of the 1913 Arroyo Seco camp meeting in which the Jesus' Name issue erupted.[33] *The Good Report* and its array of editors and contributors already looked more like a "who's who" of the forthcoming Oneness movement. The disquiet of a new issue was, decidedly, nipping at the heels of the sanctification battle, overlapping its theological divisiveness

28. McAlister, "Apostolic Faith Movement," 4; *The Good Report* 1/6 (November 1, 1913) 1; *The Good Report* became *Meat in Due Season*, spring 1914.

29. McAlister, "A Good Report," 1, and "Portland, Oregon, Mission, Cor. Front and Burnside," 8.

30. McAlister, "The Finished Work of Calvary"; cf., *The Good Report* 1/3 (1912) plus the articles "Pentecostal Testimony," 8; "Our Publications," 16.

31. Ewart, "Defending Heresies," 12, and "Work on the Coast," 6.

32. McAlister, "Sanctification Is Not a Second Work of Grace," 2, and Argue, "At Evening Time It Shall Be Light," 6–7.

33. Robeck, *Azusa Street Mission*, 300; Wacker, *Heaven Below*, 79, 146; Warner, *Maria Woodworth-Etter*, 216–17.

and interfering with its aspirations for the newly imagined Assemblies of God.[34] The Finished Work network served to effectively bring together the central figures who would, in turn, initiate the Oneness controversy.

The PAW, in fact, absorbed the impact of the debate by finding its own innovative niche—a ministerial diversity representative of the divisions in the entire movement. The 1917 PAW rosters indicate that Holiness ministers remained with the transitioning PAW, even as the Finished Work ministers also joined, in spite of their differences. In 1914 the Oneness ministers would do the same, remaining in the PAW, in spite of differences, this time straining the organization's tolerance to the limit.

### 4.3.3 The Finished Work Debate in Portland, Oregon

The assumption that Frazee was originally drawn to Portland by an association with Florence Crawford's well-known ministry[35] is almost certainly unwarranted. Rather than Crawford's ministry, Frazee had already aligned himself with Finished Work ministry, indicated by his early connection to Will C. Trotter. One of Crawford's earliest supporters, Trotter had originally moved from Los Angeles to help Crawford. But by 1911, during a divisive visit to Portland by Durham himself, Trotter became a Finished Work champion. He immediately established his own mission just three blocks from Crawford's on Ankeny Street. By 1912 he had his own camp meeting, even joint meetings with Frazee, and Trotter evidently joined the PAW, though he is said to have been later "set aside by the organization." Instead, Trotter became a charter member of the AG. But in both the PAW and AG these ministries were in competition with Crawford.[36]

James Frey, one of Trotter's "most prominent workers," converted to the Oneness camp in the fall of 1917 in Kelso, near Portland, after notably strong "opposition." It was also during this time that the FBI was interviewing Trotter about Frazee and the PAW. He, obviously, did not respond favorably. The earlier PAW disaffection would certainly not have abated

34. See *The Good Report*, vol. 2 [sic], no. 1 (June 1, 1913), "Editorial Note," 2, and "Letter to Our Readers and Correspondence," 2, with Ewart noting his earlier paper, *The Apostolic Faith*.

35. Tyson, *Chalices*, 208.

36. Robeck, *Azusa Street Mission*, 299; Ewart, *Phenomenon*, 48; FBI File #55324, Hudson Report, 9, 13; Morgan, "Crawford," 10; "Portland Camp Meeting," 2. See also AG charter members, *General Council Minutes of the Assemblies of God*, 1914, 16, and "Brother Will Trotter," 1.

with the recent AG Oneness defeat or the PAW Oneness advancement.[37] Frazee, Trotter, and Crawford, though, represent identical courses of religious passion, yet three distinct theologies, pursuing churches from one to the other.[38] Similarly, Crawford's trustee, E. W. Doak, originally loyal to Azusa, then to Crawford, would later actually become the head of the PAW in this process of shifting allegiances.

## 4.4 Haywood's Earliest PAW Influence

The evidence now also points to a far more significant Haywood role in the earliest days of his PAW involvement than previous assumed. The Finished Work doctrine probably played a pivotal part in attracting him to the PAW in 1911, especially in its contrast to the AG regarding the interracial issue, and its inclusive stance on women in ministry. He immediately assumed an official role on the PAW Board of Field Representatives, having the notoriety of leading one of the largest congregations in Pentecostalism.

As early as 1912, Alexander A. Boddy, a British Anglican priest and editor of *Confidence*, while traveling through the United States, referred to the thirty two year old Haywood as "very devout" and as "a capable speaker." "At this Mission they do know God," he wrote admiringly, "and often have Baptisms in the Holy Spirit with the Signs following. The singing was just touching." After preaching in Haywood's church, "the largest Mission Hall" in Indianapolis, Boddy penned the remarkable observation: "It reminded one of the best days of the Welsh Revival."[39]

Frazee reported to the FBI, in the summary minutes, that the PAW had been conducting its annual meetings in Indianapolis since 1913, an obvious reference to Haywood's own convention. They were not, per se, official PAW conferences, but were some of the largest gatherings of PAW ministers anywhere. Flower reported in *The Christian Evangel* in 1913 that their "large tabernacle" at Eleventh Street and Senate Avenue seated a thousand, and, by 1916, Haywood's convention attendance exceeded that number.[40]

37. "Latter Rain Falling in Kelso," 1; cf. Scism, *Northwest Passage*, 23–26, 40. Frey, in Tulsa by 1919, converted under A. Pelliociotti and his sister Nona.

38. Cf., Robeck, *Azusa Street Mission*, 300.

39. Boddy, "Indianapolis," 17.

40. *1917 PAW Minute Book*, 8; Melton, "Haywood," 107; Haywood, "The Convention," 1; "Mid-Summer Pentecostal Convention," 8; Golder, *Haywood*, 36.

Frazee increasingly recognized Haywood's exceptional talents. An early 1917 FBI report, for example, suggested that Haywood appeared to be the one actually in charge of the PAW. It also drew attention to the fact that Haywood was Black.

> Elder G. T. Haywood, the man who wrote the letter to Provost General Crowder asking military exemption for Ministers of the Pentecostal Assemblies of the World, by the direction of Rev. J. J. Frazee, of this city, is a negro and resides at Indianapolis. A fair conclusion is that the Rev. Frazee is under the direction of Haywood and others who desire to secure military exemption for Ministers of the above faith . . . The Rev. Frazee is an old man in very poor circumstances and it is unlikely that he has much influence or authority in the above organization.[41]

## 4.5 Early Competitive Rivalry of the PAW & the AG Organizers

The divisive events in Portland involving Crawford, Finished Work advocates, and the PAW, were indicative of the issue raging across the country, and translated into a competitive element between the transitioning PAW and the newly forming AG. This element of competition arose at the dawn of the emergence of the Oneness movement and the changes which were sweeping the PAW into advocacy of the Jesus' Name issue.

### *4.5.1 The Issue of a PAW Charter & the AG Claim to Organizational Priority*

The historical question of the nature and timing of the PAW charter also highlights this competitive element between the AG and the PAW. A difficult question to resolve is the issue of *how*, or even if, the PAW was officially chartered before its 1919 Indiana incorporation charter. Certainly, early in 1914, Bell, Goss, and Pinson, worried about their prospects for the newly organizing AG, confronted what they viewed as a PAW competitive ploy, the report of a PAW charter.[42] Their response came in *Word*

41. FBI File #55324, Report of Special Employee Hudson, Portland, Oregon, in "Re: Pentecostal Assemblies of the Word, Anti-Conscription," August 8, 1917, 6–7.

42. Bell, "Bible Order Versus Fanaticism," 2–3; Goss and Pinson, "Important Notice About the General Assembly at Hot Springs," 2. In lieu of state, county, or local

*and Witness,* just weeks prior to the Arkansas AG formation conference. Although the question of the type of charter remains open, the correspondence referred to a "new charter," the timing of which was to demonstrate, at the very least, their competitive positioning.

This is not to be interpreted as a supposed reference to the PAW's origins, as though a mere announcement of its founding might, in and of itself, render the PAW a concern to AG aspirations.[43] They were concerned precisely because the PAW was already a uniquely positioned formidable rival, requiring a decisive response. Therefore, Bell and the others attempted to offset a PAW threat, first, in attacking its church-based headquarters model.

> I have before me as I write a paper with the incorporate seal upon it. This paper reads, "in connection with the Assembly at Portland." This charter, therefore, makes the Portland assembly HEADQUARTERS, and the letter head before me sets forth as the officers under this *new* charter Bro. Frazee as SUPERINTENDENT, brethren F. J. Ewart, R. E. McAlister, Eld. Haywood and others as the official FIELD MISSIONARIES under the new charter.[44]

The appropriateness of incorporating was not the issue, for as far as Bell was concerned "God's word is as clear as daylight on this subject." He had received credentials from Durham's chartered local assembly in 1909, and, Bell quipped, they "have never bit me yet." "More recently" than that, he states imprecisely, "the Pentecostal Assemblies of the World have been CHARTERED." "But as Bro. Haywood wisely said," Goss adds, "concerning their chartering the Pentecostal Assemblies of the World at Portland, Ore., that 'it is not organization, but *affiliation or association*.'"[45]

Bell's arguments, though, essentially ignored the significance of the PAW's prior origins and claimed rights of priority, if not superiority, for the AG. This was especially ludicrous in light of the many Blacks who were AG heirs theologically, yet disenfranchised as organizational heirs. Bell

---

official confirmation of either a Los Angeles or Portland charter, an answer remains inconclusive. The fact, though, that the Indianapolis relocation may have required a new Indiana charter does *not* imply that a previous charter did not exist.

43. Cf. Tyson, *Early Pentecostal Revival*, 195–97.

44. Bell, "Bible Order," 3; all-caps original, italics added; Goss quotes only Haywood, but Bell also mentions Frazee regarding a charter, making this the only known reference to him outside the scant Oneness sources.

45. Goss and Pinson, "Important Notice," 2, caps and italics original; cf., discussion of chartering, *1918 PAW Minutes* in *Meat in Due Season*, February 1918, 1.

obstinately, yet revealingly, implies for the PAW to somehow get out of the way of the AG: "Come and cast your lot in with us and let us cast ours with you. Could anything be fairer?" When Bell stated, "You brethren *out there* gave us no chance to join with you," the emphasis is regional control. "We are not after getting control of other parts of the country." "We merely ask all parts of the country to COOPERATE TOGETHER IN THE LORD." That is, in spite of the consequences for its Black ministers, they were to relinquish their position historically in surrender to the AG. They had no right, in Bell's view, without previous "notice," to dare use a name like Pentecostal Assemblies of the World. "We did not get in a corner and set up something with a big name."[46]

## 4.5.2 The Racial Component in the Pre-Oneness PAW/AG Competitiveness

The Finished Work AG landscape was in the process, though, of enormous change, with the Oneness controversy just beneath the surface during this 1913 to1914 time frame. Goss, pastor in Hot Springs, Arkansas, site of the 1914 AG formation conference, Opperman, Bible school director and host of Woodworth-Etter's 1913 Hot Springs meeting, officials H. G. Rodgers, B. F. Lawrence, and E. N. Bell, and Bible school director R. B. Chisolm, were all AG organizers soon swept into the Oneness controversy.[47]

The more subtle issue in the competitive AG resistance to the PAW was the less obvious issue of race and interracial credentialing, already common in the Azusa-influenced PAW. Newman, in his book *Race and the Assemblies of God Church,* sees the AG stance as signaling "the demise of racial integration" in Pentecostalism.[48] The AG was even buttressed against the inclusion of its own Black Finished Work ministers and churches. Haywood knew its attitude of exclusion as well as anyone, joining instead a competitive body to the lily White AG, the PAW. The same ominous racial posture was evident in their earlier rejection of Mason's COGIC credentialing, expanded markedly, though, in their unwillingness to credential Blacks, even if merely to emulate or reciprocate previous

46. Bell, "Bible Order," 3.

47. Blumhofer, *Restoring the Faith,* 117, 120.

48. Newman, *Race and the Assemblies of God Church,* 9.

courtesy.[49] The strong AG element worried about the increasing numbers of Finished Work Blacks was, simply, a Whites-only AG invitation.[50]

As noted earlier, J. R. Flower, impacted by the interracial furor of the Indianapolis revival, resisted a racially open AG ministerial body.[51] His own pre-AG organizational effort in Indiana in 1913 unashamedly excluded Blacks in its formation, although Haywood was an invited speaker, not a participant.[52] With Flower playing a dominant role in the AG formation, Haywood was very much aware of the AG challenges facing Blacks, and he was quite emphatic that he had *never* joined himself. Whether to assure it was never a forgotten reality, or to imply that he had ever had the personal open option, Haywood opposed anti-interracial organization to the end.[53]

## 4.6 Arroyo Seco—1913 Emergence of Oneness Pentecostalism

The PAW had settled its commitment to interracial ministry from its inception, but the new issue which shook it and the rest of the movement to its foundations was that of baptism in Jesus' Name and the Oneness of God. These dual doctrines central to Oneness Pentecostalism began to first emerge at a landmark Maria Woodworth-Etter camp meeting in the Arroyo Seco area, near Pasadena, California, April 1913. Organized by R. J. Scott, this had also been the site of Seymour's first camp meeting in 1907, only now Finished Work leaders did not so much as invite him to the platform when he attended.[54] "We believe," Etter wrote, "it was the largest gathering of saints in the last days." Haywood was among the

49. Cf. Rodger, "The Assemblies of God and the Long Journey toward Racial Reconciliation," 53; cf., the 1917 AG, 15 percent west, 15.5 percent north, 11.3 percent east, 42.9 percent south, *1917 Combined Minutes of the General Council of the Assemblies of God*, 27ff.

50. Faupel, *Everlasting Gospel*, 257 n. 127, 303; Anderson, *Introduction*, 47; Bell, "Bible Order," 3.

51. Cf., *The Pentecost*, January-February 1909, 10; Alexander, *Women of Azusa*, 65.

52. Bundy, "Urban Realities," 247; Flower, "A Closer and Deeper Fellowship," 1; see Boddy, "Indianapolis."

53. Cf., Bundy, "Urban Realities," 248; Anderson, *Introduction*, 53; Golder, *History*, 36; Reed, *"In Jesus' Name,"* 208.

54. Borlase, *Seymour*, 223–24; Nelson, "For Such a Time," 254; Sanders, *Seymour*, 121; Alexandria, *Women of Azusa*, 174–75.

throng.[55] Miracles were reportedly in abundance. George B. Studd, for example, who "looked like a dead man" from "sciatic rheumatism," was healed instantly under the "gigantic" tent, with its "crude, unfinished, pine platform."[56]

During the course of the Arroyo Seco camp meeting, the Jesus' Name controversy emerged for the first time as the result of a baptismal sermon preached in the "vast arena" by McAlister. The Apostolic formula, McAlister asserted, was "in the name of Jesus Christ," rather than the titles of Mt 28:19, which were "never used in Christian baptism." Though many were immediately stirred, Ewart, Haywood, McAlister, and others, committed themselves over the next several months to delve into its Scriptural meaning.[57] Varied accounts report, though, that even during the camp some were rebaptized, either in a nearby creek or somewhere on the coast.[58]

Ewart suggested that the truly significant work of the Spirit at the Arroyo Seco camp included the powerful idea of a "new message" and "New Thing" which "struck fire" in their minds.[59] The interpretation of an Arroyo Seco prophecy given by China missionary Homer Faulkner, later published in Ewart's *Meat in Due Season*, signaled the Spirit's endorsement of Acts 2:38 baptism: "It is a *new thing* the Lord wants to do on the earth. Gather them in, and do not fail to preach the gospel the way Peter preached it."[60]

## 4.6.1 Earliest Successes of the Movement's Rebaptism Campaigns

Arroyo Seco emerged as the movement's shot heard round the world, the pivotal point of no return theologically. Ewart and Cook, long time PAW members, intentionally launched a campaign of rebaptisms in April 1914,

55. Woodworth-Etter, *Sign and Wonders*, 172–75, 253; Warner, "Maria B. Woodworth-Etter" 212; cf., Warner, *Maria Woodworth-Etter*, 155, 182, 186.

56. Riss, *Revival Movements*, 88–89.

57. Ewart, *Phenomenon*, 76–77. Reports of the camp in *The Good Report* made no reference to the Jesus' Name controversy, "Los Angeles Camp Meeting," 1, and "Missionary Offering at Los Angeles," 1.

58. Robeck, *Azusa Street Mission*, 318; Winehouse, *The Assemblies of God*, 44.

59. Ewart, *Phenomenon*, 76, 34; Warner, *Maria Woodworth-Etter*, 186; Woodworth-Etter later called the Oneness issue "the biggest delusion the devil ever invented," see idem, 196–97.

60. "Remarkable Prophecy," 4, italics added; cf., Blumhofer, *Restoring the Faith*, 130.

the exact time of the AG formation meetings. Earlier, in November 1913, Frank Small had baptized in Jesus' Name in Winnipeg, but not rebaptized, and some, like Haywood, had opportunity to interact with the principle initiators of the new issue.[61]

Cook was the first to be rebaptized, April 15, 1914, followed by Ewart, in Belvidere, California, accompanied by a wave of theological articles defending rebaptism, the Oneness of God, and the idea of revelation. Cook, for example, readily emphasized that the issue was "a revelation," or the Word of God revealing to, and the lifting of the veil from, their eyes to see Jesus and understand the simple truth about Him.[62] As crucial as it was for sympathetic leaders to be convinced of its theological legitimacy, strong rejection and opposition ensued, with Haywood even initially fighting it. In the months previous he had expressed his concern over the claims made for revelation.

> They trusted in their experience rather than in the work of Christ on the cross of Calvary, and the word of the living God . . . Moreover, some have become visionary and are being led by *revelations*, but this is leading into delusions that will work havoc in the ranks of the children of God except more heed is given to the word of God.[63]

Paddock suggests that Haywood thought that the Oneness message was "of the devil," until, as Ewart states, he was "convinced" otherwise. It is unclear, though, whether Ewart's depiction is suggesting that Haywood fought it with pen and voice, or merely in private discussion or perhaps only inwardly.[64]

The movement rapidly swept up the west coast, especially among PAW leaders early in 1915, including Cook, Ewart, Morse, Farrow, Studd, and probably Frazee, then into the Midwest and South.[65] Throughout 1915, much to the influence of Roberts and Haywood, Bartleman, Booth-Clibborn, Hall, Bell, Rodgers, Goss, Opperman, McAlister, and Small were all rebaptized, as well as LaFleur, Shearer, Fauss, and all the Louisiana

61. Foster, *Think It Not Strange*, 60, 52; "The Winnipeg Convention," 2; cf., Ewart, "The New Birth," 2, Cook, "Standards of Justification," 2, and Ewart, "Compromise," in *The Good Report*.

62. Cook, "A Revelation," 3, italics added.

63. Ewart, *Phenomenon*, 53; Haywood, "The Word of God," 1.

64. Paddock, *Apostolic Heritage*, 40–41; cf., Owens, *The Azusa Street Revival*, 108.

65. Ewart's account of the 1915 Portland revival does not mention Frazee, see *Meat in Due Season* 1/7 (September 1915) 1.

contingency, following Floyd and Smith's lead.[66] As increasing numbers of AG ministers embraced the Oneness movement by 1916, even more than had joined the PAW at this point, the necessity of eradicating its influence became the top AG priority.

### 4.6.2 The Impact of the Rebaptism of G. T. Haywood

With the momentum of rebaptisms building in California, Cook left for a tour of the Midwest, his home region, in January 1915, and several were rebaptized in St. Louis, including Mother Moise, whose home Bell had been using as a temporary headquarters for the new Assemblies of God.[67] In Indianapolis by late February, Cook reported: "Practically all the saints in the city came together and such a spirit of unity had not been known since the first outpouring of the Spirit."[68] Flower, who knew Cook well, tried to send Haywood a warning of Cook's intentions, probably unaware of his frequent interaction with the principle proponents, but the message was received too late.

Haywood, instead of heeding the warning, opened his church to Cook. Ewart, and Cook, and the impact of *Meat in Due Season,* had been influential in persuading him. Cook was highly respected for his role in the early Indianapolis revival, and Haywood determined to hear him out at Roberts' Oak Hill Tabernacle on Roosevelt Avenue, ten blocks north and due east four miles of his own assembly. Roberts, and his assistant, Homer White, and the Oak Tabernacle congregation were the first to be baptized in Jesus' Name east of the Mississippi, March 6, 1915, with Cook baptizing first Roberts and then White.[69] God, according to Haywood, had already been dealing with him. As Golder has noted, at some point in his search, "while he was riding the streetcar one day, the voice of God spoke to him and said, 'Walk in the light, lest a greater darkness come upon you.'"[70] White also confirms that Haywood did not respond imme-

66. Cook, "Eastern Trip," 2, and Morse, "Our Trip Down the Coast," 2; *Meat in Due Season* 1/9 (December 1915) 1–4; Floyd Interview, 47–53; Foster, *Think It Not Strange*, 61, 56.

67. Hall, "'New Issue'—Oneness Pentecostalism," 14, 15, 16; Cook was again at Moise's in May, meeting with Flower and Bell.

68. Cook, "An Eastern Trip," 2.

69. Ewart, *Phenomenon*, 53–54, 56; Homer White, Roberts' assistant, was the second baptized, Tyson, *Before I Sleep*, 47.

70. Golder, from the foreword in Garrett, *Ahead of His Times*, 18.

diately, but waited several days before requesting to be baptized. Cook's preaching is also said to have played the major role in convincing both Haywood and Roberts of the message's divine urgency. Once he believed he had heard from God, and submitted to baptism, White says that it absolutely "electrified the saints of God."[71] Mid-March Glenn Cook baptized Haywood, along with several of his leaders, including Hilda Reeder, at Oak Hill Tabernacle. The remainder of Haywood's church was baptized on Easter Sunday, April 4, 1915.[72]

Three of the largest of these baptisms were captured on camera, the first being that of Cook baptizing Roberts in Eagle Creek, with about 100 White church members. Haywood's church baptisms were divided by race, most likely to avert the threat of public reprisals, with Fall Creek the location, a section running through a portion of the downtown. The first shows Haywood in the water with a baptismal candidate, with a minister, probably S. R. Hancock, and about 150 Black church members. In the second, it appears that Cook is baptizing about 100 of Haywood's White members.[73]

"During the meeting," Cook reported ecstatically, a few weeks later, "465 were baptized by Bro. Roberts, Bro. Haywood and the writer, and since then about 100 more have been baptized in this way."[74] This account is consistent with Robert's immediate acceptance, Haywood's delay, and the hundreds of rebaptized saints which followed. By summer's end Roberts reported that "as many as seventy-one people were seeking the Lord at one time" in the spring meeting and that up through August 1915 "we have baptized 833."[75]

News of the baptisms sent shock waves throughout the movement and stunned the Assemblies of God. Seymour evidenced the disappointment of the news, and, reportedly, several Azusa members followed Haywood in rebaptism.[76] Seymour's 1915 handbook, *The Doctrines and Discipline,* included this statement under "Sound Doctrine: "We don't believe in being baptized in the name of Jesus only."

71. Wallace, *Profiles*, 373.

72. *Historical News* 10/3 (April-June 1991) 4; Tyson, *Early Pentecostal Revival*, 212.

73. Tyson, *Chalices*, 209; Garrett, *Haywood*, 58.

74. Cook, "Eastern Trip," 2.

75. S. N. Hancock and T. C. Davis were also baptized, see Cook, "The Truth About E. N. Bell," 3; Roberts, "Pentecostal Campaign at Indianapolis, Ind.," 4.

76. Sanders, *Seymour*, 121; Sanders suggests, as a "Final Blow," that the majority of Seymour's members abandoned Azusa to embrace the Oneness message (119).

> We want all of our White brethren and White sisters to feel free in our churches and Missions, in spite of all the trouble we have had with some of our White brethren in causing diversion, and spreading wild fire and fanaticism. Some of our colored brethren caught the disease of this spirit of division also.[77]

As the Azusa Street mission closed its chapter on the continued hope of interracial Pentecostalism, Haywood stepped into a movement, as of yet, very optimistic of racial aspirations, in spite of the closing doors to racial justice in the AG.

Immediately after the 1916 AG expulsion of Oneness ministers, Haywood and Lawson were invited by Mason to speak with COGIC ministers "present from all over the South," but to little avail. "It was not our purpose to argue," Haywood wrote.[78] Mason was unimpressed with what he called the "One in the Godhead People," objecting to an assertion of Lawson that Jesus was, supposedly, "no longer the Son of God." "He is not the Father of God but the Son of God," he said publicly, "nor is he his own father, for no son has ever begotten himself."[79]

## 4.7 The AG Showdown & Ministerial Expulsion

In the battle for the Assemblies of the God the final straw, after the distressing news of Haywood and Roberts, came two months later with the rebaptism of their own chairman E. N. Bell in Jackson, Tennessee in July 1915.[80] Although Bell was already backing away from the movement even before fall, in the whirl of confusion and uncertainty whirling about this dramatic event, the damage could hardly be undone. Bell's rebaptism, in and of itself, regardless of protests to the contrary, had been taken as a

77. *The Doctrines and Discipline*, as excerpted in Jacobsen, *Reader in Pentecostal Theology*, 53; cf., Haywood's eulogy of Seymour, "Death of W. J. Seymour," 7; Martin, *Seymour*, 330–31; Tinney, "Significance of Race," 60 n. 19, based on an interview with Franklin Showell, Baltimore, MD, November 11, 1978, suggests Seymour and Haywood remained friends.

78. "Memphis, Tenn.," *VW*, 1.

79. Jacobsen, *Reader in Pentecostal Theology*, 219, 221, 21, citing Mason's "The Sonship of Jesus"; Mason later refers to Lawson comments at a COGIC conference in St. Louis, which is assumed here to be the same meeting to which Haywood is referring.

80. See appendix E: "High Profile Rejection and Defection Impacting Early Oneness Pentecostalism," in French, "Early Interracial Oneness Pentecostalism," 350ff.; also Roberts, "Bro. E. N. Bell Is Baptized," 4; Reed, *"In Jesus' Name,"* 147–66.

complete endorsement.[81] Published repudiations of the movement by Bell, of course, helped immensely to assure an AG Trinitarian victory against the Oneness gains.[82] But the AG could not afford another such traumatic setback.

The inevitable showdown came at the AG General Council meeting in St. Louis in October 1916. The drastic measures enacted nullified a 1915 AG General Council meeting agreement which had allowed the use of either baptismal formula. The proverbial handwriting was on the wall and a strongly worded Trinitarian "Statement of Fundamental Truths" was passed, expelling 26.7% of their own ministry.[83] Their exit, October 7, 1916, meant that 156 of the 585 ministers of the 1916 Assemblies of God walked out, 77 of which had been part of the 531 original AG charter members.[84]

Many of the non-AG ministers, Black and White, were present, including Haywood, who could not have felt the AG betrayal more keenly. But, as noted previously, Leonard, who knew Haywood well, even interjected race into this final divisive episode.[85]

> At one point, T. K. Leonard *facetiously* referred to the "Oneness" doctrine of G. T. Haywood and his colleagues as "hay, wood and stubble," with the further remark, "they are all in the wilderness and they have a voice in the wilderness," (referring to the periodical published by Brother Haywood entitled a *Voice in the Wilderness*). Haywood turned pale and started to rise to his feet, but was pulled back into his chair by those sitting near him . . . Gilbert Sweaza, red-faced and indignant, stomped out the door. Voices from both sides were raised in protest, and it was some minutes before things quieted down.[86]

Leonard clearly managed to stun both sides of the aisle in a confrontation many have interpreted as an attempt to either ridicule Oneness

81. "A Pentecostal Convention in Los Angeles," 4; Bell, "Meat in Due Season Corrected," 2; Reed, *"In Jesus' Name,"* 151 n. 25.

82. See, for example, Bell, "Bro. Bell on the Trinity," 1; "The Great Controversy and Confusion," 6–7; Ewart, *Phenomenon*, 55.

83. Blumhofer, *Restoring the Faith*, 132–33; *Minutes of the General Council of the Assemblies of God*, October 1–10, 1915, 5; *Minutes of the General Council of the Assemblies of God*, October 1–7, 1916, 10.

84. *1914 Combined Minutes of the General Council of the AG*, 13–16; Reed, *"In Jesus' Name,"* 164.

85. Wallace, "Homer White," 2:372.

86. Brumback, *Like A River*, 58; italics added.

acceptance of Black leadership, or to demean Oneness theology on the basis of its acceptance by Blacks, or both. But it represented for Blacks a double rejection, as a Oneness minister *and* as a Black minister.[87]

Anderson suggests that the "Oneness movement fell far short of early expectations, or fears, that it might sweep the bulk of Pentecostals into its fold."[88] He also suspects that the movement represented the ultra-poor of the Pentecostal disinherited, but confirms the Midwest as the "real center of their strength."[89] By 1917 there were 142 Oneness minister with the PAW and 154 with the GAAA. The reluctance of the GAAA ministers to join the PAW, reflected the reality of the PAW's theologically diverse ministerial body and the determination not to have a repeat of their AG experience of majority opposition.[90]

## 4.8 THE 1917 TRANSITIONAL PAW'S TRINITARIAN MAJORITY

The earliest extant PAW ministerial documents are from *1917 Minute Book and Ministerial Record of the Pentecostal Assemblies of the World*, in the FBI Report #55234. Analysis reveals that, at the height of the early AG-Oneness controversy, the PAW had grown to within 11% of the size the fully Trinitarian AG by 1917, 548 PAW ministers compared to 693 AG ministers.[91] Many of these ministers had original ties to Azusa, and thirty two percent were women. Astonishingly, only 98 (18%) of these ministers went the distance and joined the merged-PAW in 1918, although at least 190 (31%) were Oneness, compared to the sixty nine percent that had remained Trinitarian.[92] Uniquely, the PAW leadership had become Oneness, while the majority of the ministers remained Trinitarian.[93]

The west was the dominant region (with fifty six percent of the ministers), California (38%) and Oregon (9%) being the largest states,

87. Cf., also, Brumback, *Like A River*, 58.

88. Anderson, *Disinherited*, 185.

89. Ibid., 187, 188; cf., Butler, *Oneness Pentecostalism*, 77.

90. Even the AG reported the formation of the GAAA, see "New Pentecostal Organization," *Weekly Evangel*, 15.

91. FBI File #55324, 28ff, *1917 PAW Minute Book*, 8–19; *Combined Minutes of the General Council of the Assemblies of God*, 1917, "List of Ordained Ministers," 27.

92. Comparative Analysis: *1917 PAW Minute Book* and *1919 PAW Minute Book*.

93. FBI File#55234, 29; Of the nineteen Field Superintendents only W. H. Aston, W. R. Farris, and H. M. Turney were not Oneness.

followed by Indiana (6%). The pre-merger PAW was approximately ninety percent White, partially substantiating Anderson's conclusion that it was "a fully integrated fellowship at every level," and "especially so after 1917." Although neither of the top PAW officials were African American, two of the fourteen officers were, G. T. Haywood and R. C. Lawson.[94]

## 4.9 The FBI's 1917 Investigation of the PAW

Intolerance and censorship of pacifism ran high during World War 1, with the Bureau of Investigation (now the FBI) investigating over a million people, organizations (such as COGIC), and publications. What had not been previously known was that the FBI had launched an investigation of the PAW, a probe which was initiated almost immediately after the Conscription Act of May 1917.[95]

### 4.9.1 Insights into Frazee-Haywood History from the FBI Report

Frazee signed the critically important registration letter for verification of PAW exemption, June 22, 1917, to the Provost General, "requesting that Ministers and Members" of the PAW "be given due recognition before any exemption board." But Frazee readily admitted that it was actually Haywood who had written the letter.[96] The FBI questioned the Frazee signature in August 1917 due to "per GTH" appearing beneath it. Clearly, Haywood, rather than PAW Secretary, Mautz, had assisted Frazee in the registration and investigation requirements. A Haywood letter prompted the FBI response that "they (the PAW) seem to be well advised," referring to Haywood's keen use of National Bill H. R. 3545, Section 4, 65th Congress.[97]

Doubts regarding the PAW's validity arose immediately when agents reported on Frazee's "*very poor* circumstances" and Portland residence which appeared to be "little more than a shack." In August 1917 an agent

94. Anderson, *Disinherited*, 191; FBI File#55234, 19.

95. Alexander, *Peace to War*, 36, 38, 41, 74, 132; cf. Wacker, *Heaven Below*, 243, 245, 347.

96. B. L. Fitzpatrick, a White minister from Haywood's church, served for the duration of the war; see Fitzpatrick, "From the Battlefield," 1; cf., Wacker, *Heaven Below*, 78.

97. FBI File#55234, Hudson Report 8–1917, 7–9, Byron Report 3–1918, 81–82.

reported being incredulous regarding Frazee's own position, being, as it appeared to him, without status, and "an old man" with little "authority." "Frazee is at present confined to his bed with a broken leg."[98]

In November a War Department memo to the Department of Justice suggested that the PAW may be merely an "alleged religious organization," comprised of assemblies "which apparently are following the policy of ordaining many new ministers in order to enable such persons to evade the provisions of the Selective Service Law."[99]

### 4.9.2 Historical Highlights of the 1917 FBI Investigation

In addition to the PAW pacifist stance, several other things, mostly misconceptions and actual errors, led to the FBI's initial concerns, including two ministers in question, Homer J. Sherman and J. W. Hitch, the PAW policy of regularly surrendering credentials for replacement, which, for Sherman, occurred in conjunction with his conscription, and the Bureau's confusion of an anti-government journal by William J. Robinson, *A Voice in the Wilderness,* which had been banned, with Haywood's monthly periodical.[100] Sherman, an El Paso, Texas pastor, had been wrongfully conscripted and incarcerated, as had one of his local ministers, J. W. Hitch, prompting a PAW petition for immediate discharge on the grounds of religious exemption.[101]

In March 1918, two spies, unknown to each other, were assigned to spy on the El Paso church, but found "nothing actionable." They were, though, ordered to "join" the assembly, which required being "baptized into the 'faith.'" Instead of finding verification of anti-government activity, it was reported that the pastor, Mrs. Tinguely, had "opened the Bible and read in it some place where it says that we are to work with the Government and help them in every way . . . and not to lead them away from their duty as they see it."[102]

98. FBI File#55234, Hudson Report, 7, 9, 14; italics added.

99. FBI File#55234, 4, 91–92.

100. FBI File#55234, 5–6, 37–70; Sherman's induction, probably in October 1917, coincided with the FBI's already ongoing investigation.

101. FBI File#55234, 4, 91–92, 18; By February 1918 Sherman was in "confinement for disobedience of orders," "disloyal statements against the government," and "preaching to other men and advising them not to obey any military orders whatsoever."

102. FBI File#55234, 98, 96.

The agents, in order to quickly gain necessary confidence and access, had to infiltrate the altars as seekers. They were quite descriptive of their experiences.

> They do speak with other tongues at the meetings, and some twist under the Power of God. I have seen this with my own eyes, so I know it is true, and the Power of God is very strong in all these members of Pentecostal (sic) . . . I went forward, and they tried to pray me thru to God and all they didn't try to do is not worth talking about, but somehow I came out O.K.
>
> Mrs. Tinguely and another woman tried to preach but were constantly interrupted by other members, who would suddenly jump out of their seats, swing their arms, do a hop scotch and scream. Once, when several of them were howling, Mrs. Tinguely jumped on to the platform, uttered several blood curdling war-whoops, then she pulled off a "Tinguely Tango" that would make Ruth St. Dennis ashamed to show her face.
>
> As soon as they were through howling over me, I tried to corner Mrs. Tinguely for a little chat, but she was so enraptured that she could only howl and jabber in the unknown tongue (which sounds very much like Arabic). One young fellow was laid out on the floor, and it took a lot of "hokus pokus" work to call his spirit back to earth. As soon as he came out of the trance, everyone went home.[103]

Sherman's military conscription had, in fact, been in error, having been credentialed with the PAW since 1915, but the Bureau had difficulty navigating the PAW's non-conformist, counter-cultural practices.[104] Nevertheless, by January 1918 Haywood could report to the newly merged PAW/GAAA "definite information . . . that all ministers are exempt from draft for military service."[105]

## 4.10 Conclusion

The PAW Frazee era, coming to near conclusion with its uniquely intriguing 1917 ministerial constituency and Trinitarian majority, positioned the movement for one of its most significant transitions of all, amalgamation into a fully Oneness interracial organization. Indeed, it had transitioned to

103. FBI File#55234, 101–3; see also, "El Paso, Texas, Mrs. Tinguly," 1.

104. FBI File#55234, 92, 86, 25, 18; Sherman, "Report from El Paso, Texas," 1; Dutcher, "El Paso, Texas," 2.

105. "Minutes," *1918 PAW Minutes, MDS*, 2.

Finished Work, then to Oneness ideology, and, as the Trinitarian majority willing withdrew, the historic PAW would transition yet again, to a Oneness-envisioned Pentecostalism in the PAW/GAAA merger in 1918.

Just at the close of the FBI probe and Frazee's sudden departure from the forward momentum of the movement, as the dust was clearing, the all-Oneness PAW emerged from Arroyo Seco's spark and the AG racial and theological battles as a viable interracial Pentecostal alternative on the landscape of American Pentecostalism.

# 5

# The Interracial Doak-Haywood Golden Era of Oneness Pentecostalism

The Oneness restorative impetus, paradoxically, served to divide them out from the AG due to an emphasis on revelation, but that commitment to divinely restored directive served, on the other hand, as the basis to unite them racially to the AG dispossessed, its Black heirs. "In a very real sense," as Blumhofer suggests, "those who accepted the revelations and consequent new teaching were *more thoroughly* Pentecostal than those who did not."[1] By 1918 Oneness horizons had broadened substantially since Arroyo Seco, and the movement was poised for the achievement of a viable Pentecost capable of incorporating integrated worship, structure, and leadership. A decade of transitional survival is adequate evidence that these were truly meaningful PAW aspirations and not merely naïve.

It is certainly possible that the PAW Trinitarian majority had willingly been dormant up to this time, patiently awaiting an outcome of the battles within the AG, at least until they might ascertain a verdict as to a Oneness PAW. They did, of course, finally abandon ship in 1918, Frazee himself enigmatically following their lead sometime after the merger of the PAW/ GAAA. Nevertheless, despite the setbacks, the merged, new PAW in 1918 was far larger than the combination of the two merging organizations. A relatively small number of ministers, PAW (89) and GAAA (154), initially joined the 1918 merger, yet, by the time of Haywood's election as Secretary, and the fully interracial Doak era of PAW leadership, the 1919 new-PAW (704) ministerial list was 65% larger.

1. Blumhofer, "Pentecostal Assemblies of the World," 884; Blumhofer, *The Assemblies of God*, 1:15, 1:237–38.

## 5.1 Formation of the GAAA by the AG Oneness Ministers

Many of the exiting AG White ministers may have prioritized the Oneness battle within the organization, perhaps hoping to initiate racial changes if they could secure an AG victory. The failure of that eventuality necessitated an immediate new course of action, resulting in the formation of the General Assembly of Apostolic Assemblies in January 1917. Many ministers, like Fauss in the south, were evidently not even yet familiar with the PAW, and many ministers did not immediately join the GAAA or know of its formation.[2]

The GAAA ex-AG ministers were hindered from the start because newly formed religious bodies were forbidden by law from obtaining government ministerial exemption. With the U.S. entry into the war in April the GAAA was eager for a solution. As they were organizing the GAAA, necessary statements of faith were drawn up, yet the simplicity of the resulting Articles of Faith was notable. They were no doubt creed-weary from their AG experience, and having just protested exclusionary creed-making so loudly, it may have shaped the basic summary form of their eighteen statements, such as "one way of entrance" by "a baptism of water and Spirit."[3] The AG *Weekly Evangel* quickly criticized the GAAA organizers whom they had only recently expelled.

The GAAA was led by D. C. O. Opperman and based in Eureka Springs, Arkansas, although it merged the next year with the PAW. Ministers were predominantly southern, comprising a major Oneness center concentrated in Arkansas, Missouri, Oklahoma, Texas, and Louisiana. Opperman's *The Blessed Truth,* which he obtained from David Lee Floyd, played an important part in unifying this region as an early center.[4] Opperman (1872–1926) was not only a noted preacher but a respected educator. Having opened his own school in Eureka Springs in 1915, the AG became its initial sponsor by 1916. It eventually became known as the "Pentecostal Literary and Training School," boasting 60 fulltime students and staff by 1917.[5]

2. Fauss, *What God Hath Wrought*, 202.

3. "New Pentecostal Organization," *Weekly Evangel*, 15; Clanton, *United We Stand*, 28–29, 30; Floyd, Interview, 67, 69; Tyson, *Chalices*, 165.

4. Treece, *Beulah*, 176; Floyd, Interview, 21–22, 50–53, 65, 67–68.

5. Blumhofer, *Assemblies of God*, 1:337, 431, 2:120; Gohr, "D. C. O. Opperman and Early Ministerial Training," 5–8, 21; Cagle, *Echoes*, 32.

The GAAA held very few events, but Opperman did host a Bible Conference early in 1917,[6] and possibly a camp meeting. When the merger with the PAW transpired, Opperman, evidently, deferred to Frazee, who was 30 years older than both Opperman and Haywood.[7] Opperman's organizational role began to diminish considerably at this point, but the establishment of the GAAA and its successful merger with the interracial PAW were no small feats, advancements which owed much to the efforts of both Opperman and Frazee.[8]

## 5.2 The 1918 PAW/ GAAA Merger

Apparently, sources typically confuse the 1918 events, times, or locales, especially Frazee's PAW withdrawal. The PAW/ GAAA merger meeting was held in St. Louis January 21–25, 1918, the second in Eureka Springs in October 1918 after Frazee's withdrawal. At the merger Frazee was acting chairman and W. E. Kidson acting secretary. Frazee was elected Superintendent, Opperman Secretary, and Goss Treasurer. Of twenty one governing Field Superintendents, four were Black, Haywood, Lawson, Douglas, and Schooler.[9] The elder Frazee, a week prior to his 67th birthday, whose efforts were indispensable to the merger's success, took the lead of the new organization, rather than the southern based Opperman. Also, they chose to retain the time-honored name, Pentecostal Assemblies of the World.

Although 31 percent of the pre-merger PAW was Oneness in 1917, the GAAA must have understood that the Trinitarian majority in the PAW would not be a factor in the merger, for that is what proved to be true. Surprisingly, though, perhaps even to Frazee, barely half of the Oneness ministers immediately joined the merged PAW/ GAAA. Even more extraordinary is the realization that the 69 percent Trinitarian majority allowed the minority takeover. Perhaps this was motivated by knowledge that large numbers of incoming Oneness members were forthcoming.

6. Tyson, *Early Pentecostal Revival*, 182; Treece, *Beulah*, 176, 172–73, with the rare Eureka Springs Photo of 140 ministers, including speakers John Dearing and Frank Muse from Idaho, and Jerry Osborn from Texas.

7. Tyson, *Early Pentecostal Revival*, 182; McClain and Foster, evidently, mix some details of 1917 and 1918, listing Goss, rather than Floyd as Secretary, see McClain, *Seek Ye First*, 49–50, and Foster, *Think It Not Strange*, 74.

8. Brickey, "Henry Green Rodgers," 3; Goss, *Winds of God*, 100–101.

9. "Minutes," February 1918, *MDS*, 3; Golder, *History*, 46; "To the Jew First," *MDS*, 1; Lovett, "Black Holiness-Pentecostalism," in *DCPM*, 80; *1918 PAW Minute Book* in Tyson, *Early Pentecostal Revival*, 288ff.

They may simply have been significantly more sympathetic with the Oneness cause than Trinitarianism in general, willing to allow the transition of the PAW into an all-Oneness organization.

After nearly a dozen years, for some, in the Azusa-based PAW, unsuited to wage an AG-like repeat battle, the majority appears to have simply relinquished their place and parted ways. Apparently, they differed considerably from their AG counterparts. By 1919, then, the withdrawing Trinitarian majority of 450 ministers were replaced by 461 Oneness independents, previously neither GAAA nor PAW. Some evidence points to the probability that a sizeable number of churches originated from this exit which were committed to independency and remained unaffiliated in the west and northwest, including possibly even Frazee himself.[10]

The uncertainties surrounding Frazee's enigmatic PAW withdrawal stem, first of all, from the lack of explanation accompanying the decision, a possible indication of its problematic nature to the movement, the most likely cause being the choice of independency, short of defection. Although problems weren't evident at the time of the merger, he withdrew before fall and was replaced in October 1918.

At the merger only minor changes were made in the Articles of Faith adopted directly from the PAW, and Frazee himself maintained top leadership.[11] Although personal and political concerns cannot be ruled out, there is a strong possibility that the shift away from PAW theological neutrality in Pentecostal issues tipped the scale for Frazee. Theological conformity would not guarantee agreement as to its organizational application.

The October election was called, at the height of the pandemic, *due to* Frazee's own withdrawal, which corresponded with a west-northwest PAW split, including all thirty four of the Portland ministers.[12] In California, 88 percent of the PAW ministers also withdrew.[13] Yet the federal census shows that Frazee remained in Portland. At least as early as September 1929 Frazee was institutionalized and ultimately sent to the Oregon State Hospital in Salem where he died June 14, 1930.[14]

10. Anderson, *Disinherited*, 125;cf., Ewart, *Phenomenon*, 80.

11. "Minutes," February 1918, *MDS*, 4.

12. Crosby, *America's Forgotten Pandemic*, 320ff; "Eureka Springs, Arkansas," *MDS*, 2.

13. See FBI File#55234, 7.

14. Jacob J. Frazee, *1920 U.S. Census*, Portland City, OR, 13A; "Oregon State Hospital Remains," by truitti, 14 March 2009, www.ancestry.com; cf., Maisel, "Oregon's Forgotten Hospital"; "Last Years of Jacob Jackson Frazee," by truitti, 10 March 2009, www.ancestry.com.

## 5.3 The Doak-Haywood Era of Interracial Worship & Leadership

PAW historian James L. Tyson suggests that this Golden Era in the movement was bold and courageous precisely because it was "more than symbolic," but rather a genuine "determined effort" to promote racial harmony. Importantly, the southern periodicals were boldly supportive of this bold move, proving that it was not merely a northern effort.[15] As Nelson said of Azusa, these accomplishments were nothing short of a "surprising historical breakthrough," established by design, in spite of the earlier abandonment of such a vision throughout much of the broader movement.

The era of the new, merged PAW in early Oneness Pentecostalism can be viewed as its Golden Era racially and structurally, with the implementation of a long envisioned interracial organization. Its AG disappointments forced the movement to mobilize independently, a fact which actually did a great deal to solidify the movement, and, paradoxically, to guarantee its future expansion.[16] Therefore, the movement's 1916 AG defeat, 1918 PAW victory, and 1919 PAOC Canadian defeat worked to secure its independency from mainstream Pentecostalism. A strong, all-Oneness PAW set the stage for the movement's own agenda of global expansion and fulfillment of interracial priorities.

The urgency of securing another chairman prevailed, in spite of the rare global flu pandemic which raged throughout the world. Another PAW Convention, therefore, convened at Opperman's October 1918 in Eureka Springs, Arkansas. Floyd, present for the E. W. Doak election, reported that Opperman actually made the nomination. Doak, like Frazee, was from the original PAW western stronghold, a fact which avoided shifting the leadership too quickly away from its base. Actually, the only order of business accomplished was the selection of Doak, and that of Booth-Clibborn as Secretary because early cancellation of the convention.

> Whereas, in the Convention of the P. A. of the World, now being held at above place: certain conditions have arisen requiring a cessation of all gatherings (public), by reason of National Order promulgated by the National authorities at Washington, DC.

15. Tyson, *Early Pentecostal Revival*, 195; see, for example, *The Pentecostal Messenger*, which was an official paper in Kinder, Louisiana edited by H. L. Henderson, see Loden, "Divisions, What For?," 3; It soon merged with *The Blessed Truth*, see Fauss, *What God Hath Wrought*, 108.

16. Bell, "The 'Acts' on Baptism," 3.

> And the work of this Convention having just begun, we deem it advisable that the Convention be adjourned until January 16th, 1919, at the City of Indianapolis, Indiana.[17]

Doak, though not even listed in 1917 as a PAW minister, assumed leadership in 1918 at the age of fifty nine, eight years younger than Frazee. Like Frazee, he has left behind no print legacy of his theology.[18] Edward Wesley Doak, whose parents were originally from Vermont, was born March 26, 1859 in Ovid, Michigan, near the Indiana state line, but grew up with his mother and a step-father ("Pitts") in Victor, Michigan.[19] The young Doak, according to ancestry data, following in his stepfather's profession, worked as a fairly successful carpenter-contractor.

Moving to Appleton, Wisconsin, he met and married Nellie A. Fuller in 1883. In 1899, his contractor business took them from Wisconsin to Hawaii, where he worked on Oahu. With the Schaepes also living in Honolulu, it is possible they first met at this time.[20] But, within a year of the outbreak of the Azusa revival, both families were intricately involved with Azusa Pentecostalism in Los Angeles.

After the Doaks moved to California, they lived there the rest of their lives, in either Pasadena or neighboring Monrovia. Like Schaepe, Doak was involved with Azusa, possibly as early as the Arroyo Seco meetings in 1907. Early in 1909, with Doak already in his late forties, Crawford made him a trustee of her Portland mission.[21] At least as early as 1913, the Doaks were connected as missionaries with *The Good Report*.

Within weeks of the rebaptism of Haywood and Roberts in Indianapolis in 1915, Doak, who had "severely" criticized and resisted the movement, was rebaptized in Los Angeles at Ewart's Arroyo Seco Camp Meeting held in April-June. Cook and Haywood were the camp speakers. Doak's rebaptism story appeared next to that of the Indianapolis rebaptisms, in the same issue of *Meat in Due Season*, in what was, otherwise, a doctrinaire article by Carrie M. Pool. Pool wrote, "I believe the word

17. An early PAW convention cancellation notice was posted in *MDS* 2/4 (November 1918) 1.

18. *U.S. Passport Applications-1795–1925*, 5 August 1913; *MDS* 1/7 (December 1913) 1; Martin, *Seymour*, 297; Tyson, *Chalices*, 219, 349.

19. *1860 U.S. Census*, Middlebury, MI, 41; *1870 U.S. Census*, Victor, MI, 22, "Doke" [sic].

20. *1900 U.S. Census*, Oahu, Hawaiian Islands, 19A; *Appleton, Wisconsin Directories*, 1884–1898, 1897, "Edward W. Doak."

21. Nellie Doak, October 14, 1944, California Death Index, 1940–1997; *1910 U.S. Census*, Pasadena, CA, 9A; 1916 Voter Registration, "retired."

of God just the way it is," then, tells the story of a 1907 Virginia "band" "convinced" of the "right way to baptize." They "all obeyed the word of God and the power fell mightily in their meetings."[22]

Following a testimonial regarding India missionary Robert Cook, and "how God has led them to baptize all the natives in the scriptural way," Pool related the story of Doak's moving Oneness conversion.

> In the afternoon service a touching incident happened: Bro. Doak, missionary from Egypt, got up and publicly confessed that he had severely criticized "this way" and also had said many things against Bros. Ewart and Cook. With tears running down his face he asked them to forgive him and said, "inasmuch as I have spoken against you, Bro. Ewart, I want you personally to baptize me." Oh, Hallelujah, this is "the good old way" wherein the apostles walked.[23]

They were, at the time, returned missionaries, having been laboring in Egypt since at least 1913, although it is not known if they originally went to the mission field even earlier. According to the Bowdans, the Doaks attended the Arroyo Seco camp meeting in April 1913. By 1916, Doak was serving as missionary secretary for *Meat in Due Season*.[24]

The 1919 Indianapolis elections solidified Doak's earlier 1918 election as Overseer, since he was a seasoned minister, but not well known. He was not currently a pastor, nor did he have the renown or leadership savvy of Haywood, but he was 21 years his senior, for Haywood was merely 38 years old. Similarly, other more well-known candidates, such as Goss, Opperman, Ewart, and even Cook, were all about Haywood's age.

The history making moment took place on January 21, 1919, G. T. Haywood was elected Secretary, a top national position, ushering in a fully interracial era of leadership in the PAW which would last until 1924.[25] It was the first time an African American had been chosen to one of the top two leadership positions in the PAW. The selection of Haywood demonstrates, too, the intentionality of a prioritization of the interracial vision, for the PAW at the time did not have a Black majority. Alexander R. Schooler, a Black pastor from Cleveland, Ohio, became Vice-General Overseer and T. C. Davis, Treasurer. This was a history making moment for the PAW.

22. Pool, "An Open Letter," 6.
23. Ibid., 3.
24. LaBlanc, *Like A Rose*, 6; *MDS* 1/13 (June 1916) 2.
25. Tyson, *Early Pentecostal Revival*, 196–97; "Important Notice," *MDS*, 1.

Haywood's parents were Raleigh slaves at the time of Doak's birth, making it all the more remarkable an achievement that Pentecostalism could give rise to such interracial possibilities in the span of their lifetimes. Doak realized the importance of assuming this responsibility by hitting the ground running. Later that year *The Blessed Truth* reported he had visited "more than twenty states since January, traveling from coast to coast" and was "acquainting himself with the work of the entire field."[26] Haywood, too, had not merely been honored with position, but was so central a figure that on January 25, 1919 they incorporated in Indiana and moved the PAW headquarters, not to Los Angeles where Doak lived, but to Indianapolis. T. C. Davis later wrote: "By the grace of God this city has become a great Pentecostal center."[27]

## 5.4. The Impact of High Profile Conversions and Defections

Several high profile defections served as sobering disappointments to the often high-spirit advocates of the Oneness cause. The most prominent of these disconcerting rejections of Oneness Pentecostalism include such well known early advocates as R. E. McAlister and L. V. Roberts. Hopes ran high as E. N. Bell, one of their most visible AG opponents, joined the ranks with great fanfare, only to vehemently renounce it within a few months.[28]

Leading up to Oneness Pentecostalism's Golden Age, in fact, three dispiriting losses occurred between 1916 and 1919 which took an enormous psychological toll on the movement. With the first of these, the AG's harsh rejection and expulsion of Oneness ministers in late 1916, the minority status of the Oneness faction within the Pentecostal movement had become obvious—a seriously disappointing realization. The second major loss came, offset by the bitter-sweet triumph of a PAW/ GAAA merger, when huge numbers abandoned the PAW in 1918. Broad based sympathies, too, were waning, and attitudes toward the movement, especially from the mainstream, were hardening. By 1919 the third fracture was in

26. "Editorial," *BT*, 2.

27. Davis, "Let's Get Acquainted," 2; The PAW directory listed the Doaks in Indianapolis, but the address was Haywood's; *1920 U.S. Census*, Santa Cruz, CA, 4B, *and* San Pedro, CA, 27A.

28. See appendix E: "High Profile Rejection and Defection Impacting Early Oneness Pentecostalism," in French, "Early Oneness Pentecostalism," 350ff.

process, this time in Canada, when the PAOC abandoned the Oneness position, necessitating the 1921 establishment of the ACOP of Canada by Frank Small.[29]

Undaunted, though, Oneness proponents rushed to highlight the numerous notable conversions to the Oneness message which occurred, such as the rebaptism of the well-known evangelist Mattie Crawford in 1921.[30] Just as the devastating news of L. V. Roberts' defection was breaking, Andrew Urshan had only just joined the PAW himself, late in 1919, and the news of the switched allegiance was, indeed, welcome. Urshan was rebaptized in Russia in early 1916, and protested the use of the word persons at the 1916 AG convention, but did not disassociate with the AG with the expulsion of its Oneness ministers.[31] With his Oneness views more and more under scrutiny, he was pressured out of the AG in 1918, after which he joined the PAW. In late 1919 he began publishing a new Oneness series of his influential *The Witness of God*, which served to popularize Urshan as a Oneness apologist and evangelist.

*The Witness of God* was filled with an array of Oneness theological defenses exemplified, for example, by the 1921 article by John Patterson, highlighting the issue of "The Essentiality of Water Baptism" for the "remission" of sins.[32] Yet the Oneness loss felt at the volatility and rejection inevitably manifested itself. Urshan himself made reference to "the few persons who have recently turned their backs" on the movement, noting that "our *old issue brethren* or rather the Pentecostal Trinitarians are reporting in their papers that the New Issue people's work is *crumbling*."[33]

## 5.5 The Setback of R. C. Lawson's Withdrawal from the PAW

At precisely this same time, though, a severely disappointing blow to the prospects of the new interracial aspirations of the PAW occurred with the unexpected 1919 withdrawal of African American leader, and Haywood's

29. See Reed, *"In Jesus' Name,"* 146 n. 47.

30. Crawford, "Spiritual Outpouring in Dayton, Ohio," 2.

31. *1916 Minutes of the General Council of the Assemblies of God*, 16; French, *Our God Is One*, 73–76. Urshan was born May 17, 1884 and emigrated from Abajaloo, Urumia in 1901, see *U.S. Passport Application*, No. 17167, October 13, 1913. By 1933 he had published 104 editions of *WG*.

32. Patterson, "Essentiality of Water Baptism," 4–6.

33. "Interesting News & Info," *WG*, 7; italics added.

early protégé, Robert Clarence Lawson. Lawson had become a powerfully influential Black leader in his own right within the movement, one of the most widely known Black ministers in Pentecost, whose loss of involvement and support could only serve to weaken PAW efforts at a time when unity was critical.

An ambiguity remains, thus far, in the records regarding the year of Lawson's birth, May 5, 1883 or 1888, in New Iberia, Louisiana, although official Lawson biographies, perhaps correctly, maintain the earlier date. Nevertheless, Lawson's own signed 1923 U.S. passport not only shows that Lawson gave his own age as thirty five, but contains an Affidavit of Birth giving the year as 1888, signed by an acquaintance from New Iberia, Mathew V. Boutte.[34]

Partial details of Lawson's biography are found in Thomas' *For the Defense of the Gospel* and in *The Silent Spokesman* by Stewart and DuPree.[35] Lawson, from an early age, due to the death of his parents, who had been itinerant ministers and missionaries, was raised by an aunt.[36] At about the age of twenty five, while traveling extensively in 1913, severe illness brought him from Canada and Chicago to Indianapolis.

> I was from the South, and I hadn't gotten the negatives of segregation out of me yet, and how they had treated me down there. And I didn't believe there could be a God when they had such prejudice in their minds . . . The Lord just let a sickness come upon me . . . I got so bad, I went to Indianapolis to see a friend of mine whose father owned a large evening place and saloon, and from there he sent me to the hospital . . . The doctors pronounced me "TB plural."[37]

He was miraculously healed, though, after his hospital roommate's elderly mother, who was a member of Haywood's Indianapolis church, invited him to come for prayer. Lawson's earliest hymn, commonly known

34. *U.S. Passport Application*, #343224, September 1923; *1900 U.S. Census*, Iberia Parish, Louisiana, 139A, no. 22; *1930 U.S. Census*, Manhattan, New York, 14B; *1920 U.S. Census*, Manhattan, New York, 3A; *1917 WW1 Registration*, June 4, 1917, Columbus, OH.

35. Thomas, "History of Robert C. Lawson," 6–23; Spellman and Thomas, *The Life, Legend and Legacy of Bishop R. C. Lawson*, 9–4; W. L. Bonner Literary Committee, *And the High Places*, 262–72; Stewart and DuPree, *The Silent Spokesman*.

36. Lawson's father, William, died in Texas, after which he lived with Nathan (age 60) and Peggy (35) Frazier, see *1900 U.S. Census*, Iberia Parish, LA, 139; "aunt Grace," Spellman and Thomas, *Legend*, 44A, 9.

37. 1952 Tape Transcription, in Spellman and Thomas, *Legend*, 41–42.

as "God is Great and Greatly to Be Praised," is widely held to have been penned after this Lawson healing. "He's balm of Gilead, the great Physician," the first stanza reads. "Now by His stripes we're healed of all diseases." The crescendo of the chorus climaxes with the title line: "God is great in my soul!"[38]

Later, in 1914, he received Spirit baptism, entered the ministry under Haywood's direct tutelage, and married Carrie F. Fields from Herbert Davis' Leavenworth, Kansas church, which had been brought into the Oneness movement through Lawson's campaigns. Shortly afterward, he took the Columbus, Ohio work of Albert and Lula Roberts, who were also originally from Haywood's church. Columbus expanded quickly into a successful interracial congregation. He travelled extensively, nonetheless, from Columbus, during which time he established strong works in San Antonio and St. Louis, as well.[39] News of Lawson's successful revivals, such as the story of Baptist minister M. R. Gregory's conversion, was plenteous in the early Oneness periodicals.[40]

An AME seminary student from Zanesville, who had a "charge" with a Methodist congregation in Columbus, Karl F. Smith, a young man destined to renowned leadership in the PAW, was Spirit filled in Lawson's church in April 1915. By 1916 Smith had become Lawson's much-needed assistant. Along with the decision to withdraw from the PAW, Lawson had decided to resign from the Columbus church, which he turned over to Smith in July 1919, probably shortly after handing over his credentials. Later, in July of 1919, R. C. Lawson decided that New York City was the city of his calling where he was to start over, prompting his immediate, aggressive launching of the church which would quickly become his most successful, rivaling any in Pentecost, including Haywood's.[41]

Lawson's most famed theological dispute was with his own mentor, G. T. Haywood, and the primary issue was that of divorce. Haywood had

38. Lawson, "God Is Great In My Soul," 39. Lawson followed Haywood in joining the pre-Oneness PAW, see *1917 PAW Minute Book*, 8ff., as did Karl Smith (Columbus), E. G. Lowe (L.A.), and Oddous Barber (Boston) and G. C. Beaver (Kansas City, KS), both from Indianapolis.

39. See the October 1916, no. 18, *VW*, "Columbus, O.," 1, 4, "The Convention," 4, and "Norwegian's Sister's Testimony," 1, "San Antonio, Tex.," and "Good Tent Meetings in Los Angeles, Cal.," 1.

40. Gregory, "Baptist Preacher's Testimony," 4; Martin Rawleigh Gregory afterward established Emmanuel Tabernacle Baptist Church of the Apostolic Faith in Columbus in 1916.

41. Smith, *Devout Man*, 5–6, 8–9, 17; racial integration, 23, 42ff.; Smith's founding of Aenon Bible College of the PAW in 1941, 42, 63–68.

published his views on divorce in *The Voice in the Wilderness* throughout 1918, concluding that divorces prior to conversion did *not* require that individuals return to their first companions or, else, remain single. "I had preached many a time," Haywood wrote, "and caused many of them to separate, thinking I was doing God's bidding."[42]

Lawson, though, was appalled, and "took a stand," emphatically and vociferously, against Haywood's new view. Such a couple, Lawson believed, *must*, indeed, dissolve their marriage and return to their first spouses, if possible, or else remain unmarried. Lawson, therefore, decided to protest by means of "open" letters of opposition, which, in Lawson's words, "precipitated a controversy" across the movement, "culminating" in a showdown at the Indianapolis annual convention.[43]

Both men, after publishing their views in letter and periodical form, published books on their views of marriage and divorce, *The Marriage and Divorce Question in the Church*, by Haywood, and Lawson's *An Open Letter on the Burning Issue of Marriage and Divorce*.[44] One of the most interesting illustrations in Haywood's book was the example of a couple at his Indianapolis church who received Spirit baptism, in spite of the fact that, against his own beliefs at the time, they were *remarried*. But crucial to the story is the fact that, also seeking Spirit baptism that evening, was Lawson himself.

Not only did it impact Haywood, he notes, but "everybody saw it." And then he adds: "Elder R. C. Lawson was there that very night seeking the Holy Ghost and seeing what God had done, went over and sat in the very same seat that he might be filled but was not successful at that time."[45] Not only does this illustration illuminate the issues surrounding the debate, in some rather interesting ways, but it dates the origin of the issue itself. Lawson sought Spirit Baptism in 1913 or 1914, and, thus, this is the timeframe in which Haywood reformulated his views on divorce.

The details regarding this convention confrontation indicate that it must have been in 1919, and, almost certainly, it would have been the earlier January convention, rather than October. This is due to the fact, as Lawson's account demonstrates, that he "had not resigned" from the

42. Haywood, "The Marriage and Divorce Question (Article No. 2)," 2.

43. Lawson, "Pentecostal Intolerance," 310; cf. Blumhofer, *Restoring the Faith*, 122, 138 n. 31.

44. Haywood, *Marriage and Divorce Question*; Lawson, *An Open Letter on the Burning Issue of Marriage and Divorce*; cf., Spellman, "Issues of Consensus and Controversy"; Stewart and DuPree, *Silent Spokesman*, 15.

45. Haywood, *Marriage and Divorce Question*, 4–5.

Columbus church, at the time, but was, in fact, "still" the pastor, even when he later withdrew from the PAW, events which took place before July 1919.[46] Establishing the timing of this event also helps pinpoint the time of Lawson's move to New York.

Neither could this have been the 1918 convention, sometimes suggested, because the events took place in "Indianapolis." But the January 1918 PAW/GAAA merger was in St. Louis, and Doak's October 1919 election took place in Eureka Springs. The showdown must have occurred in January 1919, in spite of the fact that ambiguities persist, including the fact that Robert and Carrie Lawson are included in the PAW rosters published late in 1919, whereas Smith, who was following Lawson's lead in leaving the PAW, at least at this time, is no longer included in the roster.[47]

By the next convention, October 1919, the PAW had adopted the very divorce policy to which Lawson so objected. "No person shall be ordained, or licensed, who has divorced his wife (or her husband), and remarried, *since* coming into the Body of Christ:--both of whom having been members of the Body of Christ."[48] Undoubtedly, Lawson was referencing the debate and adoption of this section of the by-laws, and, by the time the Article of Faith were published, Lawson had already withdrawn.

Haywood, Lawson reported, taught for four hours on this subject at the offending convention, to which Lawson strongly objected, especially when Doak and Haywood, in order to "muzzle all opposition," determined not to allow Lawson "anything to say" in rebuttal. Lawson recalled later that the "majority, who was of small minds," were swayed, and thus, agreed with Haywood, "with few exceptions."[49]

This issue was merely the final straw which, from Lawson's viewpoint, resulted in his being "forced out." But other critical issues also play a contributing role in Lawson's increasing dissatisfaction, two of the most significant being opposition to women preachers and his belief in required head coverings for women.

Lawson would not be dissuaded from his decision to leave the PAW. "I resigned personally to the president, Elder Doak, who was the head of the P.A.W.," Lawson explained, "by handing my credentials to him at my

46. Cf., Thomas, *Legend*, 11.

47. Thomas, *Legend*, 11; 1919–1920 *PAW Minute Book*, 17.

48. *1919 PAW Minute Book*, Article 7, Sec. 2, 6.

49. Lawson, "Pentecostal Intolerance," 310–11; cf., also, Paddock, *Godly Heritage*, 37–47.

breakfast table when he was a house guest of mine." Doak's Columbus visit had failed at its effort of appeasement.[50]

This was, indisputably, a monumental loss for the integrated PAW and its vision of interracial unity. Although Lawson does not appear to have directly opposed the interracial effort, the schism profoundly impacted it on two levels. First, Lawson's rejection of Haywood's leadership and role in the venture had far reaching implications, damaging and weakening his position with Blacks and Whites alike, but especially those Whites who might be seeking, for example, proverbial excuses or kinks in the armor in order to minimize, or even sabotage, the arrangements. Secondly, it presented the first serious Oneness competition to the PAW, other than independency, and that from a Black organizational alternative. The challenges, therefore, obviously came in both Black and White, which may be the most intriguing aspect of the paradox of Lawson's withdrawal.

Many, like Karl Smith in Columbus, joined Lawson under the auspices of the "Church of Christ of the Apostolic Faith," later COOLJC, with Smith becoming its first Secretary. Another well-known Columbus convert, Smallwood Williams, was Spirit filled under Smith's ministry in March 1919, before Lawson's actual resignation. Williams established a leading COOLJC church in D.C. beginning in 1927, but in 1957 he withdrew to form Bible Way Churches of Our Lord Jesus Christ World Wide.[51] COOLJC and BW, with 1.4 million members worldwide, rival the size of the PAW.[52]

## 5.6 Ministerial Composition of the New-Merged PAW by 1920

Indianapolis and Haywood's ministry had become the major Oneness epicenter by 1920, even as the commitment to the PAW's early vision of interracial diversity were being realized and put to the test during the six years prior to 1924. A wide-angle photograph of the October 1919 PAW Convention in Indianapolis shows a packed auditorium, including the side balconies, with an evenly mixed distribution of Blacks and Whites.

50. *1919 PAW Minute Book*, Article 6, Sec. 8; Thomas, *Defense*, 11.

51. Smith, *Devout Man*, 23; Spellman, *Pentecostal Apostolic Fellowship Crusade*, 10, 13, 15–18.

52. Barrett, *World Christian Encyclopedia*, 783; cf., *COOLJC International General Annual Convocation Minute Book and Ministerial Record of the Seventy-Ninth Session* (1998–1999) thru (2009–2010).

Of even greater significance, the PAW leadership, which had packed the platform of Tomlinson Hall, was evenly mixed racially, as well.[53] This picture had certainly not come easily.

Indianapolis, with fifty nine ministers, had the largest concentration of PAW ministers of any city in the U.S., and analysis indicates that the majority were White (63%) and associated with Haywood's church or one of its missions.[54] Los Angeles, by comparison, had only forty-one of California's ninety-nine ministers. Indiana and California were the largest PAW states, together comprising slightly more than a third of the total of PAW ministers. Oakland, with twenty nine ministers, emerged as the third largest Oneness center due to Morse's highly successful missionary school.[55]

Texas, Ohio, Arkansas, Louisiana, Missouri and Illinois had the next largest state concentration of churches and ministers, mostly scattered broadly, though, in rural areas rather than concentrated in urban areas, deterring an earlier centralization in the region. In Texas, for example, 56 ministers were located in 30 different cities, in Ohio, 46 in 18 cities, Arkansas, 41 in 16 cities, Louisiana, 40 in 23 cities, Missouri, 36 in 17 cities, and Illinois, 26 in 10 cities. The highest urban concentrations, other than Indianapolis and Los Angeles, were Boston (17), New York (15), and St. Paul (15), all others having eight or less.

Nevertheless, even with little urban centralization, by this time the south was clearly gaining a regional leadership edge with thirty nine percent, over the thirty three percent in the Midwest.[56] Texas, in particular, had become the third largest state, followed closely by Arkansas and Louisiana.

The *1919 PAW Minutes* listed a total of 641 U.S. ministers. Comparable to 1917, the 1919 percentage of women ministers in the PAW was thirty percent, with a fourth of these women ministers also being the wives of male PAW ministers.

53. Bundy, "Haywood," 249; Tyson, *Chalices*, 22–221.

54. *1919–1920 PAW Minute Book.*

55. Compare the *1917 PAW Minute Book* and *1919 PAW Minute Book.*

56. See *1919–1920 PAW Minute Book,* U.S., 641 ministers/ 400 churches; 70 percent in eight states: IN (100), CA (99), TX (56), OH (46), AR (41), LA (40), MO (36), and IL (26).

## 5.7 Wonderful!—Racial Integration and Adaptation

Even by 1917 the PAW was unfamiliar to some in the GAAA, such as Fauss, noted earlier, and S. C. McClain, who was ministering in Eureka Springs, Arkansas, which had emerged earlier as one of the most important Oneness non-urban centers.[57] McClain, born in Madison, Georgia, 1889, became an Arkansas school teacher. He later worked from about 1917–1920 in Opperman's Pentecostal Literary and Bible School. In 1919 he married Bessie A. (Sheets) Rodgers, widow of Indianapolis mission pastor Joe Rodgers. He became a prominent southern Bible teacher, a pastor in Fort Smith, Arkansas and then Albuquerque, New Mexico, as well as the author of the popular book, *Highlights in Church History: Student's Handbook of Facts in Church History.*

McClain, a White PAW minister by 1919, stated in his memoirs regarding the interracial fellowship of the period: "I thought it was *wonderful*."[58] In reference to attending the 1920 PAW Convention in Indianapolis, on the other hand, McClain admitted that the interracial meetings had taken some getting "used to it."[59] Yet McClain was quickly converted from a lifetime mentality of social segregation to viewing integration as "wonderful." "I had never seen White and colored people associate on the same level," he wrote. In spite of inherent issues with such a statement, a wide-eyed transformation was, in fact, in progress. "For the first time in my life I sat in church services and then at the dining table side by side with colored people."[60]

Even with the rapidly increasing number of Blacks joining the PAW, significantly, by 1919 only approximately eighteen percent of the PAW ministers were African American.[61] The interracial Golden Era of the PAW, therefore, had been inaugurated by a White PAW majority. Comparative analysis of the 1917 and 1919 rosters indicates, surprisingly, that possibly as few as twenty Black Oneness ministers remained from the premerger PAW. A considerable number of the Oneness African American

57. McClain, *Seek First*, 49–50; Fauss, *What God Hath Wrought*, 202.

58. McClain, *Seek First*, 68; italics added.

59. Ibid., 68, 11.

60. Ibid., 61, 72.

61. *1919 PAW Minute Book*, 11; Tyson, *Early Pentecostal Revival*, 195; Garrett, *Haywood*, 135.

ministers, including Haywood's assistant, Samuel N. Hancock, rushed to join the PAW only after the inauguration of its Golden Era after 1918.

PAW Black ministers in 1919 were concentrated in Indianapolis, Los Angeles, New York, Boston, Louisville, St. Louis, Baltimore, Grand Rapids, Cleveland, Chicago, Dayton, and Washington, DC. A few were also in the south, especially in Texas, as well as the northern states of Ohio, New Jersey, and Kansas.[62]

Adaption in the period would, of course, become increasingly difficult with the challenges of increased intensity and growth, especially as the dynamic of growth shifted into the less accommodating climate of the south. Earlier the shift had been from west to Midwest, but now the Midwest dominance was giving way to a subtle shift south, rearranging the dynamic of the balance of power. Arkansas as a center of influence waned once Goss left Hot Springs for Picton, Ontario in 1919, and after the closing of Opperman's school in 1920, resulting in the natural shifting of influence and centralization into the more dominant growth areas of Texas and Louisiana.[63]

## 5.8 Dramatic Increases in the Number of PAW Black Ministers

The PAW ministerial rosters increased by more than a third in the five year period from 1919 to 1924, climbing to a total of 1,054 ministers. Top leadership remained in the hands of Doak and Haywood, but twice the Vice Chairmanship alternated between Schooler and Opperman. Alexander R. Schooler, like Lawson and Hancock, was an early Haywood convert, who became a successful Black pastor in Cleveland, Ohio. He was not only a prolific songwriter, with numerous songs appearing in the hymnal *Bridegroom Songs*, but by 1923 he was publishing his own periodical, *Christian Unity*.

The Board of Executive Elders grew from seventeen to twenty nine, yet did not reflect the substantial growth in the number of incoming Black ministers, to nearly fifty percent. The Black board representation for the period only increased to an average of twenty five percent. Black board members included Dunlop Chenault (San Antonio), Herbert Davis (Leavenworth), Guy Jameson (Cleveland/ D.C.), F. I. Douglas (Louisville),

62. *1919 PAW Minute Book*, 11.

63. McClain, *Seek First*, 62.

and Joseph Turpin (Baltimore). The discrepancy may represent the initial surfacing of racial dissatisfaction or uneasiness, stemming from the likely unexpected disproportionate Black increases.

The bold and courageous united vision of the PAW demanded equally courageous leadership to stand up to the challenges to its success, yet Doak does not appear to have carried the marks of such boldness. His earlier actual role in the movement had been rather minimal, perhaps even untested, having been retired when elected, and not a pastor. Haywood notes that he even had to seek financial assistance on Doak's behalf.[64] A successful, highly involved pastor, like Ewart in Los Angeles where the Doaks possibly attended church, might have provided the necessary vision. Certainly, their absence from the PAW's vital center, Indianapolis, was, in itself, problematic. Ewart, though, in a bewildering development, withdrew from the PAW in 1920, due possibly to doctrinal issues, a "low profile," or general disinterest, Reed suggests.[65] Perhaps he had anticipated a more pivotal role in the organizational life of the PAW.

## 5.9 Distribution of U.S. Oneness Pentecostal Churches by 1924

Conversely, Haywood's influence increased significantly throughout the period, as reflected, first of all in his position, but also in the astounding increase in the number of Black ministers. By 1924 Black ministers represented forty seven percent of the total PAW ministerial constituency.[66] In addition to the regional shift, a shift in the racial complexity of the PAW was taking place throughout this period.

A number of other Oneness organizations had formed by this time, ten of which were small Black groups with a combined total of 180 churches, and, of the 400 PAW churches in 1924, 180 were Black churches.[67] Hispanic churches did not begin to appear in the PAW rosters until 1925, having previously been affiliated with the work in Mexico, although they were concentrated in California and Texas.

64. Haywood, "Sixth Annual Convention of the Pentecostal Assemblies of the World at Indianapolis, Ind.," 1.

65. *1919 PAW Minute Book,* 10; Reed, *"In Jesus' Name,"* 211, 196, 197 n. 64, and 191; see *The Herald of the King,* noted in *WG,* "News," vol. 2, 19th edition, July 1921, 9.

66. The (pre-schism) *1923–24 PAW Minute Book* compared to the (post-schism) *1926–27 PAW Minute Book.*

67. *1923–1924 Minutes of the General Assembly of the P.A. of W. Convention.*

A less recognized aspect of Oneness Pentecostal expansion is the fact of widespread independency with respect to the White segment of the movement. The extensive nature of White independency resulted in the approximation in size to that of the contrasting organized churches, well exceeding 200 churches by 1924. Many of these congregations simply never assimilated into the emerging organized Oneness bodies, especially in the west-northwest region and in the south. The mere election of organizational leaders was considered by many to be "POPEISM." *The Blessed Truth,* for example, as late as 1920, was attempting to explain to a vast network of independents in the south that the PAW, though an organized body, was not going to "put his servants under a bondage that will work a hindrance to the gospel."[68]

Black Oneness churches were clearly concentrated in the Midwest, north, and northeast, with a growing concentration of COOLJC churches in the east. Samuel N. Hancock (1883–1963), for example, was a well-known exemplar of the dynamic of Black Oneness regional success in Detroit. Hancock's family, sometime before 1900, moved from Kentucky to Indianapolis, where Hancock married in 1907, was Spirit filled at Haywood's church in 1912, and entered the ministry in 1914. Haywood's assistant until 1920, Hancock took Levi Miles' mission in Detroit. As the work expanded into a premiere PAW congregation, its influence led to the formation of a separate Black organization, the Pentecostal Churches of the Apostolic Faith.[69]

White Oneness church expansion in the west by this period was predominantly in California, but extended into Oregon, Washington, Idaho, and Arizona. The entire Midwest region, especially Ohio, Illinois, and Indiana, extending into the north, and the entire southern region, including the southeast, experienced the largest growth. Northeastern growth was mostly in Maine, but extended rapidly into New Brunswick, Canada.

Haywood was an exceptionally and uniquely adaptable African American to ministry in White settings in dominantly White regions. Well-known areas of Haywood's northern influence were Minnesota and Wisconsin and the initial July 1915 St. Paul revival which impacted early leaders such as Charles P. Nelson and J. P. Rullen.[70] Canadian leader Frank

68. Loden, "Divisions, What For?" 2; "Editorial," *BT,* 2.

69. *1900 U.S. Census,* Indianapolis, IN, 2B; Bertha Valentine, Annie W. Williams, see *Indiana Marriage Collection, 1800–1941,* Marion County, Indiana, 26 Dec 1907 and 28 Sept 1914; *1910 U.S. Census,* Indianapolis, IN, 14A; *1920 U.S. Census,* Indianapolis, IN, 17B; *WW1 Registration,* September 12, 1918, Order# 3111; www.pcaf.net.

70. Cf., *1919 PAW Minute Book,* 21–22; Johnson, "First Jesus' Name Pentecostal Church," 2; Reinking, "Nelson," 20; *Saint Paul Pioneer Press,* July 1915.

Small was even rebaptized there at their October convention. In December Haywood preached the Ottawa Convention in Canada in which R. E. McAlister, his brother Harvey, and their wives were all rebaptized.[71]

Unlike Mason's COGIC churches, Black Oneness churches in the south were far fewer than their expanding northern counterparts. White Oneness itinerant evangelists in the south, unlike Black ministers who were more restricted, were able to easily crisscross back and forth between states, north and south.[72] By 1924 Texas, Arkansas, Louisiana, and Missouri were clearly dominant, with Texas already experiencing unparalleled growth and rapidly becoming the largest Oneness concentration anywhere. Yet for some time, with the region's widely scattered churches, Texas and the entire southern region were apparently without a clearly coalesced center. Camp meetings, nevertheless, quickly evolved into early state centers of influence, and in Texas, for example, Dallas emerged as a strong early hub.[73]

## 5.10 Conclusion

The surrender of the PAW to its destiny as an all-Oneness organizational base after its merger with the GAAA, and the subsequent influx of previously unaffiliated Oneness ministers, propelled the entire movement into an unparalleled period of interracial, worldwide expansion. This Golden Era of Oneness Pentecostalism began the process of anchoring the young movement within the context of its roots as it finally entered a brief period of stabilization. Not only were hundreds of additional churches attracted to the invigorated PAW which had embraced afresh an interracial posture, but it captured the attention of the entire Pentecostal movement by expanding that vision to its leadership structure.

Haywood and the majority of originators of the PAW interracial structure believed that Pentecostal power via the crimson stream of blood would wash away the color line. Only then could the church experience the restored model of racial harmony intended by the Spirit. Although it

71. "Pastor Frank Small Baptized," 4; Larden, *Heritage*, 34; Ewart, *Phenomenon*, 98; "Editorial Notes," *MDS*, 3; *A Living Word*, St. Paul, MN, H. O. Scott, noted in Ewart, *Phenomenon*, 98–99, 96.

72. See appendix A: "Profiles of Early Oneness Pentecostal Pioneers."

73. Dallas was, initially, the earliest growth center in the state, with churches in Walnut Springs, Clebourne, Georges Creek, Newcastle, Alvaredo, Jacksboro, and Grand Prairie.

was a belief held in tension with the realities of the developing Oneness movement and society-at-large, the PAW had committed to such an ideal from its inception. The unraveling of that ideal would come in 1924.

Yet those years of hard fought battles and interracial successes were not merely an interlude to later Oneness history. They were the priority development of the restorative vision of both Black and White, of African American fortitude, and of a broad-based White cultural resistance of conviction.

# 6

# Redrawing the Color Line in Early Oneness Pentecostalism

The complexities of the racial issues following emancipation within the American cultural context of the late 19th and early 20th centuries were rooted in the failures of the Reconstruction era. Neither society nor Christianity provided an adequate response to escalating racism and the other-worldly counter-cultural impulse within early Pentecostalism was inconsistently applied to the issue of race. Initially the Oneness movement reacted to these failures, spearheaded in the PAW, with restorative tenacity, championing emancipation as a meaningful aspect of Pentecost as Spirit poured out on *all* flesh without partiality.

By 1924 this ideological framework collapsed as the PAW splintered into multiple race-based organizational centers mirroring the diverse segregationist mentality which permeated the broader culture. During post-Civil War Reconstruction emancipation essentially devolved into an increasing abandonment of racial justice by 1900. Edward J. Blum has described this as a racial dark cloud in his 2005 *Reforging the White Republic: Race, Religion, and American Nationalism, 1865–1898.*

## 6.1 20th Century Race Issues in Context & in Black Perspective

Blum not only argues that this was due to the political and economic expediency of reuniting with the south, but also that it was due to religious Whites who backed away from earlier commitments to Black equality.

In place of equality Jim Crow laws were implemented for the purpose of segregation and control, and they were not ruled unconstitutional and removed until 1954. Their premise was the fallacy of White superiority and of Black inferiority. "They lost the battle for America's identity," Blum concludes, "with far less hope than they had a generation earlier."[1] In Blum's view, in spite of resolute intentions, via the long fought Civil War, to defend Black equality, Evangelicalism and D. L. Moody became legitimizing influences in the rejection of radical Reconstruction due their acceptance of religious race based segregation.[2] Rather than push for interracial worship and endure social ostracism, they craved unity instead.[3]

An interesting corollary to these concerns about the role of faith in the arena of race is the recent work by J. Kameron Carter, *Race: A Theological Account.* Carter's unique emphasis begins with racism as the "core theological problem of our times." From this perspective cultural imperialism must actually be traced in church history as it has impacted and shaped both Black identity and White identity.[4]

W. E. B. DuBois was an important Black spokesman who has had a pervasive influence to the present and is critical to an understanding of African American responses to the twentieth-century racial issues. *The Souls of Black Folk,* his landmark work, quickly became the single most insightful manifesto ever written on race. DuBois' insights came to revolutionize the twentieth-century century Black perspective, especially with respect to its perceptive recognition of the Black reality of "double-consciousness." Essentially, this refers to the Black conception of self "through the revelation of the other world," i.e., the White world, resulting in Black responses as always "guarded" rather than self-assertive and strident. This *veiled* way of speaking is described as developing survival skills amidst the angst of camouflage, concealing as it interprets, so as to express one reality through another, such as story, sarcasm, and irony.[5]

Economic woes must also be recognized as reinforcing the Jim Crow world at the turn of the twentieth century. "Given a declining agricultural economy," Baer and Singer have noted, "Blacks became an easy target for White hostility." Laws were contrived in the south for providing

1. Blum, *Reforging the White Republic,* 3, 15, 18, 120ff., 93ff., 142–44, 244.

2. Ibid., 13, 119; see 119–45.

3. Ibid., 141.

4. Carter, *Race,* 5–6, 4; see also, Winn, "Book Review of *Race,*" 133–34.

5. DuBois, *The Souls of Black Folk,* 3, 204, 205, 206; Crouch and Benjamin, *Reconsidering the Souls of Black Folk,* 8; cf. Hubbard, *The Souls of Black Folk: One Hundred Years Later,* 2, 132, 138–39, 161.

and controlling "a manageable and inexpensive labor force."[6] Economic pressure clearly impacted race developments negatively, with the Black response to southern economic and racial circumstances being to migrate north.[7] During or right after the war, and certainly by 1919, a half million African Americans relocated, creating a host of new racial challenges.[8]

## 6.2 Perspectives Regarding Early Pentecostal Racial Division

What Tinney has referred to as the *a priori* understanding of early Pentecostal racial realities is essentially the culturally dominant race attitudes at work within the Pentecostal structures, such as in the all-White AG. It allowed, for example, for Seymour to be mostly ignored by historians, even in Lawrence's 1916 account. To the culture, the interracial aspects of the movement seemed more dangerous than the glossolalia.[9]

This is, of course, in contrast to Seymour and Azusa. "For him," Hollenweger has noted, "Pentecost meant more than speaking in tongues. It meant to love in the face of hate, to overcome the hatred of a whole nation by demonstrating that Pentecost is something very different from the success-oriented American way of life."[10] Historian David D. Daniels perceives of the Azusa Street revival as the fashioning of a "new racial/nonracial identity" which looked "beyond the racial divide of the era and reflected a racial vocabulary, symbolism, and vision that differed drastically from the dominant society of that day."[11]

Wacker, in pointing out racism's subtleness, noted that ritualized Pentecostal historical accounts have served to systematically eclipse women, on the one hand, and to ignore the influences of Black secular culture "on White Pentecostalism (such as jazz and folk healing arts)," on the other.[12] In this way, as Rosenior points out, Black Pentecostals, or for that

6. Baer and Singer, *African American Religion*, 224.

7. DuBois, "Let Us Reason Together," 231.

8. Baer and Singer, *African American Religion*, 38, 44; Baron, "The Demand for Black Labor," 105.

9. Tinney, "Exclusivistic Tendencies," 34, 35; Nelson, "For Such a Time," 18, 20; Nelson, "The Black Face of Church Renewal," 180; cf., Clemmons, *Mason*, 31.

10. Hollenweger, "Priorities in Pentecostal Research," 9; cf., Goff, *Fields White Unto Harvest*, 132.

11. Daniels, "God Makes No Differences in Nationality," 72.

12. Wacker, "Bibliography and Historiography of Pentecostalism," 75.

matter, female, Hispanic, or Oneness Pentecostals, were relegated to mere footnotes of history.[13] AG racial effrontery began while in COGIC, in the demand for credentials signed only by their own White ministers, and escalated into a rejection of all Black ministers, COGIC or otherwise.[14] In *Race and the Assemblies of God Church* Newman concludes that race was, indeed, "*the* dominant factor," the unspoken, overriding motivation in the AG formation.[15] Paternalism, certainly, was a contributing factor. More seriously, Newman points out, Whites viewed COGIC as not good enough for them, but just "fine for African Americans."[16] Howard Kenyon, too, argues that the socio-ethical proclivity for acceptance by Evangelicalism, the tendency toward social accommodation, and the "acquiescence to the American culture" all contributed to these AG attitudes.[17]

Hollenweger's pointed discussion, especially interpreting Lovett, suggests a White avoidance of dealing with racism's injustices, which makes it easier to ignore, excuse, or justify them. A common fatalistic excuse, referred to by Lovett, involves putting off and ignoring racial issues "until Jesus comes," as though only heaven held the needed solutions. Hollenweger adds that, in the attempt to assuage guilt and justify lack of remedial action, responsibility is relegated to the individual rather than the churches as a whole.[18]

An emphasis on individual responsibility, according to Lovett, cannot be allowed to translate into a failure by the churches themselves "to indict racism in word and deed." Nor must they conveniently conceal racism behind varied forms of denial or the shame of tokenism. As is the nature of subterfuge, denial usually works, disguising the real issues. Since racism by definition refuses to share institutional power and resources, by "blaming the victim and subjugating persons on the basis of the pigmentation of

13. Rosenior, "Toward Racial Reconciliation," 301; cf., Gerloff, "Hope of Redemption," 162–63.

14. Clemmons, *Mason*, 27, 70, 71; see also Lincoln and Mamiya, *Black Church in the African American Experience*, 81; Robeck, "Historical Roots of Racial Unity and Division in American Pentecostalism," 11; cf., also, Rodgers, "The Assemblies of God and the Long Journey toward Racial Reconciliation," 57.

15. Newman, *Race and the Assemblies of God Church*, 87, 9–10; italics added.

16. Ibid., 78, 74, 90, 97, 98–101, 116, 170.

17. Kenyon, "An Analysis of Ethical Issues," 401, 406, 404; cf., Owens, *Azusa*, 105, 97–98, 76; Butler, "Walls of Separation," 1.

18. Hollenweger, *Pentecostalism*, 29, 31.

their skin," Lovett argues that Whites find it easier to maintain the status quo than to upset the powers that be.[19]

A powerful conclusion, argued by Jennings, in his article in *The Gospel in Black and White,* is that the disturbing fact remains that the church complies with racism due to the sad and disturbing reality that it has remained unable to "mount an adequate *theological* response" to it.[20]

## 6.3 The Haywood Influence in Erasing the Color Line

Having permeated Oneness thought long before penned in melodic prose in "I See a Crimson Stream," the Haywood theological response to racism was "the blood." This was, therefore, linked critically to the all flesh aspect of Pentecost, as a washing and changing of the people of Pentecost, transforming them into the people of the Spirit. This is precisely Bartleman's meaning in referencing the interracial aspect of the Azusa Street meetings—the color line was washed away in the blood.[21]

These were two monumental Pentecostal motifs, therefore, in close proximity and application, Calvary and Pentecost, with the blood being a rich theological symbol of the all-inclusiveness of the Spirit. From this perspective, for Haywood to see a crimson stream of blood, was to see the hope it alone could bring, the hope long held for the lifting of the human spirit past the racist disappointments of the unredeemed. Such a power impacting racial change was the dream for which Haywood had worked for sixteen years constituting the "rays of hope for tomorrow" which "across our path were laid." Not as merely static points of a finely honed dogma about salvific hope, but far more broadly applied, indeed.[22]

### 6.3.1 The Impact of the Perspectives of Washington & DuBois on Haywood

Before considering Haywood's considerable role in attempting to counter the interracial back-tracking of the Oneness movement, it is helpful to

19. Lovett, "The Present," 6, 8, 3, 14.
20. Jennings, "Wandering in the Wilderness," 37–38, 4, 20; italics added.
21. Bartleman, *Los Angeles*, 49.
22. Haywood, "I See a Crimson Stream," 45.

recognize the diversity of influences on his perceptions, especially that of Washington and DuBois. Washington's influence is more clearly demonstrable in Haywood due to the articles and sketches which are related to him in *The Freeman.* According to Raymond Smock, it was Booker T. Washington who became the "leading spokesman for the race," with millions of African Americans looking to Washington "as their new Moses" during the challenges of this period of Black American history. Nevertheless, Washington's policy of acceptance of Jim Crow limitations, and thus the perceived "soft peddling" of civil rights, together with the worsening Black condition, resulted in growing Black opposition to the leadership perspective of Washington.[23]

But the *Boston Guardian* was criticized by *The Freeman* and *The Recorder* for its attacks on Washington's efforts. DuBois criticized Washington's approach as being merely accommodation, whereas DuBois wanted activism. Tony Seybert, who has referred to the early Black press as "Soldiers Without Swords," explains that "most Black newspapers tended to be conservative, supporting the ideas of Washington."[24] Haywood's *Freeman* sketches certainly lauded Washington, as did millions of other African Americans, for many years after attitudes toward his policies began to shift and became controversial among many Blacks. Haywood's perspective reflected in his 1903 *Freeman* sketches was strongly influenced by, and supportive of, Booker T. Washington. The newspaper articles which accompanied these sketches were likely Haywood's as well.[25]

The "creative conflict" between Washington and an increasing array of other Black leaders resulted in DuBois publicly breaking with Washington's leadership in 1903, after which he established the NAACP in 1906 as a political rival to his influence on African Americans. DuBois, the first African American PhD at Harvard, was outspoken in his criticisms of Washington: "Mr. Washington's programme practically accepts the alleged inferiority of the Negro races."[26] Washington, who died in 1915, had,

23. Smock, *Booker T. Washington*, 3, 120, 171, 203; cf. Bieze, *Booker T. Washington*, 16, 25, 29.

24. Seybert, "The Black Press."

25. See *The Freeman,* "Uncle Sam," January 29, 1903, 1, "union" Whites saying, "We won't work with a negro"; "Good Citizenship Must Be Encouraged," February 7, 1903, 1, bricks being hurled at Roosevelt for extending a hand to the "negro"; the 1903 attacks out of Boston on Booker T. Washington, "The Hour and the Man," February 14, 1903, 1; see also, Bundy, "Urban Realities," 238.

26. Smock, *Booker T. Washington,* 154, 166, 193; cf. Moses, *Creative Conflict in African American Thought*; DuBois, *Souls of Black Folk*, 50.

according to some, not established a platform which could counter the increasing tide of Jim Crow discriminatory laws leveled against African Americans.

W. E. B. DuBois had also clearly impacted Haywood in significant, though less obvious ways. DuBois' writings, which called the color line "*the* problem of the twentieth century," were pervasive in African American society. In the mindset of the PAW this was a period of hope that the color line would indeed be washed away, a desire partially realized in the period 1906–1924.

DuBois, too, appears to have influenced Haywood's perceptions in a manner not unlike that of millions of African Americans of the era, that is, via his 1903 history making sociological analysis of African American "double consciousness," *The Souls of Black Folk*. DuBois had become extremely impatient with Washington's inadequate methods of addressing racial concerns, which he had come to see as practically accepting the limitations set on Blacks by what he called "Whiteness."[27] Haywood was evidently less impacted by the rivalry with Washington's ideology, but does show evidence of DuBois' double consciousness influence as reflected in his monumental hymn "I See A Crimson Stream of Blood."

## 6.3.2 The Crimson Stream and the Voice in the Wilderness

The equality for which Washington, DuBois, and others were laboring on a national and political level, the PAW was embarking upon in the religious realm, although its scope was international as well. But Haywood did not consider himself dependent upon human theoretical initiative. Instead, one of the most inspiring directives which impacted the challenge facing Haywood was a Sunday vision experience, which has since become legendary, from which he emerged with the entirety of his most memorable and moving hymn–"I See a Crimson Stream of Blood."

In the face of mounting difficulties Haywood reportedly emerged from his office directly into the Christ Temple sanctuary early in 1920 having received a dramatic, life changing vision of Calvary and of a crimson stream of blood. Etching the experience into verse he wrote: "Its waves which reach the throne of God are sweeping over me!"[28]

27. DuBois, *The Souls of Black Folk*, 13, 43, 50.

28. Haywood, "I See a Crimson Stream of Blood," 45; cf. also the 1919 songs "Thank God, For the Blood" and "The Day of Redemption," in *Bridegroom Songs*, 2, 37, as well as the 1921 song "I'm Saved Today," 61. Note the lines "in vain attempt the

Nathaniel A. Urshan, son of Andrew Urshan and former General Superintendent of the UPCI, was known to speak of the indelible impression that the resulting anthem had upon him at the age of eight as a weeping Haywood sang of the cross and the crimson stream. In fact, Haywood's reputation as a singer and hymn leader was of such notoriety that members of Christ Temple from the era said that when he sang it was "like the heavens would open up."[29]

The hymn not only demonstrates the centrality of the cross in Oneness theological thought, but it clearly reflects, as well, an embedded double-meaning or explication reflecting DuBois' influence. The "sin's demands" denote the role of blood in salvation, but the blood is also celebratory "rays of hope" for a blood washed equity and integration for all people, if not in culture, certainly in the kingdom.

> On Cal'vry's hill of sorrow
> Where sin's demands were paid
> And rays of hope for tomorrow
> Across our path were laid.[30]

A crimson stream, in fact, became an iconic symbol of spiritual *and* racial possibilities, now synonymous with Haywood himself. Although the color line would be redrawn at the close of the Doak era and prove to be White, the interracial period which PAW visionaries accomplished took on a grandiose aura of enduring quality far ahead of its time. When the unspeakable redrawing of the color line began to take place, Haywood again became the protectorate of the interracial vision, although a majority of the White Oneness Pentecostals walked away.

In his role as a conscience and noted spokesman of a fledgling movement Haywood's identity, via his widely read periodical, *The Voice in the Wilderness,* was widely touted. Leonard had noted well in 1916: "They have a voice." And it was increasingly obvious. The *Indianapolis Star* reported by mid-1924, at the time of the ground breaking for the building of Haywood's impressive new Christ Temple: "The membership of the church now numbers almost 1,200."[31] Every aspect of Haywood's leadership voice

soul to free," "Christ removed it all away," "God's church is the power that's shaking this hour," and "to raise the guilty from the fall and wash their sins away."

29. Garrett, *Haywood*, 25; Peagler, *Haywood*, 61; N. A. Urshan (1920–2005) led the UPCI for twenty four years from 1978–2002.

30. Haywood, "I See A Crimson Stream of Blood," first stanza, 45.

31. "Apostolic Faith Assembly," *The Indianapolis Star,* June 13, 1924, 14; Few Pentecostal leaders enjoyed such renown. Indicative of his wide populist appeal is Ewart's

and notoriety was on the ascendancy, evidencing that emerging interracial discontent had not stemmed from displeasure with Haywood.[32]

Haywood's double-voiced "wilderness" analogy served as an expressive symbol of both the salvation cry and the lonely cry for racial justice and equity. Such wilderness difficulties for Haywood were nothing new. "We were obligated to nail up the sashes with boards," Haywood noted of segregationist attempts in 1908 and 1909 to shut down his first W. Michigan Street mission.[33] With the painful redrawing of the color line in the 1920s the emotional boarding up of the sashes once again took its toll as Haywood ultimately faced the same racial obstacles and reversals which had confronted Seymour, the Azusa Street revival, Mason, and others.

In spite of years of publicly visible effort expended in the erasing of the color line, no amount of legislation and rhetoric could keep it washed away once the return to cultural racist norms preempted original restorationist vision. But the White commitment to radical separatist theology in areas of holiness and doctrine which so profoundly shaped its theological and self-identifying underpinnings and norms in many facets of its development served to mask its abandonment in the area of race.

This tilt in the scales was a major shift from its Azusa Street ideological framework in which the interracial goal and reality constituted an eschatological sign of the validity of the Pentecostal experience and, indeed, the movement itself.[34] During the height of the interracial zeal White and Black Oneness participants from a broad spectrum of the movement had stood proudly with Haywood, as with other Black leadership, just as they had with White leadership, defying the worldliness of racism.[35]

glowing report in *The Phenomenon of Pentecost* describing Haywood's much sought after ministry at the Main Street Mission in Los Angeles: "Crowds flocked there to enjoy his wonderful Bible teaching. His knowledge of the word of God was phenomenal," see Ewart, *Phenomenon*, 50.

32. As Anthea Butler noted in her SPS presidential address, "Pentecostal Traditions We Should Pass On," 344, what obliterates the prophetic voice of liberation and holiness is very often the unwillingness "to engage the difficult issues." And so it was within the Oneness movement at the time.

33. Ford, "Integrated City Church Had Stormy History," 4.

34. Seymour's first issue of *The Apostolic Faith* reflected an identical emphasis, reporting on the multiple evidences which follow genuine Spirit baptism such as healings, miracles, and "gifts of languages" for missionary preaching. Prominent among these signs, but contrary to the social norms, was the "humble" reality of "colored people," Whites, and all "nationalities" now united by the Spirit to "worship together," and, thus, a replication of Pentecost; see "The Same Old Way," 3.

35. Nevertheless, after the initial flourishing of the interracial arrangement beginning in January 1918, the strength to engage the difficult issue of race did not endure

## 6.4 Preliminary Discussion on Redrawing an Erased Color Line

As evidence mounted of the looming racial division many were hoping that Haywood could secure a resolution which might salvage the damaged hull of the PAW. The accomplishments of the united interracial PAW had certainly astounded most observers, especially since it was evident that its relative cohesion and racial intentionality had not come easily.[36]

In Indianapolis, where the societal rejection included the dubbing of the movement as the "Gliggy Bluks," Haywood was successful nevertheless. Only someone with adequately manifest zeal could have done as much in a state which by the mid-1920s led the nation in supremacist rhetoric. *The Encyclopedia of Indianapolis* states, "Nowhere was 'Americanization' stronger or the Ku Klux Klan more active." In fact, the KKK resurgence in Indiana into the largest in the U.S. was a parallel-in-contrast to Haywood's impressive church and the interracial PAW.[37]

MacRobert coined the expression "redrawing the color line" relative to the Oneness racial division, which necessarily assumes the fact of a previously erased color line. The noteworthy intentions of the Oneness movement in interracial fervor fade in the redrawing of that which it had defied. But with societal opinion weighing so heavily in support of scrapping the entire interracial effort, the reversal could be quick and effortless. The culture would, for once, applaud them.

Throughout the first half of 1924 it was rather doubtful that anyone could halt the seemingly inevitable division, although many did try. Unity Conferences were implemented and apparently accelerated prior to the

---

past the fateful split in the Pentecostal Assemblies of the World in October 1924.

36. The one most credited with its success had been Haywood, so much so that its headquarters was relocated to Roosevelt Road in Indianapolis just a few miles northeast of the center of downtown. According to the *2000 U.S. Census* Indianapolis population was 791,926, with a metro population of 1.5 million. The Indiana state population was 6,080,485. The 2000 U.S. ethnic population was 75.1 percent White, 12.3 percent Black, 12.5 percent Hispanic, and 3.6 percent Asian. Indiana has a lower ethnic composition than the U.S. as a whole with 87.5 percent White, 8.4 percent Black, 3.5 percent Hispanic, and 1 percent Asian; see DeBarros, Phillips, and Overberg, "Census 2000." Cf., also, Rudolph, *Hoosier Faiths*, 545, listing the 1990 Indiana African America population as 165,570.

37. Barrows and Bodenhamer, *Encyclopedia of Indianapolis*, vii; Pierce, *Polite Protest*, 12; Rudolph, *Hoosier Faiths*, 547; cf. Blum, *Reforging*, 233. The Indianapolis Black population was increasing, with 34,678 by 1920 (11 percent) and 43,967 by 1930 (12 percent).

1924 PAW Conference.[38] *The Christian Outlook* reported that Mason had even attended the November 1923 conference held in Chicago. A bit of startling news, without further corroboration or detail, was printed by Haywood: "Elder C. H. Mason, General Overseer of the Church of God in Christ, acknowledged in the Unity Conference at Chicago that he was baptized in Jesus name in August 1920 in Mississippi."[39]

In the past surprisingly little public or written discussion had occurred which went on record espousing division on any basis. But southern dissatisfaction with the racial complexity of the PAW was not hidden by any means, although it was not until 1922 that public actions began to explicitly demonstrate it. By 1923 the PAW business minutes suggested that they were in "danger of being rent asunder" over certain administrative issues. The actual core reasons for the emerging problems which remained mostly unspoken had more to do with conflicting culturalisms and racial insensitivities than polity.[40] On the whole a rather minuscule amount of historical primary source material has been helpful in evaluating the exact what, how, and why of the deterioration of the interracial commitment.

The most extensive study of the movement, Reed's *"In Jesus' Name"*, devotes little attention to either the race issue within the movement or the racial divide, as is also the case with Howell's "People of the Name."[41] Roderick R. Brown, in his 2005 University of South Dakota MA thesis, "Oneness Pentecostalism and Ethnicity: A Decision Out of Step," although emphasizing a wealth of related historical materials regarding race and church history, commits only a few pages to the PAW racial divide.

Lawson, on the other hand, has addressed the racial issue directly in his writings. Clanton also focuses almost entirely upon explanations for the division in his discussion of the PAW.[42] In *The Early Pentecostal*

38. Unity Conferences were held November 1922, November 1923, and then again in about April 1924, see *Christian Outlook*, January 1923, 25, December 1923, 235, and May 1924, 370.

39. Other related information regarding the conference pointed to its failure to promote unity; see "Column of Information," 251.

40. *1923–1924 PAW Minute Book*, "Minutes of the General Assembly of the P. A. of W. Convention Held at St. Louis, Missouri, October 4 to 6 Inclusive, 1923–1924, 9. Even Haywood's own self-reflective understandings of the divisions are mostly little more than hints of otherwise unexpressed detail.

41. Reed, *"In Jesus' Name,"* 211–16; Howell, "People of the Name," 100–105.

42. Brown, "Oneness Pentecostalism and Ethnicity: A Decision Out of Step," 126–135; see also, "Oneness Pentecostalism and Race: A Decision Out of Step"; Clanton, *United*, 33–39.

*Revival,* African American PAW historian James L. Tyson devotes at least 35 pages to the racial issue, including one entire chapter, entitled "The Body Is Rent Asunder."[43]

Interesting in the discussion of the racial division is the contrast in approach between Blacks and Whites. For example, White ministers expected that their simple disavowal of racial motivation would be adequate proof that a racial division was in no way racially motivated. But such dodging of the real substance of the conflict comes across as mostly disingenuous and patronizing.

The earliest Oneness historical account by Golder, an African American, offers a very different explanation regarding the why of the events, for example, than that of Foster and Clanton. "When the White ministers left the Pentecostal Assemblies of the World," Clanton suggests, "it was not because of racial prejudice on their part." On the other hand, Golder, a protégé of Haywood's, interprets the data differently, arguing emphatically, and persuasively, that "color," indeed, was the issue.

> If the White Pentecostal brethren would have stood firm against prejudice and racial injustice, having the most powerful authority (the Holy Spirit) and the most powerful message (the Gospel of Jesus Christ), they could have been the instruments of God for the destruction of this hideous ideology. But instead of fighting it, they submitted to its influence and have been affected by it even until now.[44]

Historians, short of oppositional concession, have nevertheless substantiated Golder's assessment indicating that White Oneness Pentecostalism, as Butler said of its Trinitarian counterpart, "slowly began to dance." In similar fashion the movement resisted its own basic impulse and affirmed the racial exclusion of the dominant culture with deliberate intent.[45] Wacker adds to the equation the aspect of a growing movement which accommodates to racist assumptions of the culture. The movement failed to "provide a sustained theology of race reconciliation" which inevitably led to the same recoiling and pulling away found in society at large.[46]

43. Tyson, *Early Pentecostal Revival*, 192–95, 199–201, 240–68.

44. Clanton, *United*, 32; Golder, *History*, 65, 80, cited in Hollenweger, *Pentecostalism*, 31, and MacRobert, *Black Roots*, 73.

45. Butler, "Pentecostal Traditions," 347; italics added.

46. Wacker, *Heaven Below*, 226–27.

## 6.5 Historical Account of the PAW Racial Division (1923–1924)

Aspects of the sequence of what Reed refers to as "gradually revealed serious racial tensions" can be unclear amidst the nuanced interpretations of the events.[47] But Haywood's perspective, however sketchy or veiled, is available from before, during, and after the racial divide. He noted in late 1923, for example: "God has called for his brethren to be gathered *together*. But there are men standing in the way."[48]

The first evidence of a southern racial problem began to surface, associated with a Southern Bible Conference in Little Rock in 1922, about the time of Seymour's death and in the fifth year after the PAW merger. Kidson's suggestion years later that separation had been "talked, pro and con" for several years previous may have been an isolated reality, but there appears to be no evidence of this before or during the crisis. Kidson later insisted that they had not intended to completely separate.[49]

### 6.5.1 Southern and Separate White Meetings, Abolished Chairmanship, and Rejection of the Signature of Black Officials on Ministerial Licenses

Safety concerns and segregated public facilities excluded Blacks from southern meetings, requiring that they be held in the north, adding expense to southerners, as well as assuring that they were "outnumbered" by northerners.[50] Southerners had longed for a meeting, such as the Southern Bible Conference, although, by necessity, African American ministers would be excluded, whether or not that was the intended motive. Yet not being able to have meetings in the South was blamed for an increasing

47. T. C. Davis' appointment to sign credentials in place of Haywood, for example, may have been a move toward placing Blacks under White leadership, but it was not an attempt to have a Black minister sign the credentials of Black ministers, because Davis was White; see *1910 U.S. Census*, Indianapolis, IN, 5B; *1920 U.S. Census*, Indianapolis, IN, 25A; Tyson, *Early Pentecostal Revival*, 203; cf., Reed, *"In Jesus' Name,"* 211–12.

48. Haywood, "Unity Conference," *CO*, 235; italics added.

49. According to this perception of the conflict things somehow simply escalated; see Kidson, *The Apostolic Herald*, July 30, 5; Clanton, *United*, 37.

50. Peagler, *Haywood*, 79; Foster, *Think It Not Strange*, 73; The Southern Bible Conference, held in November 1922, was sponsored by the states of AR, MO, TX, AL, OK, TN, and LA, from which it derived its committee members.

"agitation," on the one hand, whereas Blacks resented exclusion, the actuality of which would only serve to increase suspicion that these ministers viewed segregation as a preference.

As Brown has pointed out, the southern conference caused PAW African American ministers to believe that they were being "intentionally excluded." Even more incendiary was the fact of the enormous success of the Little Rock meeting. Word spread that one of the organizers, William A. Mulford, formerly Haywood's "Assistant Secretary," wired Doak, who reportedly "took the next train" to join them. It was so widely touted that a booklet was published, inadvertently announcing an unsanctioned, repeat "Southern" gathering, to be held just prior to the 1923 PAW convention.[51]

While African Americans were stunned and angered, many White participants, evidently, failed to grasp the height of insensitivity, offense, and highly volatile course of events, that had been triggered by these actions. Conference organizer S. C. McClain, commenting later, appears to express southern regret for what they saw as mostly a "wrong impression," southerners forcing their meetings upon the entire PAW. The name was even changed to "*General* Bible Conference" for 1924. Booth-Clibborn's booklet, *A Call to the Dust and Ashes,* in spite of the furor, called for the strong support of "our own organization," the PAW: "Don't jump out . . . If the organization-ship is leaking—all hands to pumps—yours included."[52]

The stage, though, had already been set for a turbulent "voyage" throughout 1923. Historians have tended to jump quickly to the events of 1924, although the characterizations of a "volatile situation," exacerbated by "power struggles," an "undercurrent," and a "growing rift" or "wedge" between the races, are as apropos to 1923, as to the following year.[53] The threats to the 'organizational-ship' were increasingly more titanic-like. According to an "open letter" published by Haywood, within just a few months after the Southern Bible Conference, Doak announced intentions to resign, i.e., "refused re-election," "many months before" the 1923 PAW Convention in St. Louis.[54]

51. Brown, "Race," 15; Foster, *Think It Not Strange*, 75; Tyson, *Early Pentecostal Revival*, 245–46, 194; cf., Booth-Clibborn, *A Call to the Dust and Ashes.*

52. Brown, "Ethnicity," 128; Clanton, *United*, 35; "General Bible Conference," *Christian Outlook*, February 1924, 281, italics added; see also Booth-Clibborn, *Dust and Ashes*, 21.

53. Brown, "Ethnicity," 131; Tyson, *Early Pentecostal Revival*, 199, 201; Reed, *"In Jesus' Name,"* 212; Foster, *Think It Not Strange*, 76.

54. Haywood, "Open Letter," 208.

As a result, two fateful decisions were made in 1923 which would effectively torpedo the interracial aspirations of the Pentecostal Assemblies of the World. First, with Doak's resignation, a battle ensued over a replacement. Perhaps this was related to White concerns that the obvious might occur, the election of Haywood, an African American, at the precise time that race relations were so terribly strained, and the burgeoning growth of the southern Oneness region was becoming rather notable. It was, nonetheless, rather unprecedented to entirely eliminate the office of chairman as a supposed solution.

"There was a considerable amount of controversy," Haywood himself reported, "as to who should be the next Ex. Chairman." Haywood also reported that the "tension ran high." Haywood himself, in the *Christian Outlook*, explained the final, surprising decision—to replace the office of PAW chairman with a seven member interracial Board of Presbyters, comprised of Haywood, Urshan, Goss, Schooler, Booth-Clibborn, Turpin, and Davis.[55]

The second St. Louis decision, less personal to Haywood, but another major racial upset, eclipsed the struggle over the office of Chairman, with an admission that the PAW, including Haywood, had found it necessary to compromise over the issue of some who did not want an African American to sign their credentials. Haywood's "open letter" in October 1923 appears to have been an attempt to soften the blow.

> Owing to trouble among some of the Ministers in the Southern part of the country, it was decided that Credentials and Fellowship Certificates *for such cases* should be signed by Elder T. C. Davis and Howard A. Goss. In cases where it is not deemed necessary the general course will be pursued.[56]

The Minutes revealed an even more telling and injurious state of affairs than perhaps the leadership had been willing to admit in the face of such a ludicrous decision. MacRoberts' response echoes Golder's: "Are we expected to believe that a person's colour is discernible from his signature?" Golder wondered at Whites being "made to suffer," or as Paddock

55. Ibid. The arrangement, though, designated Haywood as Secretary and editor-in-chief of the *Christian Outlook*. See also, *1923–1924 PAW Minute Book*, 9. Four members were White: Urshan, Goss, Booth-Clibborn, and Davis, and three Black: Haywood, Schooler, and Turpin.

56. Haywood, "Open Letter," 208.

says, "belittled," simply because a Black man's name "appeared on his credentials."[57]

It is highly probable that such a compromise emboldened the hopes of some Whites that their African American ministerial comrades would yield to their wishes and accept further concessions. The actual resolution, the fateful "Resolution #4," suggested, or "deemed advisable," and, thus, recommended that Blacks also have their credentials signed only by Blacks, adding that the new arrangement was being mandated by "conditions" which were "no fault of the brethren."[58]

In the December 1923 *Christian Outlook* Haywood repeated explanations regarding the "no chairman" decision, but not the "no-Black-signature" debate, which was ravaging the movement. He did, though, place a brief article about KKK race hatred in the same column: "In this fight between the Ku Klux Klan and the Catholics the saints of God should remain neutral . . . To join the Klans you will have to take on race hatred." As a farewell to Doak, now an honorary Board member, but with the office of chairman now defunct, Haywood reported: "Elder E. W. Doak and wife have reached California, after motoring thirty days."[59]

### 6.5.2 The Defeat of the 1924 Texas Resolution for a Separate Black Administration and the Resulting White Walk-Out

Texas was the largest and fastest growing state in the southern region, rivaling Indianapolis and the Midwest, and quickly becoming the largest Oneness center by the later 1920s. Many of its earliest and most influential leaders had emerged from Parham's influence and ministry, rather than having self-identified with Seymour's influence and Azusa, such as Goss, Opperman, Floyd, Lyons, Hall, Osborn and Fauss. The early influence of leadership, and certainly the southern regional attitudes, impacted their interracial commitments. Yet, for all that, it was not possible to pass a separate-but-equal resolution in the PAW in 1924.

Although southern dominance and influence figured prominently into the racial tensions within the PAW in 1923–1924, northern

57. MacRobert, *Black Roots*, 74; Golder, *History*, 82–83; Paddock, *Heritage*, 49.

58. *1923–1924 PAW Minute Book*, 10; see also, Tyson, *Early Pentecostal Revival*, 243.

59. "Column of Information," *CO*, 251; *1923–1924 PAW Minute Book*, 12.

participation, or acquiescence, played a role, as well. Tensions, though, did not ensue because of a "disproportionate" number of PAW Black "officials," which was quite representative, but rather because of the rapidly increasing number of Black ministers within the PAW in ratio to the number of White ministers.[60]

As 1924 began, Haywood appears to have been quite aware that the interracial PAW was in danger of "sinking" fast. Brown has uncovered another factor which, evidently, was contributing to the deterioration of an "already volatile situation," involving White protestation to an "interracial marriage" which had occurred in Booth-Clibborn's St. Paul church. The ongoing "signature" issue, appropriately depicted by Tyson as a virtual "powder keg" of "hypocrisy" and "ignorance," continued to inflict irreparable damage to the organizational hull.[61]

"If ever there was a time that God's people should be laying aside their differences," Haywood lamented in May, "it is now." "If we cannot forgive our brethren and seek the unity of the Spirit we are not ready for the appearing of our Savoir." But "division," not "unity," was the proposal of July 8, 1924 PAW Presbyter Board meeting—"a proposed division between the colored and White," the north under Schooler, the South under Urshan.[62]

Haywood had just asked regarding the "petty differences" which were ripping away at the organization: "Can such a thing be of God?" "As brethren, and as a movement," he pleaded, "we must stand together for the name of Jesus sake." But Haywood's efforts at peacemaking and unity were clearly being ignored.[63]

The Texas ministers met in Houston just days prior to the October 1924 Chicago PAW Convention, and, energized by earlier concessions, they drafted two resolutions more destructive to racial unity than anything previously proposed, except that this time the African American ministers were prepared for them. Not only did the Texas delegation propose for the PAW to have two separate administrations, one Black, one White, but they also intended to change the name Pentecostal Assemblies of the World.[64]

60. Cf., Howell, "People of the Name," 100–101, and Golder, *History*, 65.

61. Brown, "Ethnicity," 131; Tyson, *Early Pentecostal Revival*, 243–44.

62. Haywood, "Editorials—The Time Is At Hand," 356; Haywood, PAW Board of Presbyters Meeting Handwritten Secretarial Notes, Chicago, July 8, 1924, see Tyson, *Chalices*, 295.

63. Haywood, "Division Coming," 374, "One Convention," 418, and "Editorial," 441.

64. Clanton, *United*, 36–37; Reed, *"In Jesus' Name,"* 213; Tyson, *Early Pentecostal Revival*, 247.

The southern proposal attempted to convince Whites, many of whom were absolutely opposed to these suggestions, as well as Blacks, of the rationale behind the supposed "handicap" caused by interracial unity, such as a supposed hindrance in spreading the gospel and the strain of dealing with social laws. But they were not impressed with such arguments. Tyson suggests that it was nothing less than "flagrant rebellion."[65]

Nonetheless, amidst counter proposals and attempts at appeasement, and, in what was likely an unexpected turn of events from the perspective of the Whites leading this cause, the proposals were totally rejected. The intent had not been total separation, but neither could they bring themselves to yield to a racial defeat. Instead, on October 15, 1924, the defeated White faction walked out, leaving the vast majority of the White segment of the movement in considerable disarray, and the Black ministers, and the sizeable number of remaining Whites, wounded and angry, but in full control of the PAW.

## 6.6 Post-Interracial PAW Perspectives on the Racial Division

In his popular *Witness of God*, the following month, Urshan explained the organizational rationale of withdrawing ministers: "Now we will minister to them under the 'Apostolic Churches of Jesus Christ,' the *White ministerial branch* of the P. A. W."[66] Although the PAW had soundly rejected the offending, back-to-segregation proposal, calling for two administrations in one organization, so that Whites could separate from Blacks, effort was exerted to downplay the division. Haywood, less than three months after the split, for the sake of the movement, wrote the following call to unity:

> The Pentecostal Assemblies of the World is not divided. Those who have reorganized themselves are supposed to have done so in order that the Southern brethren might not be hindered in reaching the public with their message. It should have been called the Southern Branch of the P. A. of W. However that may be, the General body stands as heretofore. There is no difference with God. All brethren shall be treated alike"[67]

65. Tyson, *Early Pentecostal Revival*, 248; Reed, *"In Jesus' Name,"* 213 n. 38.

66. Urshan, *Witness of God*, 6:8.

67. Haywood, "Editorial Page," *CO*, 4; italics added. Other, similar Haywood articles in *Christian Outlook* include "Unity and Strength," December 1923, 196, "New Organizations," October 1924, 466, "United Methodism: North and South," November 1924, 481, and "Unity," July 1925, 124.

Perhaps the lingering hope that they might still be able to rally a majority of both Black and White ministers continued to inspire them, as did their commitment to interracial organization and the loyal White segment of the PAW, now approximately 20–30% of the whole. "The P. A. of W., will always stand for the freedom of the brethren," Haywood wrote in 1926, "regardless to race or color."

The additional explanation, though, remains sufficiently ambiguous, without a means of clarification: "It is true that a large number of the brethren are the opposite race, but this was caused by many of those drawing away after they found that finances were running short, and drew many others with them who were ignorant of their devices."[68] In spite of Haywood's conciliatory explanation that the PAW was actually not "divided," for him to speak of the "supposed" motives of the withdrawing Whites belies the underlying anguish which resulted from the racial divide. Tyson's depiction of the impact upon the PAW as "rent asunder" by these events is certainly realistically and historically accurate.[69]

The *Christian Outlook*, perhaps for spiritual and social reasons, did not become the vehicle for a publicly strident critique, or even a lament, of a re-emergence and the role of the racism at play in the Oneness racial division. Although suppressed and never admitted to, Golder calls it the "demon of prejudice." He suggests that, whether from the failure to maintain their previous commitment, or due to an original absence of any meaningful commitment, a sufficient number of them "never intended that a black brother should be equal with his White brethren even in the Lord." MacRobert, additionally, interprets, as "spineless" and "bigoted," their uncritical accommodation to social "laws and customs."[70]

Brown's thesis, rather than emphasizing the historical questions surrounding the racial issues within the movement, concentrates on related race-slave history and societal race law, drawing heavily on Ayers' *The Promise of the New South* and Woodward's *The Strange Career of Jim Crow*. Holding, more or less, the interracial impulse to be fundamental to Pentecostalism, Brown concludes that the White Oneness decision for racial division was "a decision out of step," incongruent with the movement's fundamental orientation, the central tenet of "every kindred, and tongue,

68. Cf., Tyson, *Early Pentecostal Revival*, 206–7; Haywood, "To Our Brethren of Color," 3.

69. Tyson, *Early Pentecostal Revival*, 192.

70. Golder, *History*, 78–79; see also MacRobert, "Spirit and the Wall," 132.

and people, and nation" (Rev 5:9 KJV), essentially, its own restorative organizing principle.[71]

Except for that of R. C. Lawson, African American Oneness responses from this episode, and even before, though not unexpected, were exceptionally guarded, at least in print. Wacker makes the observation of Haywood's approach to the issue of race, in his *Voice in the Wilderness*, "in particular," for example, that it "seemed almost completely unmindful of such matters." But Wacker's conclusion, that race only "played a slight role" in his "theological thinking," is certainly inadequate as an explanation of Haywood's racial motivations.[72]

Quite descript of the Black Oneness responses, and Haywood, particularly, Wacker also notes: "Facing a brick wall of incomprehension at best, and hostility at worst black Pentecostals responded with resignation."[73] To use the expression of Salvation Army Captain Ballington Booth, perhaps the experience of grappling with the social dilemmas was, for African Americans of the period, a bit like "bailing the ocean with a thimble."[74] Note, as well, Stephens' suggestion:

> The southern Pentecostal press only occasionally broached the subject of race. Even periodicals edited by African-Americans, including the *Whole Truth* and *Voice in the Wilderness*, showed *remarkable inattention* to matters of racial justice . . . Yet when the press did grapple with issues of race, it must have made a strong impact upon its readers.[75]

## 6.7 Comparative Analyses of the PAW Racial Divide—Tinney, MacRobert, and Gerloff

The most exceptional of the essential analyses regarding implications of the early Oneness racial division, undoubtedly, include that of Tinney, MacRobert, and especially Gerloff's varying studies, most notably the summarized insights in "Theology En Route of Migration." Hollenweger's evaluation of MacRobert offers the salient warning regarding the

71. Brown, "Ethnicity," 136ff., 48–74; cf. Ayers, *The Promise of the New South*, and Woodward, *The Strange Career of Jim Crow*.

72. Wacker, *Heaven Below*, 234.

73. Ibid., 321.

74. Quoted in Sanders, *Saints in Exile*, 135 n. 27.

75. Stephens, "There Is Magic in Print," italics added.

temptation, in efforts at race analysis and unity, to fail to go far enough and simply "pass over to hallelujahs." "In many cases," he cautions, "Pentecostal spirituality obscures the real societal and structural relationships."[76]

Tinney's work is an excellent starting point for grappling with the difficulty of the Oneness racial division which sabotaged its interracial union. The Oneness mindset, or orientation, was actually viewed by Tinney as "a conscious break with White theological standards," which, in turn, impacted White acceptance of Black cultural influences. Whites, he suggests, were "far more influenced" by Black culture, than vice-versa, citing, as an example, "the wider acceptance of emotional display even in White churches." The movement's propensities were too radical, spiritually and socially, for the majority of its AG counterparts. Tinney argues that, "in actuality," AG and other Trinitarian rejection of the movement was "largely because of opposition to the Black cultural influences."[77]

Tinney's explanation of the Oneness racial division may best be described as pragmatic, in that he suggests that it stemmed from the culturally "competing worldviews" of Black versus White. Interestingly, though, rather than positing "blatant" or conscious racism at its core, Tinney attributes the conflict, basically, to the cultural clash originating from, and, most importantly, operating at the "*subconscious* level." Therefore, denied and suppressed, divergent culturalisms, "struggling to gain ascendancy," were the inevitable divisive spark.[78]

The acceptance and introduction of social segregation, nonetheless, unmasked the racism at the root of the conflict, inflicting a deep wound and long-term "feeling of being betrayed by Whites," which remains to the present. In Tinney's general discussion of racism elsewhere he has noted the disingenuous attempt to "simply pass off" segregation as merely the influence "of society in general," which clearly "misses the point."[79]

Instead, the root of implicit racism, as delineated by Tinney, is extremely complex. "The truth of the matter is that rigid class interests lie behind Pentecostal self-definition and expression," as well as "the supposed superiority of Whites over blacks." Unfortunately, not only have meaningful efforts at reconciliation, including repentance, *not* occurred since the Oneness racial division, but, as Tinney points outs, "one searches in vain for an attempt in White literature bearing on the ethical import

76. Hollenweger, *Pentecost Between Black and White*, 11.

77. Tinney, "Significance of Race," 64, 63.

78. Ibid., 62, 63; italics added.

79. Ibid., 63, 62.

of race." Rather than reconciliation, blame has been shifted, ironically, to African Americans in 1924 for supposedly "misunderstanding" southern segregation.[80]

Hollenweger has suggested that MacRobert's studies go "a long way to explain the *root cause* for the division between black and White churches," that is, their core cultural differences. "They are two cultures," he adds, "an oral, narrative, inclusive, black culture" and "a literary, conceptual, exclusive, White" culture. As the title indicates, MacRobert's *The Black Roots and White Racism of Early Pentecostalism in the USA* is not specifically critiquing the Oneness racial division. He does, though, offer some critical insights regarding it, albeit within the framework of the African and slave roots of Pentecostalism and the significance of race in Black Pentecostal perception and understanding.[81]

MacRobert, like Tinney, considers the Assemblies of God Oneness rejection to be predicated upon prejudice against the Black contingency and its desire to "become 'respectable.'" But he also views the 1918 PAW/GAAA merger as mostly a "marriage of convenience," which was also a term used by Whites who had been associated with COGIC. He does recognize, though, that the level of commitment in the PAW was such that "both black and White were working together and, more importantly, sharing in leadership," an indicator, it seems, of more than mere convenience.

MacRobert's mid-1980s work also popularized the descriptive expression "redrawing the color line."[82] The division is framed in terms of "racially prejudiced Whites" withdrawing in a "White exodus," due to "their unwillingness to challenge the racist mores of the South." MacRobert is quite accurate in appraisal. Unity was replaced by acrimony.[83] Ultimately, therefore, lacking the will and courage to resist, the Oneness Pentecostal movement reverted to inconsistent segregationist division, rather than retain the equality principle of Pentecost. In doing so, it yielded to a cultural racial climate rooted in a long history of "dehumanization," injustice, and a perception that interracial spirituality was unchristian and immoral.[84]

80. Tinney, "Exclusivistic Tendencies," 45; Foster, *Think It Not Strange*, 74.

81. MacRobert, *Black Roots*, e.g., "The 'New Issue' Controversy," 68–76.

82. MacRobert, *Black Roots*, 70, 71, 72.

83. Ibid., 73, 75.

84. Hollenweger, "Towards an Intercultural History of Christianity," 529, 531, 530; italics added; MacRobert, *Black Roots*, 9, 124, 73, 75.

Roswith Gerloff, in her focus upon the socio-economically dispossessed nature of Black Oneness Pentecostalism, goes into unique case study detail, beyond Robert Mapes Anderson's general assumptions of disinheritance, in order to investigate what she sees as a fundamental racial freedom resulting from its spirituality. Her views are quite insightful. She views the essence of the Black Oneness experience, for example, distinctly from the White movement, as radically providing new meaning to their lives so as to constitute "an outright protest against the prevailing social order." They utilize "the power of the gospel for liberation from *White superiority*," and, most importantly, overcome "the speechlessness of people in society."[85]

> Deprived, dispossessed and racially persecuted people became liberated and encouraged to preach, teach, heal, baptize and evangelize not in the name(s) or authority of traditions and dogmas imposed on them by historical (mainly White-Western) Christianity, but in the "Name," power or authority of "Jesus only."[86]

Haywood is viewed by Gerloff as critical to the movement's development for several reasons, including the reference to Tinney's belief that Haywood was, in fact, "devoid of prejudice." Gerloff considers Haywood to have been what she calls a bilingual theologian "capable of thinking and preaching in the language of another culture, but also of introducing a bridge-building process by which elements of one culture become incorporated into another."[87] Haywood is understood by Tinney to be the key to the Black "non-derivative character" of the movement, although employing White elements in order to circulate Black oral sources. Such elements allowed the movement to emerge on its own terms, "without asking consent from any White minister," in the precise categories of Gerlach and Hines' social analysis.[88]

Several factors are suggested by Gerloff which possibly prompted the White Oneness split, such as a "patronizing" attitude toward Blacks. She notes, too, that some must have been threatened by the expansive and perhaps unanticipated growth in the number of African American ministers

85. Gerloff, "Theology En Route," 24, 3, 5; italics added.

86. Ibid., 1.

87. Ibid., 11.

88. Ibid., 9, 5, 6, 8, drawing heavily from Gerlach and Hine, "Five Factors Crucial" and *People, Power, Change*.

in the PAW, as well as the fact that Whites adapted themselves uncritically to the Jim Crow laws.[89]

Gerloff, relying extensively on Tinney's analysis of the White Oneness racial division, also views the 1924 racial impasse in terms of causes other than race or "*rather than racial hostility*." Initially, at least, class and culturalisms, which produce "a natural and normal competition" between White and Black cultures, were to blame, "each struggling to maintain its own autonomous character."[90]

The context of Gerloff's explanation is also Anderson's assumption in *Vision of the Disinherited* that the White Oneness movement was almost composed entirely of the most impoverished and socially ostracized. From such a viewpoint is derived a sense that, as the poorest of the poor, they were ill-equipped to alter their own circumstances or deal with societal racial ills. Anderson's socioeconomic interpretive stance suggests, for example, that their interracial efforts were not so much anti-racist as "anti-intellectual."[91]

The implications suggest that, for example, the AG, already stigmatized as the dispossessed poor, resisted further stigmatization by rejecting the Oneness faction, and thus avoided a double rejection. Early interracial Oneness Pentecostalism, referred to by Anderson as "the most bi-racial wing" of the movement could similarly be characterized as having arrived at a point of avoiding a triple societal rejection, i.e., disinherited, heretical, and integrated.

Although Anderson probably overstates his case, he suggests that rather than challenge society the logical sociological escape was "other worldly religion." He concludes, therefore, that division and controversy were actually essential to the invigoration of Pentecostalism, as a continuing stimulus for growth which he sees as becoming "the very life and breath" of the movement.[92]

89. Gerloff, *Plea for British Black Theologies*, 108, 121, 110.

90. Gerloff, "Theology En Route," 23–24; italics added.

91. Anderson, *Disinherited*, 231, 224, 226, 227; Gerloff, "Theology En Route," 25.

92. Anderson, *Disinherited*, 227, 192, 193.

## 6.8 R. C. Lawson's Response to Oneness Racial Division

Although the racial split took place within the organizational structure of the PAW, the division impacted the entire movement and became its de facto modus operandi for segregating the majority of the movement. No other Oneness group even came close to approximating the interracial detail of the PAW. Robert C. Lawson essentially removed himself from the interracial equation within the PAW by establishing the COOLJC five years prior, his own separate all-Black organization, and moving his ministry to the Bronx.

This, however, did not silence Lawson, who spoke out rather definitively against the racial division in the Oneness movement at that time. Most apropos to the times, Lawson published a book on the subject of race and racism, in 1925, *The Anthropology of Jesus Christ Our Kinsman Redeemer*, as the racial problem was at its height in the movement.

He similarly addressed the race issue in later publications and sermons, as, for example, *An Open Letter to a Southern White Minister*, which defends "intermarriage." Also, posthumously, his equally persuasive sermons were published in *For the Defense of the Gospel*, edited by Arthur M. Anderson, with one message entitled: "The Greatest Evil in This World is Race Prejudice."[93]

Haywood's responsive method, on the other hand, had tended toward a much more reconciliatory demeanor, holding out hope, perhaps, of reuniting the divided races. Jacobsen suggests that these were non-responses: "Lawson decided that *silence* had lasted long enough."[94] It was, therefore, time to be emphatic.

> The egotism of race-pride . . . is causing many to think themselves better than other people; therefore, separating themselves in the body of Christ through shame of their brethren of the colored race. And because of this ungodly behavior, they are bringing upon themselves spiritual leprosy—typifying what came upon Miriam when she murmured against Moses because of his Ethiopian wife. There are many of them murmuring today, especially among our White brethren in the South, because of

93. Lawson, *An Open Letter to a Southern White Minister*; Anderson, *For the Defense of the Gospel*, including "Sparks from the Anvil," July 1947, 326–28, "Prejudice," August 1947, 328–29, "Make Full Proof of Thy Ministry," May 1956, 404, and "The Greatest Evil in This World is Race Prejudice," June 1957, 248–56.

94. Jacobsen, *A Reader*, 200; italics added.

> colored brethren occupying prominent positions in the Church of Christ. Some even go so far as refusing to take credentials signed by a Negro. What a shame![95]

*Anthropology* quotes extensively from experts on race in order to establish a "one blood" motif (from Acts 17:26, AV) for all races, requiring, therefore, "mixing the bloods of all" races in humanity's kinsman redeemer, Jesus. As such, he argues, Jesus had "Negro blood in him," thus assuring that "our Savior isn't wholly of any race."[96] Lawson sees this as guaranteeing the "absolute equality" of the races. "We thought sure," Lawson laments, "that . . . the Apostolic people would teach these groups a wonderful lesson by example. We thought they would show that the true people of God are one regardless of what nationality or race they may belong."

> But today we find that this color proposition is the one thing that is separating many from the love of God. Whenever a people or a movement have encountered this proposition and have failed to walk according to the truth of the gospel, they have lost power with God, and have failed, as an instrument in his hands, in saving the world for Christ. How can we love and abide in God whom we have not seen if we cannot love without respect of persons our brethren—not separating on any grounds or reasons.[97]

No doubt, many had longed to speak so plainly, yet, compelled by a myriad of concerns, withheld confrontation and judgment. Of course, by experience Lawson knew well the varied grounds for separation, but not grounds based upon the unfathomable—a "respect of persons," involving nothing more than the color of one's skin. Douglas Jacobsen, whose *Thinking in the Spirit* offers an important analysis of Lawson's views, suggests, by way of introduction, that no "ethnically identified group of Christians could claim the movement as their own. It belonged to everyone."[98]

According to Jacobsen, Lawson was the "first person in the pentecostal movement to address race with any degree of sustained theological attention," with expressions suggesting possible influences from Lawson's popular contemporary New York Black leader Marcus Garvey. The

95. Lawson, *Anthropology*, 33.

96. Ibid., 47, 40, 35.

97. Ibid., 34, 33.

98. Jacobsen, *Thinking in the Spirit*, 260.

historical emphasis of the *Anthropology of Jesus Christ* is a depiction of the Black race as a people undeniably worthy of the respect of every race.[99]

According to Anderson, the "typical Pentecostal attitude" toward the KKK was that of inactivity, or silence, in the face of racial injustice. Glenn A Cook, long an interracial advocate, nonetheless, made the astounding suggestion that the KKK was, "no doubt . . . at least permitted by the *Lord* to curb" Catholicism. He did, though, add the clarification that "we could not bow down and worship a fiery cross and don the hood."[100]

Lawson simply did not attempt to mollify his listeners or readers, or the "soft peddlers," by attempting to alleviate their responsibility by ignoring or shifting blame, for example, or by criticizing others, such as Haywood, or his handling of the events, or by putting the blame off on culture. Haywood and Lawson's goals were clearly the same.[101] Lawson often had wielded criticism of Haywood, but, in this situation, he exercised obvious restraint.

In a 1957 sermon on race prejudice Lawson, again, referenced what he saw as the enormous detriment of the acceptance of racist logic by the Jesus' Name church, and lamented its lack of agents of change.

> This, the Pentecostal people ought to have seen long ago and lifted up their voices against the iniquity . . . But as a whole, nothing has been said or done but all the status quo of society have been accepted or supinely submitted to and a pattern followed. Up until this day, even after the Supreme Court of the United States declared unconstitutional, unlawful and unrighteous the entire system of race segregation, no White Pentecostal movement has declared its stand and support and advocacy of this revolutionary edict, and begun to put into practice desegregation.[102]

## 6.9 Conclusion

Although the racist dilemmas of the twentieth century American context were a wilderness experience for African Americans, the restoration impulse within Pentecostalism, and especially the Azusa Street revival, built

99. On the other hand, parallel expressions between Garvey and Lawson weren't inclusive of Garvey's pan-African philosophy; see Jacobsen, *Thinking in the Spirit*, 263.

100. Anderson, *Disinherited*, 191; Cook, "The K.K.K. and Romanism," 1; italics added.

101. Cf. also, Millner, "Love Lived."

102. Lawson, "Race Prejudice," 249.

upon the all-flesh inclusive theology of Pentecost. Unfortunately, neither Christianity at-large nor Pentecostalism was able to mount an adequate theological response to racism and counter the spirit of the age. Instead, initial restorative impulses were held inconsistently and a failure to indict racism in action, as well as outright racism, signaled the death knell to interracial hopes in Pentecostal groups.

Oneness Pentecostalism remained persistent, at first, in its restorationist yearnings for original, pristine New Testament practice and continued to apply its counter-cultural orientation to the issue of race as best exemplified in the interracial PAW prior to 1925. Oneness perspective, following Haywood's lead, remained convinced that the color line of race was washed away in the crimson stream of blood. But signs of the movement's breakdown in commitment to its interracial vision appeared in the early 1920s with the expansive southern segment of the movement resisting the PAW arrangement, especially with the accompanying expansive growth of the African American segment of the PAW.

In openly divisive actions which were incongruent and completely out of step with their earlier restorative convictions, a large segment of southern ministers determined to eradicate the interracial aspect of the PAW. The Texas attempt to relegate African Americans to a separate organization was soundly defeated and 70 to 80 percent of the White ministers walked out of the convention. Haywood's efforts in the end failed, and like the earlier events within the AG, African American Oneness Pentecostals once again knew a wilderness of betrayal and the aftermath of decimated allegiances.

Comprehending the reasons or excuses for redrawing racial lines for which so much energy had been expended to erase is certainly complex and difficult. But the corporate urge for respectability, the appeal of the pragmatic, and the ever-present cultural pull ultimately led to the patronization which obliterated the restorative ideology which had kept their interracial commitments intact. For Oneness Pentecostalism this commitment meant that they were experiencing a triple rejection of social disinheritance, religious heresy, and cultural stigmatization.

Even as Haywood attempted to restore order Lawson's assessment was resoundingly emphatic—the activism of White Oneness Pentecostals in splintering the movement racially was spiritual leprosy! He called the movement to reject the cultural sin of racism and desegregate once again, an action which would not remotely begin again for more than fifty years. Lawson's appeal was based on the identical ideology which integrated the movement in 1906, a Savior Whose blood included the races of all humanity and set the church at variance with society. Like Haywood, whose interracial advocacy Lawson carefully refrained from criticizing, he remained convinced that the color line was washed away in the blood of Christ.

# 7

# The Haywood Era in Oneness Pentecostalism

## The Reshaping of Its Legacy and Organizational Context

### 7.1 Ramification of Racial Reversals in Oneness Pentecostalism

The abrupt 1924 schism within the PAW put a decisive and jolting end to the interracial era within early Oneness Pentecostalism. But the ramifications of that breach of relationship were a far-reaching impact upon organizational diffusion, non-uniformity and disunity, alienation, disruption of effort, and, of course, racial segregation and disparity. The subsequent development of the movement was characterized by destabilization and increasing division and independency throughout, beginning with the White disparate organizational attempts.

The problem was put succinctly by Haywood, as Golder noted, as having been the result of the lack of backbone. In an article entitled "Men With Backbone," he articulated the problem and condemned the practice of racial segregation.

> If ever there was a place where there should be no distinctions made between races and nationalities in their common fellowship, it ought to be in the true church of God. A secular minister said recently that the church must do its part to put down this terrible growing race hatred. To prove their sincerity in this

> matter, ministers of various churches exchange pulpits in many of the large cities of the East and the middle-west. If they can do it, what is the matter with the people who claim to have more of the grace of God than they?[1]

This rhetorical question, posed by Haywood, was at the center of the issue over racial prejudice and separation—"What is the matter?" The fact that they had "more of the grace of God" than "secular" ministers should have made a difference. Unfortunately, Oneness Pentecostalism in the last half of the 1920s was in a highly tenuous phase of development, hardly discernible to most, and obscured by urges for pragmatism and a yearning for some degree of societal normalcy.

An abrupt "walk-out" of the majority of Whites, and the immediacy of pragmatism, nonetheless, in the context of impulsive disbandment, was clearly not in the long-range best interest of the movement. Only eight years earlier, at the AG Council meeting, the Oneness proponents, though stunned by the rejection, had walked out together, Black and White, men and women. Now, with the calloused estrangement of nearly half of the entire Oneness movement in the United States, based on race, considerable havoc, and an unnecessary degree of destabilization, was wreaked upon the movement.

From no vantage point, even that of erroneous triumphalism or social accommodation, can the disruptive consequences of the rupture be even remotely justified—the subsequent abandonment of the interracial commitment, the schism from the Black PAW ministers and minority White ministers, and the reversion to all-White Oneness ministerial bodies. Perhaps the most impacting of the far-reaching ramifications, though, related to the protracted splintering and alienation. Preferment and promotion of racial segregation, in effect, ended all meaningful hope of a broadly unified movement.

On another level, neither could Oneness Pentecostalism now benefit from the advantage of a cohesive front by which, for example, it might impact the broader movement. Instead, ethnic centers of Oneness Pentecostalism in the U.S., along with their burgeoning mission centers, and the emerging autochthonous Oneness bodies around the world, developed in virtual isolation from each other, as well as from mainstream Pentecostalism and Christianity in general. While the reorganized 1925 Pentecostal Assemblies of the World was adequately resilient and prompt in establishing its new leadership, the overall long-term impact of the rift between the

1. Haywood, "Men With Backbone," cited in Golder, *Haywood*, 63.

White and Black segments of the movement has been virtually incalculable, remaining unreconciled.

The White disregard for interracial cooperation, with the resultant disintegration of the integrated PAW, on that fateful "Black Thursday," as some, such as Tyson, have dubbed it, might have inflicted even more harm, had it not been for the resolve of Black and White ministers alike in the PAW to buttress their originating principles. Certainly, those who knew Haywood best knew him as the preacher's preacher, the quintessential representative, "immaculate in dress," yet, in exemplary demeanor, likewise. This "quiet, determined man," as observers characterized him, with what Smith considered a "melancholic temperament," remained consistent and offered steady guidance to a disrupted Pentecostal Assemblies of the World.[2]

Decades of White organizational disunity and the surge of independency were part of the price of segregation belying an underlying disregard for the bond of fellowship which their common message had previously guaranteed. The galvanized organizational segregation which ensued would indeed impact the movement and the PAW for generations. Yet the indifference to the premium assets of unity which had been central to the movement did not dissuade everyone from their interracial vision or from lifting the ailing PAW from neglect to restructured organizational success.

## 7.2 The Black Majority/White Minority of the New PAW (1925)

In spite of the interracial devastation in the PAW Haywood was able to set the tone of reaction to the heavy blow of disappointment with positive advancement. Abandonment and the feeling of betrayal could not be allowed to cause the rest to falter, including the significant number of Whites who had stood with the PAW. Therefore, it is quite evident that Haywood allowed very little proverbial moss to gather in the months following the parting of the ways. The well-known healing evangelist F. F. Bosworth was one of the speakers at Haywood's 15th Annual Convention, as was A. D. Urshan, just weeks afterward and it continued to be business as usual.[3]

2. Peagler, *Haywood*, 49, citing Golder; Bundy, "Haywood," 237; Garrett, *Haywood*, 78, citing Smith.

3. The convention was held in November 1924, with Urshan as a speaker, as was F. F. Bosworth, a Trinitarian who had published his popular book *Christ the Healer* in

The Indianapolis church, too, had only just been renamed "Christ Temple." The Old Testament temple theme of God's presence and glory, the interracial 1200-member congregation, and the nearly two-thousand-seat new edifice served as a most opportune symbol of the collective pride of the entire PAW. The completion of Christ Temple, the first overflow crowd service, Thanksgiving Evening at the convention, in the face of Indianapolis' severe race restrictions, symbolized all the more the PAW's determined resolve.

> During 1924, perhaps the year of the Klans' greatest influence in Indiana, Haywood dared to break yet another taboo. In Indianapolis, the area north of Fall Creek was off-limits for African Americans . . . Haywood purchased a number of vacant lots used primarily as a dump. The city . . . assumed that any African American enterprise north of Fall Creek would fail.[4]

This is not, of course, indication that Haywood's leadership had not been tarnished or weakened by the loss of White support and the precipitous collapse of interracial harmony within the movement. In the divisional chaos Haywood himself certainly faced, not merely the brunt of White rejection, but something of an undercurrent of Black dissent and disapproval, as well, which contributed, in turn, to an ebb and flow of losses and setbacks within the PAW.

With Doak's resignation in 1923 and the decision to abolish the office of chairman, the PAW was left without a designated leader for two years. In spite of this being the crucial period in which the PAW was being rent asunder by racial division, Haywood almost certainly would have been elected chairman had the office not been eradicated. Instead, that would not occur until September 25, 1925 when the PAW completely reorganized under a preferred episcopal church government, created a Board of Bishops, and, then, elected G. T. Haywood as its first Bishop. F. K. Smith from Columbus, having recently left COOLJC to rejoin the PAW, became the General Secretary.[5]

If the peak interracial roster for 1925 was 1,200, as Tyson reports, there was evidently a resulting slow-down in ministerial expansion for both Blacks and Whites, and, possibly, the loss of a number of ministers. The percentage of loss, Black or White, would be impacted, of course, if

---

1922, see Urshan, "Indianapolis Visit," 8; also, note the reports of the Cadle Tabernacle meetings, Haywood, "Bosworth Campaign in Indianapolis," 4.

4. Bundy, "Haywood," 250; Peagler, *Haywood*, 67–68.

5. Peagler, *Haywood*, 84–85; Smith, *A Devout Man*, 26–27.

Blacks had begun to actually "outnumber" Whites in the PAW, which is an unverified, but suggested, possibility.[6] Nevertheless, by late 1926 the PAW could report only 556 ministers, indicating that the PAW had approximately 200 churches.[7] By late 1930, with 683 ministers, the PAW had approximately 250 churches.

Although only a minority of these were White churches, both of the PAW's national boards, the Board of Bishops and the Board of District Elders, continued to reflect the PAW's continued commitment to interracial organizational vision. In spite of the withdrawal of every White Board member in 1924, the PAW, with its new White minority of about 20%, immediately made G. B. Rowe and A. F. Varnell Bishops. In 1927 J. A. Rayl replaced Varnell and in 1929 A. W. Lewis replaced Rayl.[8] The PAW interracial resolve and intentionality had never encompassed a submission to White dominance, but meaningful fulfillment of an every-people-vision of Pentecostalism. The 1930 national Board of District Elders, for example, reflected a considerable White PAW presence with its 33 members boasting one Hispanic and 14 Whites.[9]

The Black/White rift appears to have resulted in temporary slowed organizational expansion within the PAW and the reorganizing White bodies. The combined total, by 1927, in the newly forming White groups was 458 ministers, inclusive of the Apostolic Church of Jesus Christ, Emmanuel's Church in Jesus Christ, and the Pentecostal Ministers Association. What is significant with this total is that it is not the estimated 600 or more White ministers that had exited the PAW in 1924. The discrepancy in the number of White ministers was due to additional organizational diffusion resulting in varied contingents, such as the PAW White minority, the emergence of lesser known new White groups, various wait-and-see factions, and a strong contingent opting for total independency.

6. Tyson, *Early Pentecostal Revival*, 248, suggesting, possibly, that the withdrawing Whites remained on the PAW rosters for some time after their withdrawal; Peagler, *Haywood*, 81.

7. See *1926–1927 PAW Minute Book*; cf., 642 in 1927 and 618 in 1928, see *1927–1928 PAW Minute Book* and *1928–1929 PAW Minute Book*.

8. Urshan, though vacating his 1924 position and joining the ACJC, also remained with the PAW into the 1930s, see *1930 PAW Minute Book*, 26; see Tyson, *Early Pentecostal Revival*, 249, *1927 PAW Minute Book*, 1, *1929 PAW Minute Book*, 1.

9. See *1930–1931 PAW Minute Book*, including, P. Banderas, N. Wall, J. Nelson, H. Alvey, G. Russell, T. Russell, E. Burrell, S. Burrow, G. Nichol, D. Dainty, B. Blunt, F. Curts, H. Curtis, B. Pettiford, and C. Lundquist; other members included, R. Cook, G. Carlisle, Bennie Nelson, H. White, N. Bibbs, B. David, A. Urshan, T. Urshan, H. Nigh, L. Spillman.

Some of the PAW White minority remained simply as a show of support, and as a protest against the majority disruption of racial unity, although many of them, at the same time, were members of all-White groups. They were, evidently, uneasy with, and regretful for, the White legacy of distrust. A photograph of the 1929 Illinois District Conference of the PAW in Centralia, for example, indicates that only five of the 32 ministers present were African American. The majority of Whites, though, in addition to their PAW membership, were part of separate White groups.[10] Foster's observation is interesting here: "Not all the White ministers of the north went along with any of these groups, preferring to stay with the Pentecostal Assemblies of the World."[11] Therefore, the withdrawal had been perceived as a southern walkout so thorough that only northern White ministers remained with the PAW.

The consequences of impetuous separation included, therefore, resentment between Whites for the irreversible damages inflicted upon their African American friends and the movement as a whole. Others, such as A. W. Lewis, and later, R. P. Paddock, were so outraged by White indifference and racial unconcern that they refused identification with White organization.[12] By the 1930s, though, many were beginning to exit the PAW for White counterparts. Nevertheless, the PAW's extensive interracial legacy includes two White Presiding Bishops, Paddock and L. C. Brisbin, of the eight Bishops to serve since Haywood.

## 7.3 White Organizational Diffusion, Separation, and Independency

The disunity and destabilization was nowhere more evident than in the divisive impact upon White Oneness Pentecostalism itself, with scores of groups forming across the country and with many opting for independency. The Oneness movement was now more closely mirroring in this regard what was also happening in Pentecostalism as a whole. The Oneness message had now become no more sufficient a rallying point of unity than the theological positions of other segments of Pentecostalism had been. But this had not become evident within early Oneness Pentecostalism until

10. Photo of 1927 Illinois PAW District Conference in *Historical News* 18/3 (April-June 1999) 4, includes Odel Cagle, Nora Baker, L. C. Hall (a PMA official, 1925 and 1926), Harry Blunt, and Ben Blunt.

11. Foster, *Think It Not Strange*, 79.

12. Paddock, *Apostolic Heritage*, 52–56.

the racial division within the closely watched Pentecostal Assemblies of the World. Nevertheless, the African Americans in the PAW, however, appear to have been both energized and, within a relatively brief time span, solidified by the difficult events of the 1924 schism.

### 7.3.1 Disparate Organizational Efforts of Exiting White Ministers

Three southern-dominated White groups, the ACJC, ECJC, and PMA, emerged early in 1925, the very groups which would eventually amalgamate into the United Pentecostal Church in 1945 twenty years later. But the process of decades evidences the representative lack of White unity and pervasive division at the time of the walk-out in 1924. Two small groups formed separately in early 1925 which totaled approximately 125–150 ministers, the Apostolic Churches of Jesus Christ in St. Louis and the slightly smaller Pentecostal Ministerial Alliance which formed in February in Jackson, Tennessee with 60 ministers.

Within eight months, the PMA was already splintered. Ministers left the PMA to form their own third group, the Emmanuel's Church in Jesus Christ, which organized in October 1925 with 50 ministers in Houston, Texas. Although organizing with few, if any, Black ministers, the ECJC reportedly established an African American ministerial policy, essentially equivalent to that rejected by the PAW just one year previous. African Americans were to be credentialed in the southern-based ECJC with "full rights," but, when large enough, they were promised a separate administrative organization, which was to work in harmony with, and therefore, *under*, the White ECJC.[13]

The ECJC was concentrated in Texas, Louisiana, and Oklahoma, originally under Lyons and G. C. Stroud. Little is known of the earliest history and ministerial roster of the ACJC, except for its founders and Missouri base. The PMA, though, was known to have been concentrated in Arkansas, Missouri, Tennessee Louisiana, Indiana, and Idaho.[14]

The substantial growth of southern Oneness Pentecostalism would, in fact, eventually secure the dominance of this all-White segment of the movement, its amalgamation into one organization, the UPCI, the attraction of Whites throughout all the other regions, and its growth into the

13. Clanton, *United*, 62.

14. See, for example, ibid., 44–137; French, *Our God Is One*, 81–83.

largest body of Oneness churches in the U.S. That eventuality would not begin to unfold in Haywood's lifetime, or even the following decade, not, in fact, until the decade of the 1940s. The fledgling ACJC and PMA, along with the other separate organizations, independents, and indigenous groups were known to Haywood, but the later well-known names of PAJA and PCI were not created until after his 1931 passing. In 1931 the PAW and ACJC, which was the now merged ECJC/ACJC, merged to become PAJC, Pentecostal Assemblies of Jesus Christ. And the PMA changed its name in 1932 to the PCI, Pentecostal Church, Inc.

In the 1920s, though, in danger of accentuated mediocrity in their divided condition, the ex-PAW White ministers who comprised these new organizations seriously needed solutions for reuniting. Unfortunately, before they would actually be united, as they had been formerly in the PAW, it would require two decades of effort and not less than ten merger attempts.

Not surprisingly, Haywood very likely held out reasonable hopes, early on, for the possibility that the majority of Whites might be reunited in the Pentecostal Assemblies of the World, at least until the prevailing preference for all-White, separatist organizational structures became more and more apparent and entrenched.

As an early positive advance in this direction, the ECJC and ACJC merged in Guthrie, Oklahoma in 1927, with about 70 ministers attending, retaining at first the name ECJC. But, in 1928, the name changed to ACJC, with "Churches" becoming "Church."[15] A convention photo included the leaders, W. H. Lyons, W. H. Whittington, and Ben Pemberton, who became chairman at the merger, as well as B. H. Hite, C. P. Williams, O. F. Fauss, Nora Baker, W. R. Pair, and one unidentified African American minister. The first ECJC chairman, Texas minister W. H. Lyons, was Spirit filled in a Millicent Goss revival in 1910 in Texas.[16] ACJC leaders Whittington and Pemberton were St. Louis pastors. Whittington, though, temporarily withdrew in November over the tentative retention of the "ECJC" nomenclature. By 1928, the ECJC elected Fauss as Chairman. The early PMA was headed first by Hall, then Goss.

The 1927 ECJC/ACJC merged roster indicates a total of 3 missionaries and 174 ministers, with 67 percent being from two southern states, Texas, with 40 percent, and Louisiana, 27 percent. Wide fluctuation in ministerial affiliation, especially new affiliation, was commonplace with

15. Clanton, *United*, 67–68; Foster, *Think It Not Strange*, 78.

16. Treece, *Beulah*, 256–57, 252; Goss, *Winds*, 145–46.

these emerging bodies. By 1929, for example, fluctuation in regional affiliation in the ACJC lowered the overall Texas percentage to a "mere" 25 percent. Texas dominance, however, in White Oneness Pentecostalism, now legendary, had clearly become established. Emerging regional, and even state, hegemony may have figured into the overall organizational morass temporarily characteristic of this ex-PAW segment of White Oneness ministers.[17]

The combined total of the three newly organized all White organizations, the ACJC, ECJC, and PMA, by 1930, with an estimated total of 600 ministers and 230 churches, was still not as large as the integrated Black, Hispanic, and White union of ministers within the reorganized 1930 PAW which had remained committed to an interracial vision. The PMA had 222 ministers in 1926, after the Tennessee churches, under Rodgers, joined in mass. And by 1930 the PMA had grown to approximately 360 ministers and 130 churches, whereas the merged ACJC/ECJC, now the ACJC, had grown to about 260 ministers in 100 churches. The ACJC and ECJC merger had reportedly anticipated uniting nearly "400" ministers, but by 1929 only 236 ACJC ministers were indicated as having joined.[18]

### 7.3.2 The Engendering of Increased Separatism and Independency

By the late 1920s, Oneness leadership among Whites was also in flux. Opperman relocated, after 1920, to Dallas, then Lodi, California, near Sacramento, where he all but disappeared from leadership. Arkansas was no longer at the center of southern regional influence. Yet he served as the head of the controversial 1922 Southern Bible Conference, exiting the PAW in 1924, but was not instrumental in the development of the emerging new groups. Tragically, the 54 year-old Indiana-born scholar and Oneness statesman was killed in September 1926, along with five other occupants of the car, when they were struck by a Southern Pacific train in Baldwin Park in California.[19]

17. *1927–1928 Minute Book and Ministerial Roster of Emmanuel's Church in Jesus Christ,* St. Louis, Missouri; although merged, the name was not change to ACJC until late 1928. Clanton, *United*, 77.

18. Clanton and Clanton, *United*, 77, 56, 41, using a church to ministers ratio of 35 percent, indicative of the PAJC/PCI, see the separate 1944 minutes.

19. Williams, "In Memory of Bro. Opperman," 2; cf., news item in *The Pentecostal Witness* 2/12 (October 1, 1926) 1.

Whereas Goss is representative of early leadership which remained intricately involved in the organizational life of the movement, Glenn A. Cook and Frank J. Ewart represent the constant, strong influence of the tendency toward independency. Cook and Ewart had been the pioneer leaders of the movement in the west, and Opperman and Goss had been officials of the earliest Oneness bodies emerging in the south. Additionally, for example, Urshan, who was clearly a loyalist to the organizational cause, nevertheless symbolized this tendency quite well, carrying on his own active, separate ministerial paper, *The Witness of God,* well into the 1930s.

Cook, however, the quintessential Oneness proponent, stated in his newly established periodical, *Messiah's Coming Kingdom,* in 1927: "We have no credentials." He admits rather gleefully to his 5,000 subscribers that, he had been "turned out by everything we have joined so far." "We can't find anything that will have us."[20]

Goss, three years younger than Haywood, lived until 1964, served as an one of the key early Oneness leaders, and served as pastor in Toronto throughout the 1920s and 1930s. He was the major figure in the development of the PCI, resulting in his being elected first General Superintendent of the UPC, after the 1945 PCI and PAJC merger forming the UPC, a position he held through 1951.

Ewart (1876–1947), on the other hand, who had played the most prominent role in the emergence of the early movement, best represents the impulse of independency in Oneness Pentecostalism. Preferring independence, Ewart withdrew from the PAW in 1920.[21] Although Ewart and his Belvedere congregation were, at times, controversial, he continued to produce some of the movement's most legendary theological works. Several have been republished periodically by the UPCI, including *The Name and The Book* (1936), *Jesus: The Man and the Mystery* (1941), *The Revelation of Jesus Christ* (n. d.), and *The Phenomenon of Pentecost* (1947).[22] By 1947, after the merger of the PAJC and the PCI, Ewart had joined the UPC while pastoring in Monterrey Park, California.[23]

Emerging Oneness organizations, as well as an array of independent Oneness congregations throughout the south, Midwest, and the west coast regions, were very much aware of the divisive disputes which raged

20. Cook, "Editorial," *Messiah's Coming Kingdom*, 2.

21. Cf., the discussion regarding Ewart in Howell, "People of the Name," 101–2.

22. "A Tribute to Frank J. Ewart," *Historical News*, 2–4.

23. *1947 Ministerial Directory of the United Pentecostal Church, Inc.*, 81.

within the earliest flagship Oneness body—the Pentecostal Assemblies of the World. Such large-scale division was incapable of fostering unity, but served rather to engender fear in organizational power, confirming what many had already strongly suspected and feared. Many closest to the disputes, such as Baker in Oregon, already shaken by the earlier Frazee defections, were sufficiently frustrated as to be compelled toward a fiercely independent Oneness posture for many years. Others apparently lost confidence in organization as a vehicle for appropriately advancing the movement, while some evidently crafted similar excuses in the fostering of further divisions.

Initially, therefore, the new race based schismatic groups held little potential for uniting diverse factions throughout the U.S. In fact, the merger of three groups, the (1) PAW and (2) ACJC (1931), which became the PAJC, and later the PAJC and (3) PCI (1945), rather than resulting in one merged organization immediately resulted in four separate groups. These were the re-chartered, salvaged PAW (1932), a re-chartered ACJC (1932), a re-chartered PAJC (1945), and the UPC (1945).

In the case of the ACJC, for example, W. H. and Maud Whittington had always strongly advocated the use of the precise name—Apostolic Church of Jesus Christ. They therefore chose to ignore the 1931 merger and reorganized a small number of churches in 1932 under the original ACJC charter.[24]

Another large splinter group during this time which separated from the PAJC was an indication of the continued proliferation of Oneness independency which began to expand in 1924. The well-known minister, L. R. Ooton (1896–1976), from Tipton, Indiana, was instrumental in the 1941 schism from the PAJC, involving several hundred ministers throughout Indiana, Illinois, Ohio, and West Virginia, with the establishing of the AMA, Apostolic Ministerial Association.

Also, another well-known leader, the head of the Texas PAJC, R. L. Blankenship, similarly led a schism in 1945 by establishing the separate Apostolic Church with a few hundred PAJC ministers. Later, with the eventual waning of some of these smaller groups, ministers were re-absorbed into the larger Oneness bodies, after this heightened degree of early separatism and independency.

The 1920s saw the origination of several large White groups, not necessarily connected to ex-PAW Whites, and they were mostly southern,

24. Crownover, "Not Vain the Weakest" 5, 21–22; Whittington, *Pentecostal Witness*, 2.

but with a Midwestern presence as well. Some of these formed in pocketed areas across the region, as alternative regional bodies, challenging, more or less, the larger, national structural networks which were attempting to emerge. The most closely networked of these, concentrated in Texas, Louisiana, Mississippi, Tennessee Indiana, and Ohio, were the Assemblies of the Church of Jesus Christ in the Midwest, the Jesus Only Apostolic Church, and the Church of the Lord Jesus Christ. By 1930 they represented a total of approximately 60 churches. The JOAC and CLJC probably emerged in the early to mid-1920s, and the AsCJC originated from a 1933 splinter from the PAJC. They merged in 1952 to form the Assemblies of the Lord Jesus Christ.[25]

Other White ministers, some of which had been in the PAW, opted for a far more loosely organized network and formed the Cleveland, Tennessee based The Church of Jesus Christ by 1927. Independency impulses were strong and numerous others began in the 1940s to splinter into enclaves of localized leadership. Usually splintering over specifics regarding Oneness doctrinal details, splinter groups usually retained a form of the original name, "Church of Jesus Christ." By the 1930s the CJC had approximately 100 churches, concentrated in Georgia, Alabama, Florida, Mississippi, Tennessee and Kentucky.[26]

Several small Sabbath-keeping churches, for example, maintained loose-knit separate fellowship short of organizational union. Another group of White ministers established a group of churches which believed in what is termed "spiritual communion" or "bread of life" teaching, essentially disavowing literal communion of bread and wine. Some of these ministers had associated with the PAW, but with probably less than 20 churches concentrated in Arkansas, Tennessee and Mississippi they established the Associated Ministers of Jesus Christ in 1933 which later became the Associated Brotherhood of Christians.[27]

Another splinter occurred over the doctrine of initial evidence. A. F. "Doc" Varnell was one of two White Bishops of the PAW appointed in

25. Now the ALJC, see Mayo, *History of the Assemblies of the Lord Jesus Christ*, 10; cf., Nelson, "History of the Assemblies of the Lord Jesus Christ"; cf., www.aljc.org; Burgess and McGee, *DPCM*, 29; Jones, *GSPM*, 651; Gerloff, *Plea*, 439; Howell, *People*, 170–71. The ALJC is now the second largest White Oneness group in the U.S.

26. CJC, see Boyd Lawson Interview, M. K. Lawson's son, Cleveland, Tennessee October 10, 1993; Holder and Cole, *Voice of the Pioneers*, 7, 22, 24–28, 36, 106, 131–34; see also, Burgess, *DPCM*, 211; Gerloff, *Plea*, 440; cf., Jackson, "The Full Gospel Church of Jesus Christ."

27. AMJC (now ABC), see *Articles of Faith of the Associated Brotherhood of Christians*, 5; Taylor, *Baptismal Passover*.

1924. He left the PAW in late 1920s and in 1934 established the Evangelistic Ministerial Alliance with about 20 churches. The EMA was concentrated in Indiana and Illinois and later changed its name to Bethel Ministerial Association. The EMA (BMA), like Varnell, disavowed the common Oneness belief in tongues as the initial evidence of Spirit baptism.[28]

Therefore, within a decade of Haywood's passing, the movement saw the proliferation of not fewer than a dozen White organizations, a factor which contributed significantly to the widespread growth of independent Oneness churches, especially throughout the Midwest and the south.[29] These smaller bodies also provided a consistent venue of ministers and established congregations for the largest of the Oneness organizations, with the upward mobility of the more successful congregations resulting in a regular flow of ministers and churches from smaller to larger Oneness groups.

These White splinter organizations, not including the PAJC and PCI, constituted quite a sizeable, and competitive, body of churches, well over 200 churches by the mid 1930s. This sudden diffusion within White Oneness Pentecostalism represented, in itself, a form of independency. But, more significantly, the strength of the early independency impulse throughout the south, Midwest, and west coast has most often been underestimated, both in relation to these early alternative groups and the resistance to organizational structure on principle embodied in the independent movement. At least in the 1920s and 1930s, the unaffiliated White Oneness churches in these regions very likely numbered well into the hundreds. The "organized" Oneness bodies could not but help become the repeated beneficiary of such a vast and growing reservoir of untapped churches and ministries.

Another glimpse into the dynamic relationship of the White movement's emerging centers, organizational impetus, and the independency impulse is evident in its growth concentrations and its largest mega-type churches. As would be expected, the four largest Oneness White congregations in the U.S., for example, are all centrally located within areas which have been major epicenters of high Oneness concentration and sustained early growth. These largest churches are in Arkansas (North

28. BMA, see Wilson, *It Makes a Difference What You Believe*; Varnell, "Fifteen Things Wrong"; Tyson, *Early Pentecostal Revival*, 249, 261.

29. The AMA and the AC emerged in the 1940s, probably initially involving a minimum of 200 churches, contributing only later, though, to the increased independency impulse.

Little Rock), Louisiana (Alexandria), California (Stockton), and Indiana (Indianapolis).[30]

Yet one of these premier centers, the First Pentecostal Church of Jesus Christ of North Little Rock, Arkansas is evidently one of the largest White Oneness congregations in the United States, if not the largest, yet part of a considerably expansive network of independent Oneness churches.[31] FPC, the most excellent exemplar of southern, long-term Oneness independency, was, originally, briefly with the ALJC, a group perhaps closest to the early independent impulse. Therefore, FPC has contributed to this heritage and benefited as the heir of a vast southern network, or rather, distinct networks extending far beyond the south, of hundreds of Oneness churches.[32]

## 7.4 Expansion of Early Oneness Pentecostalism Worldwide

Nevertheless, the protracted U.S. splintering of the movement over a period of two decades set the stage for an atmosphere of decentralized expansion within the context of the global movement. From the time of the initial rebaptisms in Jesus' Name to Haywood's untimely passing, the seventeen year period, April 1914 to April 1931, the movement was birthed from within the networks of early Pentecostalism, or, from the perspective of Oneness Pentecostal participants Ewart and Goss–the phenomenon of Pentecost and the winds of God.

As an exemplar of aggressive evangelism and expansion, few, if any, early churches could rival Christ Temple's success, commitment, and support of the Oneness movement's worldwide thrust. With proficient leaders such as Witherspoon, Haywood, Lawson, and others, as models of accomplishment, lending their genius and zeal to organization, finance, literature production and missions, the movement grew rapidly, capturing the imaginations of dispossessed, albeit eager, recruits the world over.

30. Except for Little Rock, all are UPCI churches; see The Pentecostals of Alexandria, www.thepentecostals.org; Christian Life Center, www.clministry.com; and Calvary Tabernacle, www.calvarytabindy.org. The largest Black Oneness churches, all with links to the PAW, are The Potter's House, Dallas, TX, www.thepottershouse.org; Apostolic Church of God, Chicago, IL, www.acog-chicago.org; and the City of Refuge, Los Angeles, CA, www.noeljonesministries.org.

31. See Beall, *Mission Accomplished*, and Holmes, *Oceans of Blessings*.

32. Cf. also, Ryder, "Jesus Only Movement," 10–11.

Just how astute Haywood was concerning the state of the emerging Oneness movement can be seen in his straightforward assessment preserved in an interview conducted by papers with the New York press in 1930. He estimated extremely accurately that Oneness Pentecostalism, that is, the widespread "connections" of the PAW at that time, had 250,000 in 2,000 churches. Certainly, no individual was better positioned or qualified to know the global Oneness situation.

> The Pentecostal Assembly of the World has a membership of 250,000 representing America and foreign countries. There are 2,000 churches in the connection, three of which are in Palestine, ten in Jamaica, B.W.I; two in Hawaii and four in Liberia. The connection contributes about $900 a month to foreign work. The church has missionaries in Africa, Hawaii, Japan and India.[33]

Haywood's quarter of a million estimate has proven an excellent benchmark from which to begin analysis of early Oneness expansion during the Haywood era. Obviously, Oneness Pentecostalism was considerably larger than merely the PAW exclusively, but Haywood perceived of the PAW as representative of the movement as a whole and recognized the entirety of the movement as one entity to which he ultimately owed loyalty. He was certainly correct that within the short span of sixteen years from the time of the first rebaptisms in Jesus' Name, from 1914 to 1930, more than a quarter of million, or the actual total of 260,000, comprised the Oneness movement worldwide.

Not less than thirty five Oneness organizations are known to have emerged by the dawn of the 1930s, six Hispanic with half in the U.S. and half in Mexico, eleven Black U.S, eleven White U.S., and seven other autochthonous groups. Each of the White Oneness groups, with the exception of the earlier GAAA which had merged with the PAW in 1918, organized after the racial divide in the PAW, and at least five were bodies with direct involvement in the PAW racial schism.[34]

33. These totals therefore included the entire movement worldwide, missionary-led and autochthonous, indicating that Haywood thought of the PAW as the overarching organizational symbol of the movement. Also, he continued to subsume the White constituency under the title PAW; See Allen, "Pentecostal Assemblies to End Session Friday," 7, in Tyson, *Chalices*, 347; "Leaders at Convention Here," *New York Amsterdam News*, 7; cf., Golder, *Haywood*, 68.

34. White groups: (1) GAAA (merged with/became PAW, 1918), (2) ACJC, (3) ECJC (merged with/became ACJC, 1927), (4) PAJC (merger name of PAW/ACJC, 1931), (5) PMA (renamed PCI, 1932), with lesser-known histories for the (6) JOAC,

The majority of Black Oneness Pentecostal ministers, following the lead of Haywood and Lawson, adopted Finished Work theology, coalescing within three groups by 1930, the dominant PAW, COOLJC, and the much smaller Emmanuel Tabernacle Baptist Church Apostolic Faith. Four Holiness groups emerged early on which did not accept the Finished Work ideology, the Apostolic Faith Mission Church of God, Church of God (Apostolic), Apostolic Overcoming Holy Church of God, and Oneness group of the Church of the Living, the Pillar and Ground of the Truth. And four ex-COGIC Black Holiness groups embraced the Oneness position later in the 1920s, the Glorious Church of God in Christ Apostolic, New Bethel Church of God in Christ (Pentecostal), Pure Holiness Church of God, and the Free Church of God in Jesus' Name.[35]

Interestingly, the constituency totals for White and Black segments of the movement in the U.S. by 1930, taking into account estimates for known independents as well as interracial groups, were nearly equal, with 33, 870 Black Oneness Pentecostals in about 513 churches and 33,550 Whites in 510 churches. The 1960 *Yearbook of American Churches*, although notoriously inaccurate with respect to African American updates, indicates that the gap between the size of the PAW and the size of the merged PAJC and Pentecostal Church, Inc. (formerly PMA), now having taken on the merger name of UPC, had widened significantly. While the thirty year increase from the Haywood era brought the PAW to about 50,000 in 600 churches, the UPC had 160,000 in 1,595 churches. As a matter of comparison, the 2010 PAW constituency was approaching an estimated 2 million worldwide, with approximately 2,000 U.S. churches.[36]

(7) CLJC, and (8) AsCJC (now ALJC), the (9) CJC, the (10) AMJC (now ABC), and the (11) EMA (now BMA). Hispanic groups: U.S. (1) AAFCJ, (2) ACJ, (3) ACANJC; Mexico (4) ACFCJ, (5) LWC, (6) CGSC. Other autochthonous groups: (1) AFC (Hawaii), (2) SJC (Japan), (3) TJC (China), (4) IPC (Indonesia), (5) ECSA (Russia), (6) CPC (Yugoslavia), (7) ACOP (Canada).

35. The (2) PAW (1906) and (2) ETBCAF (1916) were largely Midwestern, whereas (3) COOLJC (1919) was eastern. The (4) AFMCG (1916), (5) CGA (1897; 1919), (6) AOHCG (1920), and (7) CLGPGT (1920) were all southern-based Holiness groups. Of the ex-COGIC groups (8) GCGCA (1921) was Midwestern, (9) NBCGCP (1927) was western based, and two were southern based, (10) PHCG (c. 1927) and (11) FC-GCJN (1927).

36. Landis, *Yearbook of American Churches-1960*, 86–87; COOLJC, by comparison, was reported as having 45,000 members in 155 churches. The official PAW-released statistics have not been updated since 1998, with 1.5 million worldwide and 1750 churches in the U.S., see "The Association of Religion Data-Archives," www.thearda.com. The UPCI reported 4,063 U.S. churches in 2010, see *Directory: United Pentecostal Church International (Incorporated) 2010*, with approximately

### 7.4.1 Autochthonous Oneness Organization

The Canadian Oneness movement, originally under the PAW, established the Apostolic Church of Pentecost of Canada in 1921 under Frank Small and Goss' leadership, with churches from east to west. Originally their strength was western, with additional early leaders such as R. Dawson, E. E. Lang, O. J. Lovik, J. A. Erickson, and E. W. Stories.[37]

Beginning in 1922, in New Brunswick, an eastern stronghold was established at the Woodstock Convention, when the leader, Edgar Grant, and others, such as C. Crabtree, the Stairs and Flewelling brothers, R. Hathaway, G. Henderson, E. L. Jacques, and Leonard Parent, were re-baptized.[38] Several were originally with the Davis Sisters' St. John work, such as B. McQuarrie, W. Ring, and M. Wright, or established other early works, including R. McCloskey, S. McConaghy, S. Steeves, H. Perkins, and W. Rolston.[39]

The earliest of the autochthonous Oneness groups was established by Mexican immigrant ministers and churches which were among the earliest Oneness leaders. These Hispanic ministers emerged first in California as part of Seymour's Azusa Street revival but spread immediately into Mexico by 1914. As the Oneness Hispanic segment of the movement grew rapidly in the U.S. and in Mexico, the entirely indigenized network of ministers in Mexico organized in 1925 as the ACFCJ, Apostolic Church of the Faith in Christ Jesus.

By 1930 the more than 34 U.S. Hispanic ministers listed with the PAW from California, New Mexico, Arizona, and Chicago, including the leader, A. L. Nava, organized separately from both the PAW and ACFCJ

800,000, and a missions constituency of 1,927,480 in 24,942 churches and preaching points, see Howell, "We Had Church," 37. The AWCF, of which the PAW, but not the UPCI or COOLJC, is a part, reported a 2010 membership of 181 affiliated Oneness organizations, with 5.2 million members and 20,200 ministers, see www.awcf.org.

37. ACOP: 4,000 in 60 churches (1930); see also, "Pastor Frank Small Baptized," *MDS*, 4; Larden, *Our Apostolic Heritage*, 92–97.

38. See also appendix B: "Profiles of Early U.S. Oneness Pentecostal Pioneers."

39. Morehouse, *Pioneers*, 68–72, 24–25, 57, 76–78, 85–86, 185–86, 230–32, 301–2, 162–63, 164–69, 195–201, 242–48, 268–70. The eastern section withdrew from the ACOP in 1946 joining the UPC, with 16 New Brunswick churches, see *1947 UPC Directory*, 82–83, and Larden, *Apostolic Heritage*, 161. The "UPC of Canada" has 241 churches, Ontario, with 75, and New Brunswick, with 61, being the largest districts, see *2010 UPCI Directory*, 243–52.

that year as the AAFCJ, Apostolic Assembly of the Faith in Christ Jesus.[40] "If poor Whites and blacks were Jews and Samaritans of the new Pentecost," Ramirez has suggested regarding these disparate groups, "then Latinos were among the first gentiles, adopting many of the social and religious values of these similarly dispossessed, peripheral communities in North American society."[41]

With rapid growth in Mexico, splinter groups developed in 1926, the Light of the World Church, now, with several million members, the largest Hispanic Oneness group worldwide, and what became known as the Christian Gospel Spiritual Church. In the U.S., in 1927, two groups broke with the ACFCJ, the Apostolic Church of Jesus and the Apostolic Christian Assembly of the Name of Jesus Christ.[42]

At the time of the 1924 PAW schism in the U.S. a small group of churches in Hawaii which were Holiness sanctification adherents under Charles Lochbaum also established a separate autochthonous identity as the Apostolic Faith Churches.[43] Therefore, in addition to the separate Canadian and six Hispanic groups which had formed, three in the U.S. and three in Mexico, six other autochthonous bodies had formed by the 1930s, although in some instances doctrinal and culturally suspect to many Oneness ministers, leaders, and missionaries from the U.S., these indigenized groups were nevertheless symbols of both intrigue and pride.

Though possibly related, the Hawaiian and Japanese groups formed separately from that of the much larger Chinese movement. Intensive missionary activity produced one of the largest Oneness centers of any mission field, but it was the totally separate, indigenized forms of the movement, the True Jesus Church, which soon became the largest Oneness bodies worldwide. The leaders of the extremely aggressive True Jesus Church broke with missionaries in 1917 over Sabbath-keeping. By

40. ACFCJ: 4,800 in 50 churches, 30 "small missions" (1930); AAFCJ: 1,800 in 30 churches (1930); By 1948 the ACFCJ had 125 churches and 75 small missions in Mexico, see Gaxiola, "Pentecost in Mexico," 3, and Bowen, *Evangelism and Apostasy*, 5, 41, 69, 75; The AAFCJ had 8,000 adult members in 152 churches by 1960, see Holland, *Religious Dimensions in Hispanic Los Angeles*, 346; cf., Gaxiola, "The Serpent and the Dove," and Gill, *Toward a Contextualized Theology for the Third World*.

41. Ramirez, "Pentecostal Praxis," 3.

42. LWC: 3,200 in 45 churches (1930); CGSC: 1,000 in 25 churches (1930); ACJ: 300 in 6 churches (1930); ACANJC: 150 in 4 churches (1930); Inclusive constituency, not merely adult membership, see Gill, *Contextualized Theology*, 363, 75–89.

43. Howell, "People of the Name," 181.

1930, approximately 45,000 in 330 churches were swept into the TJC, and 129,000 in 1,000 churches by 1949.[44]

Two other Asian centers of Oneness expansion, Japan and Indonesia, were not only missionary success stories, but probably due to the Chinese influence, soon became indigenized forms as well, with the emergence of the Japanese Spirit of Jesus Church, largely a house church movement, and the Indonesian Pentecostal Church.[45]

In Eastern Europe and Russia scores of Oneness congregations were established without affiliation, due largely the challenge of communism, but several united with the Evangelical Church in the Spirit of the Apostles, in Russia, and the Christ Pentecostal Church of Yugoslavia.[46]

The autochthonous Oneness groups by 1930 had grown to an estimated 95,580 in Mexico, China, Japan, Indonesia, Russia and Eastern Europe, although close to half of the total was in China. Black, White, and Hispanic churches in the U.S. and Canada, independent Oneness congregations, and indigenized forms of the movement around the world conservatively totaled 153,000 in 1,563 churches.

### 7.4.2 Oneness Pentecostal Missionary Expansion[47]

In addition to these groups, several of the indigenized forms of Oneness Pentecostalism also resulted from a missionary presence which encouraged autochthonous independence, partly a consequence of the Oneness independency impulse, but also due to the early organizational turmoil in the U.S. Although Mexico's indigenized movement was not related to missionary activity, its proximity to the American movement and the conversion of Mexican immigrants in the U.S. was a determinative influence.

44. Kauffman, *China*, 139.

45. SJC: 7,300 in 60 churches and 30 house churches (1930); Yoshinobu and Swain, *Christianity in Japan*, 184–87; Brown, *Laity Mobilized*, 37, 98, 132, 171, 205–7; The most recent statistics are the most phenomenal, listing the SJC with 420,000 in 477 churches (and house churches) in 1995, although these are actually worldwide figures, see Barrett, *World Christian Encyclopedia*, 418. IPC: 12,000 in 130 churches (1930); Cooley, *The Growing Seed*, 64–72.

46. ECSA: 4,900 in 70 churches (1930); Hall, "Oneness Pentecostal Origins in the Soviet Union," 4–5, 22–23; "Early Pentecostals in Russia," 3–5. CPC: 1,050 in 30 churches (1930); Balca, *My Life With God*, 79–171.

47. See appendix C: "Early Oneness Pentecostal Missionaries (1914–1930)," in French, "Early Oneness Pentecostalism," 336ff.

Destabilization caused by division in the U.S. merely reinforced suspicion of creeds and man-made allegiances.

The earlier period from 1914–1921 was certainly characterized by missionary vacillation between Trinitarian and Oneness loyalties, but the later eruption of division within the Oneness movement was sufficient to cause some to return to the security and support of previous allegiances or in many cases to reach out to new areas of support and fellowship. Several Oneness missionaries, such Phoebe Holmes and Ralph Phillips, for example, who had both been in China, are known to have returned to Trinitarian groups during this period.[48] Some, such as George White in Jamaica, tired of the racial division and confusion and simply organized separately into new groups.[49]

The missionary fluidity during this time was sufficient to make it difficult at times to keep track of the varied allegiances. Scores of missionaries embraced the Oneness movement throughout the early period, but many returned to Trinitarianism as well. For a time some were active in both Oneness and Trinitarian fellowships. Missionary Robert F. Cook in Bangalore, India, for example, was variously with the AG, an independent, and then the Church of God. He was also rebaptized, according to Ewart's *Meat In Due Season,* and then led to baptize all converts in India "in the scriptural way."[50] Although he received early financial support as a "PAW mission" and was featured on a 1923 cover of the PAW's *Christian Outlook*, he does not appear to have ever credentialed with the PAW. And after 1926 Cook's vague association with the movement apparently ended.[51]

The interracial impulse, with its underlying idealism, was, in fact, a missionary impulse, tied inextricably to the fervor of Pentecost, to which early Oneness periodicals attested. Of the 58 missionaries connected, prior to 1914, with Ewart's pre-Oneness periodical *The Good Report,* 31 percent transitioned into the Oneness movement. A bit later, extant issues of *Meat in Due Season* (1915–1919) list 31 missionaries, only two of which

48. Blumhofer, *McPherson*, 22, and Urshan, *Witness of God*, 9:1.

49. Toulis, *Believing Identity*, 113.

50. Pool, "An Open Letter," 3; cf. "Robert F. Cook," *NIDPCM*, 560–61; see Conn, *Where the Saints Have Trod*, 219–22, regarding his Church of God (Cleveland, TN) involvement.

51. Cook received missionary funds from Haywood, see *The Voice in the Wilderness* 24/2 (September 1918); Reeder lists Cook as an early PAW missionary, see Reeder, *A Brief History of the Foreign Missions Department of the Pentecostal Assemblies of the World*, 24–25, as does Tyson, *Chalices*, 255, based on *Christian Outlook* articles and photos of Cook, 229, 233; The Cooks are not known to have been supported by any other Oneness periodicals, including *Blessed Truth* or the pre-Oneness *Good Report*.

were not Oneness, although it is possible that they had been rebaptized and viewed, temporarily, as part of the movement.[52]

The same holds for extant issues (1918–1921) of Opperman's *The Blessed Truth*, uncertainty exists regarding only two of the 65 missionaries listed. His mission data indicates that independency among missionaries was extensive. "There may be and probably are some other Pentecostal missionaries," he wrote, "who are one with us in the faith. I will gladly add them to our list if their names and addresses are sent to me." Only 30 of the 64 missionaries were listed in the 1919 PAW rosters, suggesting that Opperman was compiling a list of Oneness missionaries unrelated to affiliation.[53]

By comparison, the PAW roster for the same year, 1919, listed 40 current or returned missionaries or missionary couples in 1919. In the previous years, though, as extant issues (1916–1918) of *The Voice in the Wilderness* indicate, Haywood continued support for Trinitarian missionaries after the 1916 AG expulsion of Oneness ministers, at least until the time of Frazee's 1918 exit from the PAW. Even after 1924, interracial support remained a PAW norm. And Reeder, missionary "assistant secretary" to Haywood, later noted:

> Bishop Haywood was well known to the missionaries, better probably than any other man in the P.A.W. He had been in contact, either by letter or in person with many of them before there had been a P.A.W. He was missionary-minded far beyond the average . . . At least no one can deny that he had their full confidence. They felt that at all times they had the full benefit of all his powers to aid them.[54]

Analyses of primary and secondary sources indicate that there were a minimum of ninety six active Oneness missionaries and missionary couples by 1921 in China, Japan, Indonesia, Burma (Myanmar), India, Liberia, South Africa, British East Africa (Kenya), Chile, Bolivia, Ecuador, Hawaii, Alaska, Jamaica, Israel, Egypt, Armenia, Mesopotamia (Iraq), Persia (Iran), Russia, Yugoslavia (Slovakia), Czechoslovakia (Czech Republic), France, Switzerland, and Mexico. It is also known that during

52. Cf., also, Ewart's *Phenomenon of Pentecost*, which includes 22 missionaries, only 9 of which, apparently, were Oneness, and Goss' *The Winds of God*, which includes 5, only 2 of which were Oneness.

53. "Our Missionaries," *BT*, 3; see also, *1919 PAW Minute Book*.

54. The PAW, for a short time, evidently, implemented support directly to "nationals," rather than traditional American missionaries, so that by 1930, only 11 out of 30 listed PAW missionaries were actually traditional, see Reeder, *A Brief History*, 15.

the 1920s at least an additional sixty eight missionaries and missionary couples, including 12 American-financed national ministers, were added to the roster of Oneness missionaries of the early era, which included the additional countries of Greece, Hungary, Poland, Estonia, and Cuba.[55]

In the early 1920s the PAW sponsored, at the most, 20–25 missionaries annually, which decreased after 1924, and the later ACJC (ECJC), PMA, and ACOP supported even fewer, evidence, not of missionary attrition, but rather of rapid mission indigenization.[56] The racial division, certainly, resulted in missionary woes, such as organizational overlapping, short-term confusion, a jeopardizing of financial provision, defection and an acceleration of mission independency. Even the re-merger of the PAW/ACJC was promoted by Urshan in 1932 as for "the greater help to our missionaries," one indicator of the earlier missionary conditions.[57]

Nevertheless, at least 164 Oneness missionaries were sent out during the early era, 1914–1930, to 28 countries, Hawaii, and Alaska. The majority of these missionaries, evidently, were "independent," which is another indicator of the extent of Oneness missionaries "not yet accounted for" from this early period. The largest concentration of missionaries, 35 percent, was in China, with the second largest, 21 percent, in Africa, centered in South Africa and Liberia, with a few in Kenya. Europe, Russia, and the Middle East received 16 percent, with 9 percent in India, 7 percent in Jamaica, 4 percent in Japan, and 4 percent in Hawaii. And, in addition to the indigenized forms already noted, evidence suggests that several of the neighboring countries, such as Sierra Leone and Nigeria, were also being evangelized and impacted by these same missionaries.[58]

Allan Anderson's study of early Pentecostal missionaries, *Spreading Fires: The Missionary Nature of Early Pentecostalism*, includes approximately 243 missionaries in 43 countries, of which 29 (12 percent) are known to have joined the Oneness movement.[59] Many of the Oneness missionaries, though, not included in the study, were catalysts of expansion, yet their names appear on no early Oneness rosters. For example,

55. See 1930 PAW Minute Book.

56. Clanton, *United*, 49, 63, 95–96.

57. Urshan, "Merger," 7.

58. See *The Good Report*, *The Voice in the Wilderness*, *The Blessed Truth*, *Meat in Due Season*, *Christian Outlook*, and Reeder's *Brief History*. The largest known collection of *The Good Report*, *Meat In Due Season*, *The Voice in the Wilderness*, and *The Blessed Truth*, 1913–1921, contains only 29 issues, or partial issues, a fraction of the originally released publications.

59. Cf., Anderson, *Spreading Fires*.

Elmer B. Hammond received Spirit baptism in 1907 as a Salvation Army officer stationed in Hawaii. "The Lord told me I would have to leave the Army," he wrote to Azusa, "as I could not glorify God and be under men—I would have to be led by the Spirit."[60]

By 1912 Elmer and Hattie Hammond, and Corabelle Hammond, his sister, later married to Frank Small in Winnipeg, were in Hong Kong, where they were the first rebaptized in Jesus' Name in 1914. He, in turn, baptized thousands in China. Robert Hammond, his younger brother, in California, was one of Ewart and Morse's early associates. The Chinese Oneness movement was initiated by these early missionaries, mostly single women missionaries, such as Alice Kugler, who later married Daniel Sheets, and who worked closely with Hammond.[61] Missionary efforts such as these resulted in a significant impact on the varied regions such as China, which continues to boast a notable Oneness constituency, especially the autochthonous TJC churches.

By 1930 the Oneness Pentecostal organizational-based missionary movement exceeded 62,000 constituents. Yet another 35,000 could be found within the independent Oneness missionary endeavors, that is, more than a third of all Oneness missions at the time. All totaled, U.S. Oneness constituencies, missionary constituencies, and autochthonous constituencies, the estimated number of Oneness Pentecostals, as Haywood had pointed out, was more than a quarter of a million in 1930, 260,000 in 2,660 churches.[62]

## 7.5 Death & Legacy of G. T. Haywood

The death of Haywood at the relatively young age of fifty was an unexpected loss which impacted every segment of the movement to which he had been such an inimitable figure from its origins. One of G. T. Haywood's robust worship choruses, "We Will Walk Through the Streets of the City," was likely one of his earliest since it was undated, appearing in

60. Hammond, "Baptized in Honolulu," 3, and "Missionary Letters," 1.

61. Elmer Hammond (d. June 16, 1916), see Sheets, *Nuggets of Gold*, 13–14; Denny, "From Hong Kong, China," 1, and Hult, "Pentecost in China," 4. Hattie Hammond later remarried Charles Wesley Storey and returned to China in 1920, Tracy O. Hammond Interview, Freemont, IN, November 2006; Bays, "The Protestant Missionary Establishment" 52–54.

62. Allen, "Pentecostal Assemblies to End Session Friday," 7; cf., Haywood's 2,000 church estimate used by Urshan in 1933, see *The Witness of God*, January 1933, 2.

earliest versions of *The Bridegroom Songs*. The song's musical emphasis of the phrase "*through* the streets" is lilted and reiterated as a bold promise, one held in excited anticipation of "loved ones who've gone on before." And the refrain, not unlike his own bequeathed legacy, evokes a consolation in the face of his own final life-claiming illness.

> We now walk thru the valley and shadow,
> Thru a world full of labor and strife;
> But some day we shall walk with our Savior
> Robed in everlasting life.[63]

Golder included the sheet music of this song in his Haywood biography as a most apropos final tribute to his life and legacy. "I have been true to God," Haywood is said to have whispered to S. N. Hancock in his final days. "I have loved the brethren, I have done all I could for them, now I am tired and weary, and I want to go home."[64] True to God Haywood would leave behind an enduring legacy in his beloved Pentecostal Assemblies of the World. Like America's heartland recovering from months of drought in 1930, Haywood could see signs of revived vigor in the PAW, including White Bishops, Rowe and Lewis, and fourteen White District Elders, including H. L. Alvey, standing with him.

The Indianapolis ministry legacies included notables like Hancock, Lawson, Schooler, and Tobin, but also the impact on lives such as Arthur E. Boring (Greensburg), Charles V. Taylor (Shelbyville),[65] and Herman G. Basore, who received Spirit baptism at Haywood's in 1913.[66] His friend L. V. Roberts came from Newark, Ohio in 1913 and started Oak Hill Tabernacle in 1914,[67] the year Lena O. Spillman (1879–1953) was Spirit filled, later starting Christian Tabernacle.[68] Joseph Rodgers' 1912 Apostolic Faith Helping Hands Mission owed much to Haywood, though Rodgers was

63. Haywood, "We Will Walk Through the Streets of the City," stanza #1, 68; Golder, *Life and Works*, 69; see also, Garrett, *Haywood*, 192.

64. Hancock's sermon quoted in Garrett, *Haywood*, 175, and included in Hancock's article to the PAW, "Haywood Funeral," *CO*, 52–54.

65. *1930 PAW Minute Book*; see "What is Drought?" National Drought Mitigation Center, http://archive.is/noIro.

66. Interview, Robert W. Basore, February 6, 2009.

67. Davis, "Revival at Oak Hill Tabernacle," 4; Davis, "Let's Get Acquainted," 2; cf., also, Cordell, *Indianapolis Star*, 1.

68. James D. and Lena Spillman, *1920 U.S. Census*, Indianapolis, 9A; *1930 U.S. Census*, Indianapolis, 7B; "Tribute to a Pioneer—Lena Spillman," in Dean, *Kentucky Pentecostal Heritage*, 2:19–22, 120; Boyer, "Pastor, Mate on Duty for Duration," 2.

killed in a 1918 scaffolding accident.[69] He influenced Alvey in 1920 to start First Friendship Apostolic Church near Fountain Square,[70] and later Greek immigrant Alexander B. Anderson (1895–1963) in his early ministry.[71]

Haywood, too, was leaving an impressive literary legacy for the generations after him. Jacobsen is, of course, quite right in recognizing the magnitude of his unique contribution: "G. T. Haywood's publications contain the most wide-ranging theological vision produced by any first generation Pentecostal leader from either the Trinitarian or the Oneness wings of the movement."[72] He branched out considerably to touch on themes such as ecclesiology, worship, typology, tithing, healing, creation, divorce, remarriage, eschatological prophetic events, and gifts of the Spirit.[73] Few could match his prolific pen with its theological scope, exemplified in the many articles published for more than a dozen years in *The Voice in the Wilderness* (1910–1922) and eight years in the *Christian Outlook* (1922–1930).

With Haywood's passing the loss of such a busy pastor, preacher, writer, publisher, songwriter, counselor, and administrator could not help but be sorely felt, yet never replaced. His theological acumen reflected in his many books helped shape a movement, from Godhead and Christology classics, such as *The Finest of the Wheat,* [74] *The Victim of the Flaming Sword*, *Divine Names and Titles of Jehovah,* and *Feed My Sheep,*[75] to soteriological studies such as *The Birth of the Spirit.*[76] Few, since, have approximated the wide-range contributions to such a multiplicity of theological topics,[77] as to include a widely read speculative creation study for

69. Rodgers, "Bro. Jos. Rodger's Mission, Indianapolis," 2; "Bro. Joe Rodgers," 2.

70. *1900 U.S. Census*, Perry County, Anderson Township, 3B; *1910 U.S. Census*, Troy, Indiana, 12B; 1918 World War 1 Registration, 265; *1930 PAW Minute Book*, 8.

71. *1920 U.S. Census,* Indianapolis, 5A; *1930 U.S. Census,* Indianapolis, 8A; Cole, *You Too Can Make It*, 21–23; Anderson, "I Am the Way and the Truth" [translation] and "The Voice of the Gospel" [translation].

72. Jacobsen, *Thinking in the Spirit*, 197.

73. Haywood, *The Resurrection of the Dead*; *Christian Stewardship*; and *The Marriage and Divorce Question.*

74. Haywood, *The Finest of the Wheat*, 2–3.

75. Haywood, *Divine Names and Titles of Jehovah*; and *The Victim of the Flaming Sword.*

76. Haywood, *The Birth of the Spirit in the Days of the Apostles.*

77. Haywood, *The Teachings of the Apostolic Church According to the Bible*, *Ezekiel's Vision*, and *The Old and New Tabernacle Compared*, in Goodloe, *God's Word,* 5.

combating evolution, *Before the Foundation of the World,* with illustrative drawings of dinosaurs drawn by his own hand.[78]

"I want to go home," was his request, having served so many for so long with extraordinary breadth of ministry and historic import. In his last days, not only was the true nature of his condition probably unknown, Haywood was evidently himself unaware of the extent of the severity of his own deteriorating health. Reportedly, the PAW Convention in New York City in August of 1930 was especially fatiguing for Haywood due to strong eastern resistance led by Grimes. Tyson reports, for example, that Grimes was "very vocal."[79] In contrast Haywood has been characterized as the model of "diplomacy and tact," with Urshan referring to him as "so humble." A Christ Temple convention photo, also from August, though, shows an inordinately stressed, if not ailing, leader of the Pentecostal Assemblies of the World.[80] Evidently, Haywood may have actually been exhibiting evidence of inherited heart disease which had already been taking its toll.

A three month trip to Jamaica which Haywood began in January 1931 resulted in over exertion and his collapsing in New York City upon his return in March. Managing to finally return to his home in Indianapolis, G. T. Haywood died on April 12, 1931, which, according to the death certificate, resulted from "acute cardiac dilatation" underscored by "cardio vascular venal disease."[81]

With the headlines "Thousands Mourn At Bishop Haywood's Funeral" the Indianapolis *Recorder,* for which Haywood once worked, noted that Haywood's funeral was one of the largest in Indianapolis history. He also noted that the services had what he thought to be an "unusually large number of White citizens" in attendance.[82] Honored by Blacks and Whites alike, the eulogies, and the more than 10,000 attendees, were a moving tribute to his scope of vision.

78. Jacobsen, *Thinking in the Spirit,* 197; *Before the Foundation of the World.*

79. Tyson, *Early Pentecostal Revival,* 274, 277; see also, Howell, "People of the Name," 108, noting that a Grimes faction "questioned the financial operations."

80. Tyson, *Chalices,* 348, in which Haywood "appears" ill, also, 316, 344; cf., Tyson, *Early Pentecostal Revival,* cover, and Golder, *Haywood,* 59.

81. Peagler, *Haywood,* 86–87; Garrett, *Haywood,* 153; *Death Certificate,* Marion County Health Department, in Garrett, *Haywood,* 151; see also Paddock's suggestion that he "preached himself to death," *Apostolic Heritage,* 51.

82. Stanley, "Pentecostal Assemblies' Bishop Goes to Final Resting Place," 1, 8; Garrett, *Haywood,* 158.

In a separate article, *The Recorder* noted again the exceptional memorial, "Honor Fitting Nation's Head Accorded Haywood at Burial," in which the reporter appropriately recognized Haywood as one "who played his part so infinitely well."[83] Hancock, who had been one of his closest associates, rushed to Haywood's side in April. And as the main funeral speaker he eulogized the life of G. T. Haywood as having been propelled by the "zeal of God" and "driven by the Spirit." Twenty-three years of ministry, from 1908, according to Hancock, were marked with difficulties "because of the actions of his brethren." "God said, I will take you away from the shame, reproach, and persecution. You have *fought* for twenty-three years, come and rest."[84]

The legacy of G. T. Haywood has been enduring and far-reaching, capable of rising above stereotypical limits and caricature to a realm of near legendary status within the movement which he not only helped originate but definitively shaped. To a great extent Haywood's legacy was accomplished as the quintessential preacher, regardless of race, via his leadership skills, his handling of Scripture, his writings, and his music. All of these contributed to the wide ranging success of the movement in Indianapolis and the Midwest as a Oneness epicenter and in the interracial vision which characterized Oneness Pentecostalism from its inception. And the most tangible evidence of his legacy to the present, of course, is the Pentecostal Assemblies of the World itself.[85]

Seven months after Haywood's death, in an attempt to fulfill the interracial dream he had upheld in his lifetime, the PAW merged, once again, with an all-White GAAA-heir, the ACJC. The PAW Bishops had already decided, in honor of Haywood, to forego selection of a Presiding Bishop until 1932. Expectations of "making history," following the severe blow of losing such an icon, certainly motivated their efforts. As MacRobert has

83. Stanley, "Honor Fitting Nation's Head Accorded Haywood at Burial," 1.

84. Funeral Sermon, in Garrett, *Haywood*, 179.

85. This is illustrated in the *Encyclopedia of African American Religions* inclusion of sixteen PAW leaders and six other Black Oneness leaders: PAW–Floyd Ignatius Douglas, Morris Ellis Golder, Samuel Joshua Grimes, Samuel Nathan Hancock, G. T. Haywood, John Silas Holly, Austin Augustine Layne, Benjamin Thomas Moore, Oscar Harwood Sanders, Alexander R. Schooler, David Thurman Shultz, Francis L. Smith, Karl Franklin Smith, Willie May Ford Smith, Freeman N. Thomas, and Joseph Marcel Turpin; Others–William Lee Bonner, Henry Chauncey Brooks, Sherrod C. Johnson, Robert Clarence Lawson, Jasper Roby, Jr., and S. McDowell Shelton; see Murphy, Melton, and Ward, *Encyclopedia of African American Religions*.

stated, "It looked as if the dead phoenix of interracial Oneness Pentecostalism was rising from the ashes of American racism."[86]

"As we review it today," states Smith's biography, regarding the merger, "we cannot say what lay deep in the hearts of the men who broached the ideas." But, it adds, "If intents on both sides of the race line had been sincere, it would have succeeded . . . Racism once again caused . . . a bitter disappointment to those who had thought there would be a real merger of the two bodies."[87] The efforts of integration were thwarted and, by 1937, the entire union dissolved. Thanks to the foresight, though, of those who re-established the charter of the PAW, the PAW itself was saved.[88]

## 7.6 Conclusion

Although almost ninety years of racial division has impacted the development of the Oneness movement, in spite of some evidencing of limited interracial sentiment, a meaningful analysis of the failed interracial vision and the writing of a new interracial chapter remain palpably unfulfilled endeavors. The ramifications of the early racial reversals not only altered the PAW forever, but galvanized the developing White segments of the movement into decades of segregated, diffuse factions. For a period of years after the rift, 20 to 30 percent of the PAW ministers were White, but evidently a significant portion were also members, at the same time, of new White organizational bodies. The interracial vision had dissipated and an interracial era abruptly brought to a close.

Until the 1940s even the White segment of Oneness Pentecostalism was characteristically diffuse in spite of noble efforts to the contrary and only able to reunite and amalgamate slowly over a period of more than two decades. Successful mergers often resulted in new divisions and new splinter groups. It was, in fact, just such a critical schism which ended up

86. MacRobert, *Black Roots*, 76.

87. Smith, *A Devout Man*, 31.

88. Most of the remaining 1937 African American leadership, and some Whites, including Paddock, left the PAJC to join the PAW under Samuel J. Grimes. Another nine years would pass before merger efforts would be renewed between the now all-White PAJC and the all-White PCI. For the most part, though, White ministers who had joined the PAJC from the PAW did not return to the PAW, Howell, "People of the Name," 112–14; The PAJC passed a resolution opposing interracial marriage and requiring "that any of our ministers performing such marriages be disfellowshipped," see "Minutes of the Sixth Annual Conference," *The Pentecostal Outlook*, November 1937, 21, 3; Smith, *A Devout Man*, 32; Clanton, *United*, 101–2.

preserving the PAW after its attempt to re-merge with Whites who had previously splintered the organization. Re-establishing the PAW saved the organization from complete dissipation when, once again, the 1930s interracial failure of the PAJC was complete.

For varied reasons a considerable segment of the Black Oneness churches as well as large segments of the White movement had never joined the PAW and the final outcome of the PAW schism was increased division throughout Oneness Pentecostalism. Its failure was a failure for the movement as a whole. And Black Oneness factions rarely, if ever, moved toward the merger and organizational unity model which to some degree emerged slowly within segments of White Oneness factions. The diverse segments of the movement, except where the option of amalgamation was realized, were left to function independently of one another, for the most part, in the rather unsympathetic theological terrain of Evangelicalism's harsh reality. Yet within this context the movement both adapted and flourished globally.

By the time of Haywood's passing the organizational landscape was equally divided into Black, Hispanic, White, and autochthonous Oneness Pentecostalism. And in its Asian expressions the movement was clearly experiencing its most expansive growth and nuanced indigenization. Most observers at the time were somewhat startled and perplexed by these developments—with a movement which had grown in little more than a decade and half to 260,000 and at least thirty five separate organizational groups by the first half of the 1930s. In the face of increased racial schism, separatism, and independency, an accompanying intensified missionary zeal and indigenization had also occurred. Within a span of a dozen years a robust Oneness Pentecostalism with not less than 160 missionaries could be found in more than thirty two countries around the world.[89]

89. By 1930, then, 26 percent of the Oneness constituencies were in the U.S., with 74 percent in more than 31 other countries, with 37 percent within missionary-led segments and 37 percent within autochthonous segments of the Oneness Pentecostal movement.

# 8

# Conclusion

## "Some Day, Some Happy Day!"

### 8.1 The Finest of the Wheat

When G. T. Haywood wrote *The Finest of the Wheat* in the defense of Oneness theology and practice his popular work resonated with the familiar vernacular of the original, characteristic Oneness mindset. The most significant ideological concepts, as well as the most common, were steeped in imagery and motifs of the Old Testament.

> Our souls are being "fed with the finest of the wheat." Daily there cometh down from heaven to us "our daily bread." The beauties of the revelation of "the Father and Son" in Christ; the New Birth of water and Spirit . . . and many other heretofore hidden mysteries of God, truly have become "hidden manna" to our hearts.
>
> But that is not all. He has also promised us "honey out of the rock." All these promises are ours. The test of our loyalty to Christ has come. The trials are hard and many, yet there is a sweetness in it all.[1]

The manna, the bread, and the wheat of Psalm 81:16 represented powerful corollary truths for them, just as the honey in the rock foreshadowed

1. Haywood, "Finest of the Wheat," 1, and Haywood, *Finest of the Wheat*, in Goodloe, *God's Word*, 38–93.

the test of truth which they all faced. For early Pentecostals the hermeneutic of direct application of figurative discourse to daily life and doctrine interpreted the finest of the wheat as the fulfillment of the Spirit's very best in the last day harvest of truth. It is not difficult to see how this became broadly applicable to every aspect of their spiritual existence, especially as the finest display of new spiritual unity was being substantiated in a transformational all-flesh, integrated Pentecost. What made it the *finest* was that it was viewed as precisely what the Spirit intended. What made it all the sweeter was the fact that it was a counter-cultural, shared, and integrated dissatisfaction with the yield of previous inferior religious harvests.

Haywood made use of this impacting metaphor in his quintessential hymn, "O Sweet Wonder," uniting the element of the promise of sweet honey with the theological uplifting of the Name of Jesus and His Deity.[2] As a result the metaphoric refrain of sweet wonder served to hearten Oneness proponents throughout the movement who readily interpreted symbolic and restorative significance into the context of their own ideological and interracial ardor.

On the other hand, these lilting aspirations were, therefore, all the more stunning and disappointing in the midst of the corresponding failures which ultimately transpired during these inaugural years of the movement, an admixture of interracial accomplishment, tension, and failure. In fact, few could have foreseen the far-reaching ramifications of the eventual racial divide within Oneness Pentecostalism, including the considerable degree of destabilization and organizational diffusion which ensued. Haywood's influence was demonstrably effective, though, even in death, with yet another official attempt at interracial unity in 1931. Although its déjà-vu like failure was not surprising by any means, it can, nevertheless, be seen as the evidence of the fading interracial vision, its finale upon the stage of early Pentecostalism.

The opening act of interracial cooperative union, though, had been nowhere better expressed liturgically than in Haywood's sweet wonder hymn and in the succinct lyrical expression, "How I adore Thee! O how I love Thee!" The Jesus-centrism is dominant and unmistakable. Booth-Clibborn's classic composition, "Down from His Glory," was likewise reflective of the definitional parameters of the emerging Oneness

2. Although actually entitled "Jesus the Son of God," and written in 1915, it is known more commonly by the song's refrain, "O Sweet Wonder." It has remained one of the movement's most enduring anthems, see Haywood, "Jesus the Son of God," 5.

movement, devotionally focused upon issues of the centrality of Christ, the God-Man motif, and Christ as the totality or fullness of God.[3]

Oneness Pentecostalism, therefore, was quick to coalesce theologically, attested to, for example, by the long list of its detractors and defectors, and, by 1919, it had established itself as an atypical, interracial, non-Trinitarian segment of the Pentecostal movement. Observers could clearly delineate the distinct difference between the one God manifest in the flesh in Oneness thought from an incarnate divine person-among-persons in the Trinity. The immediate early insistence, therefore, upon both Jesus' Name baptism and Spirit baptism was predicated, not merely on apostolic precedent, but upon the interpretive significance of these theological tenets from the Oneness perspective.

The intent of this work has been to solve as many of the riddles regarding the inaugural years of the early Oneness movement as possible, or at least remove some of the dust of obscurity, but, at the same time, to grapple with the historical reality and long-range ramifications of race unity and race division. Interestingly, although tumultuous, the success of the inaugural years 1913 to 1931 was clearly *not* impeded by its well-known interracial commitments, for in many respects the movement's early global expansion was rather remarkable.

In the short span of eighteen years the movement's global presence was already well established, from the U.S. and Canada, to the rapidly expanding missionary base, to the varied autochthonous forms of the movement. Oneness Pentecostalism was poised for astounding success around the world. All of this transpired in spite of, or perhaps due to, its investment in the interracial paradigm, highlighting its recognition of, and commitment to, the centrality of its own Black roots and influences, as well as the theological components which undergirded such an important race mindset in an utterly resistant societal framework.

To some extent this was due to the fact that it was uniquely centralized around the interracial Pentecostal Assemblies of the World, that is, until the 1924 racial turmoil and altered mindset which resulted in its splintering into the diffuse segments which came to characterize Oneness Pentecostalism for more than two decades. That diffusion, in fact, characterizes the movement still, in that it shattered, not its expansion, but rather its cohesion racially, structurally, and globally. Mere independent

3. Booth-Clibborn, "Down From His Glory," 97, including "My God and Savior came, and Jesus was His name" and "O, how I love Him! How I adore Him!" Cf., also, Grimes, "The Great I Am," 84, "the great eternal Wonder."

organizational successes have not been able to recover the valuable benefits of the interracial, international aspects of the unique unity of this earliest era.

It will not do, therefore, to treat the early interracial era as though it were merely a momentary, empty historical pretense of negligible import and, as a result, largely ignore the details which were indeed significance laden. It would be historical amnesia to fail to take into account the originating years of the PAW as an Azusa derivative, a thorough going interracial body from the start. With the PAW's assimilation into the Oneness movement, complete by 1918, a race relationship resulted which included both leadership structure and worship. Even decades after its failure the Black majority PAW still remained committed to an interracial ideal. Therefore, with its evangelistic and global successes already secured, it is startling that such a unity could be so utterly abandoned in favor of segregated, separated entities and futures.

## 8.2 The Restoration Context of Early Oneness Pentecostalism

Another crucial influence which more thoroughly inculcated Oneness perceptions than almost any other segment of the movement is that of the restoration impulse. Its thorough-going restorationism was, in fact, central to the ideological framework in which its oppositional theology developed. An even more pointed fact is that its initial interracial vision was intricately and thoroughly linked with its original restorationist impulse, the same impulse which had stirred and motivated its earliest theological passion. The influence and importance of its Black roots and of the Black experience within the movement's development is anticipatory of the interracial emphasis which dominated early on.

The Oneness movement emphasized and upheld racial unity for more than twenty years, although the PAW commitment pre-dated the emergence of a theologically distinct Jesus' Name Pentecostalism. With the interracial PAJC finale extending from 1931 to 1937, the PAW's years of evidentiary interracial success spanned more than *thirty* years, from its 1906 founding to about 1937. Clearly, therefore, it was an interracial dream, vision, and inspired hope, though imperfectly executed and flawed. Most had not even "thought through" the "how" of making it work for the long term. The impulse, nonetheless, was rooted in belief in a divine imperative, nurtured as an inner desire to fulfill a Pentecostal ideal in a world of prejudice.

> No more our brave and gallant youths,
> Shall tremble of tomorrow;
> Behold, sweet liberty and truth,
> Has broke the chains of sorrow.[4]

These are the poetic lines of Indianapolis' famed Aaron Belford Thompson, friend of G. T. Haywood, from his 1907 *Harvest of Thoughts*. Such thought of emancipation, sweet in its divine derivation, was essentially the context of Oneness zeal and of "living the real love of God." Breaking such chains was a reality to which early adherents actually aspired as proof to the world of the genuine success of Pentecost and of the spiritual restoration believed to be taking place in the Oneness movement.

The interracial unity that had failed in Parham's ministry, resulting in his racial rejection of the validity of Seymour's revival, and the later unraveling of racial unity at Azusa itself, was accomplished to a great extent, though temporarily, in the visionary dream of Oneness integration and unification. Neither the broader movement's insistent segregationist tactics, nor the Parham racist influences, nor the southern cultural resistances were deterrents to Oneness determination to go-it-alone on the race issue. It was so part and parcel with their restorationist zeal as to foster a reorientation within the movement away from the segregationist mentality in hope of a genuine unity within a genuinely restored Pentecostalism.

## 8.3 The Obscurity, Transition, and Acquisition of the PAW

When Cook suggested of Indianapolis, at the beginning of the Midwest Azusa in 1907, "this will be a center of power," little did anyone realize at that early juncture just how accurate he had been. The emergence of a Oneness epicenter in Indianapolis corresponded closely with Frazee's leadership ascendency in the PAW, with both regions, the Midwest and the west, becoming pivotal to the movement's ultimate success. This research has provided insights which have lifted Frazee and his leadership era from virtual obscurity, clarifying the nature of the Oneness inundation of the ministerial fellowships of both the Assemblies of God and the Pentecostal

4. Thompson, "Emancipation," stanza 5, 46.

Assemblies of the World. Uniquely, Oneness gains in Portland, as in the PAW itself, were leadership gains, with Frazee himself being swept into the movement, an eventuality in the AG which fell short of accomplishment.

The commonly acknowledged battle for the AG in the period 1914–1916 was accompanied by what turned out to be the far more significant battle, more accurately depicted as an acquisition, the winning of the PAW to and for the Oneness cause. Uncovering earlier PAW ministerial documentation in the FBI reports and the accompanying *1917 PAW Minute Book* has significantly enhanced an understanding of the events, especially the nature of the transition of the PAW from a Trinitarian majority to complete acquisition by a Oneness majority in 1918. The events transpiring in the PAW were quite distinct from the battle for the AG, especially the PAW's ministerial diversity both theologically and racially, its interracial priorities, and its western dominance, all of which set it apart from the southern dominated AG.

Even prior to the surfacing of the Oneness issue, though, a definite leadership scuffle had developed between the PAW and the AG, with Ewart, Haywood, and Frazee in the west and Midwest vying for the more inclusive hegemony of the race-conscious PAW, and Bell, Pinson, and Flower in the south content with exclusive polity. The red hot embers of the erupting Oneness conflict simply carried these already volatile differences to an entirely unforeseen new level. To some extent, as well, the racial issue co-opted the Oneness issue within the debate in the AG, so as to become an opportune excuse in camouflage for the abandonment of its own Finished Work African American ministers.

As the conflict was enlarged the unabashed racial disregard became more and more engraved upon the collective consciousness of Oneness participants, Black and White, shaping their blossoming interracial resolve. Nevertheless, when Oneness theological and racial hopes were dashed in the AG, the move was on for the fulfillment of a new Oneness Pentecostal future rooted in aspirations of meaningful unity. The detection of an unmistakable Trinitarian majority at this time in the PAW, sympathetic enough to Oneness aspirations to bow out and relinquish control, was made to order for uniting these forces. All that remained was for the White ministers who had previously placed their hopes in the AG to shift the battle to the PAW and become adequately prepared to go the distance in securing a meaningful interracial structure. The PAW Oneness minority somehow became convinced that they could win the day and, amazingly, that is what they did.

The earlier AG wrangling and disputation was replaced in the PAW strategy with apparent good will in the Oneness acquiescence of the organization, when, by necessity, the majority of the original PAW ministers withdrew in 1918, replaced by an even larger number of basically unaffiliated Oneness ministers.[5] Amidst the characteristic fluidity of the period, there is no evidence, either, that this withdrawing Trinitarian majority made any move to join the organizational structures already in existence, but likely followed the common path of independency. With the loss of Oneness momentum within the broader movement, the resolve of such Trinitarians, who may have been on the fence or even sympathetic in varying degrees to Oneness objectives, was solidified, nonetheless, to veer away from the uncertainties of a now aging new issue.

## 8.4 Racism and the Pentecostal Loss of Interracial Vision

Oneness Pentecostalism received the nudge of rejection from its Trinitarian counterparts to recognize its potential as a viable movement in its own right. The interracial vision was as good a starting point as any and became the inaugural distinguishing theme of its determination to overcome racial division within its own organizational efforts. The full-blown integration of the PAW, therefore, had been bolstered by insights gleaned from the pros and cons of past mistakes, inspiration imparted by the courageous efforts of past participants, and the hope derived from past achievements in spite of the odds. A further source of encouragement derived from the groundswell of 460 Oneness ministers who quickly joined the PAW, although they had up to this time remained outside the organizational fray. Reflected in the roster of more than 700 ministers which had joined the PAW by 1919, this means that nearly twice the number of Oneness ministers joined for the first time than had been in the earlier combined PAW/GAAA.

The first order of business, therefore, had been the institution of a fully integrated leadership *in addition to* the ideal of interracial worship in the life of the church. On the other hand, unfortunately, it had proceeded without much in the way of an articulated blueprint for just *how* to proceed. They might as well, then, have been holding their breath in the uncertainty of the historic moment, for assuredly little advance, outside

5. The 1917 PAW, interestingly, was almost as large as the 1917 AG.

assistance could be had in a culture steeped in racist assumptions. Voices of support and encouragement in the era were non-existent, while ample resistance and opposition could be cited for not making it work. In fact, the most ready and consistent excuse for failure has remained the quick referral to the lack of any personal responsibility based upon the excuse of simply being products of the times and culture. Thus, it was better to have tried and failed, so it goes, than to never have tried at all.

To what extent the tide of detractors and defectors may or may not have also been similarly infected by racial motivations is not known. For many, any abandonment of the cause was a demonstration that neither the movement, nor its ambitious vision, could ultimately succeed. This was especially obvious in the detractors who assumed that its theological novelty would assuredly blow over like a temporary storm. While theological rejection from without served as a motivator, any internal rejection of the racial impulse and/or effort only served to discourage. From Haywood's perspective, for example, Lawson's departure from the PAW efforts, regardless of motive, at this crucial moment was especially detrimental.

Succeed they did, nevertheless, for a time, both in initiating the dream and expanding their base evangelistically. Oneness beliefs, of course, were not viewed by outsiders as adequately orthodox, and this contributed to an even greater extent to the Oneness separatist expansion in isolation, although that too was at least partially self-imposed. Therefore, their praises were not sung, their story was not told, and their exuberance neither felt nor emulated, especially within a Pentecostalism which had both predicted a Oneness demise and continued to nurse the guilt of its own racial failure. Instead, developing Oneness Pentecostalism was more or less ignored by the broader movement.

It is possible that the movement, in the angst of interracial uncertainties in the era, hoped for a larger degree of acceptability which simple cultural adaptability could provide, although they do not seem to have recognized it as such. Oneness expansion actually contributed to this state of affairs, in that the integrated organizational leadership of the PAW initially thrived. The African American PAW ministerial numbers literally quadrupled, resulting in their dominance not only of the eastern region, but of portions of the Midwest and northern region, as well as many of the urban centers. Several dynamics were brought into play as these efforts materialized, including the effect of west coast losses from the PAW after the merger, and the South's inability to coalesce around a major center of leadership with the shift of balance away from Arkansas and the roles of Goss and Opperman.

Most importantly, the movement remained without a distinctly articulated Christian response to racism around which to unify, having been motivated essentially by an unarticulated impulse of spiritual derivation, but which seldom confronted culture verbally with a logic of race equality. They were clearly inadequately prepared to overcome the culturally normative abnormalities regarding race which surrounded them on a daily basis. As the growth in the south began to explode, the challenges were mounting, without adequate response efforts to stem the negative appeals regarding the difficulties of racial societal dilemmas. Clearly, the E. W. Doak leadership during this era could not match these challenges, nor was it centralized enough, to offset the growing resistance to integration from increasingly prominent southern ministers and leaders who were maneuvering these stormy challenges for the first time, many of whom simply did not have the necessary conviction to weather them.

By 1924 the interracial union unraveled amidst a renewal of latent race prejudice and naiveté which not only separated the majority of the White ministers from the PAW, but literally splintered the White movement into multiple factions. It would require decades of effort, well into the 1930s and 1940s, to reunite even a minority of these elements of the fractured movement. The redrawing of the color line essentially guaranteed the movement's initial splintering and diffusion, rather than its unity—its persistently characteristic feature to the present. And it inflicted upon itself generations of self-imposed intra-movement isolation, further ostracizing what was already a widely ostracized form of Pentecostalism.

## 8.5 "But, O Lord, How Long?"

"If ever there was a place" is, fittingly, Haywood's own expression for motivating and prodding Pentecostals toward decisive character and action regarding the racial crisis which divided and devastated them nearly ninety years past.[6]

> When shall the day dawn when right de-thrones wrong?
> My Jesus, I'm waiting, but, O Lord, how long?[7]

6. Haywood, "Men of Backbone," in Golder, *Haywood*, 63: "*If ever there was a place* where there should be no distinction made between races and nationalities in their common fellowship, it ought to be in the true church of God." Italics added.

7. Haywood, "O Lord, How Long?," 15.

Haywood meant, of course, that a genuine Pentecostalism held the key necessary to right the wrongs and forge a true equity in the expectant now. He was, in fact, acknowledging for the movement at-large the ever present worth of racial reconciliation and renewed unifying vigor. Of course, "if ever there was a place," referred to the expectancy that a Spirit led Oneness Pentecostalism was the most logical place for the righting of interracial wrong. Not only in the ethos of Haywood's "how long" imagery, but within the scope of this entire historical study, the question evoked is, if it worked within the context of the early twentieth century originating passion, why not in the twenty-first century? That is, the pursuit of a unifying passion has been modeled, already, within a context of daring to move beyond mere *hallelujahs* to the *hows* and the *how longs* of the implementation of Pentecost. Surely, of all the varied characteristics of the early movement, this is the distinctive feature most worthy of repeat emulation.

Haywood's question rhetorically and symbolically addresses the necessity of the de-throning of agendas which may be illegitimately deemed more important than reconciliation. An understandable impatience is evidenced in the question, too, speaking of the anticipation of eschatological solutions, of possibilities actualized by intervening positive action. Wrong can, and will, be righted, just as visionaries take it upon themselves to be participants in the process.

Both history and the participants in that past have the potential of speaking into the present via an enlightenment of the present circumstance with the unfolding of insight from the lessons within the events in their proper context. For example, Haywood's query, "but, O Lord, how long," begs the question as to the renewal of an interracial vision of consequence within Oneness Pentecostalism which has maintained its pervasive denominational racial division. Surely human motivations and longings do not change so considerably as to render their own early historic voices valueless. Regardless of intent of application within a given setting, much is to be derived from the comprehension of any era truly committed to racial justice and harmony.

First and foremost, the voices of the Oneness era of interracial unity have spoken forcefully of meaningful reconciliation which pushes past merely limited localized rhetoric to the recognition of the core issues of repentance for, and denunciation of, racism, and a prioritizing of a righteous and holy race response to the sin of prejudice in culture.[8] Again, though,

8. Cf., West, "A Critical Exploration of the PCCNA's Rhetorical Vision for Racial Unity," 2–6.

in terms of intra-movement applicability, unless these take the form of sincere denominational gestures, which ultimately comprise their priority vision, fundamental articles of faith, and "living the real love of God," they will likely be of little consequence.

Yet meaningful race equity and the legitimacy of hopefulness are ageless Christian priorities, unworthy of politicizing and sidelining, but with reconciliation as the contemplated finest hour and sweetest success. Even outside observers of the movement have opined of the potential and possibilities inherent in such an unparalleled legacy of racial unity.

> Haywood reached across the racial divide of his day and earned the respect of both Blacks and Whites. Thirty years after his death, when the nation was engulfed in racial turmoil and violence, Indianapolis was spared much of that, and civic leaders attributed this to the legacy of Haywood. *If that legacy were repeated on a wide scale, the new century could be the Church's finest hour.*[9]

Another energetic Haywood favorite, "Some Day," also expressed in song a common early Pentecostal confidence that all solutions would materialize at the linear end of the age regardless of momentary circumstances. Therefore, even if no earlier reconciliation comes, the eschatological better day of cosmic restitution is envisioned as God's means of final justice.

> There'll be no curse, no sin, nor sighing,
> Some day, some day, some happy day,
> Nor shall be heard the voice of crying,
> Some day, some day, some happy day.[10]

Certainly, though, the lyrically suggested "some day" resolution was never intended to apply to the search for solutions to the racial divide as a sort of endorsement of entrenched warring racial allegiances of varying stripes or the indefinite suspension of responsibility.[11] These double-conscious, spiritual-earthly expressions of the soul were not the putting off of essentials to some distant other day, either devotionally or racially. They were, rather, evidence of both hope and certitude. The courage, therefore,

9. Note the following example, Roberts, "Pentecostalism's Greatest Test Could Be Her Finest Hour," http: //www.agts.edu/encounter/articles/2010summer/roberts.htm; italics added; cf., Bernard, "Future of Oneness Pentecostalism," 143.

10. Haywood, "Some Day," 6.

11. Cf., "Pentecostal Partners: Racial Reconciliation Manifesto," Memphis, Tennessee October 17–19, 1994, www.pentecostalworldfellowship.org/pub /manifesto.html.

of these first generation Pentecostals to take responsibility for racial and spiritual equity in the face of enormous cultural challenges should, at the very least, instruct and inspire. The early narrative of pioneer interracial vision serves as a present challenge to the status quo of social accommodation and self-serving pragmatism. It may very well be that a revitalized passion for ending the voice of crying with respect to inequity will be able once again to glean from this earlier paradigm—daring to hope for a possible new and meaningful racial reconciliation someday—*some happy day.*

# Appendix A

# Profiles of Early U.S. Oneness Pentecostal Pioneers

## Regional Summary of the Movement's Earliest Leadership

### A.1 West & Northwest Region

Southern California formed the early center of emerging Oneness movement and its key leadership which initially formed around the ministry of Frank J. Ewart in Los Angeles. Hispanic Oneness churches first emerged in California in joint association with the ACFCJ and PAW, then the U.S. AAFCJ, with leaders such as Antonio Nava, Francisco Llorente, Marcial Cruz, and Juan Navarro. The earliest Black leadership from the region included Edward S. and Mattie Lee and William and Maggie Bowdan.

The earliest White PAW leadership (3.3.2) was Los Angeles based including William H. Pendleton (3.4.2), E. W. Doak, Glenn A. Cook, George B. Studd, Frank Bartleman, Fred and Sarah Poole, John Schaepe, E. G. Lowe, and George Farrow.[1] In Arizona the earliest Oneness minister was Guy R. Homes.[2]

1. George Farrow was born in Montana in 1885, see, *1918 WW1 Registration*; After rebaptism by Ewart in L.A. in January 1915 he worked with Frazee in Portland, home of his wife, Lulu Brumwell, probably among the earliest rebaptized there, see Farrow, "Letter to Lulu Brumwell," 11; By 1920 he had established the Turlock, CA church and written "It's All In Him," one of the movement's most popular hymns.

2. By 1914 Guy Homes was in Mesa, AZ, but his brother R. L. Homes in Phoenix

In northern California by 1917–1918 a major center developed around Harry Morse's Oakland work and the Oakland-Stockton-Sacramento area.[3] The movement up the northwest coast formed another important center in Portland, Oregon around the leadership of J. J. Frazee. Subsequent to Frazee's 1918 PAW withdrawal the largely White northwest region began to revitalize slowly from independency with leadership such as that of Andrew C. Baker, Oregon City, Oregon, Fred Scott, Harry Judd, and Ralph Bullock.[4]

Throughout the area the ministries of Robert G. Hammond (3.3.2) and William E. Booth-Clibborn were significant, as was that of W. L. Stallones whose ministry impacted Arkansas, Idaho, and Maine before he went to California.[5] In Idaho by 1917 the earliest Oneness ministers included Frank and Marie Muse and John H. Dearing. After the 1921 conversion of Mattie Crawford scores were rebaptized in her revivals in the region, as well as those of Kenneth A. Wine and A. D. Hurt, in Idaho and Washington, including Frank Yadon.[6]

---

did not join the movement, see, *1917 PAW Minute Book*, 12; *1919 PAW Minute Book*; Wallace, *Old-Time Preacher Men*, 115–21. Homes exited the PAW in the sweep of post-merger independency by 1919, but established a Oneness work in Phoenix by 1922, cf. Wesson and McCarty, *Apostolic Pioneers of Arizona*, 23.

3. Originally from Wisconsin, Harry Morse (1879–1963) worked in Stockton before 1900, but returned prior to 1910 as a pastor, see, Wallace, *Profiles*, 2:283; Haney, *Man of the Hills*, 32. Morse was a key leader in the expansion of the movement in the region, see Morse, "Our Trip Down the Coast," 2. Harry and Maude Morse were part of the pre-merger, pre-Oneness PAW, see, *1917 PAW Minute Book*, 15, and already on the Ninth St. location where they started the popular Missionary Training School. Several leaders, such as Oscar Vouga, originated from Morse's work, see, Wallace, *Profiles*, 2:244–46.

4. "From Oregon City," 1, "Andrew C. Baker . . . has received a revelation of the great truth of baptism in the name of Jesus Christ." Cf., Scism, *Northwest Passage*, 48–49.

5. R. G. Hammond, see, Larden, *Heritage*, 77. Booth-Clibborn was rebaptized while evangelizing in Wilburton, OK, August 1915, after *Meat in Due Season* "was placed in my hands," see, "A Preacher's Testimony," 3, "Hugh York of Hartford, Arkansas . . . baptized me . . . I turned around and baptized him." He wrote *Christ—The Mystery of God* in about 1919 and the famed "Down From His Glory" in 1921. Stallones, "Brother Wilner Levoy Stallones," 3.

6. Treece, *Beulah*, 173; Yadon, *Northwest*, 4–5; Scism, *Northwest Passage*, 79; Wiens, *Great Northwest*, 123, 131–32.

## A.2 East & Northeast Region

A large nucleus of Black Oneness churches emerged in the region whereas the comparative growth of White churches remained slow. Key leaders in the region included R. C. Lawson in New York and S. C. Johnson[7] in Philadelphia with COOLJC and a growing number of PAW leaders in several states, such as Guy Jameson, Smallwood Williams, and James A Morris in D.C.,[8] Peter J. F. Bridgers and Samuel J. Grimes in New York, and Joseph Turpin in Baltimore.

Due to the influence of Oddous Barber and C. R. Wilkes, Boston initially became an interracial center with the 1917 campaigns of L. C. Hall and Haywood in which hundreds, including R. G. Cook, were rebaptized.[9] White church growth in the east was largely further north into Maine and New Brunswick, beginning with Dearing's move from Idaho to Charleston, Maine by 1920. Due to Dearing's influence, what was known as the Woodstock Convention swept a large percent of the New Brunswick Pentecostal ministers into the Oneness movement in 1922. With Woodstock only twelve miles east of Maine's U.S. border, the entire area was impacted.[10] Since this time New Brunswick has remained an important regional center of the Oneness movement.

The first Oneness church in Maine was established in Bangor in 1922 by twin sisters from Georgia, Susie Davis (1884–1962) and Carro Davis (1884–1976), who had been Spirit baptized at Urshan's Chicago mission in 1910. By 1924 they had established their premiere work in Saint John, New Brunswick.[11]

7. Johnson later founded the Church of The Lord Christ of the Apostolic Faith.

8. Morris later founded Highway Christian Church of Christ.

9. Ralph G. Cook (1899–1981) left Boston by 1919, worked with Haywood, then pastored in Bloomington, IN, Louisiana, Arkansas, Foxboro, MA, and Ohio. He was UPC Asst. Gen. Supt. (1963–1971); See Wallace, *He Stands Tall*, 67ff, and Cook, "Let's Get Acquainted," 3.

10. Dearing (1880–1940) was born in Farmington, WA, see, Treece, *Beulah*, 173, 176; Wallace, *Old-Time Preacher Men*, 27–33; Morehouse, *Pioneers*, 37–41; Wallace, *Profiles*, 1:114–16. Leonard Parent, in "Let's Get Acquainted," 3, 16, confirms that the first rebaptisms were in 1922; cf., Morehouse, *Pioneers*, 70–71; Reynolds and Morehouse, *From the Rising of the Sun*, 30–52.

11. Attendees of the 1916 AG General Council meetings, they were a part of the Oneness walk out, see, Larden, *Heritage*, 87–88; Also, Morehouse, *Pioneers*, 33–36, 203; Peters and Pickard, *Prevailing Westerlies*, 390–93, 574–75, 156; Pickard, *The Davis Sisters*.

## A.3 North & Midwest Region

Like Haywood's work in Indiana, several high profile African American churches impacted the northern region which was quickly becoming a burgeoning center of African American Oneness Pentecostalism. These included flagship works such as that of Samuel N. Hancock in Detroit, John S. Holly in Chicago, and, in Ohio, E. F. Akers in Dayton, Karl F. Smith and Martin R. Gregory in Columbus, and A. R. Schooler in Cleveland. Haywood's interracial ministry played the key role in the initial development of St. Paul as a northern Oneness center,[12] with other leaders in the region such as L. C. Hall and Andrew D. Urshan as key figure in Chicago and Wisconsin.

In Indiana, in addition to the White expansion of the movement in Indianapolis in the ministries of such leaders as Lena O. Spillman, Oscar C. Hughes, L. V. Roberts, T. C. Davis, and H. L. Alvey, other areas of influence in the region included the ministries of G. B. Rowe, A. F. Varnell and the EMA (now BMA), and L. R. Ooton. And the north and Midwest evidenced considerable growth in both the Black and White segments of the movement, as far west as Kansas,[13] and especially in Illinois,[14] Indiana and Ohio, exemplified in the ministries of James A. Frush (5.5) in Newark,

12. Early pastors in St. Paul include H. O. "Bert" Scott and Eric S. Stone, photographed in the July camp meeting, see, also, "St. Paul-Minneapolis," *Meat in Due Season,* September 1917, vol. 1, no. 7, 4, as well as Harvey McAlister, Gilbert Sweaza, William Booth-Clibborn, and, in 1934, S. G. and Jessie Norris.

13. Herbert Davis (5.9) in Leavenworth, an African American, and Harry Nigh in Council Grove, White, were among the earliest pioneers. Davis, Spirit filled in California, was in Kansas before 1919 and on the PAW Board of Elders by 1920, see, *1917 & 1920–21 PAW Minute Book;* Chalfant, "History of Truth Tabernacle UPCI, Leavenworth, Kansas."

14. The earliest works in Illinois included that of S. S. Grant in Pinckneyville (after 1917), Hira Byers in Iola (1918), J. O. Underwood in Bellville (1920), and Pearl B. Champion in Carbondale (after 1919); Historical Committee of the Illinois District United Pentecostal Church International *Our Pentecostal Heritage,* 1, 36; "In Memoriam," *Pentecostal Herald,* March 1972, 21; "In Memoriam," *Pentecostal Herald,* September 1977, 20; Cagle, *Echoes*, 35ff.

Ohio,[15] Homer L. White (4.7) in Athens, Ohio and Decatur, Illinois,[16] and W. T. Witherspoon in Columbus.[17]

## A.4 South & Southwest Region

Several southern and eastern Black churches were already divided from the PAW interracial efforts even before 1919 having coalesced in the south around the Holiness ministries of Frank W. Williams' AFMCG and W. T. Phillips' AOHCG in Alabama and Thomas J. Cox and the CGA in Kentucky and the Carolinas. Although few in number there were some notable Black PAW ministries in the south including that of Floyd I. Douglas in Louisville,[18] Dunlop Chenault in San Antonio, and Austin A. Layne's work in St. Louis, founded by Lawson, the city's first Black Oneness church.

Further south a sizeable number of White churches formed independent associations in Tennessee, Mississippi, and Georgia around the ministries of E. E. Partridge and H. A. Riley in the AMJC (now ABC) and the CJC churches spearheaded by E. L. Farris, M. K. Lawson, and B. R. Hawthorne. The early JOAC, CLJC, and AsCJC with concentrations of churches in the Midwest and south, especially Texas and Louisiana, highlighted the ministries of leaders such as R. B. Bingham, Sr., L. A. Parent, J. T. Payne, and J. L. Pipkin.

The integrated PAW and early splinter groups had almost no representation in the Carolinas, Alabama, Georgia and Florida and only a small number of churches in five others. Some of the earliest known pioneers

15. Stanley R. Hanby, an early leader, was converted under Frush in 1916, see, Doggette, *One Man's Journey Through Life With God*, 1–3.

16. White (1892–1973) was Spirit filled in 1912 at T. K. Leonard's Findlay convention at which Haywood was speaker, see, Wallace, *Profiles*, 2:370–72; In 1915 he was the second rebaptized east of the Mississippi with L. V. Roberts whom he was assisting, see, Tyson, *Before I Sleep*, 47; cf., *1917 PAW Minute Book*, 11, 19. He and Karl Smith were "roughed up" for interracial street preaching in Athens, see, Smith, *A Devout Man*, 10, and Wallace, *Profiles*, 2:373. He assumed the pastorate in Decatur, IL in 1923.

17. William Thomas Witherspoon (1880–1947) received Spirit baptism in 1912 in Pittsburg, moved to Columbus in 1914 where he heard Haywood and embraced Oneness theology, and by 1917 established a church. He was PAJC Chairman 1938–1945; see, Clanton, *United*, 301–2; Wallace, *Profiles*, 271–74. Stanley Chambers, later Superintendent of the UPC (1967–1978), was Spirit filled in Witherspoon's church in 1930, see Bentley, *Ship Ahoy*, 15.

18. Douglas, from Bardstown, KY, was Spirit filled and called to ministry in Louisville in 1911, then joined the PAW in 1912, see, La Monte McNeese, "FAC Council History," www.facdytn.org/History.com.

were T. C. Montgomery and Lester E. Partee in Mississippi,[19] Alford Ball, Horace and Thomas J. Skirvin, Jess Collins, and Roy A. Johnson in Kentucky,[20] and Myrtle Marple, W. H. Forbush, J. D. Grover, and C. C. Zuefle in West Virginia.[21]

Somewhat larger centers formed in Tennessee where early leaders included H. G. Rodgers, J. C. Brickey, E. J. Douglas, A. D. Gurley, and A. N. Graves.[22] Likewise, in Oklahoma the earliest churches were in Dewar, Pawnee, and Sallisan, after which early works were started by temporary Texas transplant Jerry E. Osborn. Theodore Smith, who was rebaptized after hearing Haywood in Cincinnati, started early works in Skiatook, Sperry, and Morris, and Arthur T. Duck, from Arkansas, was in Tulsa by 1922.[23]

The fourth largest concentration of early southern Oneness churches was in Missouri which benefited from the itinerant north-south evangelism of Whites able to traverse regions indiscriminately, such as the ministry of Odell Cagle.[24] The movement first emerged in St. Louis with the early ministries of Mother Moise, Mother Barnes, and Ben Pemberton, with early significant works also led by B. H. Hite and W. H. Whittington.[25]

19. Montgomery founded the UPCI Tupelo Children's Mansion, see Montgomery, *A Brief Story of My Life*; *Historical News,* October-December 1998, vol. 18, no. 1, 3; Holder and Cole, *Voice of the Pioneers-Pentecostal,* 7, 22, 24–28, 36.

20. With works in Olive Hill, Gent, and Lawton, 1917–1920; See, "Skirvin," see, *1919 PAW Ministerial Record,* 21; Dean, *Kentucky Pentecostal Heritage,* 2:10, 18, 31; 1:22–23; *Historical News,* January-March 1987, 3.

21. In Charleston and Huntington, see, Scott, "A Tribute to a Pioneer," 7, 14.

22. Rodgers (1864–1950), Brickey (1890–1939), Douglas (1888–1959), Gurley (1889–1976), Graves (1893–1975); See, Wallace, *Tennessee,* 16–20, 25–31, 84–99, 33–39, 168–81; Douglas, "Early Days of My Ministry," 3; Wallace, *Profiles,* 47–59, 71–90.

23. Osborn in Wildcat, Russell, and Carter, by 1921, see, Treece, *Beulah,* 155, 177–186, 194; Smith, previously in Neosho, MO, was in Skiatook by 1919, see, Booker, "Floyd Interview," 21–22; Martin, *Tulsa Story,* 12, 17–18, 21–29; *1919 PAW Minute Book,* with listing for Charles V. Bettis, Lewis H. Hulvey, and James Duca, 11, 16, 14.

24. See, Cagle, *Echoes of the Past,* 34–59; Born in Alabama in 1900 Charles Odell Cagle moved to Cardwell, MO in 1912 where his family was Spirit filled in H. H. Hite's tent meetings in 1917, vii, 12, 16; Studying at Opperman's Arkansas school 1918 to 1920, 27–33, he later ministered in Illinois, Missouri, Arkansas, 34–89.

25. By 1900 Moise (1850–1930) had established a home for girls and a mission in St. Louis. Barnes (1854–1939) came to assist her sometime before 1910 and worked with her into the late 1920's. Ben Pemberton (1891–1963) was Spirit filled in 1909 in Iola, MO and, by 1913, was working with Moise; See, Lenore Barnes and Mary G. Moise. *1910 U.S. Census,* St. Louis, MO, EDN270, 14A; Lenore Barnes, *1930 U.S. Census,* St. Louis, MO, EDN96–189, 4A. B. H. Hite (1888–1948), from Kentucky, was Spirit baptized in 1912 in Nashville, rebaptized in 1916, and evangelized extensively

Early in the 1920's Louisiana became one of the largest areas of Oneness growth behind only that of Texas and Arkansas. Reportedly, every AG minister but one was rebaptized at the Elton Bible Conference in December 1915 after the teaching of David Lee Floyd, Charles A. Smith, and Howard A. Goss.[26] Some of the early key pioneers in the state include Robert L. LaFleur, Harvey Shearer, and Bennie Baggett, with Merryville and DeQuincy two of the earliest revival centers.[27] Among the early pioneers were W. F. Haley in Provencal and Crisp Reason in Tioga and Alexandria, and by 1925 a key Louisiana leader was S. L. Wise.[28]

As the movement's early center Arkansas' role in early Oneness Pentecostalism is legendary even though it was not able to maintain its leadership edge in the region with key changes in leadership, Howard A. Goss leaving Hot Springs for Picton, Ontario in 1919 and D. C. O. Opperman closing his Bible School and leaving for California in 1920. Other early pioneers include David Lee Floyd, C. P. Kilgore,[29] Clarence T. Craine,[30] S.

---

before starting a St. Louis mission by 1921, see, also, Hall, "Early Pentecostals in St. Louis," 10, 18; Wallace, *Old-Time Preacher Men*, 181–195; Wallace, *Tennessee*, 21–24.

26. As early as 1907 there was a report of Spirit baptism in Louisiana resulting from simply "reading" *The Apostolic Faith* from Azusa Street, see, "New Orleans, Louisiana," *The Apostolic Faith*, vol. 1, no. 10, Sept. 1907, 2. See, also, Floyd, "Interview," 47–53; Tenney, *The Flame*, 14–18, 24; Fauss, *What God Hath Wrought*, 65–67, 179, 181–82, 185–86.

27. See, Gillis, *History of the First United Pentecostal Church of DeQuincy*, 4ff; Fauss, *What God Hath Wrought*, 57–63.

28. Spirit baptized in a Smith and LaFleur 1913 Texas tent meeting, Wise was rebaptized at the Elton Bible Conference, see, Tenney, *The Flame*, 28–29; Nation, *Spenser Leslie Wise*, 15, 27, 32, 37, 48–53, 60, 68–71.

29. In 1920 in Social Hill, AK near Malvern Kilgore received Spirit baptism in a Roxie Hughes revival and he started ministry in 1922 in Friendship, AR, later ministering throughout Arkansas, Texas, Oklahoma, and California; See, Shoemake, *Blanche Faye*, 2–4, 7, 55; Wallace, *Old-Time Preacher Men*, 198.

30. Craine (1889–1976) was Spirit filled at Goss' work in Malvern in 1909, attended Opperman's school in Joplin in 1910, and was rebaptized in Hot Springs in January 1915, after receiving a tract on Jesus' Name baptism late in 1914; His earliest ministry included Hot Springs, Eureka Springs, and Green Forest; See, Martin, *Tulsa Story*, 37; Wallace, *Profiles*, 61–64.

C. McClain in Fort Smith, Ben Blunt,[31] G. C. McDaniel,[32] G. H. Brown, H. E. Reed, and C. A. Pyatt.[33]

By the mid-1920's Texas had quickly grown into the largest center of Oneness Pentecostalism anywhere with Dallas, initially, the earliest growth center. Among the earliest pioneers in the Dallas area were W. H. Lyons and Jerry Osborn.[34] Another prominent early pioneer was R. L. Blankenship. Evidently, although Houston soon developed into one of the largest Oneness centers, its earliest church which was founded by A. A. Matney and C. W. Dowden was not established until 1921.[35] One of the most prominent of the early leaders in the south, Oliver F. Fauss (1898–1980), established a premiere work in Houston by 1928.[36]

31. In 1908 at Redfield, AR Blunt (1891–1953) experienced Spirit baptism at Madge Kinneson's church and was rebaptize in early 1917 along with W. E. Kidson in Quincy, Illinois by Earl D. Hill from Mt. Vernon. He ministered throughout Arkansas, Missouri, and Illinois; See, Wallace, *Profiles*, 2:49–57.

32. McDaniel (1887–1955) was Spirit filled in Goss' Malvern tent meeting in 1909 (as was Ethel (Wright) Goss), was rebaptized when L. C. Hall was pastor in Malvern in 1915, and began his early ministry in Thornton and Pine Bluff; See, Wallace, *Profiles*, 135, 141.

33. Reed, "The Birth of Water and Spirit," 1, 2; "Bible School in Hot Springs," 2; Wallace, *Profiles*, 172–74. C. A. Pyatt, see, *The Blessed Truth*, December 15, 1918, vol. 3, no. 18, 4.

34. As Osborn's congregation observed from the shore, Goss rebaptized him in c. 1916 in Walnut Spring, Texas. In 1917 he was a speaker in Eureka Springs at the only GAAA Bible Conference ever held; See, Treece, *Beulah*, 173, 251–52; Goss, *Winds of God*, 145.

35. Matney, "The Founding of Jesus' Name Pentecostal Churches in Houston Area," 2–3; Wallace, *Profiles*, 2:281–82.

36. O. F. Fauss (1898–1890) spent his early ministry in Louisiana in Pine Wood, DeQuincy, and Kinder and went to Bronson, Texas in 1919. He was Spirit baptized in Ganado, Texas in 1911 and rebaptized at the Elton Bible Conference, Elton, Louisiana in December 1915; See, Fauss, *What God Hath Wrought*, 1, 64, 28, 36; *1918 WW1 Registration*, Order #2601; *1919 PAW Minute Book*, 14; *1920 U.S. Census*, Kinder, LA, 4A.

# Appendix B

# Early Oneness Pentecostal Missions (1914–1930)

## B.1 Early Oneness Missionary Activity—A Context of Fluidity

Even with the limited scope of primary sources for the earliest Oneness period, it is demonstrable that the movement attracted numerous missionaries and their respective mission constituencies into the Oneness Pentecostal fold. The following is a composite list of 164 such missionaries drawn from early Oneness sources which indicate that more than half (59 percent) had converted in the earliest period and mostly before the 1920's. Many of these were drawn into the movement while in the midst of missionary labors around the world.

The premier missionary analysis of this same period in Anderson's *Spreading Fires* encompasses about 254 missionaries of which twenty eight became involved with Oneness Pentecostalism.[1] A few of the early missionaries who joined the movement were only involved with Oneness Pentecostalism temporarily, such as Robert Cook, although the fluidity of their association with the movement remains somewhat obscure.[2] For example,

1. Anderson, *Spreading Fires*. Only Bernt and Magna Bernsten, early missionaries to China, are specifically noted in Anderson as possibly Oneness, see, 30, 54, 64, 125, 133. Additionally, though, twenty eight of the other missionaries referenced (11 percent) were also involved in the movement.

2. The most obscure data relative to early Oneness missionary involvement and/or

some missionaries, such as B. O. Moore, who may not have remained with the movement indefinitely, nonetheless, had considerable and prolonged early involvement and often high profile early association with Oneness Pentecostalism, although much of the details remain sketchy.

Also, although the vast majority of Oneness missionaries from the Haywood period of the movement prior to 1931 were already in their respective fields before the 1920's, the missionary data gleaned from *The Christian Outlook* of the interracial PAW suggests that approximately 35–40 missionaries were being supported between 1922 and 1926.

Another interesting fact has to do with the large number of non-Oneness missionaries which Haywood continued to support via *The Voice in the Wilderness* and his local Indianapolis congregation before the all-Oneness merger of the PAW and GAAA. Eighteen missionaries or missionary couples were listed in three extant issues between 1916 and 1918 who were not known to have ever been directly associated with the Oneness movement.[3] Also, many Oneness missionaries received funds from each of the Oneness groups which emerged from the 1924 PAW split.

Data regarding these early missionaries is derived from the following:

| | |
|---|---|
| BT | *The Blessed Truth*, D. C. O. Opperman, ed. |
| CO | *The Christian Outlook*, G. T. Haywood, ed. |
| ECJC | *ECJC Minute Book and Ministerial Roster 1927–1928* |
| GR | *The Good Report*, Frank J. Ewart, ed. |
| MB | Missionary Biography |
| MDS | *Meat In Due Season*, Frank J. Ewart, ed. |
| PAW | *PAW Minute Book and Ministerial Record 1919–1920; +1930–1931* |
| PhP | *Phenomenon of Pentecost*, Frank J. Ewart |

temporary involvement includes only a few of the early missionaries, Robert F. Cook (India), B. O. Moore and C. F. and Marie Juergensen (Japan), Mary A. Posey (China), and Joseph K. Blakeney (South Africa). Also, a few missionaries due to their later unknown affiliation are not included although they were listed early (1914–1915) as missionaries with *The Voice in the Wilderness*: Estelle Bernauer (Japan), L. M. Anglin and Adolph Hiencke (China), and P. R. Rushin (Philippines).

3. See, the following issues of *The Voice in the Wilderness*, No. 18, October 1916—*China:* George Hansen, H. L. Lawler, H. J. Mader, Olive Maw; *South America:* R. S. McBride, Daniel Berg; *Africa:* Anna Richards, John Perkins; *India:* Miss C. B. Herron, Edith Kirschner; No.19, December 1916—*China:* T. & Drusie R. Mallot, Lettie M. Ward, J. Raymond Benning; *South Africa:* Jacob O. & Lily Lehman; No. 24, June 1918—*Africa:* Bertha Sutley, Anna Richards; *South America:* Lucy Leatherman; *India:* Robert R. Cook; *China*: Olive E. Maw. By the June 1918 issue Haywood was speaking of those missionaries who had "accepted the message."

| | |
|---|---|
| PT | *The Present Truth*, L. V. Roberts, ed. |
| R-T | *Brief History*, Hilda Reeder; *Chalices of Gold*, James L. Tyson |
| VW | *The Voice in the Wilderness*, G. T. Haywood, ed. |
| WG | *The Winds of God*, Howard A. Goss |
| | * – single or widowed (otherwise, all listings are missionary couples) |
| | **m** – subsequent married name |
| | **nm** – national minister receiving U.S. missionary finances |

## B.2 96 Oneness Missionaries between 1915 and 1921

| Missionary | Country | Source |
|---|---|---|
| Aikenhead, May* (m: Burnside) | China | ACOP |
| Bass, Earnest R. | China | MDS, R-T |
| Bateson, Albert | China | BT, PAW |
| Beddell, Saul | Persia | GR |
| Berntsen, Bernt, & Magna | China | BT, PAW, WG |
| Biddle, Willard S.* (Mrs.) | China | ACOP, BT, CO |
| Blakeney, Joseph K. | South Africa | MDS, GR |
| Booker, Melvia | China | BT, PAW |
| Bottomley, Golden (Harrison)* (Mrs.) & Albert (d. 1918) | China | BT, MDS, PAW |
| Burnside, W. H., & May (Aikenhead) | China | BT, CO, R-T, PAW |
| Clark, J. E., & Clark, Margaret* (Mrs.) | India | BT, PAW, VW |
| Condrajian, Harry | Turkey (Armenia) | BT |
| Cook, Robert F. (only until 1926) | Bangalore, S. India | R-T, VW |
| Coote, Leonard W. | Japan | BT, CO, ECJC, MB, MDS, PhP, PMA |
| Cound, George | China | BT, CO, ECJC |
| Denny, Frank, & Lillian | China | BT, GR, MDS, PAW, PhP, VW |
| Dickson, Louie* (Miss) | Palestine | ACOP, BT, CO, PMA |
| Doak, E. W., & Nellie | Egypt | BT, GR, MDS, PAW, VW |

| Missionary | Country | Source |
|---|---|---|
| Doyal, George H. | China | BT |
| Early, James M. (d. 1921) | Liberia | BT, PAW |
| Edkins, E. | South Africa | BT, PAW, VW |
| Faulkner, H. L. | China | GR, MDS |
| Gray, Frank, & May (Heath) (CMA Missionary 1902–1906) | Japan | BT, MB, MDS, PAW |
| Grimes, Samuel J. | Liberia | BT, CO, R-T |
| Gunstad, N. O., & Marie | Chili, Bolivia | BT, CO, GR, VW |
| Habacker, Tillie* (Miss) | China | BT, PAW |
| Hammond, Elmer B. (d.1916) & Hattie (m: Storey) | China | GR, MDS, VW, MB |
| Hammond, Corabelle* (m: Small) | China | BT, GR, MDS, PAW |
| Haish, Cora* (Miss) | China | BT, R-T, PAW |
| Harrison, Addell * (Mrs.) | China | BT, MDS, PAW |
| Heidal, A. | China | BT |
| Hensley, Carl M., & Mabel E. | China | BT, CO, MB, PAW, PhP, PMA |
| Hofer, Lyda* (Miss) | China, India | GR, VW |
| Holmes, Phoebe* | China | ACJC, BT, MDS, PAW, VW, PMA |
| Hult, Alma C. | China | BT, CO |
| Iry, Mae* (Mrs.) | China | ACJC,BT,CO,ECJC, MB, PMA |
| Jacobs, A. (nm) | India | BT, PAW+, VW |
| James, John D. | China | BT, MDS, VW |
| Johns, Clarence | Hawaii | BT |
| Johns, H. J. | Hawaii | BT, MDS |
| Joyner, Paul M. | Palestine | BT, PAW |
| Juergensen, C. F., & Marie | Japan | BT, MDS, PAW, VW |
| Kelly, George (rebaptized 1927) | China | GR, MB, PhP, WG |
| Kok, Anna* | China | BT, CO |
| Kugler, Alice S.* (m: Sheets) | China | BT, CO, ECJC, MDS, PAW, PMA |
| Lazarus, Boba | Persia | BT, GR |
| Lee, Henry (nm) | Jamaica | CO, MB |
| Lowther, Willa B. | China | BT |

| Missionary | Country | Source |
|---|---|---|
| McCarty, Dorothea L.* | India | ACJC, BT, CO, ECJC, GR, MDS, VW, PMA |
| McCullough, D. | Palestine | BT |
| McLean, Hector, & Sigrid (with PMU until 1927) | China, Burma | BT, PAW |
| Mayton, Paul, & Agnes | Czechoslavokia | PAW |
| Merrin, W. H., & Edith E. | India | BT, PAW |
| Miller, Clyde T. | British East Africa | BT, CO, R-T |
| Mocuacueng, Oliphant (nm) | South Africa | PAW |
| Molongoane, F. N. (nm) | South Africa | PAW |
| Moore, George M. | South Africa | BT, CO, PAW |
| Moore, Barney. S. | Japan | MS, PT, VW |
| Moore, A. O. | India | ECJC, PMA |
| Morgan, Chonita | Mexico | MB, AAFCJ |
| Nichols, Nettie D.* | China | GR, MDS |
| Phillips, Ralph | China | BT, CO, PAW |
| Posey, Mary A. | China, Hawaii | MDS |
| Pyatt, C. A. | China | BT |
| Raby, Anna* | China | BT, CO, PAW, R-T |
| Ramsey, F. S. | China | BT, GR, MDS, PhP, PAW, VW |
| Randall, H. E. | Egypt | BT, GR, MDS, PAW |
| Reynolds, Arthur | China | BT, CO, ECJC |
| Ross, Arthur D. | Africa | BT, PAW |
| Roth, Peter A., & Minnie M. | Switzerland | BT, CO, PAW |
| Russell, Nina R. | Jamaica | MB |
| Sheets, Daniel Keefer, & Alice Sarah (see, Kugler) | China | MB, PhP, PAW |
| Sherman, H. J. | Mexico | MDS |
| Sly, L. B. | Uruguay, Ecuador, Cuba, Colombia | ACJC, BT, R-T, PAW |
| Smith, William Bodie | Jamaica | MB |
| Sonnenberg, Robert, & Alice (Iry) | China | BT, CO, ECJC, MB |
| Sonnenberg, Lydia | China | PAW |
| Spooner, Kenneth E. M. | South Africa | MDS, VW |

| Missionary | Country | Source |
|---|---|---|
| Steinberg, Edgar C. | China | BT, MDS, PMA, VW |
| Stieglitz, Elizabeth (Harrison)* | China | BT, MB, PAW, PhP, PMA, R-T |
| Storey, Charles W., & Harriet M. | China | BT, MDS, PAW, VW |
| Tefre, Henry, & Olive | India | ACJC, ECJC |
| Thebe, Jeremiah R. | South Africa | PAW |
| Tinker, Jessie* (Miss) | India | MS, PAW |
| Urshan, Andrew D. | Persia | BT, GR, MDS, PhP, VW |
| Urshan, Timothy D. | Palestine | BT, CO, ECJC, PAW, PMA |
| Walker, Manuel | Mexico | MB, AAFCJ |
| Watson, Arthur (d. 1925) | Jamaica | BT, CO, PAW |
| Weaver, H. C. | Hawaii | BT, CO |
| White, George, & Melvina (nm+) | Jamaica | MB, PAW+, R-T |
| Wick, Emma L.* | South Africa | BT |
| Wingard, A. | China | BT |
| Wortham, Ruth | Alaska | BT |
| Wright, Ada* | South China | BT |
| Yest, Nicholas, & Mary | China | CO, VW, PAW |

## B.3. 68 Additional Missionaries between 1922 and 1930[4]

| | | |
|---|---|---|
| Allison, Samuel | Liberia | CO |
| Anderson, Carry | China | CO |
| Antha, A. T. (nm+) | South Africa | PAW+ |
| Badger, Llewellyn | South Africa | Com PAW |
| Balca, Jan (nm+) | Yugoslavia, Hungary | MB |
| Bohlokoane, C. M. (nm+) | South Africa | PAW+ |
| Broadnax, Rosa Lee* | Jamaica | PAW+ |
| Brown, Lloyd D. | East Africa (Kenya) | CO |
| Brown, Walter * (Mrs.) | China | CO |
| Budge, J. G. (nm+) | South Africa | PAW+ |
| Cheatham, S. Eugene | Liberia | CO, R-T |
| DuToit, J. F. (nm+) | South Africa | PAW+ |
| Fleming, R. A. | Japan (by 1929) | R-T |
| Georges, D. D. | Greece | CO |
| Georges, D. H. | Jamaica | CO |
| Gray, Pekro | Liberia | CO |
| Holmes, Aaron, & Pearl | Liberia | MB, COOLJC |
| Huba, Anton | Czechoslovakia | MB |
| Huba, John | Czechoslovakia | MB |
| Hull, W. L. | Iraq, Israel | ACOP |
| Ivanhoff (nm+) | Russia | CO, PAW+ |
| Jamieson, Caleb | Jamaica | PAW+ |
| Johns, Clarence | Hawaii | CO |
| Johnson, L. M. | China | CO |
| Johnson, Ted | China | ACOP |
| Joseph, N. John (nm) | India | CO |
| King, Elsie | China | PMA |
| Lerch, John | Hungary | PAW+ |

4. In 1928 the restructured PAW implemented a short-term missionary support program for national ministers in key leadership roles in various countries, which included a total of twelve national ministers by 1930 based upon the *PAW Minute Book and Ministerial Record 1930–1931*. These missionaries were mostly in South Africa, Jamaica, Eastern Europe, Liberia, and India. The extra designation of "nm+" is used to denote these specific missionaries. Also, the designation "PAW+" is used for the remaining new missionary listings from the *1930 Minute Book*.

| | | |
|---|---|---|
| Ledbetter, L. R. | Africa | CO, R-T |
| Leonard, Garland, & Eleanor | China | ACJC, PMA |
| Long, M.* (Mrs.) | Estonia | CO |
| Lye, Alice* | China | ACOP |
| Lye, Florence* | China | ACOP |
| McCune, Henry | China | R-T |
| MacGregor, William B. | India, Jamaica | CO, ECJC, R-T |
| Matson, Joseph | China | ACOP |
| Mayton, Paul, & Agnes | Czechoslavakia | PAW |
| Miller, Cleophas (Clyde Miller's son-died in Kenya) | Kenya | CO |
| Mingard, Adolph | China | CO |
| Morabe, Barry E. (nm+) | South Africa | PAW+ |
| Morar, Samuel (nm+) | India | PAW+ |
| Moses, Willie (nm+) | South Africa | PAW+ |
| Nann, Otto L. (nm+) | India | PAW+ |
| Paulson, S.* (Miss) | South Africa | CO |
| Paulson, S.* (Mrs.) | South Africa | CO |
| Phelps, C. W. | Cuba | CO |
| Phelps, Raymond | China | R-T |
| Porter, Elizabeth* | Liberia | CO |
| Powar, J. Benj. (nm+) | India | PAW+ |
| Rezniczek, Joseph | India | ACJC, MB, PMA, PAW+ |
| Robinson, Ophelia* | Liberia | MB |
| Sikora, John, & Susanna (nm) | Estonia | CO, R-T |
| Silverstein, A. | Bulgaria | CO |
| Smisek, Karol (nm+) | Yugoslavia | PAW+ |
| Spence(r)* (Mrs.) | China | CO, R-T |
| Stapleton, Nina A.* | Jamaica | CO |
| Stiles, C. D. | Hawaii | CO |
| Stromquist, A. E. | Japan | ACOP |
| Swanepoel, J. H. (nm) | South Africa | CO, R-T |
| Teasley, Pearl | Liberia | MB, COOLJC |
| Thomas, J. B. | Iraq, Israel | ACJC, PMA |
| Tucker, Cordelia* | Liberia | CO, PAW+ |

| | | |
|---|---|---|
| Walent, Adam | Yugoslavia | CO |
| Sier, Wier (nm+) | Liberia | PAW+ |
| Wilson, Nathan | Jamaica | PAW+ |
| Wilson, R. M.* (Mrs.) | Jamaica | PAW+ |
| Wise, Henrietta | India | ECJC |
| Wright, Rosa Lee | Liberia | MB, COOLJC |

# Bibliography

## Primary Sources

### Books, Pamphlets, Ancestry Records


Alvey, Herbert. *1900 U.S. Census*. Anderson, IN, Perry Co., EDN106, 3B.

———. *1910 U.S. Census*. Troy, IN, EDN136, 12B.

———. 1918 World War 1 Registration, #265.

Anderson (Angelopoulos), Alexander. *1920 U.S. Census*. Indianapolis, IN, EDN27, 5A.

———. *1930 U.S. Census*. Indianapolis, IN, EDN49–115, 8A.

Anderson, A. B. "I Am the Way and the Truth." [translation] Greek Tract, n.d.

———. "The Voice of the Gospel." [translation] Greek Tract, n.d.

Anderson, Arthur M., ed. *For the Defense of the Gospel*. New York: COOLJC, 1971.

"Articles of Faith—1945." *Codified Rules and Ministerial Record of the PAJC at Indianapolis, IN*.

*Articles of Faith of the Associated Brotherhood of Christians*. Hot Springs, AR: Goslee Printing, n.d.

Balca, Jan. *My Life with God: Autobiography of Jan Balca*. Hazelwood, MO: printed by Samuel Balca, 2005.

Barber, Oddous. *1900 US Census*. Indianapolis, IN, Marion Co., EDN70, 12B.

———. *1910 US Census*. Indianapolis, IN, Marion Co., EDN102, 9A.

Barnes, Lenore. *1930 U.S. Census*. St. Louis, MO, EDN96–189, 4A.

Barnes, Lenore, and Mary G. Moise. *1910 U.S. Census*. St. Louis, MO, EDN270, 14A.

Bartleman, Frank. *The Deity of Christ*. Los Angeles: by the author, 1926.

———. *From Plow to Pulpit: From Maine to California*. Los Angeles: by the author, 1924.

———. *How Pentecost Came to Los Angeles: As It Was in the Beginning*. Los Angeles: by the author, 1925.

Bell, E. N. *The Truth about the Godhead with Comments on the Water Baptism Formula*. Springfield, MO: Gospel Publishing House, n.d.

Booth-Clibborn, William. "The Baptism in the Holy Spirit, Part 1." *AG Heritage* 10/4 (Winter 1990–1991) 6–7, 22–24.

———. *A Call to the Dust and Ashes*. St. Paul: by the author, 1922.

———. *Christ—The Mystery of God*. N.p.: by the author, c. 1919.

———. "Down from His Glory." In *Victory Songs No. 4 (Booth-Clibborn)*. Chicago: Tabernacle, n.d.

"Brief Record of Minutes 1907–1917." In *PAW Minute Book and Ministerial Record 1917–1918*. Portland, OR.
Cagle, Odell. *Echoes of the Past*. Stockton, CA: Apostolic, 1972.
Cockrum, William M. *History of the Underground Railroad*. Oakland City, IN: J. W. Cockrum, 1915.
Cook, Glenn A. *1870 U.S. Census*. Lincoln, IN, Hendricks Co., 30.
———. *1880 U.S. Census*. Brownsburg, IN, EDN146, 5B.
———. *1900 U.S. Census*. Chicago, IL, Cook Co., EDN308, 3B.
———. *1910 U.S. Census*. Chicago, IL, Cook Co., EDN1250, 12B.
———. "The Azusa Street Mission." Los Angeles: Belvedere Christian Mission, n.d.
Cotton, Emma. "The Inside Story of the Azusa Street Outpouring." *Message of the Apostolic Faith*, April 1939, 1.
Davidson, Asa Elsworth. *1920 US Census*. Portland, OR, 2B.
Davis, T. C. *1910 U.S. Census*. Indianapolis, IN, EDN36, 5B.
———. *1920 U.S. Census*. Indianapolis, IN, 25A.
*Discipline of the Pentecostal Holiness Church, 1945*. Franklin Springs, GA: Pentecostal Holiness Church, 1945.
Doak, Edward W. *1860 U.S. Census*. Middlebury, MI, 41.
———. *1870 U.S. Census*. Victor, MI, 22.
———. *1900 U.S. Census*. Oahu, Hawaiian Islands, EDN11, 19A.
———. *1910 U.S. Census*. Pasadena, CA, EDN519, 9A.
———. *1920 U.S. Census*. San Pedro, CA, EDN311, 27A.
———. *1920 U.S. Census*. Santa Cruz, CA, EDN230, 4B.
———. Appleton, Wisconsin Directories, 1884–1898, 1897.
———. "Index to Register of Voters." Pasadena City, Precinct No. 46, Los Angeles Co., California, 1916.
———. U.S. Passport Applications 1795–1925, 5 August 1913.
Doak, Nellie. *California Death Index, 1940–1997*. Los Angeles, October 14, 1944.
*Doctrines and Disciplines of the Azusa Street Apostolic Faith Mission of Los Angeles*. Los Angeles, CA: 1915.
ECJC Minute Book and Ministerial Roster, 1927–1928. St. Louis, Missouri.
Eldridge, George N. *1850 US Census*. Orrington, ME, Penobscot Co., 215.
———. *1880 U.S. Census*. Calais, ME, Washington Co., EDN169, 18B.
———. *1910 U.S. Census*. Pasadena, CA, EDN313, 7A.
Ewart, Frank J. *The Phenomenon of Pentecost*. Houston, TX: Herald, 1947.
Farrow, George R. "Letter to Lulu Brumwell." January 11, 1915.
Fauss, O. F. *What God Hath Wrought: The Complete Works of O. F. Fauss*. Hazelwood, MO: Word Aflame, 1985.
———. *1900 U.S. Census*. Waynoka, OK, Woods County, EDN243, 2A.
———. 1918 WW1 Registration Card, Order #2601.
———. *1920 U.S. Census*. Kinder, LA, EDN18, 4A.
FBI Report #55234. Publ. M1085. "Investigative Case Files of the Bureau of Investigation 1908–1922."
Flower, Alice Reynolds. "When Pentecost Came to Indianapolis." *AG Heritage* 5/4 (Winter 1985–1986) 5–7.
Floyd, David Lee. *1900 U.S. Census*. Red River Co., Texas, EDN100, 22A.
———. Interview with Larry Booker (1979–1980). Unpublished Transcript. Miami, Oklahoma.

Frazee, Jacob J. *1860 US Census.* Van Buren, IA, 287.
———. *1900 U.S. Census.* LaJunta, CO, Otero Co., EDN82, 18B.
———. *1910 U.S. Census.* Rialto, CA, EDN113, 12B.
———. *1920 U.S. Census.* Portland, OR, EDN44, 13A.
———. *Iowa State Gazetteer.* "Mount Zion Directory: 1884–1885." 1266.
Frazee Letter to Sherman. October 1917. FBI Report #55234, Publication M1085, 92.
Frazee, Louvica Anna (Brizendine). *1900 US Census.* Burlington, IA, EDN3, 4B.
Frush, James A. *1910 U.S. Census.* Bowling Green, OH, EDN48, 1B.
———. *1920 U.S. Census.* Newark, OH, EDN143, 10B.
*General Council of the Assemblies of God—Combined Minutes 1914.* Hot Springs, AR.
*General Council of the Assemblies of God—Combined Minutes 1915.* St. Louis, MO.
*General Council of the Assemblies of God—Combined Minutes 1916.* St. Louis, MO.
*General Council of the Assemblies of God*—Combined Minutes 1917. St. Louis, MO.
*General Council of the Assemblies of God*—Combined Minutes 1919. Chicago, IL.
"The Gliggy Bluks' Water Carnival." *Enrichment* 11/2 (2006) 34.
Goodloe, Harry W., Sr., ed. *God's Word: Exhorted, Revealed, Prophecied.* Indianapolis: Christ Temple, n.d.
Goss, Ethel E. *The Winds of God.* New York: Comet, 1958; revised by Ruth Goss Nortje, Hazelwood, MO: Word Aflame, 1977.
Grimes, Susan Kathleen. "The Great I Am." In *The Bridegroom Songs.* Indianapolis: Voice in the Wilderness, 1926.
Grimes, Samuel Joshua. 1918 WW1 Registration Card, #2942.
———. "Manifest of Alien Passengers for the U.S." S.S. Athenia, New York, 1924, 4.
———. "Naturalization Application," #3419718, New York, 1931.
———. 1942 WW2 Registration, New York.
Hancock, Samuel Nathaniel. *1900 U.S. Census.* Indianapolis, IN, EDN15, 2B.
———. *1910 U.S. Census.* Indianapolis, IN, EDN177, 4A.
———. 1918 WW1 Registration, September 12, 1918, Order# 3111.
———. *1920 U.S. Census.* Indianapolis, IN, EDN64, 17B.
———. *Indiana Marriage Collection, 1800–1941*, Marion Co., IN, Annie W. Williams, September 28, 1914.
———. *Indiana Marriage Collection, 1800–1941*, Marion Co., IN, Bertha Valentine, December 26, 1907.
Harris, Thoro. *1880 U.S. Census.* District of Columbia, EDN3, 1A.
———. *1910 U.S. Census.* Chicago, IL, Cook Co., EDN633, 9A.
———. *1917–18 WWI Registration Card.* No. 3711.
———. "Baptized in Jesus' Name." *The Present Truth* 1 (1916) 1.
Haywood, Ben. *1850 Schedule 2: Slave Inhabitants.* Raleigh, NC, Wake Co., July 1850.
———. *1860 Schedule 2: Slave Inhabitants.* Raleigh, NC, Wake Co., June 1860, 3, 5, 14, 17, 18.
———. *1880 U.S. Census.* Greencastle, IN, EDN152, 401A.
———. *1900 U.S. Census.* Marion, Co., Indianapolis, IN, EDN84, 12A.
———. *1910 U.S. Census.* Marion Co., Indianapolis, IN, EDN263, 7A.
———. Fall Creek Renovation Notification. *Indianapolis Star*, May 27, 1910.
Haywood, G. T. *1900 U.S. Census.* Marion Co., Indianapolis, IN, EDN84, 12A.
———. *1910 U.S. Census.* Marion County, Indianapolis, IN, EDN74, 4A.
———. *1920 U.S. Census.* Marion County, Indianapolis, IN, EDN66, 6B.

———. *1931 Certificate of Death*. Marion County Health Department, Indianapolis, IN, April 12, 1931.

———. "Baptized into the Body." In *The Bridegroom Songs*. Indianapolis: Voice in the Wilderness, 1926.

———. *The Birth of the Spirit in the Days of the Apostles*. Indianapolis: Voice in the Wilderness Publishers, n.d.

———. *The Birth of the Spirit in the Days of the Apostles*, n.d. In *The Life and Writings of Elder G. T. Haywood*, edited by Paul D. Dugas, 67–90. Portland, OR: Apostolic, 1968.

———, ed. *The Bridegroom Songs*. Indianapolis: Voice in the Wilderness, 1926.

———. *Brief History of Christ Temple Church*. December 1924. In Morris E. Golder, *History of the Pentecostal Assemblies of the World*, 36. Indianapolis, 1973.

———. *Christian Stewardship*. Indianapolis: Voice in the Wilderness, n.d.

———. "The Day of Redemption." In *The Bridegroom Songs*. Indianapolis: Voice in the Wilderness, 1926.

———. *Divine Names and Titles of Jehovah*. Indianapolis: Voice in the Wilderness, n.d.

———. *Ezekiel's Vision*. Indianapolis: Voice in the Wilderness, n.d.

———. *The Finest of the Wheat*. Indianapolis: Voice in the Wilderness, n.d.

———. "I See a Crimson Stream of Blood." In *The Bridegroom Songs*. Indianapolis: Voice in the Wilderness, 1926.

———. "I'm Saved Today." In *The Bridegroom Songs*. Indianapolis: Voice in the Wilderness, 1926.

———. *Index to Marriage Record 1901–1905*. County Clerk's Office, Marion County, Indiana, OS Page 555.

———. "Jesus Our All in All." In *The Bridegroom Songs*. Indianapolis: Voice in the Wilderness, 1926.

———. "Jesus, the Son of God." In *The Bridegroom Songs*. Indianapolis: Voice in the Wilderness, 1926.

———. *The Marriage and Divorce Question in the Church*. Indianapolis: Christ Temple, c. 1928.

———. "O Lord, How Long?" In *The Bridegroom Songs*. Indianapolis: Voice in the Wilderness, 1926.

———. *The Old and New Tabernacle Compared*. Indianapolis: Voice in the Wilderness, n.d.

———. PAW Board of Presbyters Handwritten Secretarial Notes. Chicago, July 8, 1924.

———. *The Resurrection of the Dead*. Indianapolis: Voice in the Wilderness, n.d.

———. "Some Day." In *The Bridegroom Songs*. Indianapolis: Voice in the Wilderness, 1926.

———. *The Teachings of the Apostolic Church according to the Bible*. Indianapolis: Voice in the Wilderness, n.d.

———. "Thank God, For the Blood." In *The Bridegroom Songs*. Indianapolis: Voice in the Wilderness, 1926.

———. "These Signs Shall Follow Them." In *The Bridegroom Songs*. Indianapolis: Voice in the Wilderness, 1926.

———. *The Victim of the Flaming Sword*. Indianapolis: Voice in the Wilderness, n.d.

———. "We Will Walk Through the Streets of the City." In *The Bridegroom Songs*. Indianapolis: Voice in the Wilderness, 1926.

Haywood, G. T., and Fern Reneick Smith. "The Name of God." In *The Bridegroom Songs*. Indianapolis: Voice in the Wilderness, 1926.

"Haywood, Gen. Robert W." *Wake Co., North Carolina Archives Obituaries*. Mary J. Haywood, August 29, 1857. http://files.usgwarchives.org/nc/wake/obits/h/haywood7980b.txt.

Haywood, Sherwood." *Wake Co., North Carolina Archives Obituaries*. October 5, http://files.usgwarchives.org/nc/wake/obits/h/ haywood17109ob.txt.

*Historical News* 18/3 (April–June 1999) 4.

Kickler, Troy L. "North Carolina History Project." John Locke Foundation, 2008. http://www. northcarolinahistory.org/encyclopedia/18/entry.

Kidson, W. E. *History of Pentecostal Organizations*, n.d. Cited in vol. 1 of *The Encyclopedia of American Religions*, edited by J. Gordon Melton. Tarrytown, NY: Triumphant, 1991.

Lane, Lunsford. *The Narrative of Lunsford Lane, Formerly of Raleigh, N.C., Embracing an Account of His Early Life, the Redemption by Purchase of Himself and Family from Slavery, and His Banishment from the Place of His Birth for the Crime of Wearing a Colored Skin*. Boston: J. G. Torrey, 1842.

Lawrence, B. F. 1917 World War 1 Registration, no. 199.

———. *1920 U.S. Census*. Tulsa, OK, EDN235, 5A.

———. *1930 U.S. Census*. St. Louis, MO, EDN8, 4A.

———-. *The Apostolic Faith Restored*. St. Louis: Gospel Publishing House, 1916.

Lawson, Robert C. *1900 U.S. Census*. Iberia Parish, LA, EDN33, 22A.

———. 1917 WW1 Registration Card, June 4, 1917, Columbus, OH.

———. *1920 U.S. Census*, Manhattan, NY, EDN1408, 3A.

———. *1923 U.S. Passport Application*, #343224, September 1923.

———. *1930 U.S. Census*. Manhattan, NY, EDN24, 14B.

———-. *The Anthropology of Jesus Christ Our Kinsman*. Piqua, OH: Ohio Ministries, 1925; reprint, 2000.

———. "God Is Great in My Soul." In *The Bridegroom Songs*, edited by G. T. Haywood, 39. Indianapolis: Voice in the Wilderness, 1926.

———-. "The Greatest Evil in This World Is Race Prejudice." June 1957. In *For the Defense of the Gospel*, edited by Arthur M. Anderson, 248–56. New York: COOLJC, 1971.

———. "Make Full Proof of Thy Ministry." May 1956. In *For the Defense of the Gospel*, edited by Arthur M. Anderson, 404. New York: COOLJC, 1971.

———. *An Open Letter on the Burning Issue of Marriage and Divorce*. New York: Church of Christ, n.d.

———. *An Open Letter to a Southern White Minister*. Piqua, OH: Ohio Ministries, 1949; edited, 1995.

———. "Pentecostal Intolerance." March 1937. In *For the Defense of the Gospel*, edited by Arthur M. Anderson, 310. New York: COOLJC, 1971.

———. "Prejudice." August 1947. In *For the Defense of the Gospel*, edited by Arthur M. Anderson, 328–29. New York: COOLJC, 1971.

———. "Sparks from the Anvil." July 1947. In *For the Defense of the Gospel*, edited by Arthur M. Anderson, 326–28. New York: COOLJC, 1971.

Lee, Edward. *1900 US Census*. Fresno, CA, EDN5, 5A.

———. *1920 US Census*. Los Angeles, CA, EDN337, 6B.

Lloyd, Ernest B. *1890 Oklahoma Census*. Hennessey, OK, 25.

———. *1895 Kansas Census*, 1.

———. *1910 US Census*, Indianapolis, IN, EDN93, 2A.

McClain, S. C. *Seek First the Kingdom*. Edited by Robin Johnston. Hazelwood, MO: Word Aflame, 2005.

Mautz, John. *1920 US Census*. San Antonio, CA, 3B.

*Ministerial Directory of the United Pentecostal Church, Inc., 1947*. St. Louis, MO: Pentecostal, 1947.

Parham, Charles F. *A Voice Crying in the Wilderness*. Cited in "Baptism," *Apostolic Faith*, October 1912, 4–5. Baxter Springs, KS: by the author, 1902.

Parham, Charles F. 1918 WWI Registration Card, September 7, 1918.

———. *1900 U.S. Census*. Empire City, Cherokee Co., Kansas, 5.

———. *Biography Index*. Sept 1955–Aug 1958, vol. 4. New York: H. W. Wilson Company, 1960.

———. *Who's Who in America*. Vol. 7, 1977–1981. Chicago: Marquis Who's Who, 1981.

Parham, Sarah E. *The Life of Charles F. Parham*. Baxter Springs, KS: Apostolic Faith Bible College, 1930.

*PAW Minute Book and Ministerial Record 1917–1918*. Portland, OR.

*PAW Minute Book and Ministerial Record 1919–1920*. Indianapolis, IN.

*PAW Minute Book and Ministerial Record 1923–1924*. Indianapolis, IN.

*PAW Minute Book and Ministerial Record 1926–1927*. Indianapolis, IN.

*PAW Minute Book and Ministerial Record 1927–1928*. Indianapolis, IN.

*PAW Minute Book and Ministerial Record 1929–1930*. Indianapolis, IN.

*PAW Minute Book and Ministerial Record 1930–1931*. Indianapolis, IN.

*PAW Minute Book and Ministerial Record 1939–1940*. Indianapolis, IN.

Pendleton, William Henry. *1900 US Census*. Los Angeles, CA, 22.

*Pentecost*. J. R. Flower, ed. March 1910, 1.

*The Pentecostal Outlook*. November 1937, 13.

Poole, Fred. *1910 U.S. Census*. Los Angeles, CA, EDN183, 3B.

———. *1920 U.S. Census*. Visalia, CA, EDN232, 1A.

———. *1930 U.S. Census*. Chico, CA, EDN43, 7B.

Prentiss, Henry. *Index to Marriage Record 1906–1910*, Marion Co., IN, County Clerk's Office, Book 49, 261.

———. *1880 US Census*. Beverly Manor District, Augusta Co., VA, EDN14, 131A.

———. *1910 US Census*. Marion Co., Indianapolis, IN, EDN101, 3A.

———. 1918 WWI Registration Card, Chicago, IL, #1645.

———. *1920 US Census*. Wayne Co., Detroit, MI, EDN510, 16B.

———. *1930 US Census*. Wayne Co., Detroit, MI, EDN19, 2A.

Pryor, Hattie E. "The Water Way." In *The Bridegroom Songs*. Indianapolis: Voice in the Wilderness, 1926.

"Re: Pentecostal Assemblies of the Word, Anti-Conscription." Report of Special Employee Hudson, Portland, Oregon, August 8, 1917. FBI Report #55234, Publ. M1085, "Investigative Case Files of the Bureau of Investigation 1908–1922."

Reeder, Hilda. *A Brief History of the Foreign Missionary Department of the PAW*. Indianapolis: Foreign Missionary Department of the Pentecostal Assemblies of the World, 1951.

Roberts, Della. *1900 U.S. Census*. Franklin, OH, 6A.

Roberts, L. V. *1880 U.S. Census*. Bowling Green, OH, EDN181, 17A

———. *1900 U.S. Census*. Miflin, OH, EDN40, 16A.

———. *1910 U.S. Census*. Bowling Green, OH, EDN48, 1B.

———. *1930 U.S. Census*. Indianapolis, IN, EDN49-1, 5B.
Schaepe, John G. *1930 U.S. Census*. Christy, AZ, EDN7-55, 8B.
Sheets, Alice Kugler. *Nuggets of Gold: Blessings, Health, Long Life*. Houston: Herald, c. 1947.
Shumway, Charles William. "A Critical Study of the Gift of Tongues." AB thesis, University of Southern California, 1914.
Smith, John W. V. *A Brief History of the Church of God Reformation Movement*. Anderson, IN: Warner, 1976.
Spillman, Lena. *1920 U.S. Census*. Indianapolis, IN, EDN28, 9A.
———. *1930 U.S. Census*. Indianapolis, IN, 49-1, 7B.
Studd, George B. *1930 U.S. Census*. Los Angeles, CA, EDN19-1268, 8A.
Taylor, Charles E., Jr. *Baptismal Passover*. By the author, 1971.
Thompson, Aaron Belford. "Emancipation." In *Harvest of Thoughts*, 46. Indianapolis: by the author, 1907.
———. *Harvest of Thoughts*. Indianapolis: by the author, 1907.
Urshan, Andrew D. *Pentecost as It Was in the Early 1900s*. Portland, OR: Apostolic, 1923; rev. ed., April 1987.
———. U.S. Passport Application, No. 17167, October 13, 1913.
Varnell, A. F. "Fifteen Things Wrong with the Doctrine, that Teaches Speaking in Tongues Is the Initial First Evidence of Receiving the Holy Ghost." Tract, Santa Ana, CA, n.d.
Wilson, James L. *It Makes a Difference What You Believe*. Indianapolis: Bethel Ministerial Association, n.d.
Woodworth-Etter, Maria. *Sign and Wonders*. Indianapolis: by the author, 1916.

## Periodicals

"A. G. Garr Revival." *Meat in Due Season*, February 1917, 1.
Allen, Cleveland G. "Pentecostal Assemblies to End Session Friday." *New York News*, August 27, 1930, 1. In James L. Tyson *Chalices of Gold: A Narrative and Pictorial History of the Pentecostal Assemblies of the World*, 347. Warren, OH: by the author, 1990.
"Apostolic Faith Assembly." *The Indianapolis Star*, June 13, 1924, 14.
"Apostolic Faith Movement." *The Good Report*, May 1911, no. 1, 4.
Argue, A. H. "At Evening Time It Shall Be Light." *The Good Report* (Ottawa, Canada), vol. 1, no. 3, 1912, 6–7.
"Arrested for Jesus' Sake." *The Apostolic Faith*, December 1906, vol. 1. no. 4, 3.
"Baptized into One Body." *The Good Report*, December 1, 1913, vol. 1, no. 7, 3.
Bartleman, Frank. "Why I Was Re-baptized in the Name of Jesus Christ." *Meat in Due Season*, December 1915, 1.
Bell, E. N. "The 'Acts' on Baptism in Christ's Name Only." *The Weekly Evangel*, June 12, 1915, 1, 3.
———. "Bible Order versus Fanaticism." *Word and Witness*, March 20, 1914, 2–3.
———. "Bro. Bell on the Trinity." *Weekly Evangel*, November 6, 1915, 1.
———. "The Great Battle for the Truth." *The Christian Evangel*, August 9, 1919, 1–2.
———. "The Great Controversy and Confusion." *The Christian Evangel*, September 6, 1919, 6–7.

———. "Meat in Due Season Corrected." *Weekly Evangel*, September 18, 1915, 2.
———. "Questions and Answers." *Weekly Evangel*, August 11, 1917, 9.
———. "The Sad New Issue" *Word and Witness*, June 1915, 3.
"'Bluk' Apostle and One of the Bluks." *Indianapolis Morning Star*, June 5, 1907, 20.
"Bluk Crowd Runs Over." *Indianapolis Star*, June 10, 1907, 12.
"Bluk Divides Home." *Indianapolis Morning Star*, June 4, 1907, 1.
"Bluk Feet, Little and Big, Scrubbed." *Indianapolis Star*, June 16, 10.
"Bluks Appeal to Police." *Indianapolis Star*, June 17, 1907, 3, 7.
"Bluks Invade Allen Chapel and Stop Sermon." *Indianapolis Star*, April 24, 1908, 1.
Boddy, Alexander A. "Indianapolis." *Confidence*, vol. 6, no. 1, January 1913, 17.
Booth-Clibborn, William. "A Preacher's Testimony." *Meat in Due Season*, December 1915, vol. 1, no. 9, 3.
———. "Should a Christian Physically Defend Himself?" *Meat in Due Season*, June 1916, vol 1, no. 13, 2.
"Bosworth Campaign in Indianapolis." *Christian Outlook*, January 1925, 4.
"Bro. Joe Rodgers." *The Voice in the Wilderness*, September 1918, no. 24, 2.
"Brother Will Trotter." *Weekly Evangel*, April 3, 1915, 1.
"Column of Information." *Christian Outlook*, December 1923, 251.
"Color Line Obliterated." *The (Portland) Morning Oregonian*, December 31, 1906, 9. Cited in *The Women of Azusa Street*, by Estrelda Alexander, 65. Cleveland: Pilgrim, 2005.
"Columbus, O." *The Voice in the Wilderness*, October 1916, no. 18, 1, 4.
"Concerning Registration for Military Service." *Weekly Evangel*, June 2, 1917, 8.
"Controversy Languishes—Evangelism Spreading." *Weekly Evangel*, June 9, 1917, 7.
"The Convention." *The Voice in the Wilderness*, September 1916, no. 18, 1, 4.
Cook, Glenn A. "An Eastern Trip." *Meat in Due Season*, June 1915, vol. 1, no. 6, 2.
———. "Editorial." *Messiah's Coming Kingdom*, Los Angeles, 1927, no. 2, 2.
———. "The K. K. K. and Romanism." *Messiah's Coming Kingdom* (Los Angeles), December 1928, no. 9, 1.
———. "Pentecost in Lamont, Okla." *The Apostolic Faith*, January 1907, vol. 1, no. 5, 1.
———. "Pentecostal Power in Indianapolis." *The Apostolic Faith*, February-March, 1907, vol. 1, no. 6, 3.
———. "Receiving the Holy Ghost." *The Apostolic Faith*, November 1906, vol. 1, no. 3, 2.
———. "A Revelation." *Meat in Due Season*, September 1915, vol. 1, no. 7, 3.
———. "Son Conducts Funeral." *Indianapolis Star*, September 20, 1909, 7.
———. "Standards of Justification." *The Good Report*, September 1913, 2.
———. "The Truth about E. N. Bell." *Herald of Truth*, August 1947, 3.
Cook, Ralph G. "Let's Get Acquainted." *Pentecostal Outlook*, October 1939. In *Historical News*, Summer 2003, 3.
Cordell, Richard. *Indianapolis Star*, August 23, 1911, 1.
Crawford, Mattie. "Spiritual Outpouring in Dayton, Ohio." *The Blessed Truth* (Columbus City, Iowa), vol. 6, no. 10, October 1, 1921, 2.
"Davis City Camp-Meeting Report." *Weekly Evangel*, August 28, 1915, 2.
Davis, T. C. "Let's Get Acquainted." *The Pentecostal Outlook*, December 1939.
———. "Revival at Oak Hill Tabernacle." *Apostolic Herald*, January 1927.
"Days Statistics: Births." *Indianapolis Star*, June 29, 1910, 12.

Denny, Frank. "From Hong Kong, China." *Meat in Due Season*, September 1915, vol. 1, no. 7, 1.

"Desire the Bluks to Go." *Indianapolis News*, June 17, 1907, 1.

Dutcher, Brother. "El Paso, Texas." *Meat in Due Season*, March 1917, vol. 2, no. 1, 1.

"Editorial." *The Blessed Truth*, October 1, 1919, vol. 4, no. 19, 2.

"Editorial." *Christian Outlook*, September 1931, 96.

"Editorial." *Meat in Due Season*, March 1917, vol. 2, no. 2, 2.

"Editorial Notes." *Meat in Due Season*, December 1915, vol. 1, no. 9, 3.

"El Paso, Texas, Mrs. Tinguly." *Meat in Due Season*, November 1918, vol. 2, no. 4, 1.

Ewart, Frank J. "Compromise." *The Good Report*, September 1913, 3.

———. "Defending Heresies." *The Good Report* (Ottawa, Canada), vol. 1, no. 3, 1912, 12.

———. "Great Revival in Hoxie, Ark." *Meat in Due Season*, vol. 1, no. 2, 1917. In *Historical News*, October-December 1994, vol. 14, no. 1, 1.

———. "Identification with Christ." *Meat in Due Season*, June 1916, vol. 1, no. 13, 4.

———. "The New Birth." *The Good Report*, September 1913, 2.

———. "The One Great Experience." *The Present Truth*, vol. 1, 1916, 2.

———. "The Work on the Coast." *The Good Report* (Ottawa, Canada), vol. 1, no. 3, 1912, 12.

"Eureka Springs, Arkansas." *Meat in Due Season*, November 1918, vol. 2, no. 4, 2.

"The Fire Is Still Falling" *The Voice in the Wilderness*, no. 24, October 1918, 4.

Fitzpatrick, Bracken, L. "From the Battlefield." *The Voice in the Wilderness*, no. 24, October 1918, 1.

Flower, J. Roswell. "A Closer and Deeper Fellowship." *The Christian Evangel*, July 19, 1913, vol. 1, no. 1, 1.

———. "God Honors Faith." *The Pentecost*, February 1, 1910, vol. 2, no. 3, 1.

"For Disturbing Service." *Indianapolis News*, March 4, 1908, 7.

"Fresh Blaze in Indianapolis." *Word and Witness*, February 20, 1913, 3.

"From Oregon City." *Meat in Due Season*, June 1916, vol. 1, no. 13.

"A Full Gospel Convention." *The Good Report*. September 1, 1913, vol. 2 (*sic*), no. 4, 4.

Gaxiola y Gaxiola, M. J. "Pentecost in Mexico." *The Pentecostal Herald*, February 1948, 3.

"General Bible Conference." *The Christian Outlook*, February 1924, 1.

"'Gliggy Bluk' Meeting Set." *Indianapolis Star*, November 4, 1911, 7.

"Gliggy Bluk Pleads Own Case and Pays 3 Fines." *Indianapolis Star*, March 5, 1908.

"Gliggy Bluk Preacher Fined for Contempt." *Indianapolis Morning Star*, March 5, 1908, 16.

"Gliggy Bluks Are Fined." *Indianapolis Star*, April 25, 1907.

"Gliggy Bluks Bathed at Fall Creek Waters." *Indianapolis News*, June 17, 1907, 7.

"Gliggy Bluks Meet." *Indianapolis Morning Star*, April 17, 1907, 1.

"Good Citizenship Must Be Encouraged." Illustration. *The Freeman*. February 7, 1903, 1.

"Good Tent Meetings in Los Angeles, Cal." *Meat in Due Season*, September 1917, vol. 1, no. 22, 1.

Goss, Howard A. "The Blessed Revival at Malvern, Arkansas." *The Bridegroom's Messenger*, December 15, 1909.

Goss, Howard A., and M. M. Pinson. "Important Notice about the General Assembly at Hot Springs." *Word and Witness*, April 2–12 1914, 2.

Gregory, Martin R. "A Baptist Preacher's Testimony." *Meat in Due Season*, February 1917, vol. 1, no. 16, 4.

Hammond, Elmer B. "Baptized in Honolulu." *The Apostolic Faith*, vol. 1, no. 7, April 1907, 3.

———. "Missionary Letters." *Good Report*, November 1913, vol. 1, no 6, 1.

Haywood, G. T. "The Alabaster Box." *The Voice in the Wilderness*, no. 18, October 1916, 1.

———. "Bend the Sapling." Illustration. *The Freeman*, October 9, 1909.

———. "Bosworth Campaign in Indianapolis." *The Christian Outlook*, January 1925.

———. "Can He Make It?" Illustration. *The Freeman*, January 2, 1904, vol. 17, no. 1.

———. "The Convention." *The Voice in the Wilderness*, no. 18, October 1916, 1.

———. "The Dangers of Denying the Father." *The Christian Outlook*, April 1932, 3.

———. "Death of W. J. Seymour." *The Voice in the Wilderness*, 1922, vol. 2, no. 13, 7.

———. "Division Coming." *Christian Outlook*, June 1924, 374.

———. "Editorial." *Christian Outlook*, September 1924, 441.

———. "Editorial—The Time Is at Hand." *Christian Outlook*, May 1924, 356.

———. "Editorial Page." *Christian Outlook*, January 1925, 4.

———. "The First Easter Morn." Illustration. *The Freeman*, April 10, 1909.

———. "Fools and Their Money Soon Part." Illustration. *The Freeman*, August 7, 1909.

———. "A Formidable Foe." Illustration. *The Freeman*, June 20, 1903, vol. 16, no. 24.

———. "God's House." *The Voice in the Wilderness*, September 1916, no. 18, 2.

———. "The Great Controversy." *Meat in Due Season*, June 1915, vol. 1, no. 6, 1.

———. "Home Life." Illustration. *The Freeman*, December 4, 1909.

———. "The Inevitable Consequences." Illustration. *The Freeman*, June 26, 1909.

———. "It Looks Like a Case of Dr. Jekyll and Mr. Hyde." Illustration. *The Freeman*, May 16, 1903, vol. 16, no. 19.

———. "Jesus Is Both." *The Voice in the Wilderness*, September 1916, no. 18, 1.

———. "The Land of Promise." Illustration. *The Freeman*, February 8, 1908, 1.

———. "Liberia—Shall It Be Like This?" Illustration. *The Freeman*, May 1, 1909.

———. "The Marriage and Divorce Question (Article No. 2)." *The Voice in the Wilderness*, October 1918, no. 23, 2.

———. "Men with Backbone." *Christian Outlook*, April 1928.

———. "A Modern Goliath." Illustration. *The Freeman*, November 2, 1907.

———. "The Name of Names." *The Voice in the Wilderness*, no. 19, December 1916, 1, 2.

———. "The Negro Looks Quite as Well as Any in That Bunch." Illustration. *The Freeman*, January 23, 1904, vol. 17, no. 3.

———. "The Negro Path to Success." Illustration. *The Freeman*, February 29, 1908, 1.

———. "New Organizations." *Christian Outlook*, October 1924, 466.

———. "One Convention." *Christian Outlook*, August 1924, 418.

———. "The One True God." *Christian Outlook*, April 1932, 3.

———. "The One True God." *Meat in Due Season*, December 1915, vol. 1, no. 9, 2, 3.

———. "The One True God." *The Present Truth*, vol. 1, 1916, 3.

———. "An Open Letter." *Christian Outlook*, October 1923, 208.

———. "Revelation of the Ages" Ad. *Christian Outlook*, April 1923, 16.

———. "The Review of Some Articles." *The Voice in the Wilderness*, September 1916, no. 18, 2–3.

———. "Rose of Sharon." *The Voice in the Wilderness*, September 1916, no. 18, 1.

———. "The Sixth Annual Convention of the Pentecostal Assemblies of the World at Indianapolis, Ind." *The Blessed Truth*, October 1, 1921, vol. 6, no. 10, 1.

———. "The St. Louis Council at St. Louis, MO." *The Voice in the Wilderness*, no. 19, December 1916, 1.

———. "That Alabaster Box." *The Voice in the Wilderness*, September 1916, no. 18, 1.

———. "To Our Brethren of Color." *Christian Outlook*, January 1926, 3.

———. "To the Graduate." Illustration. *The Freeman*, June 19, 1909.

———. "Trinitarianism." *The Voice in the Wilderness*, September 1916, no. 18, 2.

———. "United Methodism: North and South." *Christian Outlook*, November 1924, 481.

———. "Unity." *Christian Outlook*, July 1925, 124.

———. "Unity and Strength." *Christian Outlook*, December 1923, 196.

———. "Unity Conference." *Christian Outlook*, December 1923, 235.

———. "Water Baptism." *The Messenger*, no. 2 (1915) 2.

———. "Wedding Garment." *The Voice in the Wilderness*, September 1916, no. 18, 1, 4.

———. "What Credit Is It for an Elephant to Crush an Infant." Illustration. *The Freeman*, January 9, 1904, vol. 17, no. 1.

———. "What Have I Done." Illustration. *The Freeman*, September 11, 1909.

———. "The Word of God." *The Good Report*, November 1, 1913, vol. 1, no. 6, 3.

———. "The Word of God." *The Voice in the Wilderness*, September 1916, no. 18, 2.

"Haywood Funeral." *Christian Outlook*, May 1931, 52–54.

Hezmalhalch, Tom. "In Indianapolis, Ind." *The Apostolic Faith*, vol. 1, no. 7, April 1907, 1.

"Hit Brother Cook." *Indianapolis Star*, June 17, 1907, 3, 7.

"The Hour and the Man." Illustration. *The Freeman*. February 14, 1903, 1.

Hult, Alma. "Pentecost in China." *Meat in Due Season*, vol. 1, no. 22, 1, 4.

"Important Notice." *Meat in Due Season*, February 1919, vol. 2, no. 8, 1.

"Indiana Missionary Convention." *The Apostolic Faith*, January 1908, vol. 1, no. 12, 1, 2.

"Indianapolis, Ind." *The Apostolic Faith*, June 1908, vol. 2, no. 14, 1.

"Interesting News & Info." *The Witness of God*, vol. 2, 13th ed., January 1921, 7.

"Invade the Bluks' Temple." *Indianapolis Star*, April 25, 1908, 1.

"James A. Frush." *Historical News*, Summer 2003, 2.

"Judge Discharges Man Who Laughed in Church." *Indianapolis Star*, January 5, 1915, 11.

Kidson, W. E. *The Apostolic Herald*, July 30, 5.

"Latter Rain Falling in Kelso." *Meat in Due Season*, September 1917, vol. 1, no. 22.

Lawrence, B. F. "Meat in Due Season Corrected." *The Weekly Evangel*, August 11, 1917, 9.

"Leaders at Convention Here." *New York Amsterdam News*, August 27, 1930, 7.

"Letter from E. N. Bell to J. C. Brickey." August 20, 1920, 1–4.

Loden, W. R. "Divisions, What For?" *The Pentecostal Messenger* (Kinder, LA), October 1, 1919, 3.

"Los Angeles Camp Meeting." *The Good Report*, June 1, 1913, 1.

McAlister, R. E. "The Finished Work of Calvary." Supplement to *The Good Report*, n.d., 4pp.

———. "A Good Report." *The Good Report*, May 1911, no. 1, 1.

———. "Sanctification Is Not a Second Work of Grace." *The Good Report* (Ottawa, Canada), vol. 1, no. 3, 1912, 2.

"Mayor Will Protect 'Gliggy Bluks.'" *Indianapolis News*, June 19, 1907, 1.
"Memphis, Tenn." *The Voice in the Wilderness*, no. 19, November 1916, 1.
"Mid-Summer Pentecostal Convention." *The Christian Evangel*, July 19, 1913, 8.
"Minutes" (PAW/GAAA Merger). *Meat in Due Season*, February 1918, 3.
"Minutes of the Sixth Annual Conference." *The Pentecostal Outlook*, November 1937, 21, 3.
"Missionary Offering at Los Angeles." *The Good Report*, August 1, 1913, 1.
"Missionary Report." *The Voice in the Wilderness*, October 1916, no. 18, 2.
"Missionary Report." *The Voice in the Wilderness*, December 1916, no. 19, 3.
Morse, Harry. "Our Trip Down the Coast." *Meat in Due Season*, June 1915, vol. 1, no. 6, 2.
———. "A Woman's Place in the Body." *The Good Report*, June 1, 1913, vol. 2, no. 1, 2.
"Negro Bluk Beats Demon from Girl." *Indianapolis Sunday Star*, May 5, 1907, 1.
"Negro Bluk Kissed." *Indianapolis Star*, June 3, 1907, 3.
"Negro Bluk 'Blows.'" *Indianapolis Morning Star*, June 5, 1907, 20.
"Negro Preacher on Trial in Police Court." *Los Angeles Express*, June 12, 1906.
"New Orleans, Louisiana." *The Apostolic Faith*, September 1907, vol. 1, no. 10, 2.
"New Pentecostal Organization." *The Weekly Evangel*, January 20, 1917, 15.
"News." *The Witness of God*, vol. 2, 19th ed., July 1921, 9.
"Norwegian's Sister's Testimony." *The Voice in the Wilderness*, October 1916, no. 18, 1.
"Oddy Asks Divorce Because of Bluks." *Indianapolis Morning Star*, June 6, 1907, 3.
"The Old-Time Pentecost." *The Apostolic Faith*, vol. 1, no. 1, September 1906, 1.
Opperman, D. C. O. "Brother Bell Is on Both Sides of Fence." *The Blessed Truth*, October 1, 1919, vol. 4, no. 18.
"Our Missionaries." *The Blessed Truth*, vol. 4, no. 22, December 1919, 3.
"Our Publications." *The Good Report*, 1912, vol. 1, no. 3, 16.
"The Outpouring of the Spirit in Los Angeles." *Pentecostal Testimony* 2/3 (1912) 15.
Parent, Leonard. "Let's Get Acquainted." *Pentecostal Outlook*, October-November 1940, 3, 16.
"Pastor Frank Small Baptized." *Meat in Due Season*, December 1915, vol. 1, no. 9, 4.
Patterson, John. "The Essentiality of Water Baptism." *The Witness of God*, vol. 2, 22nd ed., October 1921, 4–6.
"Pentecost Among the Young People." *The Apostolic Faith*, December 1906, vol. 1, no. 4, 1.
"Pentecost in San Jose and Portland." *The Apostolic Faith*, May 1907, vol. 1, no. 8, 4.
"Pentecost in Indianapolis." *The Apostolic Faith*, July-August, 1908, vol. 2, no. 5, 4.
"Pentecostal Convention." *The Good Report*, November 1, 1913, vol. 1, no. 6, 2.
"A Pentecostal Convention in Los Angeles." *Weekly Evangel*, September 18, 1915, 4.
"The Pentecostal Movement and Conscription Law." *The Weekly Evangel*, August 4, 1917, 6.
*The Pentecostal Witness*. October 1, 1926, vol. 2, no. 12, 1.
"Police Visit Bluks." *Indianapolis Morning Star*, May 13, 1907, 12.
"Police Are Spectators at Bluks' Meeting." *Indianapolis News*, June 11, 1907, 4.
"Police Have No Power to Stop Bluks' Meetings." *Indianapolis News*, June 20, 1907, 8.
Pool, Carrie M. "An Open Letter." *Meat in Due Season*, June 1915, vol. 1, no. 6, 3.
"Portland, Oregon Mission, Cor. Front and Burnside." *The Good Report*, May 1911, no. 1, 8.
"Portland Camp Meeting." *The Good Report*, August 1, 1913, 2.

Reed, H. E. "Bible School in Hot Springs." *The Blessed Truth*, October 1, 1921, vol. 5, no. 10, 2.

———. "The Birth of Water and Spirit." *The Blessed Truth*, August 15, 1918, vol. 3, no. 1, 1, 2.

"A Remarkable Prophecy." *Meat in Due Season*, June 1915, vol. 1, no. 6, 4.

Roberts, L. V. "Bro. E. N. Bell Is Baptized." *Meat in Due Season*, September 1915, vol. 1, no. 7, 4.

———. "More Blessed Revival Fires: Fresh Blaze in Indianapolis." *Word & Witness*, February 20, 1913, 3.

———. "Pentecostal Campaign at Indianapolis, Ind." *Meat in Due Season*, September 1915, vol. 1, no. 7, 4.

———. "The Present Truth." *The Present Truth*, 1916, vol. 1, 1.

———. "A Statement." *The Pentecostal Evangel*, February 19, 1921, 23.

———. "They Saw Giants Over There." *The Present Truth*, vol. 1, 1916, 4.

Rodgers, Joseph. "Bro. Jos. Rodger's Mission, Indianapolis." *The Voice in the Wilderness*, November 1916, no. 19, 2.

Rosa, Adolph. "In San Francisco." *The Apostolic Faith*, February-March, 1907, vol. 1, no. 6, 3.

"The Same Old Way." *The Apostolic Faith*, September 1906, vol. 1, no. 1, 3.

"San Antonio, Tex." *Meat in Due Season*, September 1917, vol. 1, no. 22, 1.

Schaepe, John G. "The One Name." *The Present Truth*, 1916, vol. 1, 6.

"Second General Convention." *The Blessed Truth*, August 15, 1918, vol. 3, no. 11, 4.

"Seek New Religious Speech." *Indianapolis Morning Star*, February 1, 1907, 5–6.

Sherman, H. J. "Report from El Paso, Texas." *Meat in Due Season*, February 1917, vol. 1, no. 16, 1.

Smock, Celia. "Reminiscences of God's Faithfulness." *The Pentecost*, July 1909, vol. 1, no. 8, 4.

"St. Paul-Minneapolis." *Meat in Due Season*, September 1917, vol. 1, no. 7, 4.

Stanley, Gabriel. "Honor Fitting Nation's Head Accorded Haywood at Burial." *The Recorder*, vol. 34, no. 29, April 25, 1931, 1.

———. "Pentecostal Assemblies' Bishop Goes to Final Resting Place." *The Recorder*, April 18, 1931, 1, 8.

Studd, George B. "The One Baptism." *Meat in Due Season*, March 1917, 1.

"Stutterer Speaks at 'Glug' Service." *Indianapolis Morning Star*, April 18, 1907, 15.

"To the Jew First." *Meat in Due Season*, March 1917, vol. 2, no. 1, 1.

"Tongues at Allen Chapel." *Indianapolis News*, April 24, 1908, 7.

"Trance Followed Sermon by Cook." *Indianapolis Star*, April 24, 1907, 3.

"Twenty-Five Receive Holy Spirit in Indianapolis." *The Weekly Evangel*, January 20, 1917, 15.

"Uncle Sam." Illustration. *The Freeman*, January 29, 1903, 1.

"Unusual Noise." *The Apostolic Faith*, November 1906, vol. 1, no. 3, 1.

Urshan, Andrew D. "Indianapolis Visit." *Witness of God*, January 1925, 61st ed., vol. 7, 8.

———. "Questions and Answers about the Merger." *Pentecostal Outlook*, April 1932, 7.

———. *The Witness of God*. January 1933, 2.

———. *The Witness of God*. November 1924, 59th ed., vol. 6, 8.

*The Voice in the Wilderness*. G. T. Haywood, ed. Vol. 2, no. 9, 1921, 36. In Morris E. Golder, *History of the Pentecostal Assemblies of the World*, 36. Indianapolis: by the author, 1973.

Westfield, Winifred. "What Is Truth?" *The Present Truth*, vol. 1, 1916, 1–2.

"Whites and Blacks Mix in a Religious Frenzy." *Los Angeles Daily Times*, September 3, 1906, 11.

Whittington, W. H. *Pentecostal Witness*, January 1932, 2.

Williams, Mary. "In Memory of Bro. Opperman." *The Pentecostal Witness*, November 2, 1926, vol. 3, no. 1, 2.

"The Winnipeg Convention." *The Good Report*, June 1, 1914, 2.

"Young Mob Assails Bluks' Temple." *Indianapolis Star*, June 17, 1907, 3, 7.

## SECONDARY SOURCES

Alexander, Estrelda. *The Women of Azusa Street*. Cleveland: Pilgrim, 2005.

Alexander, Paul. *Peace to War: Shifting Allegiances in the Assemblies of God*. Telford, PA: Cascadia, 2009.

Allman-Baldwin, Lysa. "Black History, Food and Wine in Eureka Springs." *The Examiner*, part 4. June 12, 2009. http://www.examiner.com/cultural-travel-in-kansas-city/black-history-food-and-wine-eureka-springs.

Anderson, Allan H. "The Dubious Legacy of Charles Parham: Racism and Cultural Insensitivities Among Pentecostals." *Pneuma* 27/1 (Spring 2007) 51–64.

———. *An Introduction to Pentecostalism*. Cambridge: Cambridge University Press, 2004.

———. *Spreading Fires: The Missionary Nature of Early Pentecostalism*. Maryknoll, NY: Orbis, 2007.

———. "To All Points of the Compass: The Azusa Street Revival and Global Pentecostalism." *Enrichment* 11/2 (Spring 2006) 164–72.

Anderson, Robert Mapes. *The Vision of the Disinherited: The Making of American Pentecostalism*. New York: Oxford University Press, 1979.

Armstrong, Zella. *Notable Southern Families*. Vol. 2. Baltimore: Genealogical, 1997.

Arnold, Marvin M. *Pentecost Before Azusa*. Cincinnati: Bethesda Ministries, 2002.

Ashe, Samuel A'Court. *History of North Carolina*. Spartanburg, SC: Reprint Company, 1971.

Ayers, Edward. *The Promise of the New South: Life After Reconstruction*. New York: Oxford University Press, 1992.

Baer, Hans A., and Merrill Singer. *African American Religion in the Twentieth Century: Varieties of Protest and Accommodation*. Knoxville: University of Tennessee Press, 1992.

Ball, Matthew. "West Side Story: The Heritage of One Indianapolis Congregation." *Indiana Apostolic Trumpet*, April 10, 2009.

Baron, Harold M. "The Demand for Black Labor." In *Racial Conflict, Discrimination and Power*, edited by William Barclay, Krishna Kumar, and Ruth P. Simms, 105. New York: AMS, 1976.

Barrett, David B., and Todd M. Johnson. "Annual Statistical Table on Global Mission." *International Bulletin of Missionary Research* 27/1 (January 2003) 24–25.

Barrett, David B., Todd M. Johnson, and Peter F. Crossing. "Christianity 2010: A View from the New Atlas of Global Christianity." *International Bulletin of Missionary Research* 34/1 (January 2010) 29–36.

———. "Missiometrics 2006: Goals, Resources, Doctrines of the 350 Christian World Communities." *International Bulletin of Missionary Research* 30/1 (January 2006) 27–30.

Barrett, David B., George T. Kurian, and Todd M. Johnson, eds. *World Christian Encyclopedia*. Vol. 1. 2nd ed. Oxford: Oxford University Press, 2001.

Bassett, John Spencer. *Slavery and Servitude in the Colony of North Carolina*. Johns Hopkins University Studies in Historical and Political Science. Baltimore: Johns Hopkins University Press, 1896.

———. *Slavery in the State of North Carolina*. Johns Hopkins University Studies in Historical and Political Science. Baltimore: Johns Hopkins University Press, 1899.

Bays, Daniel. "The Protestant Missionary Establishment and the Pentecostal Movement." In *Pentecostal Currents in American Pentecostalism*, edited by Edith L. Blumhofer, Russell P. Spittler, and Grant A. Wacker, 52–54. Chicago: University of Illinois Press, 1999.

Beall, Juanita Holmes. *Mission Accomplished: The Story of Bishop A. O. Holmes*. North Little Rock, AR: N.p., 1986.

Bedell, Kenneth B., ed. *Yearbook of American and Canadian Churches, 1993*. Nashville: Abingdon, 1993.

Beisner, E. Calvin. *"Jesus Only" Churches*. Grand Rapids: Zondervan, 1998.

Bentley, Judith. *Ship Ahoy: The Life and Times of Stanley and Catherine Chambers*. Bridgeton, MO: Bentley Educational Ministries, 2001.

Bernard, David K. "The Future of Oneness Pentecostalism." In *The Future of Pentecostalism in the United States*, edited by Eric Patterson and Edmund Rybarczyk, 143. Lanham, MD: Lexington, 2007.

———. *A History of the Christian Church: A.D. 1900–2000*. Vol. 3. Hazelwood, MO: Word Aflame, 1999.

———. *The Oneness of God*. Hazelwood, MO: Word Aflame, 1983.

Bieze, Michael. *Booker T. Washington and the Art of Self-Representation*. New York: Peter Lang, 2008.

Bigham, Darrel E. "The Black Press in Indiana, 1879–1985." In *The Black Press in the Middle West, 1865–1985*, edited by Henry Lewis Suggs, 55. Westport, CT: Greenwood, 1996.

Blum, Edward J. *Reforging the White Republic: Race, Religion, and American Nationalism, 1865–1898*. Baton Rouge: Louisiana State University Press, 2005.

Blumhofer, Edith L. *Aimee Semple McPherson: Everybody's Sister*. Grand Rapids: Eerdmans, 1993.

———. *The Assemblies of God: A Chapter in the Story of American Pentecostalism*. 2 vols. Springfield, MO: Gospel, 1989.

———. "D. C. O. Opperman." *The New International Dictionary of Pentecostal and Charismatic Movements*, edited by Stanley M. Burgess and Eduard M. Van Der Maas, 946–47. Grand Rapids: Zondervan, 2002.

———. "Pentecostal Assemblies of the World." In *Dictionary of Christianity in America*, edited by Daniel G. Reid et al., 884. Downers Grove, IL: InterVarsity, 1990.

———. *Restoring the Faith: the Assemblies of God, Pentecostalism and American Culture*. Chicago: University of Illinois Press, 1993.

———. "Thomas F. Zimmerman: A Look at the Indiana Roots." *Assemblies of God Heritage* 10/4 (Winter 1990–1991) 5.

———. "Thomas F. Zimmerman: The Making of a Minister." *Assemblies of God Heritage* 10/4 (Winter 1990–1991) 4.

Blumhofer, Edith L., Russell P. Spittler, and Grant A. Wacker, eds. *Pentecostal Currents in American Pentecostalism*. Chicago: University of Illinois Press, 1999.

Bodenhamer, David J., and Robert G. Barrows, eds. *Encyclopedia of Indianapolis*. Indianapolis: Indiana University Press, 1994.

Booker, Larry. "Azusa Street: The Jesus' Name Factor." *Pentecostal Herald*, August 2006, 24–25.

———. "Jesus' Name Baptism and the Azusa Revival." *Pentecostal Herald*, December 2006, 30–33.

Boora, Kulwant Singh. *Apostolic and Post Apostolic Baptism*. 2 vols. Bloomington, IN: Xlibris, 2010.

———. *Oneness and Monotheism*. Bloomington, IN: AuthorHouse, 2009.

———. *The Oneness of God and the Doctrine of the Trinity*. Bloomington, IN: AuthorHouse, 2009.

Borlase, Craig. *William Seymour: A Biography*. Lake Mary, FL: Charisma, 2006.

Bowen, Kurt. *Evangelism and Apostasy: The Evolution and Impact of Evangelism in Modern Mexico*. Buffalo, NY: McGill-Queen's University Press, 1996.

Boyd, Gregory A. *Oneness Pentecostals and the Trinity*. Grand Rapids: Baker, 1992.

Boyd, William K. *The Federal Period, 1783–1860*. History of North Carolina 2. Chicago: Lewis, 1973.

Boyer, Isabel. "Pastor, Mate on Duty for Duration." *The Indianapolis Star*, April 3, 1982, 2.

Brady, Carolyn M. "Indianapolis at the Time of the Great Migration, 1900–1920." In *Black News and Notes* 65/1 (August 1996) n.p. http://www.carolynbrady.com/indymigration.html.

Brickey, Mary. "Henry Green Rodgers." *Historical News*, July-September 2000, 3.

Brown, Neil. *Laity Mobilized: Reflections on Church Growth in Japan and Other Lands*. Grand Rapids: Eerdmans, 1971.

Brown, Roderick R. "Oneness Pentecostalism and Ethnicity: A Decision Out of Step." MA thesis, University of South Dakota, 2005.

———. "Oneness Pentecostalism and Race: A Decision Out of Step." Urshan Graduate School of Theology Symposium, 2005.

Brumback, Carl. *God in Three Persons: A Trinitarian Answer to the Oneness of "Jesus Only" Doctrine Concerning the Godhead and Water Baptism*. Cleveland, TN: Pathway, 1959.

———. *Like A River: Early Years of the Assemblies of God*. Springfield, MO: Gospel, 1977.

———. *Suddenly from Heaven*. Springfield, MO: Gospel, 1961.

Bundy, David D. "Alexander Alfred Boddy." In *The New International Dictionary of Pentecostal and Charismatic Movements*, edited by Stanley M. Burgess and Eduard M. Van Der Maas, 437. Grand Rapids: Zondervan, 2002.

———. "Documenting 'Oneness Pentecostalism': A Case Study in the Ethical Dilemmas Posed by the Creation of Documentation." *Summary of Proceedings, Fifty-Third Annual Conference of the American Theological Library Association*, Margaret Tacke Collins, ed., June 9–12, 1999.

———. “G. T. Haywood: Religion for Urban Realities.” In *Portraits of a Generation: Early Pentecostal Leaders*, edited by James R. Goff Jr. and Grant Wacker, 239. Fayetteville, AR: University of Arkansas Press, 2002.

———. “Pentecostal Churches.” In *The Encyclopedia of Indianapolis*, edited by David J. Bodenhamer and Robert G. Barrows, 1085–88. Indianapolis: Indiana University Press, 1996.

———. “Spiritual Advice to a Quaker: Letters to T. B. Barratt from Azusa Street, 1906.” *Pneuma* 14/2 (Fall 1992) 163–66.

———. “Thomas Ball Barratt.” In *The New International Dictionary of Pentecostal and Charismatic Movements*, edited by Stanley M. Burgess and Eduard M. Van Der Maas, 436. Grand Rapids: Zondervan, 2002.

Burgess, Stanley M., and Gary B. McGee, eds. *Dictionary of Pentecostal and Charismatic Movements*. Grand Rapids: Zondervan, 1988.

Burgess, Stanley M., and Eduard M. Van Der Maas, eds. *The New International Dictionary of Pentecostal and Charismatic Movements*. Grand Rapids: Zondervan, 2002.

Butler, Anthea D. “Pentecostal Traditions We Should Pass On: The Good, the Bad, and the Ugly.” *Pneuma* 27/2 (2005) 344.

———. *Women in the Church of God in Christ: Making a Sanctified World*. Chapel Hill: University of North Carolina Press, 2007.

Butler, Daniel L. *Oneness Pentecostalism: A History of the Jesus' Name Movement*. Los Angeles: n.p., 2005.

Cain, Barbara T., Ellen Z. McGrew, and Charles E. Morris, eds. *Guide to Private Manuscript Collections in the North Carolina State Archives*. 3rd ed. Raleigh: Division of Archives and History, 1994.

Carlisle, George. “The World's Saturday Night.” *Historical News* 19/2 (January–March 2000) 4, 3.

Carter, J. Kameron. *Race: A Theological Account*. Oxford: Oxford University Press, 2008.

Castleberry, Joseph L. “Pentecostal History from Below.” *Pneuma* 28/2 (Fall 2006) 271–74.

Cebula, Judith. “Celebration Will Attempt to Recapture Racial Harmony.” *The Indianapolis Star*, May 25, 1996, A17.

Cecelski, David S. *The Waterman's Song: Slavery and Freedom in Maritime North Carolina*. Chapel Hill: University of North Carolina Press, 2001.

Cerillo, Augustus, Jr. “The Beginnings of American Pentecostalism: A Historical Overview.” In *Pentecostal Currents in American Protestantism*, edited by Edith L. Blumhofer, Grant A. Wacker, and Russell P. Spittler, 244. Champaign: University of Illinois, 1999.

———. “Frank Bartleman: Pentecostal ‘Lone Ranger’ and Social Critic.” In *Portrait of a Generation: Early Pentecostal Leaders*, edited James R. Goff Jr. and Grant Wacker, 107, 113–14. Fayetteville: University of Arkansas Press, 2002.

Chalfant, William B. *Ancient Champions of Oneness*. Rev. ed. Hazelwood, MO: Word Aflame, 2001.

Charles, Deborah. “Obama Speaks on Fatherhood at Church.” *USA Today*, June 15, 2008.

Clanton, Arthur L. *United We Stand*. Hazelwood, MO: Pentecostal, 1970; revised, Arthur L. Clanton and Charles E. Clanton. *United We Stand: Jubilee Edition*. Hazelwood, MO: Word Aflame, 1995.

Clemmons, Ithiel C. *Bishop C. H. Mason and the Roots of the Church of God in Christ.* Lanham, MD: Pneuma Life, 1996.

Coffin, Levi, and William Still. *Fleeing for Freedom: Stories of the Underground Railroad.* Chicago: Ivan R. Dee, 2004.

Cole, Helen A. *You Too Can Make It.* Russellville, AR: World's Unlimited for Christ, 1994.

Conn, Charles W. *Where the Saints Have Trod.* Cleveland, TN: Pathway, 1959.

Cook, Philip L. *Zion, Illinois: Twentieth-Century Utopia.* Syracuse: Syracuse University Press, 1996.

Cooley, Frank L. *The Growing Seed: The Christian Church in Indonesia.* Jakarta: Christian Publishing House, 1981.

*COOLJC International General Annual Convocation Minute Book and Ministerial Record of the Seventy-Ninth Session (1998–1999).* New York: COOLJC, 1999.

Cox, Harvey. *Fire from Heaven: The Rise of Pentecostal Spirituality and the Reshaping of Religion in the Twenty-First Century.* New York: Addison-Wesley, 1995.

Crosby, Alfred W. *America's Forgotten Pandemic.* New York: Cambridge University Press, 2003.

Crouch, Stanley, and Playthell Benjamin. *Reconsidering the Souls of Black Folk* Philadelphia: Running Press, 2002.

Crownover, Raymond. "Not Vain the Weakest: A History of the Apostolic Church of Jesus Christ." Paper presented at Gateway College of Evangelism, St. Louis, 1978.

Dalcour, Edward L. *A Definitive Look at Oneness Theology: Defending the Tri-Unity of God.* Lanham, MD: University Press of America, 2005.

Danielou, Jean. *The Development of Christian Doctrine Before the Council of Nicea.* Edited and translated by John Baker. Theology of Jewish Christianity 1. London: Darton, Longman & Todd, 1964.

Daniels, David D. "God Makes No Differences in Nationality: The Fashioning of a New Racial/Nonracial Identity at the Azusa Street Revival." In *Enrichment* 11/2 (Spring 2006) 72.

Dayton, Donald W. *Theological Roots of Pentecostalism.* Grand Rapids: Zondervan, 1987.

Dean, Lloyd. *Kentucky Pentecostal Heritage.* 2 vols. Morehead, KY: N.p., 1998–2000.

DeBarros, Anthony, Cheryl Phillips, and Paul Overberg. "Census 2000: Indiana." *USA Today.* http://www.usatoday.com/graphics/census2000/indiana/state.htm.

Dillon, Jewel Yadon. "Harry Morse." In *Profiles of Pentecostal Preachers,* edited by Mary H. Wallace, 2:284. Hazelwood, MO: Word Aflame, 1984.

*Directory: United Pentecostal Church International (Incorporated).* Hazelwood, MO: 2010.

Doggette, Ruth. *One Man's Journey Through Life With God.* By the author, n.d.

Douglass, Frederick. "Oration of Frederick Douglass." *American Missionary* 39/6 (June 1885) 165.

DuBois, W. E. B. "Let Us Reason Together." *The Crisis* 18 (September 1919) 231.

———. *The Souls of Black Folk.* Chicago: A. C. McClurg, 1903; reprint, Herbert Aptheker, 1973.

Dugas, Paul D. *The Life and Writings of Elder G. T. Haywood.* Portland, OR: Apostolic, 1968.

DuPree, Sherry Sherrod, and Herbert C. DuPree. "The Explosive Growth of the African American Pentecostal Church." In *Yearbook of American and Canadian Churches, 1993*, edited by Kenneth B. Bedell, 7–10. Nashville: Abingdon, 1993.

Eaton, Clement. *A History of the Old South: The Emergence of a Reluctant Nation*. 3rd ed. New York: Macmillan, 1975.

Erickson, Millard J. *God in Three Persons: A Contemporary Interpretation of the Trinity*. Grand Rapids: Baker, 1995.

———. *The Word Became Flesh: A Contemporary Incarnational Christology*. Grand Rapids: Baker, 1991.

"Ernest Haywood Collection of Haywood Family Papers, 1752–1967." Southern Historical Collection, Wilson Library, University of North Carolina. http://www.lib.unc.edu/mss/inv/h/Haywood,Ernest.html.

Espinosa, G. "Apostolic Assembly of the Faith in Jesus Christ." In *The New International Dictionary of Pentecostal and Charismatic Movements*, edited by Stanley M. Burgess and Eduard M. Van Der Maas, 321. Grand Rapids: Zondervan, 2002.

Faupel, D. William. *The Everlasting Gospel*. Sheffield, UK: Sheffield Academic Press, 1996.

———. "The Restoration Vision in Pentecostalism." *Christian Century* 107/29 (October 17, 1990) 938–41. http://www.religion-online.org/showarticle.asp?title=818.

Fee, Gordon. *Gospel and Spirit: Issues in New Testament Hermeneutics*. Peabody, MA: Hendrickson, 1991.

"The First Occasional Symposium on Aspects of the Oneness Pentecostal Movement." Harvard Divinity School, Cambridge, MA, July 5–7, 1985.

Fogelson, Robert. *The Fragmented Metropolis*. Cambridge, MA: Harvard University Press, 1967.

Ford, Lynn. "Integrated City Church Had Stormy History." *Indiana Black History News*, February 1990, 4. http://www2.indystar.com/library/factfiles/history/black_history/.

Foster, Fred J. *Think It Not Strange*. St. Louis, MO: Pentecostal, 1965; revised, *Their Story: 20th Century Pentecostals*. Hazelwood, MO: Word Aflame, 1981.

Franklin, John Hope. *An Illustrated History of Black Americans*. New York: Time-Life, 1970.

French, Talmadge L. "'In Jesus Name': A Key Resource on the Worldwide Pentecostal Phenomenon and the Oneness, Apostolic or Jesus' Name Movement." *Pneuma* 31/2 (2009) 267–73.

———. "Oneness Pentecostalism in Global Perspective: The History, Theology and Expansion of the Oneness Movement." MA thesis, Wheaton College Graduate School, 1998.

———. *Our God Is One: The Story of the Oneness Pentecostals*. Indianapolis: Voice and Vision, 1999.

Fudge, Thomas A. *Christianity Without the Cross: A History of Salvation in Oneness Pentecostalism*. Parkland, FL: Universal, 2003.

Garrett, Gary W. *The Chronicles of Pentecostalism and the Apostolic Movement*. Springfield, MO: Apostolic Christian, 2003.

———. *A Man Ahead of His Times: The Life and Times of Bishop Garfield Thomas Haywood*. Springfield, MO: Apostolic Christian, 2002.

Gathercole, Simon J. *The Pre-Existent Son: Recovering the Christologies of Matthew, Mark, and Luke*. Grand Rapids: Eerdmans, 2006.

Gaus, Laura Sheerin. *Shortridge High School 1864–1981 in Retrospect.* Indianapolis: Indiana Historical Society, 1985.

Gaxiola, Manuel J. "The Serpent and the Dove: A History of the Apostolic Church of the Faith in Christ Jesus in Mexico, 1914–1974." MA thesis, Fuller Theological Seminary, 1978.

Gerlach, Luther P., and Virginia H. Hine. "Five Factors Crucial to the Growth and Speed of a Modern Religious Movement." *Journal for the Scientific Study of Religion* 7 (1968) 23–40.

———. *People, Power, Change: Movements of Social Transformation.* Indianapolis: Bobbs-Merrill, 1970.

Gerloff, Roswith I. H. "Blackness and Oneness (Apostolic) Theology: Cross Cultural Aspects of a Movement." First Occasional Symposium on Aspects of the Oneness Pentecostal Movement, Harvard Divinity School, Cambridge, MA, 3–5 July 1984.

———. "Hope of Redemption: The Religious, Cultural and Socio-Political Significance of Oneness (Apostolic) Pentecostalism in Jamaica." In *Experiences in the Spirit: Conference on Pentecostal and Charismatic Research in Europe at Utrecht University, 1989*, edited by Jan A. B. Jongeneel, 162–63. New York: Peter Lang, 1990.

———. "A Plea for British Black Theologies." PhD thesis, University of Birmingham, 1989.

———. *A Plea for Black British Theologies: The Black Church Movement in Britain in Its Transatlantic Cultural and Theological Interaction.* 2 vols. New York: Peter Lang, 1992.

———. "Theology En Route of Migration: The Inner Dynamics of the Pentecostal Oneness (Apostolic) Movement from North America to the Caribbean to Britain and Beyond." Society for Pentecostal Studies, Fresno, California, November 1989.

Gill, Kenneth D. "Book Review, Thomas A. Fudge, *Christianity Without a Cross*." *Pneuma* 26/1 (Spring 2009) 149–50.

———. *Toward a Contextualized Theology for the Third World: The Emergence and Development of Jesus' Name Pentecostalism in Mexico.* New York: Peter Lang, 1994.

Gillis, Sharon Rose Berry. *History of the First United Pentecostal Church of DeQuincy (1915–1983).* DeQuincy, LA: FUPC, 1983.

Goff, James R., Jr. "Charles Parham and the Problem of History in the Pentecostal Movement." In *All Together In One Place: Theological Papers from the Brighton Conference on World Evangelism*, edited by Harold D. Hunter and Peter D. Hocken, 186–91. Sheffield, UK: Sheffield Academic Press, 1993.

———. *Fields White unto Harvest: Charles F. Parham and the Missionary Origins of Pentecostalism.* Fayetteville: University of Arkansas Press, 1988.

———. "Parham, Charles Fox (1873–1920)." In *The New International Dictionary of Pentecostal and Charismatic Movements*, edited by Stanley M. Burgess and Eduard M. Van Der Maas, 955. Grand Rapids: Zondervan, 2002.

Goff, James R., Jr., and Grant Wacker, eds. *Portrait of a Generation: Early Pentecostal Leaders.* Fayetteville: University of Arkansas Press, 2002.

Gohr, Glenn W. "D. C. O. Opperman and Early Ministerial Training." *AG Heritage* 10/4 (Winter 1990–91) 5–8, 21.

———. "Franklin Small." In *The New International Dictionary of Pentecostal and Charismatic Movements*, edited by Stanley M. Burgess and Eduard M. Van Der Maas, 1075. Grand Rapids: Zondervan, 2002.

Golder, Morris E. *History of the Pentecostal Assemblies of the World.* Indianapolis: N.p., 1973.

———. *The Life and Works of Bishop Garfield Thomas Haywood.* Indianapolis: N.p., 1977.

Grenz, Stanley J. *The Named God and the Question of Being: A Trinitarian Theo-Ontology.* Louisville: Westminster John Knox, 2005.

*Guide to Research Materials in the North Carolina State Archives: County Records.* 11th ed. Raleigh: Division of Archives and History, 1997.

Gurley, Ken. "Howard Goss and the Revival in Alvin." *Vision: South Texas UPCI* (November–December 2005) 9–10.

Hall, J. L. "Contending for the Faith." Part 3. *Pentecostal Herald*, May 1997, 13–17.

———. "Early Pentecostals in Russia." Part 2. *Pentecostal Herald*, December 1991, 3–5.

———. "Early Pentecostalism in St. Louis, Missouri." Part 1, *Pentecostal Herald*, October 1994, 10.

———. "Oliver F. Fauss." In *Dictionary of Pentecostal and Charismatic Movements*, edited by Stanley M. Burgess and Gary B. McGee, 304–5. Grand Rapids: Zondervan, 1988.

———. "Oneness Pentecostal Origins in the Soviet Union." Part 1. *Pentecostal Herald*, November 1991, 4–5, 22–23.

———. "The 'New Issue'—Oneness Pentecostalism." *The Pentecostal Herald*, February 1995, 14–15.

———. "The Restoration Impulse: The Shaping of Oneness Pentecostalism." Symposium on Oneness Pentecostalism, St. Louis, MO, January 11–13, 1996.

———. *Restoring the Apostolic Faith: A History of the Early Pentecostal Movement.* Hazelwood, MO: Word Aflame, 2007.

Haney, Kenneth. "Azusa Street Revival." *Pentecostal Herald*, April 2006, 7–8.

Haney, Olive. *The Man of the Hills—Served in the Valley: The Biography of Clyde J. Haney.* Stockton, CA: N.p., 1985.

Hanks, Patricia, ed. *Dictionary of American Family Names.* Vol. 1. New York: Oxford University Press, 2003.

Hansford, Catherine McDaniel. "Grover C. McDaniel." In *Profiles of Pentecostal Preachers*, edited by Mary H. Wallace, 136–42, Hazelwood, MO: Word Aflame, 1983.

Haywood, Hubert Benbury, Sr. *Sketch of the Haywood Family in North Carolina.*

"Haywood, Jane F." Wake County Estate Records. Est. #53, Folder #1 and #2, microfilm.

Herskovits, Melville J. *The Myth of the Negro Past.* Boston: Beacon, 1958.

Historical Committee of the Apostolic Assemblies of the Faith in Christ Jesus, eds. *Historia la Asamblea Apostolica de la Fe Cristo Jesus (1916–1966).* Rancho Cucamonga, CA: Secretaria de Education Cristina, 1966.

Historical Committee of the Illinois District United Pentecostal Church International, eds. *Our Pentecostal Heritage.* Bloomington, IL: Illinois District UPC, 1962.

Holder, Eugene, and W. L. Cole. *Voice of the Pioneers-Pentecostal: North Mississippi and North Georgia.* Marietta, GA: Open Bible Tabernacle, 2000.

Holland, Clifford L. *The Religious Dimensions in Hispanic Los Angeles.* South Pasadena, CA: Wm. Carey, 1974.

Hollenweger, Walter J. "The Black Roots of Pentecostalism." In *Pentecostalism After a Century*, edited by Allan H. Anderson and Walter J. Hollenweger, 32ff. Sheffield, UK: Sheffield Academic Press, 1999.

———. *Pentecost Between Black and White*. Belfast: Christian Journals, 1974.

———. *The Pentecostals*. Minneapolis: Augsburg, 1972.

———. "Priorities in Pentecostal Research: Historiography, Missiology, Hermeneutics and Pneumatology." In *Experiences in the Spirit: Conference on Pentecostal and Charismatic Research in Europe at Utrecht University, 1989*, edited by Jan A. B. Jongeneel, 9. New York: Peter Lang, 1990.

———. "Towards an Intercultural History of Christianity." *International Review of Missions* 76/304 (October 1987) 526ff.

Holmes, Agnes. *Oceans of Blessings*. North Little Rock, AR: N.p., 2002.

Horn, J. Nico. "The Experience of the Spirit in Aparteid." In *Experience of the Spirit*, edited by Peter Huizing and William Bassett, 122. New York: Seabury, 1974.

Howell, Bruce. "We Had Church." *Pentecostal Herald*, January 2010, 37.

Howell, Joseph. "The People of the Name: Oneness Pentecostalism in the United States." PhD diss., Florida State University, 1985.

Hubbard, Dolan. *The Souls of Black Folk: One Hundred Years Later*. Columbia, MO: University of Missouri Press, 2003.

Hunter, H. D. "Andrew (Bar-) David Urshan." In *Dictionary of Christianity in America*, edited by D. G. Reid, 1208. Downers Grove, IL: InterVarsity, 1990.

———. "Baptism in the Spirit." In *Dictionary of Christianity in America*, edited by D. G. Reid, 108–9. Downers Grove, IL: InterVarsity, 1990.

Hurtado, Larry W. *Lord Jesus Christ: Devotion to Jesus in Earliest Christianity*. Grand Rapids: Eerdmans, 2003.

Hyatt, Eddie L. *The Azusa Street Revival: The Holy Spirit in America: 100 Years*. Lake Mary, FL: Charisma, 2006.

Inscoe, John C. *Mountain Masters, Slavery, and the Sectional Crisis in Western North Carolina*. Knoxville: University of Tennessee Press, 1989.

Jackson, D. B. R. "The Full Gospel Church of Jesus Christ." MA thesis, University of Delaware, 1973.

Jackson, Eric R. "The Endless Journey: The Black Struggle for Quality Public Schools in Indianapolis, Indiana1900–1949." EdD diss., University of Cincinnati, 2000.

Jackson, Mary, ed. *Tennessee District Heritage*. Jackson, TN: Tennessee District UPCI, 2000.

Jacobsen, Douglas. *A Reader in Pentecostal Theology: Voices from the First Generation*. Bloomington: Indiana University Press, 2006.

———. *Thinking in the Spirit: Theologies of the Early Pentecostal Movement*. Bloomington: Indiana University Press, 2003.

Jennings, Willie James. "Wandering in the Wilderness: Christian Identity and Theology Between Context and Race." In *The Gospel in Black and White: Theological Resources for Racial Reconciliation*, edited by Dennis L. Okholm, 37–38, 41. Downers Grove, IL: InterVarsity, 1997.

Johnson, Vernon R. A. "The First Jesus' Name Pentecostal Church in Wisconsin." *Historical News* (Fall 2002) 2.

Johnston, Robin. *Howard Goss: A Pentecostal Life*. Hazelwood, MO: Word Aflame, 2010.

Johnstone, Patrick, and Jason Mandryk, eds. *Operation World*. Carlisle, UK: Paternoster, 2001.

Jongeneel, Jan A. B., ed. *Experiences in the Spirit: Conference on Pentecostal and Charismatic Research in Europe at Utrecht University, 1989*. New York: Peter Lang, 1990.

Kauffman, Paul E. *China: The Emerging Challenge*. Grand Rapids: Baker, 1982.

Kay, Marvin L., and Lorin Lee Cary. *Slavery in North Carolina (1748–1775)*. Chapel Hill: University of North Carolina Press, 1995.

Kay, William K., and Anne E. Dyer. *Pentecostal and Charismatic Studies*. London: SCM, 2004.

Kendrick, Klaude. *The Promise Fulfilled*. Springfield, MO: Gospel Publishing House, 1961.

Kenyon, Howard N. "An Analysis of Ethical Issues in the History of the Assemblies of God." PhD diss., Baylor University, 1988.

Kinzie, Fred E. *Handbook on Receiving the Holy Ghost*. Hazelwood, MO: Word Aflame, 1997.

Knox, George L. *Slaves and Freemen: The Autobiography of George L. Knox*. Lexington: University Press of Kentucky, 1979.

Landis, Benson Y., ed. *Yearbook of American Churches—1960*. New York: National Council of Churches of Christ in the U.S.A., 1959.

Larden, Robert A. *Our Apostolic Heritage*. Calgary: Apostolic Church of Pentecost of Canada, 1971.

Larkin, Clarence. *Dispensational Truth*. Philadelphia: N.p., 1920.

Lear, Walter J. "U.S. Health Professionals Oppose War." *Social Medicine* 2/3 (July 2007) 131.

LeBlanc, Deborah Sims. *Like A Rose: Life, Times and Messages of the Late Bishop Frank R. Bowdan, D.D. (1910–1976)*. Los Angeles: n.d.

Lee, Shayne. *T. D. Jakes: America's New Preacher*. New York: New York University Press, 2005.

Lincoln, C. Eric, and Lawrence H. Mamiya. *The Black Church in the African American Experience*. Durham, NC: Duke University Press, 1990.

Linder, Bartley J. *The "Godhead," How Many?* Kerrville, TX: Illuminations, 1997.

Lindquist, Frank J. *The Truth About the Trinity and Baptism in Jesus' Name Only*. Minneapolis: Northern Gospel, 1961.

Longenecker, Richard N. *The Christology of Early Jewish Christianity*. Studies in Biblical Theology 17. Naperville, IL: Alec R. Allenson, 1970.

Lovett, Leonard. "Black Holiness-Pentecostalism." In *Dictionary of Pentecostal and Charismatic Movements*, edited by Stanley M. Burgess and Gary B. McGee, 80. Grand Rapids: Zondervan, 1988.

———. "Black Holiness-Pentecostalism: Implications for Ethics and Social Transformation." PhD diss., Emory University, 1978.

———. "Black Origins of the Pentecostal Movement." In *Aspects of Pentecostal-Charismatic Origins*, by Vinson Synan, 135ff. Plainfield, NJ: Logos, 1975.

———. "The Present: The Problem of Racism in the Contemporary Pentecostal Movement." *Cyberjournal of Pentecostal Charismatic Research*. http://www.pctii.org/cyberj/cyberj14/lovett1.html.

McCready, Douglas. *He Came Down from Heaven: The Preexistence of Christ and the Christian Faith*. Downers Grove, IL: InterVarsity, 2005.

McDonnell, Kilian, ed. *Presence, Power, Praise: Documents on the Charismatic Renewal*. Collegeville, MN: Liturgical, 1980.

McDonnell, Kilian, and George T. Montague. *Christian Initiation and Baptism in the Holy Spirit*. Collegeville, MN: Liturgical, 1991.

McGee, Gary B., ed. *Initial Evidence: Historical and Biblical Perspectives on the Pentecostal Doctrine of Spirit Baptism*. Peabody, MA: Hendrickson, 1991.

———. *People of the Spirit: The Assemblies of God*. Springfield, MO: Gospel Publishing House, 2004.

Macchia, Frank D. *Baptized in the Spirit: A Global Pentecostal Theology*. Grand Rapids: Zondervan, 2006.

———. "From Azusa to Memphis: Evaluating the Racial Reconciliation Dialogue Among Pentecostals." *Pneuma* 17/2 (Fall 1995) 203–18.

MacRobert, Iain. *The Black Roots and White Racism of Early Pentecostalism in the USA*. London: MacMillan, 1988.

———. "The Spirit and the Wall: The Black Roots and White Racism of Early Pentecostalism in the USA." MA thesis, University of Birmingham, 1985.

Madison, James H. *The Indiana Way: A State History*. Bloomington: Indiana University Press, 1986.

Maisel, David. "Oregon's Forgotten Hospital." *The Oregonian*, January 9, 2005.

Martin, David. *Pentecostalism: The World Their Parish*. Oxford: Blackwell, 2002.

Martin, Don. *The 1st Pentecostal Church of Garden City/1st Pentecostal Church of Tulsa Story*. Tulsa, OK: N.p., 2002.

Martin, Larry. *The Life and Ministry of William J. Seymour*. Joplin, MO: Christian Life, 1999.

Matney, A. A. "The Founding of Jesus' Name Pentecostal Churches in Houston Area." *Historical News*, July–September 1995, 2–3.

Mayo, Lou D. *History of the Assemblies of the Lord Jesus Christ*. Memphis: Apostolic Word, 1989.

Melton, J. Gordon. "Garfield Thomas Haywood." In *Biographical Dictionary of American Cult and Sect Leaders*, 106. New York: Garland, 1986.

Melton, Gordon, and John Krol, eds. *National Directory of Churches, Synagogues, and Other Houses of Worship*. Vol. 2. Washington, DC: Gale Research, 1994.

Menzies, William W. *Anointed to Serve: The Story of the Assemblies of God*. Springfield, MO: Gospel Publishing House, 1971.

Metaxas, Eric. *Amazing Grace: William Wilberforce and the Heroic Campaign to End Slavery*. Grand Rapids: Zondervan, 2007.

Miller, John W. *Indiana Newspaper Bibliography*. Indianapolis: Indiana Historical Society, 1982.

Miller, Thomas William. *Canadian Pentecostalism: A History of the Pentecostal Assemblies of Canada*. Mississauga, ON: Full Gospel, 1994.

Millner, Marlon. "Love Lived: The Body as Pentecostal Theology in Robert Lawson's 'Anthropology of Jesus Christ Our Kinsman.'" MDiv thesis, Harvard Divinity School, 2005.

———. "One, One, One . . . One Way to God? A Review Essay of 'In Jesus' Name': The History and Beliefs of Oneness Pentecostals." *Pneuma* 31/2 (2009) 275–82.

Montgomery, T. C. *A Brief Story of My Life*. N.p: n.d.

Moore, Leonard J. *Citizen Klansmen: The Ku Klux Klan in Indiana, 1921–1928*. Chapel Hill: University of North Carolina Press, 1991.

Morehouse, Joyce Macbeth. *Pioneers of Pentecost*. Doaktown, NB: N.d.

Moses, Wilson Jeremiah. *Creative Conflict in African American Thought*. New York: Cambridge University Press, 2004.

Murley, Mike. "Unionists to Secessionists: Whig Unionists and the Rise of Disunion in North Carolina (1840–1861)." http://www.geocities.ws/rowdy_pards/articles/AntebellumNC.html.

Murphy, Larry, J. Gordon Melton, and Gary L. Ward, eds. *Encyclopedia of African American Religions*. New York: Garland, 1993.

Nation, Edna. *Spenser Leslie Wise: A Biographical Sketch*. Florissant, MO: N.p., 1991.

Neal, Nina. *Keepers of the Flame: A History of the Oneness Pentecostals of New Castle, Indiana*. Newcastle, IN: Bryant, 1998.

Nelson, Douglas J. "The Black Face of Church Renewal." In *Faces of Renewal*, edited by Paul Ebert, 180–84. Peabody, MA: Hendrickson, 1988.

———. "For Such a Time as This: The Story of Bishop William J. Seymour and the Azusa Street Revival." PhD diss., University of Birmingham, 1981.

Nelson, Jacob P. "Charles Peter Nelson." In *Profiles of Pentecostal Preachers*, edited by Mary H. Wallace, 2:295–304. Hazelwood, MO: Word Aflame, 1984.

Nelson, Joseph A. "History of the Assemblies of the Lord Jesus Christ." Paper presented at Indiana Bible College, Indianapolis, October 18, 1994.

Newman, Joe. *Race and the Assemblies of God Church*. Youngstown, NY: Cambria, 2007.

Nickel, Thomas R. *Azusa Street Outpouring*. Hanford, CA: Great Commission, 1956.

Norris, David S. "Creation Revealed." In *The Spirit Renews the Face of the Earth: Pentecostal Forays in Science and Theology of Creation*, edited by Amos Yong, 74–92. Eugene, OR: Pickwick, 2009.

———. *"I Am": A Oneness Pentecostal Perspective*. Hazelwood, MO: Word Aflame, 2009.

Okholm, Dennis L., ed. *The Gospel in Black and White: Theological Resources for Racial Reconciliation*. Downers Grove, IL: InterVarsity, 1997.

Olson, Roger E. "A Wind that Swirls Everywhere." *Christianity Today*, March 2006, 52–54.

Oneness Studies Institute. "Report of the Oneness Studies Institute, 2009." Raleigh, NC. May 2009.

"Oneness-Trinitarian Pentecostal Final Report, 2002–2007." *Pneuma* 30/2 (Fall 2006) 203–24.

Owens, Robert R. *The Azusa Street Revival: Its Roots and Its Message*. Lanham, MD: Xulon, 2005.

Paddock, Ross P. *Apostolic Roots: A Godly Heritage*. Piqua, OH: Ohio Ministries, 1992.

Palma, Anthony D. *Baptism in the Holy Spirit*. Springfield, MO: Gospel Publishing House, 1999.

Pankey, William. "President Obama Graces Church that Most Others Shun." *The Examiner*, March 27, 2010. http://www.examiner.com/pentecostal-in-chicago/president-obama-graces-church-that-most-others-shun.

Patterson, Eric, and Edmund Rybarczyk, eds. *The Future of Pentecostalism in the United States*. Lanham, MD: Lexington, 2007.

Payne, Wardell J., ed. *Directory of African American Religious Bodies*. Washington, DC: Howard University Press, 1991.

Peagler, Victoria M. *Garfield Thomas Haywood (1880–1931): From Migrant's Son to an Internationally Renowned Churchman*. Dayton, OH: Wright State University, 1993.

"Pentecostal Partners: Racial Reconciliation Manifesto." PCCNA, Memphis, TN, October 17–19, 1994. www.pentecostalworldfellowship .org/pub/manifesto.html.

Peters, James E., and Patricia Pickard. *Prevailing Westerlies: The Pentecostal Heritage of Maine*. Shippensburg, PA: Destiny Image, 1988.

Pickard, Patricia P. *The Davis Sisters: Their Influences and Their Impact*. Bangor, ME: N.p., 2009.

Pierce, Richard B. *Polite Politics: The Political Economy of Race in Indianapolis, 1920–1970*. Indianapolis: Indiana University Press, 2005.

Poewe, Karla, ed. *Charismatic Christianity and the Global Culture*. Columbia: University of South Carolina Press, 1994.

Poewe, Karla, and Irving Hexham. *New Religions as Global Cultures*. Boulder, CO: Westview, 1997.

Pyatt, Timothy D., ed. *African-Americans in North Carolina and at the University of North Carolina at Chapel Hill*. Chapel Hill: Center for the Study of the American South, 1995.

Ramirez, Daniel. "Pentecostal Praxis: A History of the Experience of Latino Immigrants in the Apostolic Assembly Churches of the United States." Society for Pentecostal Studies, Lakeland, FL, November 9, 1991.

Reed, David A. *"In Jesus' Name": The History and Beliefs of Oneness Pentecostals*. Journal of Pentecostal Theology Supplement Series 31. Dorset, UK: Deo, 2008.

———. "Oneness Pentecostalism." In *The New International Dictionary of Pentecostal Charismatic Movements*, edited by Stanley M. Burgess and Eduard M. Van Der Maas, 936–44. Grand Rapids: Zondervan, 2002.

———. "Origin and Development of the Theology of Oneness Pentecostalism in the United States." PhD diss., Boston University Graduate School, 1978.

———. Review of *A Definitive Look at Oneness Theology* by Edward L. Dalcour. *Pneuma* 28/1 (2006) 166–69.

Reed, Vernita Craine. "T. Richard Reed." In *Old-Time Preacher Men*, edited by Mary H. Wallace, 199. Hazelwood, MO: Word Aflame, 1992.

Reeves, Kenneth V. *The Holy Ghost With Tongues*. Granite City, IL: N.p., 1966.

Reid, D. G. "Frank Bartleman." In *Dictionary of Christianity in America*, edited by D. G. Reid, 119. Downers Grove, IL: InterVarsity, 1990.

Reinking, Julia. "Charles Nelson: His Azusa Street Legacy Lives On." *Pentecostal Herald*, April 2006, 18–20.

Reynolds, Ralph, and Joyce Morehouse. *From the Rising of the Sun*. New Westminster, BC: Conexions, 1998.

Richardson, James C. *With Water and Spirit: A History of Black Apostolic Denominations in the U.S.* Martinsville, VA: Spirit, 1980.

Rider, James D. "The Theology of the 'Jesus Only' Movement." ThD thesis, Dallas Theological Seminary, 1959.

Riggs, Ralph M. "Heaven On Earth." In *Touched By the Fire*, edited by Wayne E. Warner, 36. Plainfield, NJ: Logos, 1978.

Riss, R. M. "Finished Work Controversy." In *The New International Dictionary of Pentecostal and Charismatic Movements*, edited by Stanley M. Burgess and Eduard M. Van Der Maas, 638. Grand Rapids: Zondervan, 2002.

Ritchey, Tony. "God's Fairness to People of All Faiths: A Respectful Proposal to Pentecostals for Discussion Regarding World Religions." *Pneuma* 28/1 (2006) 105–19.

Robbins, R. G. "Azusa Street Mission." In *Dictionary of Christianity in America*, edited by Daniel G. Reid, 98. Downers Grove, IL: InterVarsity, 1990.

Robeck, Cecil M., Jr. *The Azusa Street Mission and Revival: The Birth of the Global Pentecostal Movement*. Nashville: Nelson, 2006.

———. "Azusa Street Revival." *The New International Dictionary of Pentecostal and Charismatic Movements*, edited by Stanley M. Burgess and Eduard M. Van Der Maas, 207–8. Grand Rapids: Zondervan, 2002.

———. "Azusa Street Revival Timeline." *Enrichment* 11/2 (Spring 2006) 104.

———. "Frank Bartleman." In *Dictionary of Pentecostal and Charismatic Movements*, edited by Stanley M. Burgess and Gary McGee, 304–5. Grand Rapids: Zondervan, 1988.

———. "Frank Bartleman." In *The New International Dictionary of Pentecostal and Charismatic Movements*, edited by Stanley M. Burgess and Eduard M. Van Der Maas, 366. Grand Rapids: Zondervan, 2002.

———. "Garfield Thomas Haywood." *The New International Dictionary of Pentecostal and Charismatic Movements*, edited by Stanley M. Burgess and Eduard M. Van Der Maas, 693. Grand Rapids: Zondervan, 2002.

———. "John G. Schaepe." In *The New International Dictionary of Pentecostal and Charismatic Movements*, edited by Stanley M. Burgess and Eduard M. Van Der Maas, 1042. Grand Rapids: Zondervan, 2002.

———. "The Past: Historical Roots of Racial Unity and Division in American Pentecostalism." *Cyberjournal for Pentecostal Charismatic Research*. http://www.pctii.org/cyberj/cyberj14/robeck.html.

———. "Pentecostal Origins from a Global Perspective." In *All Together In One Place: Theological Papers from the Brighton Conference on World Evangelism*, edited by Harold D. Hunter and Peter D. Hocken, 166–80. Sheffield, UK: Sheffield Academic Press, 1993.

———. "Racial Reconciliation at Memphis: Some Personal Reflections." Society for Pentecostal Studies, Toronto, Canada, March 1996.

———. *Witness to Pentecost: The Life of Frank Bartleman*. New York: Garland, 1985.

Roberts, Terry. "Pentecostalism's Greatest Test Could Be Her Finest Hour." *Enrichment* 7 (Summer 2010) n.p. http://www.agts.edu/encounter/articles/2010summer/roberts.htm.

Rodgers, Darrin J. "The Assemblies of God and the Long Journey toward Racial Reconciliation." *Heritage* 28 (2008) 53.

Rodgers, Mary Brickey. "Henry Green Rodgers." *Historical News* 19/4 (2000) 3.

Rosenior, Derrick R. "Toward Racial Reconciliation: Collective Memory, Myth and Nostalgia in American Pentecostalism." Parallel session papers of the Society for Pentecostal Studies, Cleveland, TN, March 2007.

Ross, Bob L. *The Trinity and the Eternal Sonship of Christ: A Defense Against "Oneness" Pentecostal Attacks on Historic Christianity*. Pasadena, TX: Pilgrim, 1993.

Rucker, James. "Heroes and Hard Times: Exploring the Taproots of African-American Folk Culture." In *Piedmont Council of Traditional Music, Raleigh, NC* concert program. March 2003. http://www.sparkyandrhonda.com/taproots.html.

Rudolph, L. C. *Hoosier Faiths: A History of Indiana Churches and Religious Groups*. Bloomington: Indiana University Press, 1995.

Rutkow, Ira. *James A. Garfield*. New York: Times Books, 2006.

Sanders, Cheryl J. *Saints in Exile: The Holiness Pentecostal Experience in African American Religion and Culture*. New York: Oxford University Press, 1996.

Sanders, Rufus G. W. *William Joseph Seymour: Black Father of the Twentieth Century Pentecostal/Charismatic Movement*. Sandusky, OH: Xulon, 2003.

Schneider, Rob. "The Changing Face of Indianapolis: 1920–1929: Ku Klux Klan Dominance Marked an Ugly Era for City." December 28, 1999. http://www2.indystar.com/library/factfiles/history/black_history/.

Scism, Ellis, and Stanley Scism. *Northwest Passage: The Early Years of Ellis Scism, 1909–1949*. Hazelwood, MO: Word Aflame, 1999.

Segraves, Daniel L. "Oneness Theology." In *Encyclopedia of Pentecostal and Charismatic Christianity*, edited by Stanley M. Burges, 341–45. New York: Rutledge, 2006.

Seybert, Tony. "The Black Press: Soldiers Without Swords." *The Black Voice News*, March 29, 2005. http://www.blackvoicenews.com/index.php?option=com_content&task=view&id=37990&Itemid=24&date=2007-08-01.

Shoemake, Blanch Faye. *Blanche Faye: Pioneer Pentecostal Experiences a Witnessed through the Eyes of a Child*. Chula Vista, CA: N.p., 2007.

Simmons-Henry, Linda, ed. The *Heritage of Blacks in North Carolina*. Vol. 1. Charlotte: North Carolina African-American Heritage Foundation, 1990.

Sims, Charles A. *From Grace to Glory: The Life and Ministry of Bishop Morris E. Golder*. Columbus, IN: N.p., 2002.

Smith, Aaron J. *A Devout Man: Biography of Karl F. Smith (1892–1972)*. Chapel Hill, NC: Professional, 1998.

Smith, Franklin Carter, and Emily Anne Croom. *A Genealogist's Guide to Discovering Your African-American Ancestors*. Cincinnati: Betterway, 2003.

Smith, Timothy L. "The Disinheritance of the Saints." *Religious Studies Review* 8/1 (January 1982), 15–28.

Smock, Raymond W. *Booker T. Washington: Black Leadership in the Age of Jim Crow*. Chicago: Ivan R. Dee, 2009.

Spellman, Robert C. "Issues of Consensus and Controversy Within and Amongst Mainline Black Pentecostal Church Organizations." Society for Pentecostal Studies, Dallas, TX, November 8, 1990.

———, ed. *Pentecostal Apostolic Fellowship Crusade Journal*. New York: Church of Our Lord Jesus Christ of the Apostolic Faith and Bible Way Churches, 1989.

Spellman, Robert C., and Mable L. Thomas. *The Life, Legend and Legacy of Bishop R. C. Lawson*. New York: N.p., 1983.

"Stallones, Brother Wilner Levoy." *Historical News* 19/14 (October–December 1999) 3.

Stark, Rodney, and William Sims Bainbridge. "Of Churches, Sects, and Cults: Preliminary Concepts for a Theory of Religious Movements." *Journal for the Scientific Study of Religion* 18/2 (1979) 117–31.

Stephens, Randall J. "There Is Magic in Print: The Holiness-Pentecostal Press and the Origins of Southern Pentecostalism., Part II." *Journal of Southern Religion* 5 (2002) n.p. http://jsr.fsu.edu/2002/stephens2.htm.

Stewart, Alexander C., and Sherry Sherrod DuPree. *The Silent Spokesman: Bishop Robert Clarence Lawson*. Gainesville, FL: Displays for Schools, 1994.

Strachen, Hew. *The First World War*. Vol. 1. New York: Viking, 2003.

Synan, Vinson. *Aspects of Pentecostal-Charismatic Origins*. Plainfield, NJ: Logos, 1975.

———. "The Future: A Strategy for Reconciliation." *Cyberjournal for Pentecostal Charismatic Research*. http://www.pctii.org/cyberj/cyberj14/synan.html.

———. *The Holiness-Pentecostal Movement in the United States*. Grand Rapids: Eerdmans, 1971.

———. "The Role of Tongues as Initial Evidence." Society for Pentecostal Studies Papers, Guadalajara, Mexico, November 11–13, 1993.

Taylor, William E., ed. *A Shared Heritage: Art by Four African Americans*. Indianapolis: Indianapolis Museum of Art, 1996.

Tenney, T. F. *The Flame Still Burns: A History of the Pentecostals of Louisiana*. Tioga, LA: Focused Light, 1989.

Thomas, Mable L. "History of Robert C. Lawson." In *For the Defense of the Gospel*, edited by Arthur M. Anderson, 6–23. New York: COOLJC, 1971.

Thornbrough, Emma Lou. *The Negro in Indiana*. Indianapolis: Indiana Historical Bureau, 1957.

Thurman, Howard. "On Viewing the Coast of Africa." In *Deep River and the Negro Spiritual Speaks of Life and Death*. Richmond, IN: Friends United, 1975.

Tinney, James S. "Black Origins of the Pentecostal Movement." *Christianity Today*, October 8, 1971, 4–6.

———. "The Blackness of Pentecostalism." In *The Black Church: A Community Resource*. Washington, DC: Institute for Urban Affairs and Research, 1977.

———. "Exclusivist Tendencies in Pentecostal Self-Definition: A Critique from Black Theology." *Journal of Religious Thought* 36/1 (1979) 32–49.

———. "The Significance of Race in the Rise and Development of the Apostolic Pentecostal Movement." First Occasional Symposium on Aspects of the Oneness Pentecostal Movement, Harvard Divinity School, Cambridge, MA, July 5–7, 1984.

———. "A Theoretical and Historical Comparison of Black Political and Religious Movements." PhD diss., Howard University, 1973.

Toulis, Nicole Rodriguez. *Believing Identity of Jamaican Ethnicity and Gender in England*. Oxford: Berg, 1997.

Trask, Thomas, E. "The Azusa Street Revival." *Enrichment* 11/2 (Spring 2006) 16.

Treece, Betty. *Come to Beulah Land: The Pioneer Preacher Jerry Earl Osborn (1879–1964)*. Lake Charles, LA: N.p., 1997.

"A Tribute to Frank J. Ewart." *Historical News* 8/2 (1989) 2–4.

Turner, William C. "Black Evangelicalism: Theology, Politics, and Race." *Journal of Religious Thought* 45/2 (1989) 40–56.

Tyson, James L. *Before I Sleep: A Narrative and Photographic Biography of Bishop Garfield Thomas Haywood*. Indianapolis: Pentecostal, 1976.

———. *Chalices of Gold: A Narrative and Pictorial History of the Pentecostal Assemblies of the World*. Warren, OH: N.p., 1990.

———. *The Early Pentecostal Revival*. Hazelwood, MO: Word Aflame, 1992.

U.S. Department of Commerce. "Religious Bodies: 1936." *U.S. Bureau of the Census*, 2 vols. Washington, DC: Government Printing Office, 1941.

Vondey, Wolfgang. "Pentecostalism and the Possibility of Global Theology: Implications of Theology of Amos Yong." *Pneuma* 28/2 (2006) 289.

The W. L. Bonner Literary Committee. *And The High Places I'll Bring Down: Bishop William L. Bonner, The Man and His God*. New York: The W. L. Bonner Literary Committee, 1999.

Wacker, Grant. "Bibliography and Historiography of Pentecostalism." In *Dictionary of Pentecostal and Charismatic Movements*, edited by Stanley M. Burgess and Gary B. McGee, 75. Grand Rapids: Zondervan, 1988.

———. *Heaven Below: Early Pentecostalism and American Culture*. Cambridge, MA: Harvard University Press, 2001.

———. "The Travail of a Broken Family: Radical Evangelical Responses to Early Pentecostalism." Society for Pentecostal Studies, Lakeland, FL, November 7–9, 1991.

Wallace, Mary H. *He Stands Tall.* Hazelwood, MO: Word Aflame, 1980.

———, ed. *Old-Time Preacher Men.* Hazelwood, MO: Word Aflame, 1992.

———. *Profiles of Pentecostal Preachers.* Vol. 1. Hazelwood, MO: Word Aflame Press, 1983.

———. *Profiles of Pentecostal Preachers.* Vol. 2. Hazelwood, MO: Word Aflame, 1984.

Walsh, Arlene M Sanchez. *Latino Pentecostal Identity: Evangelical Faith, Self and Society.* New York: Columbia University Press, 1983.

Ware, S. L. "Restorationism in Classical Pentecostalism." In *The New International Dictionary of Pentecostal Charismatic Movements*, edited by Stanley M. Burgess and Eduard M. Van Der Maas, 1019–21. Grand Rapids: Zondervan, 2002.

Warner, Wayne E. "Maria B. Woodworth-Etter: Prophet of Equality." In *Portraits of a Genertion: Early Pentecostal Leaders*, edited by James R. Goff and Grant Wacker, 199–218. Fayetteville: University of Arkansas Press, 2002.

———. *Maria Woodworth-Etter: For Such A Time as This.* Gainesville, FL: Bridge-Logos, 2004.

West, Nathaniel. *The Thousand Years: Studies in Eschatology in Both Testaments.* Grand Rapids: Kregel, 1993.

West, Russell W. "A Critical Exploration of the PCCNA's Rhetorical Vision for Racial Unity: Fighting Pentecostal Racism with Saul's Armor or David's Sling?" September 27, 1999. http://www.pccna.org/documents/1999West.pdf.

Wesson, G. E., and Tim R. McCarty. *Apostolic Pioneers of Arizona.* Kearney, NE: Morris, 2002.

Wiens, Grace. *Unto You and Your Children: A Story of Pentecostal Pioneers to the Great Northwest.* Hazelwood, MO: Word Aflame, 1977.

Wilson, L. F. "George B. Studd." In *The New International Dictionary of Pentecostal and Charismatic Movements*, edited by Stanley M. Burgess and Eduard M. Van Der Maas, 1108. Grand Rapids: Zondervan, 2002.

Willmott, H. P. *World War 1.* New York: Dorling Kindersley, 2003.

Winehouse, Irwin. *The Assemblies of God: A Popular Survey.* New York: Vantage, 1959.

Winn, Christian T. Collins. "Book Review of *Race: A Theological Account.*" In *Pneuma* 32/1 (2010) 133–34.

Woodward, C. Vann. *The Strange Career of Jim Crow.* New York: Oxford University Press, 1955.

Yadon, Charlie M. *Historical Record of the Oneness Movement in the Northwest.* Puyallup, WA: N.p., 2002.

Yong, Amos. *The Spirit Poured Out on All Flesh: Pentecostalism and the Possibility of Global Theology.* Grand Rapids: Baker, 2005.

———, ed. *The Spirit Renews the Face of the Earth: Pentecostal Forays in Science and Theology of Creation.* Eugene, OR: Pickwick, 2009.

Yoshinobu, Kumazawa, and David L. Swain, eds. *Christianity in Japan, 1971–1990.* Tokyo: Christian Literary Society of Japan, 1991.

# Name Index

I



J



K



L

## T



## U

# Subject Index

## H



## I



## J



## K



## L



## M

## N



## O

www.ingramcontent.com/pod-product-compliance
Lightning Source LLC
LaVergne TN
LVHW010934100826
845153LV00001B/37

* 9 7 8 1 4 9 8 2 2 6 8 5 1 *